BANKING ON SELF-HELP GROUPS

BANKING ON SELF-HELP GROUPS

Twenty Years On

AJAY TANKHA

www.sagepublications.com
Los Angeles • London • New Delhi • Singapore • Washington DC

Jointly published in 2012 by

SAGE Publications India Pvt Ltd
B1/I-1 Mohan Cooperative Industrial Area
Mathura Road, New Delhi 110,044, India
www.sagepub.in

ACCESS Development Services
28, Hauz Khas Village
New Delhi 110 016
www.accessdev.org

SAGE Publications Inc
2455 Teller Road
Thousand Oaks, California 91320, USA

SAGE Publications Ltd
1 Oliver's Yard
55 City Road
London EC1Y 1SP, United Kingdom

SAGE Publications Asia-Pacific Pte Ltd
33 Pekin Street
#02-01 Far East Square
Singapore 048763

Published by Vivek Mehra for SAGE Publications India Pvt Ltd, typeset in 10/12pt Sabon by Tantla Composition Services Private Limited, Chandigarh, and printed at G.H. Prints Pvt Ltd, New Delhi.

Library of Congress Cataloging-in-Publication Data
Tankha, Ajay.
    Banking on self-help groups : twenty years on / Ajay Tankha.
        p. cm.
    Includes bibliographical references and index.
    1. Self-help groups—India—Evaluation. I. Title.

HV547. T36   332.2′80954—dc23   2012   2012019653

ISBN: 978-81-321-0964-8 (PB)

The SAGE Team: Rudra Narayan Sharma, Aniruddha De, Rajib Chatterjee and Dally Verghese

CONTENTS

TABLES AND BOXES

TABLES

Boxes

APPENDICES

FOREWORD

When the first self-help groups (SHGs) were linked to banks in Udaipur in 1992, several high-profile visitors from Reserve Bank of India (RBI), Indian Institute of Management, Ahmedabad (IIM-A), Swiss Agency for Development and Cooperation (SDC) and National Bank for Agriculture and Rural Development (NABARD) flocked to the small village of Sakroda to ask the bewildered group of women about their experience with the ₹ 5,000 loan that they had received from the local bank branch—What will they do with the loan? How will they lend among their members? Who will manage their books? Indeed, it was the first time that an informal group of poor women were dealing with a bank; it was the first time for the NGO as well to be facilitating such a loan, and the intelligent questions by the visitors were difficult both to comprehend and to respond to by this group squatting on the floor of the house of the SHG leader. Every time a new SHG got linked to a bank branch, there would be a local cheque presentation ceremony and group photographs of the SHG leader accepting the ₹ 5,000 cheque from the collector with the regional manager of the bank, District Development Manager (DDM) of NABARD, the NGO head and the lead bank. I was the NABARD DDM in Udaipur in those days, and was instructed to put in maximum efforts in finding groups, metamorphosing them into SHGs (or at least that is what I did) and pushing banks to link them with 'some kind of' credit.

As one more effort towards downscaling finance, NABARD started the SHG–Bank linkage programme (SBLP) as a pilot to link 500 SHGs with formal bank credit. In February 1992, a copiously detailed 14-page circular on 'SHG–Bank Linkage Programme' issued to commercial banks arrived in my office with clear instructions to report breakthroughs under the programme. While the circular had a lot of details, it was purposely also kept vague in some areas. Groups of rural folk with less than 20 members were to be formed as SHGs by NGOs; after saving for six months and rotating the kitty, they were to be linked to banks to receive a loan of up to four times of their savings. Although not stated, this was to be a term loan to the SHG; the group could be of men or women, but whether they should be poor or not was not emphasized; the purpose of the loan from the groups to their members could be for any emergent purpose. The loans would be collateral free. There was no promotional cost for SHG formation mentioned in the circular. To get this pilot off the ground, there were several issues that needed to be sorted out. Sensitization of the NGOs was the first major task. NGOs had previously never played a financial facilitation role, and did not know banks' functioning well. Designing the application for an SHG loan, an agreement between the bank, the SHG and the NGO and other paperwork needed to be sorted. Training of NGOs (later called Self-Help Promoting Institutions [SHPIs]) on maintenance of books of accounts and on bank requirements and procedures became a necessity. In the initial stages, NGOs, largely dependent on grants, were unsure of taking this additional burden and responsibility without any bottom line benefit to them. On the other hand, the banks in those times, severely beleaguered with high non-performing assets (NPAs), were not particularly exultant, with high and mounting bad debts already from loans under Integrated Rural Development Programme (IRDP). They were not keen to lend to informal groups without collateral; they weren't sure if these loans were term loans or working capital; they weren't sure if SHGs were eligible for loans if their members were defaulters; they weren't sure of who would be liable if the SHG defaulted. Initially, the pilot was only open to commercial banks as their balance sheets were much stronger than regional rural banks (RRBs) or co-ops. It took quite a while for the pilot to take off. I was quite happy that 12 of the first 50 SHGs linked to banks in the country were from Udaipur district, even though it meant many more important visitors making frequent trips to the district.

From a pilot project, SBLP became a more mainstream programme within NABARD and a separate department—Micro-Credit Innovations Department (MCID)—was established to manage and monitor the programme. Subsequently, more resources were assigned to the programme for capacity building, sensitization, exposure visits and module development among others. Some promotional costs were also subsequently allowed to NGOs for group formation. In the initial years, the progress was slow and sluggish, and only in early years of this century did it pick up some steam. While it took almost 12 years for the first one million groups to get linked to banks, it took less than 24 months to link the next one million. As of March 2011, with almost 5 million SHGs representing 70 million poor households and a bank loan outstanding of ₹ 306 billion, it has, over the last 20 years, become the largest programme in the world providing financial services to the poor.

While NABARD initiated the SHG linkage programme essentially as an outreach programme to link the unreached with formal finance, at their level the NGOs looked at it as more than just a financial linkage model.

Given that women were outside the ambit of formal finance more than men, their focus was on forming women SHGs. And given the growing women focus, the issues of empowerment and gender and access to entitlements and rights got further integrated into the ambit of what could be done with the SHG programme. Several large programmes got designed by NGOs/INGOs and donors using SHG linkage as an entry point to achieve empowerment of the poor, and in some cases, by federating SHGs into community organizations. In the hands of the NGOs, the SHG programme has helped to evolve further. The Credit and Savings for Household Enterprise (CASHE) programme, which I managed as a part of my portfolio in later years at Cooperative for Assistance and Relief Everywhere (CARE), focused substantially on the gender and empowerment agenda. When the IRDP gave way to the Swarnajayanti Gram Swarozgar Yojana (SGSY) programme, the SHG model was adopted and tweaked into a hybrid livelihoods promotion programme and subsidies were introduced in a programme which had so far remained quite market-based. This was reinforced under the World Bank–supported Indira Kranthi Patham (IKP) programme in Andhra Pradesh, the Aajivika programme in Bihar and in a few other states. This model has been further evolved under the new National Rural Livelihoods Mission (NRLM) programme being currently rolled out by the Government of India (GOI) in which SHGs would be the building bricks on which community-based federations will be erected.

Over the last 20 years, the SHG programme has come a long way, and in its 20-year-run, while covering a large number of poor households, it has evolved significantly. However, there have been a few drawbacks which have hindered its accelerated growth, like the pace we have witnessed in the alternate Microfinance Institution (MFI) model, which till 15 months ago, grew at almost 100%. Some factors that impeded the growth of the SHG movement that come to mind include the continued reluctance of banks to lend to SHGs, incapacities at the SHPI level and quality of SHGs. That lending to SHGs qualified as priority sector lending was perhaps the biggest incentive to lend to these groups, besides the fact that recoveries from SHG loans were significantly better than other priority sector portfolio segments. Banks have remained largely reluctant in making second/third loans to SHGs or in upping the quantum of loans beyond a threshold level. NABARD or any donor agency never made a serious enough effort or investment to develop at least a few very large SHPIs capable of supporting and managing a large base of SHGs, like how Small Industries Development Bank of India (SIDBI) invested in creating a few large MFIs. With most SHPIs being small and local and not too savvy in financial facilitation, the quality of SHGs formed and their management grossly suffered. SHG quality was not systematically tracked through a good management information system (MIS), and so while a large number of SHGs were being formed, not all were getting linked. Further, to overcome the regional skew issue, strategies were not strong, resulting in Andhra Pradesh claiming to have two-fifths of all SHGs in the country linked to banks. Technology wasn't leveraged enough to further reduce transaction costs or make the linkage process more efficient. Creative ideas of how the savings accrued in the SHG model could further benefit members haven't still been figured out. I'm hoping that in the second phase, which is being designed, both NABARD and the GOI will learn from all these diverse experiences and will have a way of sifting what worked and what didn't and to invest in those positive takeaways that will give the programme a new thrust.

Within ACCESS, as a part of its mission to build and contribute to sector learning and sector knowledge, for 2011, it was thought appropriate to invest in documenting on the diversity of experiences of different stakeholders associated with the SHG programme across the last 20 years. After a few consultations with sector leaders, the idea of a comprehensive study of the two decades of the SHG programme was considered appropriate. I am happy that ACCESS was able to associate Ajay Tankha, a highly respected researcher, with this overwhelming assignment. Ajay, who has previously worked in NABARD and has significant knowledge of group-based financial delivery programmes in other parts of the world as well, has also undertaken several important research studies on SHGs, particularly looking at the financial viability, promotional costs and impact. I am thankful to Ajay for agreeing to take up this important study. For accomplishing the task, Ajay undertook field visits, interviewed sector leaders associated with the SHG programme and did an extensive literature review. I thank Ajay for painstakingly assimilating all the varied experiences of stakeholders despite the complexities of assimilating varied pieces of information, data and research. As always, Ajay's great writing, analysing and narration skills have helped to produce a high-quality document.

Ajay was significantly helped in his study by some tall leaders from the sector. At the outset, I would like to thank Professor Malcolm Harper, who has been associated with the SHG programme right from the time it was started by NABARD in 1992 (also the first visitor to my Udaipur SHGs). Malcolm helped to read, critique and suggest towards improvement of content and analysis, while basking in his autumn farmhouse in England. His comments and critique invariably always help to improve and enhance any content. I am also very grateful to C.S. Reddy and his team at APMAS, who made a huge contribution to the data analysis and content of the study voluntarily. The last minute coming on board of the APMAS team is deeply appreciated. C.S. has been a past colleague, and his deep knowledge of SHGs has been a very valuable contribution to the study. I'd also like to thank Phani Priya, who provided research assistance to Ajay for the study.

This study would not have been possible without the support of several key stakeholders. I am personally grateful to NABARD to be the first to agree with the idea of this study. Within NABARD, I would like to thank Dr Prakash Bakshi, Chairman, for supporting the study and Dr Kulkarni, Dr Kumbhare and Dr Suran from MCID, besides the Department of Economic Analysis and Research team, who provided all the information and data for the report. I'd also like to thank Gesellschaft für Internationale Zusammenarbeit (GIZ), for coming on board with their support for the study. Ramakrishna has been particularly helpful in contributing to the design of the study, participating in the planning consultations, helping in fixing meetings with key stakeholders and providing important inputs and information. I am also grateful to the World Bank for their support to the study. Particularly I would like to thank Parmesh Shah, Lead Rural Development Specialist (South Asia Region), and Biswajit, Samit Das and Sitaram, his colleagues in India. I would also like to thank Henk at Cordaid for immediately agreeing to support this study. Finally, I would like to thank Plan India, particularly C.P. Arun, for its support and suggestions in bringing out the study. These are all important stakeholders associated with the SHG 'movement' and their support, in some measure, validates the idea of the SHG study initiative and this will also ensure better dissemination and use of the study.

Finally, I would like to thank my own colleagues who contributed to the completion of the study. At the outset, I would like to profusely thank Amulya, our east zone vice-president, who was Ajay's pick to support the report writing. Amulya, even though at the expense of other priorities, provided super support to Ajay in terms of research, content writing and reading and suggesting modifications in the report; I was often copied on their early morning email communication. Amulya's support immensely helped Ajay, and I'm glad that the study is finished now, and that he can get back to his priorities. Swati and Srinivas largely anchored and assisted Ajay in the field visits, cleaned up the notes, and provided gap information. In the final stages, it was Hardeep who helped with the proofs and coordinated the printing. And finally, I'd like to thank Radhika, Executive Director, ACCESS-ASSIST, in providing the overall coordination to help smoothen the process of the report writing. This period is typically busy for ACCESS, and the fact that the team could provide efficient professional inputs and support is appreciated. I can always count on my team to straddle complexities, and still be able to deliver.

A lot of effort has gone into the study, and I hope that the analysis of the 20 years of the SHG programme helps in informing and influencing the future directions that this important programme takes as it evolves into its next phase. I am happy that ACCESS has been able to bring out another document to add to its knowledge series.

Vipin Sharma
CEO
ACCESS Development Services

ACKNOWLEDGEMENTS

The purpose of this study is to trace the origins of banking SHGs in India and analyse the methodology of SHGs in financial intermediation as it has evolved over the years. An attempt has been made to piece together a comprehensive study that documents and reports the growth of this phenomenon, and to highlight key themes of interest to policymakers and practitioners. The existence of a large number of actors and stakeholders and the rapid rate of growth of innovations around SHGs, in the financial sphere as well in economic and social activities, has made this a challenging task. Microfinance as a discipline, if it can be called that, and SHGs as institutions, if they can be thus described, have many linkages in terms of development interventions and discourses such that the themes and debates touched by them are numerous. As there is extensive material available on almost every aspect of the functioning of SHGs and the SHG–Bank Linkage Programme (SBLP) from virtually every part of the country, it has not been possible to include, synthesize and present all available ideas and outputs.

In writing this volume, I have had the good fortune of receiving the support of a large number of development professionals without whom it would not have been possible to undertake the task at hand. It is more than likely that I have not been able to give expression to all their views and seek their indulgence for any deficiencies in coverage and presentation.

I am extremely obliged to Vipin Sharma, CEO, ACCESS Development Services, for having entrusted me with the task of producing this study, for sharing his ideas and for his unstinting support. I owe a special debt to Malcolm Harper, a father figure in the microfinance world in India, for reading the entire draft of the book and providing his erudite and constructive comments. I was fortunate to have the support of C.S. Reddy, who apart from long discussions, volunteered to go through all the chapters along with Andhra Pradesh Mahila Abhivruddhi Society (APMAS) colleagues— G. Bhaskara Rao, K. Raja Reddy and S. Ramalakshmi—who in turn contributed with helpful comments and materials.

During the course of the study, I was privileged to meet with three of the leading architects of SBLP. Mr Y.C. Nanda, former Chairman, NABARD, was kind enough to discuss the study design and share his own assessment of SBLP and subsequently provided detailed comments on the draft of the book. Aloysius Fernandez of MYRADA, who pioneered the idea of SBLP among NGOs in India, and Hans Dieter Seibel of the University of Cologne, one of the original designers and advocates of bank linkage, too, were generous with their time and materials.

I am thankful to the sponsors for their interest in the study. Prakash Bakshi, Chairman, NABARD, and senior staff S.L. Kumbhare, B.S. Suran and K J.S. Satyasai; Detlev Holloh and Ramakrishna Regulagedda from GIZ; Parmesh Shah and Sitaramchandra Machiraju from the World Bank gave useful advice based on their technical knowledge and field experience.

A large number of policymakers, practitioners, SHG experts and professionals in related subject areas were consulted, each of whom has contributed significantly in the preparation of this study. I am indeed grateful to Thanksy Thekkekara, Government of Maharashtra; Reddy Subrahmanyam, Government of Andhra Pradesh; B. Rajsekhar, G.V.S. Reddy and Usha Rani, Society for Elimination of Rural Poverty (SERP); Sarada Muraleedharan, Jagajeevan, Hemalatha and Ramya, Kudumbashree; Pradeep Kumar Jena and Usha Padhee, Government of Odisha; Arabinda Padhee and Subrat Kumar Biswal, Targeted Rural Initiatives for Poverty Termination & Infrastructure (TRIPTI); Rashmi Patel, Mission Shakti; D. Murali Mohan, Tamil Nadu Corporation for Development of Women (TNCDW); Mukesh Chandra Saran and Ajit Ranjan, Bihar Rural Livelihood Project (BRLP); K.K. Gupta and B.M. Pattnaik, NABARD; Sudha Kothari, Kalpana Pant and Alka Pardeshi, Chaitanya; Kaushalya Thigale, Gramin Mahila Swayamsiddha Sangha (GMSS); Anshu Bhartia, Friends of Women's World Banking (FWWB); D. Narendranath and Souparno Chatterjee, Professional Assistance for Development Action (PRADAN); Chandra Singh, MYRADA; L.H. Manjunath, K.V. Bhat, Manorama Bhat G.V., Mamata Harish Rao, Dinesh and Vishal, Sri Kshetra Dharmasthala Rural Development Project (SKDRDP); Girish Sohani, BAIF Research Foundation; Ram Sowmithri, Apt Source Corporate Services Pvt. Ltd; S. Sadananda, IDPMS; H.S. Veershekharappa, Institute for Social and Economic Change; R. Selvanathan, Sarvodaya Nano Finance Ltd; Anil Singh, NEED; B. Uma Maheshwara Rao, Indur Intideepam MACS Federation (IIMF); Madhvi Desai, Ananya, Y. Savitha, Sanghamithra Financial Services; Joslin Thampi, Bullock Cart Workers Development Association (BWDA); V. Badrinarayanan, Hand in Hand; B. Narendranatha Reddy, Andhra Bank; Selvam Veeraraghavan, Indian Bank; G.C. Pande, State Bank Institute of Rural Development; Dasarathi Tripathy, Block Mahila Sanchayika Sangha (BMASS), Jagannath Prasad; Govind Dash, Gram Utthan; Nayana Mohanty, Swayanshree Mahila Samabaya Ltd; Sharada Patel, Sanginee Secondary Cooperative; Jugal Kishore Pattnaik, Mahashakti Foundation; Jharana Mishra, Bharat Integrated Social Welfare Society (BISWA); Sanjaya

Kumar Parida, BISWA Social Security Services Pvt. Ltd; Asish Kumar Sahu, Credible Microfinance Ltd; and Banabasini Biswal, DSWO, all of whom gave their time and helped with information about their work and views on important issues. Besides, leading consultants M.S. Sriram, Girija Srinivasan, N. Srinivasan, Ramesh S. Arunachalam, M.S. Sundara Rajan and Vinod Vyasulu all contributed their ideas and useful suggestions.

I am also grateful to the organizations covered in the study for their cooperation in providing the necessary data and to the participants of a Roundtable organized by ACCESS Development Services on the theme 'Next Phase of Development of the SHG Programme' in September 2011, during which it was possible to meet and benefit from the views of a large crosssection of important stakeholders.

At ACCESS, I am especially grateful to Amulya Mohanty who was an invaluable and constant source of support, provided extensive research inputs and was a most useful sounding board for ideas. He took the lead in the preparation of Chapter 5, and contributed significantly to the preparation of Chapter 4. Radhika Agashe, as task manager, ensured prompt attention to all study requirements. Amulya and V. Chiranjeevi arranged full logistical support in Bhubaneshwar and Hyderabad respectively, and joined in visits in connection with the study. B. Srinivas and Swati Gaur accompanied me on visits to various organizations, collated data and prepared useful notes. Albert Rozario researched and helped to compile the case studies. Deepak Goswami facilitated additional data collection. Hardeep Kaur helped in liaison with the printer and Lalitha Sridharan took efficient care of all administrative arrangements.

The study would not have been completed without the contribution of Phani Priya, independent researcher, who, as in the past, tirelessly helped with data analysis and research support. Pritha Sen provided editorial assistance at short notice.

Most importantly, I would like to thank Usha, Mrinalini and Rukmini for their patience and continued support.

The original version of the book was written during September–November 2011 for release during the Microfinance Summit in December 2011. It has subsequently been revised and updated to include coverage from the *Microfinance State of the Sector Report 2011* and data from the NABARD publication *Status of Microfinance in India 2010–11* which was made available in the latter half of January 2012. The views contained in the book are of the author who is solely responsible for any errors in reporting, interpretation and analysis.

Ajay Tankha
New Delhi
29 February 2012

ABBREVIATIONS

APDPIP	Andhra Pradesh District Poverty Initiatives Project
APMAS	Andhra Pradesh Mahila Abhivruddhi Society
APRACA	Asia-Pacific Rural and Agricultural Credit Association
APRPRP	Andhra Pradesh Rural Poverty Reduction Project
ASA	Action for Social Advancement
ASCA	Accumulating Savings and Credit Association
ASSEFA	Association of Sarva Seva Farms
ASSSL	Apni Sahakari Sewa Samiti Ltd
AWS	Aadarsha Welfare Society
AWWs	*Anganwadi* Workers
BCs	Business Correspondents
BFs	Business Facilitators
BFL	BWDA Finance Limited
BISWA	Bharat Integrated Social Welfare Agency
BLFs	Block-level Federations
BMASS	Block Mahila Sanchayika Sangha
BMBCCSL	Bagnan Mahila Bikash Cooperative Credit Society Limited
BPL	Below Poverty Line
BRLPS	Bihar Rural Livelihoods Promotion Society
BWDA	Bullock Cart Workers Development Association
CAFRAL	Centre for Advanced Financial Research and Learning
CAGR	Compound Annual Growth Rate
CAIM	Convergence of Agricultural Interventions in Maharashtra
CAPART	Council for Advancement of People's Action and Rural Technology
CARE	Cooperative for Assistance and Relief Everywhere
CASHE	Credit and Savings for Household Enterprise
CB	Commercial Bank
CBMFI	Community-Based Microfinance Institution
CBO	Community-Based Organization

CBS	Core Banking Solution
CCA	Convergent Community Action
CCLs	Cash Credit Limits
CDA	Cluster Development Association
CDE	Centre for Development Education
CDF	Cooperative Development Forum
CECOEDECON	Centre for Community Economics and Development Consultants Society
CGAP	Consultative Group to Assist the Poor
CGMST	Chaitanya Grameen Mahila Swayamsidha Sangh Trust
CHASS	Changanassery Social Service Society
CIDA	Canadian International Development Agency
CIF	Community Investment Fund
CLAs	Cluster Level Associations
CLFs	Community-level Financial Systems
CmF	Centre for Microfinance
CMG	Credit Management Groups
CMMFI	Community-managed Microfinance Institution
CMRC	Community Managed Resource Centre
CPC	Central Processing Cell
CRP	Cluster Resource Persons
CS	Capital Support
CSP	Customer Service Point
CYSD	Centre for Youth and Social Development
DBCDC	D. Devaraj Urs Backward Classes Development Corporation
DCCB	District Central Co-operative Bank
DDM	District Development Manager
DFID	Department for International Development
DGRV	Deutscher Genossenschafts- und Raiffeisenverband e. V. (German Cooperative and Raiffeisen Confederation – reg. assoc.)
DHAN	Development of Humane Action
DPIP	District Poverty Initiatives Project
DRDA	District Rural Development Agency
DWCD	Department of Women and Child Development
DWCRA	Development of Women and Children in Rural Areas
ENABLE	National Network Enabling Self-Help Movement
EPVG	Extreme Poor and Vulnerable Group
FAO	Food and Agriculture Organization
FARR	Friends' Association for Rural Reconstruction
FWWB	Friends of Women's World Banking
GIS	Geographic Information System
GIZ	Gesellschaft für Internationale Zusammenarbeit

GMSS	Gramin Mahila Swayamsiddha Sangh
GOI	Government of India
GRADES	Governance and strategy, Resources, Asset quality, Design of systems and implementation, Efficiency and profitability and Services to SHGs and SHG performance
GRAM	Gram Abhyudaya Mandali
GTZ	Gesellschaft für Technische Zusammenarbeit
HCSSC	Holy Cross Social Service Centre
HDFC	Housing Development Finance Corporation
HiH	Hand in Hand
HIVOS	Humanistisch Instituut voor Ontwikkelingssamenwerking (Humanist Institute for Development Cooperation)
HUDCO	Housing and Urban Development Corporation
ICDS	Integrated Child Development Services
ICICI	Industrial Credit and Investment Corporation of India
IDA	International Development Association
IFAD	International Fund for Agricultural Development
IGA	Income Generation Activity
IIM-A	Indian Institute of Management, Ahmedabad
IIMF	Indur Intideepam MACS Federation
IKP	Indira Kranthi Patham
INAFI	International Network of Alternative Financial Institutions
IRDP	Integrated Rural Development Programme
IRV	Individual Rural Volunteer
ISMW	Indian School of Microfinance for Women
JLG	Joint Liability Group
JVK	Jana Vikash Kendra
KADFC	Karnataka Agriculture Development Finance Company Limited
KBCDC	Karnataka Backward Classes Development Corporation
KBS	Kenduadihi Bikash Society
KDFS	Kalanjiam Development Financial Services
KJS	Kajala Janakalyan Samity
KYC	Know Your Customer
MACS	Mutually Aided Cooperative Society
MACTS	Mutually Aided Cooperative Thrift Society
MARI	Modern Architects for Rural India
MAVIM	Mahila Arthik Vikas Mahamandal
MBT	Mutual Benefit Trust
MCID	Micro-Credit Innovations Department

MCP	Micro Credit Plan
M-CRIL	Micro-Credit Ratings International Limited
MDGs	Millennium Development Goals
MF	Microfinance
MFDEF	Microfinance Development and Equity Fund
MFI	Microfinance Institution
MFO	Microfinance Organization
MI	Micro Insurance
MIS	Management Information System
MMS	Mandal Mahila Samakhya
MoRD	Ministry of Rural Development
MPOWER	Mitigating Poverty in Western Rajasthan
MS	Mandal Samakhya
MWCD	Ministry of Women and Child Development
MYRADA	Mysore Resettlement and Development Agency
NABARD	National Bank for Agriculture and Rural Development
NABFINS	NABARD Financial Services Limited
NBH	National Housing Bank
NBFC	Non-banking Finance Company
NBJK	Nav Bharat Jagriti Kendra
NCAER	National Council of Applied Economic Research
NGO	Non-governmental Organization
NPAs	Non-performing Assets
NPL	Non-performing Loan
NREGA	National Rural Employment Guarantee Act
NREGS	National Rural Employment Guarantee Scheme
NRLM	National Rural Livelihoods Mission
NRLP	National Rural Livelihoods Project
OSHC	Odisha Self-Help Cooperative
OXFAM	Oxford Committee for Famine Relief
PACS	Primary Agricultural Credit Societies
PANI	People's Action for National Integration
PAR	Portfolio At Risk
PBG	Pragati Bandhu Group
PDS	Public Distribution System
PEACE	People's Action for Creative Education
PEDO	People's Education and Development Organisation
PLA	Participatory Learning and Action
PLF	Panchayat-level Federation
PRADAN	Professional Assistance for Development Action
PREM	People's Rural Education Movement
PRI	Panchayati Raj Institution
PWDS	Palmyrah Workers Development Society
RASS	Rashtriya Sewa Samithi

RBI	Reserve Bank of India
RCT	Randomized Controlled Trial
RFA	Revolving Fund Assistance
RGMVP	Rajiv Gandhi Mahila Vikas Pariyojana
RGVN	Rashtriya Gramin Vikas Nidhi
RLF	Revolving Loan Fund
RMK	Rashtriya Mahila Kosh
ROSCA	Rotating Savings and Credit Association
RSETIs	Rural Self Employment Training Institutes
RRB	Regional Rural Banks
SAGs	Self-help Affinity Groups
SAPAP	South Asia Poverty Alleviation Programme
SBI	State Bank of India
SBLP	SHG–Bank Linkage Programme
SDC	Swiss Agency for Development and Cooperation
SERP	Society for Elimination of Rural Poverty
SEVA	Social Education and Voluntary Action
SEWA	Self Employed Women's Association
SFMC	SIDBI Foundation for Micro Credit
SGSY	Swarnajayanti Gram Swarozgar Yojana
SHG	Self-help Group
SHGPF	Self-Help Group Promotional Forum
SHPA	Self-help Promoting Agency
SHPI	Self-help Promoting Institution
SIDBI	Small Industries Development Bank of India
SJSRY	Swaran Jayanti Shahri Rozgar Yojna
SKDRDP	Sri Kshetra Dharmasthala Rural Development Project
SKS	Swayam Krushi Sangham
SLBC	State Level Bankers' Committee
SMBT	Sarvodaya Mutual Benefit Trust
SMCS	Swayamshree Micro Credit Services
SMS	Sreema Mahila Samity
SNFL	Sarvodaya Nano Finance Limited
SNLP	SHG Nonfarm Livelihood Project
SNU	Swayam Niyantrana Udyamam
SOC	Sector Own Control
SPMS	Sri Padmavathi Mahila Abhyudaya Society
SRI	System of Rice Intensification
SRLM	State Rural Livelihood Mission
SRTT	Sir Ratan Tata Trust
SSV	Sakh Se Vikas
TAHDCO	Tamil Nadu Adi Dravidar Housing and Development Corporation
TNCDW	Tamil Nadu Corporation for Development of Women

ToT	Training of Trainers
TRIPTI	Targeted Rural Initiatives for Poverty Termination and Infrastructure
TWDC	Tamil Nadu Women's Development Corporation
UBTMS	Uttar Banga Tarai Mahila Samity
UNDP	United Nations Development Programme
VA	Voluntary Agency
VDOs	Voluntary Development Organizations
VLSA	Village Savings and Loan Associations
VO	Village Organization
VVV	Vikas Volunteer Vahini
WFP	World Food Programme
WSHGs	Women SHGs
WWB	Women's World Banking
ZS	Zilla Samakhya

OVERVIEW

1

1.1 Background

Development interventions are of many types and are implemented through many different institutions and agencies. This book is about a special institutional intervention that has touched the lives of hundreds of millions of people in India and created an unmatched resource built upon the social mobilization and empowerment of women. Self-help groups (SHGs) have become a familiar presence in the countryside and have also been successfully promoted in urban areas. Indeed, with the massive social capital embodied in them, SHGs can be considered to have emerged as a significant part of the development infrastructure. It, however, remains an open question whether SHGs were originally intended to fill the institutional gap in the delivery of financial and non-financial services and welfare schemes to the poor. At the same time, SHGs generally have been promoted as an effective channel and means for the delivery of microfinance, which for some time held out the promise globally as a 'magic bullet' for poverty reduction. As the number of SHGs has multiplied in the past 20 years or so, so have the types of activities and innovations that have been designed around them. As a result, the SHG movement represents a rich diversity of interventions and outcomes difficult to classify and analyse. Within the larger SHG 'movement', however, the programme for linking SHGs with banks has been a core innovation that has been the mainstay of SHG development over time.

The SHG movement in India took shape in the 1980s as several NGOs experimented with social mobilization and organization of the rural poor into groups for self-help. The SHG–Bank Linkage Programme (SBLP) under the leadership of the National Bank for Agriculture and Rural Development (NABARD), the apex bank for agriculture and rural development in the country, which built upon these experiments, completed two decades of existence in February 2012. It is, therefore, time to attempt a comprehensive

1

assessment of the accomplishments and shortcomings of SHGs and community institutions built upon them, and to chart their progress in microfinance and other developmental initiatives. The SHG movement has come to mean more than merely the provision of financial services to their group membership, which is composed mainly of poor women. However, it is the role of SHGs in financial intermediation that holds great promise as a means of financial inclusion and mainstreaming of poor families as well as a development model with wider application.

The role of SHGs as financial intermediaries emerged from a pilot programme, with NABARD support, to link 500 SHGs to the banking system in 1992. It is now a major global microfinance programme with an outreach to nearly 7.5 million SHGs having savings accounts with banks as on 31 March 2011 and nearly 4.8 million SHGs with outstanding loans from the banking system. While the NGOs played a pivotal role in innovating and developing the SHG–bank linkage model in the initial years, state governments have contributed to the rapid scale-up and growth of SBLP with banks emerging as development partners. A wide range of SHG-based federations and community institutions have also been formed in an attempt to support livelihoods and empowerment of the rural poor. These in turn have been facilitated and mediated by varying degrees of state government, donor, bank and NGO support; the legal and regulatory environment for their financial operations; and the larger socio-economic context. Indeed, the evolutionary paths of SHGs have been extremely diverse which also further represent differing degrees of success and sustainability. Over the years SHGs have both been lauded for their role in enabling women to participate in income-generating activities and to take up leadership roles in the community, as well as berated for involving women as an instrumentality of the state in a limited service delivery agenda. Thus, the role played by SHGs and other stakeholders in the provision and extension of financial services to the poor, along with addressing other wider objectives, merits a thorough investigation.

SBLP has several positive features, though it also faces several challenges for its continued growth and development. SHGs have been an important means of bringing some financial services to poor sections of the rural population. The programme has brought millions of poor into contact with mainstream banking, and 80% to 90% of SHG members are women. There is a consensus that by joining SHGs, saving regularly and availing loans, women members have been able to reduce their dependence on moneylenders and have realized empowerment benefits and also modest economic benefits. Besides, the programme has shown impressive rates of loan recovery by banks at well over 90%, which is higher than recoveries under other components of their loan portfolio. However, in recent years these levels of performance are being found to be difficult to sustain.

There are concerns that SBLP has been confined mainly to the southern region of India and has not expanded uniformly to the resource-poor regions, though some eastern states are now picking up. Also, it is widely accepted that apart from the major government programmes, funds for SHG promotion are relatively scarce. Related to this is the question of the quality of SHGs that have been promoted and their ability to undertake the increasingly large number of responsibilities that are often thrust upon them. Besides, SHGs are now largely promoted under government programmes for delivering credit with only a limited focus on savings. A major issue has been the effect of government subsidies under the Swarnajayanti Gram Swarozgar Yojana (SGSY), the asset-based poverty alleviation programme, and interest subsidies provided by several state governments in respect of SBLP. In fact, the Rangarajan Committee on Financial Inclusion (GOI, 2008) was of the opinion that subsidy on interest rates cuts at the very root of the self-help character of SHGs, and would be better redirected towards capacity building input and marketing support to SHGs.

The exponential growth of the number of SHGs, particularly in the early years of this century, has been closely followed by the even more sensational growth of the clientele of microfinance institutions (MFIs) largely using the Grameen methodology based upon smaller joint liability groups, often including members of the existing SHGs, especially in certain southern states of India. The tension and competition between the leading MFIs and the state-supported SHGs as sources of credit have been exacerbated in terms of issues related to client outreach, multiple borrowing, over-lending and coercive recovery in Andhra Pradesh and other southern states. As such, their future has become inextricably linked, and overlaps, comparisons and trade-offs with the MFI model have become a factor in the future and growth of the SHG model. The intensive promotion of SHGs by the Andhra Pradesh government (with multilateral agency support), which is being replicated closely in some other states, also provides for a greater financial intermediation role for SHG-based federations as also dedicated sources of funds independent of the banking system. It has, therefore, also become necessary to take a fresh look at the SHG-based model of financial services delivery to the poor as it is placed after the recent crisis in microfinance in India; and to re-energize the SBLP and other SHG programmes through necessary investments by concerned stakeholders.

Accordingly, this book undertakes a critical assessment of the growth of the SHG movement in the country over the last two decades, the role and experiences of different actors and the various challenges faced by them, along with a study of the enabling factors and constraints to SHG development in the country. It reviews the outstanding issues and examines the promise of new government initiatives on rural livelihoods based on SHGs. The learning from this exercise will serve to contribute to new thinking in microfinance policy and necessary initiatives for the effective functioning of SHGs and their institutions.

1.2 RESEARCH AND DOCUMENTATION ON SHGS

Thousands of reports, articles and case studies exist in respect of one aspect or the other of SHGs. These report both positive and negative experiences of the implementation of the programme and serve to provide useful learning for policy purposes. NABARD has itself conducted and sponsored impact evaluations and its regional offices have brought out state-level studies on SHG–bank linkage. Under the rural finance programme of Gesellschaft für Technische Zusammenarbeit (GTZ; now called GIZ), a major action research agenda has been implemented along with the preparation of thematic studies relevant for the banking system. NGOs such as Mysore Resettlement and Development Agency (MYRADA) and Development of Humane Action (DHAN) Foundation have documented their SHG models as also produced commentaries on microfinance in India (Fernandeg, 2003). Some states like Rajasthan and West Bengal have brought out state-level reports covering the microfinance sector and the self-help movement respectively that cover SHGs. Finally since 2006, the *Microfinance State of the Sector Reports*, sponsored by ACCESS, have provided an up-to-date and comprehensive account, on an annual basis, on the fate of the microfinance sector, including SBLP.

However, very few substantive studies have been undertaken of SHGs in microfinance in India. The earliest major study of these 'new middlewomen' was by Harper et al. (1998). In 2002, NABARD commissioned a set of six reports on various aspects of SHG banking to mark 10 years of bank linkage. Tankha (2002) provided perhaps the first comprehensive stocktaking of SHGs as financial intermediaries in India. The Consultative Group to Assist the Poor (CGAP) conducted analyses on SHG sustainability in 2003. Thereafter, the NCAER-GTZ study (NCAER, 2008) and the EDA Rural Systems–APMAS Lights and Shades study (EDA Rural Systems, 2006) have been the major reference studies on the impact of SHG FDA Rural Systems, 200 bank linkage and the strengths and weaknesses of SHGs in various domains. APMAS has dominated ratings and action research on federations in Andhra Pradesh and elsewhere. It has documented SHG federations (APMAS, 2007); and in collaboration with Deutscher Genossenschafts- und Raiffeisenverband e.V. (DGRV) (Salomo et al., 2010) prepared practical guidelines for their sustainability. ACCESS and Rabobank too have contributed recently to the study of development costs and sustainability of federations in six states (Srinivasan and Tankha, 2010). At present, studies towards an evaluation of the SHG programme in eight states are being undertaken by National Network Enabling Self-Help Movement (ENABLE), a national network of SHG resource organizations.

1.3 OBJECTIVES

The book contains outputs and findings of a study conducted by the author in the latter part of 2011 for ACCESS Development Services. It is based on secondary research undertaken for the study and the author's own extensive engagement with primary research on SHGs in the past.

The study has dual objectives. It undertakes both a substantive historical examination of the evolution of SHGs and their federations in India as well as a comprehensive review of ongoing issues and recent concerns related to their microfinance operations. The study provides a typology of the SHGs engaged in financial intermediation over the past two decades and the objectives with which they have been formed and supported. It revisits the key objectives of NABARD in selecting the SHG methodology as a programme for the unbanked poor and assesses the outreach and performance of the SBLP through time series data in respect of diverse physical and financial indicators.

It also examines the progress of both state government initiatives and those of other self-help promoting agencies (SHPAs)[1] in developing replicable models for financial intermediation and microfinance plus activities. The study highlights cases of institutional innovations by SHPAs that serve to illustrate the versatility of the agency of the SHG. It analyses the rationale of models of financial intermediation through SHGs and SHG-based institutions that have emerged given the limitations posed by the regulatory environment and the opportunities and challenges presented by market forces. In particular, it covers the experience of financial federations of SHGs, their relevance and quality and the constraints to their effective functioning. Similarly, it examines the role for SHGs and SHG federations in government-supported poverty alleviation and wider livelihoods development programmes.

The study focuses on three core issues pertaining to SHGs. These relate to (*a*) cost-effectiveness, (*b*) sustainability and (*c*) impact, i.e., the development cost of SHGs and SHG-based institutions; the sustainability of SHGs models, and community institutions fostered by them, along with the viability of the SBLP for the participating banks; and the impact of credit through SHGs in terms of poverty targeting, livelihood and income generation, and gender and social empowerment.

- The cost of promotion of SHGs, and subsequently of SHG federations, has been a concern of the donor community towards its continued financial support to NGOs. Promotion cost also forms the basis of a critique of the SHG model that emphasizes the high initial costs of the SHG-intermediated delivery model as compared to retailing of credit through MFIs. The findings of various field studies reporting SHG development costs, and recent promotional cost estimates of various SHPAs, are interpreted and benchmarked.

---

[1] The terms SHPAs and SHPIs (self-help promoting institutions) are used interchangeably in the book.

- The financial and organizational sustainability of the SHGs is often called into question. The analysis covers aspects such as the quality of SHGs, their financial performance and governance. Also analysed is the efficacy of institutional innovations, such as SHG federations, aimed at their long-term functioning. Evidence of viability of lending to SHGs by different banking agencies and findings related to the transaction costs incurred by both parties are also examined.
- The contested issue of the impact of SHGs on the lives of their members is evaluated through a discussion of several large and small studies on the subject including those by NABARD, NCAER, CGAP and other research institutions in terms of a range of relevant impact parameters.

Finally, the study reviews the existing state of affairs in respect of the SHG banking and addresses the question of what should be the next phase in the development of SHGs. It identifies the policy gaps and opportunities that exist for SHGs to be mainstreamed further into the formal financial system. The study also discusses elements of strategy and design being adopted by the National Rural Livelihoods Mission (NRLM) as also the plans of NABARD for the future development of SHGs. It concludes with a discussion of proposals and institutional arrangements for the continued growth of SHGs as an agency for change in the rural sector of India.

The book is based mainly on secondary research covering all players on the SHG stage. Besides, customized data was obtained from 10 NGOs and 6 government programmes for the purpose of the study. This was supplemented by visits to SHGs and their associations, meetings with leading SHG promoters and interviews with key stakeholders and experts. Individual and group consultations were also conducted with various stakeholders including NABARD, World Bank, state government agencies, banks, MFIs and technical support and donor agencies. The book also draws upon an extensive review of the substantial literature on SHGs and the writings of leading researchers and practitioners, including those of the author, in analysing the issues, experiences and prospects of the SHG movement.

1.4 Organization

The book has been organized into nine chapters. Following this introductory chapter, Chapter 2 traces the origin of SHGs, and the different features and typologies of SHGs. Further, it examines the origins of the SHG movement in India and evolution of the SBLP with its multiple and varied stakeholders. Chapter 3 reviews the physical and financial progress under the SBLP over almost two decades since its inception. Drawing upon the experiences of 10 leading NGO promoters, Chapter 4 examines how NGOs and SHGs have come together for financial intermediation through various structures and institutions, such as federations, that have been developed over the years. Chapter 5 has a look at the role of SHGs under half a dozen government livelihoods programmes of different states. Also taken up for review is the design and implementation plan of NRLM which has a special role for SHGs and their federations.

Chapters 6, 7 and 8 are the thematic chapters that cover a critical examination of research on costs, sustainability and impact of SHGs. Chapter 6 contains a detailed review of estimates of cost of promotion for SHGs and the economics of federations. Chapter 7 examines the evidence, based on a host of studies, of organizational and financial sustainability of SHGs and the SBLP. This includes issues related to quality of SHGs and SHG federations, viability of lending to SHGs by banks and the role of SHG federations in providing sustainable financial services. Chapter 8 covers the area of impact of SHG-based microfinance programmes on SHG members. It provides a discussion of the methodology of impact assessment and a critical examination of impact studies of SHGs. (Case studies of outcomes at individual member and SHG level are given in Appendix 10.)

The concluding chapter (Chapter 9) brings together an analysis of the current situation in respect of SHGs and banks in financial intermediation, expectations of NRLM, the role of NABARD and the imperatives of strategy and design for the next phase of SHG development.

Without anticipating the findings of the book, it can be suggested that the SHG movement stands at a crossroads. With the passage of time a fresh set of imperatives and possibilities necessitate a second round of innovation with the SHG model—an SHG initiative—much as the original Grameen model gave way to a more versatile range of products under Grameen II. The dominant role of government in SHG promotion, including the implementation of NRLM in 12 states, while providing much needed resources for expansion may, however, limit the space for NGO initiatives. At the same time, it has become necessary for NABARD, to reinvigorate the SBLP with fresh ideas in terms of institutional structures, delivery channels and financial products for the poor. It is hoped that the present study and analysis can help to contribute in a small way to a fresh thrust to the development of SHGs.

ORIGINS AND EVOLUTION OF SHG–BANK LINKAGE

2

The term 'self-help group' can be used to describe a wide range of financial and non-financial associations. A large number of informal and formal groups of various types, largely unregistered, are to be found in villages and cities throughout the world. These groups are engaged in financial, non-financial, social, cultural and economic activities. Of particular interest has been the role of such informal groups in the effective provision of enhanced financial services to their members by relying on social rather than physical collateral.

It is possible to distinguish between two broad approaches. Of these, the 'model' of the Grameen Bank of Bangladesh has attracted universal acclaim in its ability to deliver useful microcredit services to individual clients organized into *joint liability groups* (*JLGs*). The replication of the Grameen model by thousands of MFIs has been accepted as a major development success. Alternate approaches to the use of groups in the delivery of financial services have focused on the ability and potential of small groups to manage and lend their accumulated savings, and externally leveraged funds, to their members by following the principles of *self-help and mutual benefit* to their collective advantage. In such approaches the groups in effect act as financial intermediaries or 'mini banks' with the members both as owners and users.

2.1 ORIGINS OF SELF-HELP GROUPS

One of the important and fascinating traditional means of financial intermediation has been through the medium of different forms of financial self-help groups or mutual aid savings associations—the rotating savings and credit association (ROSCA), and its more evolved form, the accumulating savings and credit association (ASCA).[1]

These associations continue to be important sources of finance for people in urban and rural areas of developing countries of South and South East Asia, Africa and Latin America and the Caribbean. In India too, such informal groups are to be found—though rather more in urban areas, particularly in south India—in the form of *chits* or chit funds, and variously as *nidhi*s, *bishi*s or *shomiti*s in other areas such as Maharashtra, Gujarat, Assam and Uttar Pradesh. The prevalence of informal *financial* self-help groups in rural areas is somewhat limited.[2] The *chit* funds of southern India are a more widespread phenomenon whose subscribers are mainly the non-poor. Harper et al. (1998) reported that in the Indian rural scenario, chit funds or ROSCAs were ubiquitous.[3] In addition, there is a variety of groups such as *mahila mandal*s, village development groups, water user groups and youth groups, which are fairly common. Some of these groups have been involved in thrift and credit activity as well.

Many of the established international donors and NGOs such as United Nations Development Programme (UNDP), Oxford Committee for Famine Relief (OXFAM), ActionAid and Plan International have supported informal groups or community organizations in a programme of 'poverty lending' which gave higher priority to social outreach than financial sustainability. Revolving loan fund grants, earmarked for these groups were managed and held in trust by NGOs until community capacity for self-management was developed. These larger village-based groups were engaged in an integrated development model with health, education and natural resource management as other components.

The NGO sector in India had gained momentum in the 1980s with its socio-economic programmes, especially in developing and promoting people's organizations and community-centred activities. NGOs like Bhagavatula Charitable Trust in Andhra Pradesh, Self Employed Women's Association (SEWA) in Gujarat and Centre for Youth and Social Development (CYSD) and People's Rural Education Movement (PREM) in Odisha played a significant role in women's empowerment by forming informal

---

[1] ROSCAs are time-bound associations in which members contribute to a fund that is given in part or wholly to each member in turn. ASCAs need not be time bound and may *accumulate* their funds through loans at interest to members and others. Profits may be distributed periodically or retained. Bouman's (1995) authoritative paper on ROSCAs, ASCAs and various hybrid forms of such associations uses the term 'self-help groups' to describe these traditional and ongoing financial arrangements.

[2] ROSCAs were found to continue to exist in rural Alwar district of Rajasthan during the SHG Light and Shades study in 2005 (Sinha et al., 2009).

[3] Further, that rural bank managers and NGO staff found it comparatively easy to convert them into on-lending groups.

groups and promoting savings in the form of cash and kind by women members of village households.

Village development groups were piloted by various NGOs in India in the mid-1980s notably by MYRADA. These groups, through mutual consensus, worked towards providing access to credit to their members. MYRADA taught the group members the importance of cultivating weekly savings and giving loans to each other from their savings. These groups were called *credit management groups* (CMGs). MYRADA staff provided training on how to organize meetings, set an agenda, keep minutes and other areas vital to successful business ventures. The members were linked together by a degree of affinity based on relationships of trust and support; they were also often homogeneous in terms of income or of occupation. In 1987, they were renamed as self help groups (Fernandez, 1992).[4] These groups were among the first of their kind, i.e., the *self-help groups* (SHGs) as we know them today.

Similarly in Maharashtra (and other states) under the Integrated Child Development Services (ICDS) programme, *mahila mandals* were established by government with the help of NGOs such as Chaitanya, which in turn looked for new avenues for capacity building and promoting financial access of the group members. In 1987 the NGO Professional Assistance for Development Action (PRADAN), which was working on a pilot on the effectiveness of the government's poverty alleviation programme in Rajasthan, introduced savings in groups that had been provided with a grant for fodder purchase to deal with the drought conditions. In 1989, International Fund for Agricultural Development (IFAD) piloted the Tamil Nadu Women's Development Project in Dharmapuri district, based on an innovative idea that promoted an informal group-based system of lending and saving. After women paid contributions into a communal account, they could access loans from local commercial banks participating in the scheme.[5] MYRADA and other NGOs participated in this process that contributed to the evolution of the formal linkage of commercial banks to these SHGs.

However, it was only in 1992 that NABARD, the apex bank for agriculture and rural development in India, formally set up a pilot on the modalities for the linkage of SHGs to banks. It provided the framework for the operations of these groups as well as the training and capacity building support at all levels for participating banks, the NGO promoters and the SHGs along with refinance support to the banks that lent to SHGs. The emergence of the SHG–bank linkage model is described in Section 2.3.

---

[4] This was done following receipt of a grant from NABARD, details of which are discussed in Section 2.4.

[5] Available online at http://www.ifad.org/events/op/2008/microfinance.htm (accessed on 6 September 2011).

2.2 Types and Role of SHGs

Features of SHGs

The SHGs that thus came to be promoted by Indian NGOs, banks and government agencies can be described as a form of ASCA. This form of SHG is effectively a micro bank as it raises equity and deposits, as well as external funds, and on-lends them. Harper et al. (1998) had described Indian SHGs as on-lending groups *which collect their own equity capital, and savings deposits, from their owners, who are also the members and the customers, they lend out their money to the members, at interest rates which they decide, and they accumulate profits which they choose either to distribute to the owners, or to add to the fund at their joint disposal.*[6]

The principal features of existing SHGs can be stated as follows:

- An SHG is generally an informal homogeneous group formed through a process of self-selection based on the affinity of its members.
- It is owned by its members and operated on principles of self-help, solidarity and mutual interest.
- Most SHGs are women's groups with membership ranging between 10 and 20.
- SHGs have well-defined rules and by-laws, hold regular meetings and maintain thrift and credit discipline in the financial intermediation of own and borrowed funds.
- SHGs are self-managed and characterized by participatory and collective decision-making and pooling of their savings and other resources.
- The group has a code of conduct to bind all the members.
- All the members are required to be regular in savings, repayment of loans and attending meetings.
- The groups generate a common fund where each member contributes an equal amount of savings on a regular basis.
- The group decides the amount to be saved, its periodicity and the purpose for which loan is given to the members.
- All transactions must happen only during the group meeting.
- Loanees are decided by consensus.
- Loan procedures are simple and flexible.
- The group decides the rate of interest to be paid/charged on the savings/ credit to members and the repayment period.
- The group functions in a democratic way allowing free exchange of views and participation by members.

---

[6] It may, however, be argued that Indian SHGs, especially those promoted by government agencies, are not necessarily voluntary associations of people like ASCAs.

- The group maintains basic records and books of accounts.
- The group opens a savings account with the bank in the name of the SHG to be jointly operated by two or three designated leaders of the SHG.

As indicated earlier, NABARD has been a major force in the development of the role for SHGs in the financial system in the form that it is today. NABARD has pioneered the SHG–bank linkage model which positions the SHGs as financial intermediaries to enable the flow of bank loans to poor members without physical collateral. The essential role of SHGs and process of their mainstreaming under the bank linkage model is briefly set out in Box 2.1. The SHG–bank linkage model as it has developed in India is now a major model of microcredit globally. It has evolved over a period of about 25 years since the first SHGs of MYRADA received NABARD support and 20 years since the launch of the pilot project for SHG–bank linkage. A more detailed examination of how the model has emerged is taken up in the Section 2.3.

Box 2.1: SHG—A Concept

An SHG is a group of about 10 to 20 people from a homogeneous class, who come together for addressing their common problems. They are encouraged to make voluntary thrift on a regular basis. They use this pooled resource to make small interest bearing loans to their members. The process helps them imbibe the essentials of financial intermediation, including prioritization of needs, setting terms and conditions and accounts keeping. This gradually builds financial discipline in all of them. They also learn to handle resources of a size that is much beyond their individual capacities. The SHG members begin to appreciate that resources are limited and have a cost. Once the groups show this mature financial behaviour, banks are encouraged to make loans to the SHG in certain multiples of the accumulated savings of the SHG. The bank loans are given without any collateral and at market interest rates. Banks find it easier to lend money to the groups as the members have developed a credit history. The groups continue to decide the terms of loans to their own members. Since the groups' own accumulated savings are part of the aggregate loans made by the group to its members, peer pressure ensures timely repayment and replaces the 'collateral' for the bank loans. Apart from financial help in the time of need the group provides social security to its members.

Source: Adapted from Introduction by Y.C. Nanda in Kropp and Suran (2002) and NABARD (2006).

Promoters and Types of SHGs

Apart from the rotation of own funds and on-lending of external grants and borrowed funds, SHGs may be engaged in a range of social and economic activities that go beyond the immediate financial operations. Besides, SHGs are seen as means of enabling the development of women, of building their capacities for economic activity and their political and social empowerment. SHGs promoted by NGOs—as also women's departments of government and under different bilateral and multilateral projects—invariably have the empowerment of women as central to their development agenda.

SHG promotion has also been directed at poorer households and communities. Thus, wealth ranking, vulnerability mapping and other poverty targeting criteria have generally been a part of the process of SHG formation for NGOs. Alternately, attempts are made primarily to cover marginalized communities and tribal and scheduled caste groups.

For government agencies too, SHG promotion under the below poverty line (BPL) focused SGSY, income generation projects such as Swa-Shakti with objectives of economic empowerment and promoters such as ICDS with women's awareness, life skills and social issues, is part of a wider development agenda. In several states, SHGs have been provided with revolving fund grants for their lending activities. They have also received handouts like television sets and gas connections. Further, several women SHGs or similar formations encouraged to undertake thrift activity have been set up under a range of sectoral projects, thereby incorporating a limited gender component in the project design.

Commercial banks, regional rural banks and cooperative banks too have been engaged in promotion of SHGs with own staff or with the help of agents and volunteers. This is apart from the key role performed by them in linking SHGs to the financial system (described in greater detail in Chapter 3) and in providing the loan component of the funding for asset formation for individuals and groups through SHGs under the SGSY programme. The biggest thrust in SHG formation in recent years has been through the mega programmes of SHG promotion and support in several states such as Andhra Pradesh, Kerala, Bihar and Odisha. These programmes have attempted to use the SHGs as building blocks for a more comprehensive livelihoods strategy that goes beyond financial intermediation. As a result of all these efforts the SBLP has grown to cover nearly *7.5 million SHGs with savings accounts in banks and nearly 4.8 million SHGs with loans outstanding as of 31 March 2011.*

A large proportion of SHGs have been brought together in federations at village, village cluster, block and higher levels. A recent study (Salomo et al., 2010) quoting July 2010 estimates by APMAS indicates that the number of SHG federations in the country is 163,852. Out of these, 158,166 are primary-level federations and the rest are secondary- and tertiary-level federations. The purpose of these federations has been to strengthen the groups and their members in their negotiations with external agencies, in their efforts to realize better market access and bargaining power—as also facilitate the withdrawal of the promoting NGOs. This in turn has raised a fresh set of issues and possibilities in respect of institutional development and in terms of operational challenges.

In the two decades and more of SHG promotion and linkage with the formal financial system, there has been an ongoing process of evolution and change in the SHGs, as they and their promoters grapple with the complexities of sustaining the growth and relevance of the movement, which has brought them to where they are today. Box 2.2 below gives a broad typology of SHGs engaged in financial intermediation in India as distinguished by their origin and source of funding.

Box 2.2: Typology of SHGs

1. *Pre-existing groups:*
   - ROSCAs/ASCAs identified by banks and accessing bank loans
2. *Promoted by NGOs/NGO-MFIs:*
   - With support from international and national and donor agencies
   - With grant support from NABARD and government sources
3. *Promoted by banks:*
   - By bank staff
   - By farmer's clubs
   - By individual rural volunteers and agents
4. *Promoted by District Rural Development Agency (DRDA)/government departments and agencies/local governments:*
   - By women development departments through ICDS functionaries
   - By other government departments, e.g., animal husbandry, forests, tribal affairs
   - Under SGSY by DRDAs in different states
   - By project management under mega programme of government (with or without multilateral agency support)
   - By municipalities and panchayats
5. *Promoted by existing SHGs and their federations*
   - Self-promoted 'copy cat' SHGs formed by SHG members themselves
   - By individual agents, paid for by the groups

Source: Adapted from Tankha (2002).

SHGs and Grameen Groups

It is instructive also to contrast the SHGs with other small groups set up under what can be called the 'Grameen model' based on solidarity groups or JLGs (as it emerged in Bangladesh and spread out throughout the world) wherein groups of women are similarly brought together to access loans and other financial services. Box 2.3 provides a summary of the two systems. Certain differences are in evidence. There is clearly a heavier self-management load of membership in an SHG. SHG members collectively take decisions

Box 2.3: 'Indian' SHGs and 'Bangladesh' Solidarity Groups

Bangladesh Solidarity Group System

Prospective clients are asked to organize themselves into 'Groups' of five members which are in turn helped by the MFI to organize into 'Centres' of around five to seven such Groups. The MFI checks that all members are poor, and are not related. The members make regular savings with the MFI, and also take regular loans. Groups and Centres perform tasks such as,

- holding regular weekly Centre-level meetings, supervised by an MFI worker who maintains the records for collection of savings and repayments;
- organizing contributions to one or a number of group savings funds, which can be used by the group usually only with the agreement of the MFI;
- guaranteeing loans to their individual members, by accepting joint and several liability, by raising group emergency funds and by accepting that no members of a Group will be able to take a new loan if any members are in arrears;
- arising from the above, appraising fellow members' loan applications, and ensuring that their fellow members maintain their regular savings contributions and loan repayments.

Indian SHG System

The members form a group of around 10 to 20 members. The group may be promoted by an NGO, government, bank or by an MFI or it may evolve from a ROSCA or other locally initiated grouping. The process of formal 'linkage' to an MFI or bank usually goes through the following stages:

- The SHG members decide to make regular savings contributions. These may be kept by their elected head, in cash, or in kind, or they may be banked.
- The members start to borrow individually from their Groups, on terms and at interest rates decided by the Groups themselves.
- The SHG opens a savings account, in the Group's name, with the bank or MFI, for such funds as may not be needed by members, or in order to qualify for a loan from the bank.
- The bank or MFI makes a loan to the SHG, in the name of the Group, which is then used by the Group to supplement its own funds for on-lending to it members.

Source: Adapted from Harper (2003b).

about loans to be given to their members and their terms and tenure and interest rates. They are also required to act as bookkeepers to maintain books of accounts. Alternately, relatives or outsiders may be charged with undertaking this function, with or without a fee, and act as guides for SHGs in financial matters.

The place of savings in group operations is also different in the two systems. Grameen groups were basically formed to access microcredit. Small supplementary funds were also started for emergencies, and later savings too generally became a part of the system. SHGs were planned as thrift, or small savings, groups to generate funds for internal rotation in the first instance. These funds were supplemented by funds leveraged from banks on the basis of a multiple of SHG savings. Thus SHGs were 'savings first' and 'savings-led' rather than credit-led groups. However, banks have been more focused on using SHGs as a way of aggregating poor people's loan requirements, rather than encouraging savings and enabling the 'graduation' of SHG members to individual accounts.

2.3 EVOLUTION OF SHG–BANK LINKAGE

The present forms taken by SHGs have involved a process of evolution since the 1980s which saw NABARD along with leading NGOs and advisers from GTZ shape and define a methodology and delivery structure aimed at providing a supplementary channel as a source of finance for the households beyond the reach of the conventional banking system. It is necessary, therefore, to have a closer look at the origins and objectives of the financial intermediation role of SHGs and how it emerged over the years.

Need for Alternative Approaches for Banking with the Poor

For 20 years or so after Independence, the emphasis of government was on promoting cooperatives to help provide the credit needs of farmers, big and small, and the needs of other sections of rural society were largely overlooked. After the nationalization of major commercial banks in 1969 and the thrust towards social banking, a major expansion of commercial rural and semi-urban bank branches took place with the objective of improving the access of poorer households to financial services. Regional rural banks (RRBs) were set up in 1975 as low-cost institutions which were intended to serve the poorer sections of society.[7] However, bankers were not convinced that the poor were bankable and that lending to the poor could be a viable activity. Poverty alleviation programmes, such as the Integrated Rural Development Programme (IRDP) which was started in 1980, and which supported asset creation at the household level for BPL families through subsidy-cum-bank loan were implemented with little enthusiasm by bankers. Weaknesses in the design of the IRDP led to mis-targeting and

---

[7] The clients of RRBs were to be those families with incomes somewhat less than half the levels represented by the official poverty line!

abysmally low recoveries over the years, being exacerbated by political decisions to waive loan repayments. This left banks with unpaid loans and losses in their IRDP portfolio.

NABARD, which had been formed in 1983 as the apex bank for agriculture and rural development, had the task of finding ways and means to strengthen the credit delivery system to the unbanked poor and to bring about an improvement in recoveries of loans given under rural credit programmes. It piloted two types of innovations for this purpose. The first, with the help of the International Development Association (IDA) of the World Bank group, was to strengthen the rural bank branches to reach and serve their clients in far-flung villages. This was undertaken by helping to improve their mobility and logistical support through provision of motorcycles to rural bank managers. Complementary to this was another small programme called Vikas Volunteer Vahini (VVV) which was aimed at spreading awareness of credit among rural borrowers, sensitizing bankers to their needs, addressing the problem of poor repayment of bank loans and creating, through 'friends of banks clubs',[8] a bridge between the bankers and the poor clients.

Some of the findings of NABARD's own researches at the time were that

> the procedures of rural banks were complicated with high transaction costs for both banks and the poor; the standardized credit products such as production loans were inappropriate; tiny savings existed, but the poor had no opportunity to deposit them; and that collateral requirements of banks did not meet the needs of the poor. (Seibel, 2005)

As a result, NABARD, jointly with the Canadian International Development Agency (CIDA), funded action research in 1987 into CMGs formed by the Bangalore-based NGO, MYRADA. During the period 1983 to 1985, MYRADA had found that the strength of the groups promoted by it came from the affinity among their members. MYRADA built upon this affinity through a package of training modules to help the members manage their groups. However, when the groups wanted to borrow money they found that banks would not lend to such unregistered groups, but only to individuals. MYRADA approached NABARD in 1985–86, and was sanctioned ₹ 1 million as a research and development grant to match their savings and for institutional capacity building training as part of a pilot experiment to assess whether the groups could function as institutions with functions that

---

[8] These clubs, renamed as 'farmers' clubs' are still in existence on a small scale and play a role in helping banks to form and support SHGs.

went beyond savings and credit (Fernandez, 2003). The name of the CMGs was changed to SHGs on NABARD's advice.

Feasibility Studies on Linkage Banking

At the institutional and policy level the combined efforts of NABARD as the lead agency in India, Asia-Pacific Rural and Agricultural Credit Association (APRACA)[9] as an important regional network and communication forum and GTZ as the German technical assistance agency contributed to the development of the concept of linkage banking. In this section a brief discussion is undertaken on the emergence of SHG banking in India. It draws upon the work of Hans Dieter Seibel (Seibel, 2005, 2006) who was both a leading designer of bank linkage as well as chief chronicler of the early years of India's SBLP. The NGO side of the story is provided by Aloysius Prakash Fernandez of the NGO MYRADA, the unquestioned pioneer of innovation in linking SHGs to banks who documented their evolution from being CMGs to Self-Help Affinity Groups (SAGs) (Fernandez, 1992, 2003).

In Germany, researchers, building on a wide variety of earlier studies of 'self help groups'[10] and informal finance, had been attempting to upgrade these groups with the objective of integrating them into the national financial system, through an appropriate legal framework. Linkage banking as conceived had two components—'upgrading' of groups as informal financial intermediation agencies and 'downgrading' banks—a reference to the simplification of their procedures and delivery mechanisms for the benefit of the new clients (Seibel, 2005).

In 1985, GTZ decided to carry out feasibility studies of linkages between banks and these informal groups. The first set of studies was carried out in western Africa, where informal financial groups were found to exist in large numbers. However, with the undeveloped banking infrastructure there were no banks that could function as partners. This led them to turn their attention to Asia and to present the bank linkage model at the APRACA Regional Workshop in Nanjing in May 1986.

The linkage approach was subsequently adopted by APRACA at the Sixth General Assembly in Kathmandu, December 1986, as its main programme and supported by a GTZ regional project.

---

[9] APRACA is an association of central banks, rural development banks and rural commercial banks, established in 1977 with support from FAO and a mandate to promote innovations in rural finance.

[10] The concept of SHGs was not new in Germany. In fact, as noted by Seibel (2005) it dates back at least to the origin of the savings and credit groups of the emerging cooperative movements around 1850. German researchers saw the SHGs essentially as informal cooperatives.

Seibel (2005, 2006) identifies the key elements of the approach as,

- building on the existing formal and non-formal financial infrastructure, including SHGs as informal financial intermediaries;
- savings-based credit linkages with banks;
- informal groups holding savings and credit accounts in banks;
- NGOs (self-help promoting institutions [SHPIs]) as facilitators;
- flexible models of cooperation between SHGs, NGOs and banks as autonomous business partners, each with its own existing financial and institutional resources and interest margin to cover its transaction costs.

APRACA, with special programme support by GTZ played the role of a lead agency in promoting SHG-banking in Asia and the Pacific. It was recommended at the Nanjing workshop that each member country would form a task force to conduct a survey of SHGs and, in case of identified potential, to formulate suitable national programmes involving banking through SHGs.

The SHG–bank linkage strategy was first attempted as a pilot[11] in Indonesia during the late 1980s. The Central Bank of Indonesia had authorized its public and private banks to accept informal groups as customers and lend to them without insistence on physical collateral. Repayment rates of SHGs during the pilot phase were 100%.

Findings of NABARD Survey

In 1987 a study team—led by NABARD and comprising other Indian members of APRACA—conducted a survey of 46 SHGs of the rural poor spread over 11 states and associated with 20 promoting institutions, including MYRADA, findings of which were published in March 1989 (NABARD, 1989).[12] The SHGs covered in the case studies represent a variety of groups like savings and credit groups, joint farming groups, irrigation groups, a

---

[11] During the first half of 1987, feasibility studies were carried out with GTZ support in Indonesia, Philippines and Thailand and concluded in each country with a national workshop. In Indonesia, Bank Indonesia as the central bank, together with Bank Rakyat Indonesia as the government's agricultural bank and Bina Swadaya, a prominent NGO, adopted the approach in a pilot project (Seibel, 2006). The feasibility studies, and the resulting guidelines for a flexible linkage model to be adjusted to the circumstances in each country, were presented in 1987 at the 10th Foundation Anniversary of APRACA in New Delhi and published as Kropp et al. (1989).

[12] The 1987 study of SHGs by NABARD was in response to the adoption of 'Linking Banks and Self-help Groups' as the main programme of APRACA, a decision taken in Kathmandu in 1986 which provided the background for the adoption of the term and the savings-based strategy.

sericulture farming group, social forestry groups, trade groups and non-farm activity groups. All SHGs had more than 20 members and some 45–50 members. Various interesting practices of self-management of savings and credit by the groups were observed. All these groups saved, governed and managed their funds themselves, quite often with the help of an NGO.

The major findings of the NABARD study were:

- Almost all the sample SHGs were formed with an emphasis on self-help in order to promote objectives like freedom from exploitation, economic improvement and raising resources for development.
- By and large the sample SHGs were of target groups consisting of vulnerable sections of society. Homogeneity in terms of caste and economic activity played a significant role in organizing the poor into SHGs.
- Most groups evolved flexible systems for governing their working and managing their common resources in a democratic way.
- The SHGs evolved a variety of instruments to promote thrift among their members. Some SHGs were observed to have an emergency fund based on membership fees or surplus funds from their economic activities.
- Internal loans were generally provided on the basis of trust in borrowing members without any paperwork or security. The recovery of these loans was excellent.
- Majority of the SHGs were cohesive groups having features similar to those of formal bodies.
- Women's groups were successful in both savings mobilization and credit management, and in promoting income-generating activities.

The study observed that most of the SHGs were passing through an evolutionary stage with a very low resource base. Most groups were heavily dependent on NGOs. *It suggested that NGOs be actively involved in any scheme of linkage with banking institutions.* The absence of a legal status of SHGs was seen as a major constraint in the development of linkages between SHGs and banks. Another question that was raised was whether the SHGs could stand on their own after the withdrawal of NGOs. Finally, it suggested that given the diverse nature of SHGs, flexible models of linkages would be appropriate for various situations and that action research projects would be needed evolving appropriate linkage models.

Policy Changes and Pilot Project on SHG–Bank Linkage

On the basis of the findings of the above research survey and APRACA discussions, NABARD after a policy dialogue with the Reserve Bank of India (RBI) prepared a pilot project for linking informal groups to banks.

NABARD opted for an approach which used the existing infrastructure of banks and social organizations, was savings-driven rather than credit-led and favoured bank rather than donor resources in the provision of credit (Seibel, 2006). Accordingly, NABARD launched in 1992 a pilot project for linking 500 SHGs with banks with the objective of financing SHGs as financial intermediaries at the grass-roots level linked to banks across the country for both savings mobilization and credit delivery.

RBI and NABARD took the following three major policy decisions:

- Banks could lend to SHGs without ascertaining the purpose for which the loan was being taken by the eventual borrower.
- Banks would undertake lending to groups without physical collateral.
- Banks would be allowed to lend to unregistered groups.

Appendix 1 gives details of important circulars that set out the framework pertaining to the linking of SHGs with banks. A feature of this approach was that it moved away from the subsidy-oriented thinking associated with poverty alleviation programmes and at the same time attempted to bring about a viable means of improving the access of the rural poor to the banking system.

The process was started by the RBI in July 1991 advising scheduled commercial banks[13] of the proposed NABARD pilot project to cover 500 SHGs.[14] It provided the selection criteria for SHGs and asked the banks to actively participate in the project. NABARD's landmark circular of 26 February 1992 on the pilot project detailed the objectives of SHG–bank linkage. It envisaged that a non-formal agency of credit supply to the poor, in the form of 'Self-Help Group' of the poor could emerge as a promising partner of the formal agencies. Under the linkage project, the main advantage to the banks would be externalization of a part of the work items of the credit cycle—assessment, supervision and repayment, less paper work and reduced transaction costs. Improved recoveries and margins would lead to a wider coverage of the target group. A larger mobilization of small savings would also be possible. For the SHGs the advantage would lie in the access to larger financial resources and better technology and skill upgradation through bank schemes. The circular also allowed banks to lend to NGOs or Voluntary Agencies (VAs) for on-lending to SHGs, thus creating an alternative variant or 'model' of SHG–bank linkage to the direct bank-to-SHG route that was being piloted. However, the circular/scheme was restricted only to one savings and one loan product.

---

[13] The project was extended to cooperative banks and regional rural banks in 1993.
[14] The size of the SHGs was indicated as 10 to 25 persons. This was later, in October 1994, modified to limit the size to only 20 persons in order to avoid attracting the provisions of the Companies Act.

The 1992 circular also proposed that the rate of interest on the bank loan to the SHG would be 12% per annum and that the banks' loans would be refinanced at subsidized rates to encourage this new form of lending. Since the SHGs would not be in a position to offer any collateral security other than group savings, RBI vide the circular of July 1991 had already relaxed the security norm under the pilot project. The pilot phase was extended until 31 March 1995 to be followed by a two-year experimental phase.

The pilot project made steady progress over the years. Beginning with 255 SHGs linked with banks during 1992–93, by 31 March 1996 around 4,750 SHGs were linked with bank loan of ₹ 60.58 million and NABARD refinance of ₹ 56.61 million covering 28 commercial banks, 60 RRBs and 7 cooperative banks in 16 states and 1 union territory.[15] The quick studies conducted by NABARD to assess the impact of the linkage project showed encouraging and positive trends like increase in loan volumes and savings, shift to production activities, excellent recovery percentage, reduction in the transaction cost[16] for both banks and the borrowers, large participation of women, besides leading to gradual increase in the income level of the SHG members. The linkage thus held promise of the reduction of transaction costs of banks through the externalization of costs of servicing individual loans and also ensuring their repayment through the peer pressure mechanism.

These experiences clearly showed that the rural poor

- could save,
- were not concerned much with cost of credit,
- wanted timely and adequate credit,
- were the best judge of their credit needs and
- were good users and repayers of credit in groups.

These positive findings paved the way for the expansion of the SBLP.

SHG–Bank Linkage as Normal Business Activity

The basic objectives of linking SHGs with banks were

- to evolve a supplementary credit strategy for reaching the poor,
- to build mutual trust and confidence between banks and the rural poor and
- to encourage banking activities (both thrift as well as credit).

---

[15] From NABARD circular dated 1 October 1996 (Appendix 1).

[16] A study in three states of south India during the pilot phase estimated the reduction in transaction cost of banks to an extent of 41%, as compared to normal individual lending. (Findings of Puhazhendhi, 1995—as quoted in Satish, 2005.)

Based on this successful approach, it was decided to use SHGs as intermediaries between the banks and the rural poor for the mutual benefit of both parties. RBI constituted a working group under the chairmanship of S.K. Kalia, Managing Director, NABARD with a view to studying the functioning of SHGs and NGOs for expanding their activities and deepening their role in the rural sector. The working group in its report[17] viewed the linking of SHGs with the banks as a cost-effective, transparent and flexible approach to improve the accessibility of credit from the formal banking system to the unreached rural poor and a solution to the twin problems being faced by the banks, viz. recovery of loans in the rural areas and the high transaction cost in dealing with small borrowers. *Accordingly, it was decided to extend the SHGs linkage programme beyond the pilot phase as a normal business activity of banks to improve the coverage of the rural poor by the banking sector and to make it part of their corporate strategy.*[18]

Other recommendations aimed at mainstreaming bank linkage in the operations of banks were advised vide RBI circular dated 2 April 1996 and NABARD circulars dated 1 October 1996 and 7 October 1996 (see Appendix 1). It was clarified that SHG members who had defaulted could not obtain loans from the banks but could do so from the group's own internal fund rotation. However, SHGs with a few defaulters of bank loans could receive loans from banks.[19]

The bank linkage programme, as envisaged and implemented by NABARD, had a strong foundation in the involvement of NGOs that had promoted informal groups in rural areas and could undertake to prepare them for bank linkage. Most of these NGOs were working with formations different from SHGs. In response to the needs and possibilities of bank linkages, they began to form SHGs of smaller sizes that could engage in savings and credit, for eventual linkage with the formal banking system. The social capital that such SHG formation drew upon in the form of local affinities and traditions of cooperation and mutual help was further cemented to facilitate the linkage programme. SHGs not only drew upon social capital but enhanced it, making it possible for the emerging groups to engage in a range of activities beyond the narrow confines of thrift and credit. Recognizing these possibilities, the pioneering NGOs with the help of several multilateral and bilateral donor programmes were able to undertake a substantial programme of SHG formation within an integrated approach

---

[17] See NABARD (1995).

[18] RBI circular RPCD. No. PL. BC 120/04.09.22/95-96 dated 2 April 1996.

[19] This provision pertained to the problems created by the fact that a fair number of SHG members were already covered by the banking system under the IRDP many of whom were, willfully or compulsorily, in default to the banks on the loans taken by them. Several such borrowers of the IRDP, and later of SGSY loans, continue to be defaulters in bank records.

to development that included a host of economic and social activities. At the same time it could be suggested, at least in retrospect, that in scaling up from a pilot to a mainstream programme of the banks, there was not much by way of changes or additionality in terms of design or preparedness to embark on this major initiative—involving much capacity building at different levels in its implementation and which was further fuelled by target-driven growth.

2.4 The Challenge of Capacity Building

Capacity building was thus a major challenge faced by NABARD upon extension of the SBLP. As a result it established a credit and financial services fund, with assistance from Swiss Agency for Development and Cooperation (SDC) (Kropp and Suran, 2002) with the objective of supporting banking and financial institutions to undertake innovations in credit delivery for rural borrowers, particularly the unreached poor. The fund provided the initial funding requirement for promotion, capacity building and NABARD refinance to banks. In 1998 NABARD formed the Micro-Credit Innovations Department (MCID) with microcredit innovation cells in the regional offices. *MCID formulated a 10-year vision of credit linking one million SHGs, covering a population of 100 million poor by 2008.* Capacity building efforts at several levels for realizing the vision became a major element of NABARD's support for the SBLP. It included consultations with banks, NGOs and government officials, preparation of training modules for different categories of personnel and sponsoring of training programmes for bankers, NGOs and other promoters of SHGs. It also provided for financial support for self-help promoting institutions (SHPIs) and RRBs in formation of SHGs. In this effort it received extensive technical support from GTZ and other agencies. Thus, GTZ has been involved in the conceptual development of the linkage model and its initial piloting in India and Asia, as well as in subsequent support for capacity building and strengthening of SHG–bank linkage. SDC and GTZ were the two main agencies that provided financial and technical support to NABARD for grounding the SBLP. SDC was a source of major support for NABARD's experimentation and SDC funds were used by NABARD for training, studies, visits abroad, etc. Government of India announced in the year 2000–01 the establishment at NABARD of a start-up fund called the Microfinance Development Fund with an initial corpus of ₹ 1 billion, with 40% contributions each from RBI and NABARD and 20% from commercial banks, which was aimed at providing promotional grants to SHPIs and funding support for capacity building, exposure and awareness building. Though off-take from the fund was and has continued to be slow and limited, this was redesignated as Microfinance Development and Equity

Fund (MFDEF) in 2005–06 and the corpus increased to ₹ 2 billion to also cover capital/equity support to MFIs. This was further increased to ₹ 4 billion during 2010–11.

2.5 MAJOR INSTITUTIONAL PLAYERS AND SUPPORT AGENCIES

The entry of NABARD to support SHG activities in the early 1990s encouraged the NGOs, with the help of bankers, to strengthen their SHG programmes. However, as the concept was new to them, only a few organizations were involved in SHG promotion. As the SBLP gained momentum after 1999 in southern India, SHGs became popular in each and every state as a cost-effective credit delivery system. NGOs realized that SHGs were a viable means for socio-economic development of the rural poor, especially women, and started promoting SHGs in their respective operational areas.

At the same time, SHGs attracted the attention of state governments, who undertook, through departmental initiatives, a major programme of SHG promotion. Notable among the state governments was Andhra Pradesh, which provided incentives for SHG formation under the Podupulakshmi programme.[20] These initiatives had in turn been inspired by successes achieved by experiments such as at Chevella and particularly in undertaking anti-liquor programmes in 1990s. The women's departments of several states were also active in SHG formation. The IFAD project involving the Tamil Nadu Corporation for Development of Women (TNCDW) was a particular case in point, which first provided the resources for SHG promotion to a large number of NGOs in Tamil Nadu. Similarly, women's empowerment was a major thrust of the Maharashtra Rural Credit Project undertaken by Mahila Arthik Vikas Mahamandal (MAVIM), also with support from IFAD. Government of Kerala implemented Kudumbashree project in 1998. The UNDP–South Asia Poverty Alleviation Programme (SAPAP) project in Andhra Pradesh was succeeded by the World Bank-supported Velugu project in 2002 in two phases, the latter phase of which is being currently implemented as the Indira Kranthi Patham (IKP) programme. World Bank has also been supporting Government of Bihar's Jeevika Project from 2007 for rural livelihoods and in 2009 the Targeted Rural Initiatives for Poverty Termination and Infrastructure (TRIPTI) project for poverty reduction in 10 coastal districts of Odisha.

In Rajasthan, Odisha, Madhya Pradesh and several other states, the Department of Women and Child Development actively promoted

---

[20] Around 200,000 SHGs were understood to have been formed under this programme during a two-year period—1997 to 1999.

the formation of SHGs through training of ICDS functionaries. Under the auspices of the Department of Women and Child Development, Government of Odisha, a platform for women's empowerment 'Mission Shakti' was launched in 2001 to accelerate the SHG movement in the state. Further, projects for economic empowerment of women through SHGs were implemented in the form of Swa-Shakti (1999) and Swayamsiddha (2001) projects. While Swa-Shakti Project (Rural Women's Development and Empowerment Project) was a World Bank/IFAD assisted project which was implemented in 35 districts in the states of Bihar, Haryana, Karnataka, Gujarat, Madhya Pradesh and Uttar Pradesh as a centrally sponsored scheme, Swayamsiddha project was implemented in 650 blocks of 35 states/union territories.

In 2003 the 'Sakh Se Vikas' (SSV) programme in Rajasthan focusing on building SHGs and federations was initiated by the Sir Ratan Tata Trust (SRTT), which has emerged as the leading Indian donor agency. Subsequently, Centre for Microfinance (CmF) was established in Jaipur not only to upscale the microfinance interventions and provide technical support to existing microfinance players in Rajasthan but also act as nodal agency for the SSV programme. Recently, in collaboration the Government of Rajasthan, SRTT is involved in Mitigation of Poverty in West Rajasthan (MPOWER) through SHGs and their federations in West Rajasthan. In association with PRADAN in Jharkhand, since 2004 SRTT has been facilitating the promotion and capacity building of SHGs and working towards their food security and income enhancement. It has also supported Community Banking Programme of Kalanjiam Foundation (2007–10). Since 2008, it has taken up Sukhi Baliraja Initiative in the distressed districts of Maharashtra to alleviate agrarian distress among farmers by promoting microenterprises through microcredit support to the SHGs. In order to expand its activities, SRTT has partnered with Government of Maharashtra and IFAD through the Convergence of Agricultural Interventions in Maharashtra (CAIM) programme since 2010.

In addition, the revamped IRDP, called SGSY, introduced in 1999 had in its design a clearer role for SHGs in the delivery of loans for asset creation for poverty alleviation, as against the direct individual beneficiary model practiced earlier. The promotion of groups and provision of credit and subsidy were carried out under rigid targets that were fixed every year. Under the SGSY, DRDAs were to support NGOs in formation and training of SHGs for the programme, through reimbursement of expenses undertaken by them. Grading criteria were established for these SHGs as screening devices for bank linkage. *Nor was SHG promotion confined to projects and initiatives aimed at linking these institutions to the banking system. In watershed and farm forestry projects, and projects involving agriculture-based activities SHGs or similar formations in the form of 'user groups' also were actively promoted.* These groups were predominantly of women and served to add a gender dimension to project activities. Most of these common interest groups and user groups were also encouraged to undertake thrift activity as both a desirable saving mechanism as well as to engender social cohesion and enhancement of social capital.

Though a number of large, medium and small players were involved in taking the SHG movement forward, the contribution of a few major players is worth mentioning in funding of microcredit programmes and building capacity of the SHGs and their resource institutions.

National Bank for Agriculture and Rural Development (NABARD)

Being the largest player, NABARD has been instrumental in facilitating various activities under SHG movement at the ground level, involving NGOs, bankers, other formal and informal entities and even government functionaries, directly or indirectly. This has been done through training and capacity building of all these entities, promotional grant assistance to SHPIs, Revolving Fund Assistance (RFA) to NGO-MFIs, Equity/Capital Support (CS) to MFIs to supplement their financial resources and 100% refinance against bank loans for SHGs. NABARD continues to extend grant support to NGOs, RRBs, District Central Co-operative Banks (DCCBs), Farmers' Clubs and individual rural volunteers (IRVs) for promoting and nurturing SHG. New SHPIs were identified even while support to existing ones continued. In order to fine-tune the strategies for up-scaling support to the microfinance sector, NABARD conducted awareness creation and sensitization programmes and arranged exposure visits for SHG members, NGO, bankers, trainers and Panchayati Raj Institution (PRI) representatives, NABARD staff, government officials and micro-entrepreneurs throughout the year. As of March 2011, with the support of NABARD, 2.66 million participants had been trained with a cumulative fund support of ₹ 510.6 million; 205,798 participants were trained during 2010–11. In 2010–11, NABARD spent about ₹ 101 million towards capacity building of partner institutions as against ₹ 99.3 million in 2009–10.[21] *Though NABARD contributed by making available financial support to cover part of the costs of SHG promotion incurred by NGO promoters, this was comparatively small in relation to the investment undertaken by international donors who emerged as the mainstay of NGO funding for SHG-based and other activities.* Since the launching of the pilot project by NABARD, the cumulative amount of refinance disbursed by it up to 31 March 2011 was ₹ 154.07 billion. During 2010–11, a sum of ₹ 474 million was released from the MFDEF for support to the microfinance sector, of which ₹ 299.5 million

---

[21] NABARD, *Annual Report 2010–2011.*

was grant support for promotional activities and ₹ 174.5 million for capital support and revolving fund assistance to MFIs for on-lending to SHGs.

The branches of commercial banks, RRBs and cooperative banks too played a major role in promoting SHGs, directly or with the help of agents and volunteers, in order to meet targets set by higher levels of management even though by and large there was still limited acceptance of the programme on the part of bankers. All the above developments contributed to the accelerated growth of SHGs from about 1999 onwards. With the announcement of the target of 1 million SHGs to be bank-linked by 2008, SHG formation and linkage became target-oriented, and brought forth a surge of SHGs linked to banks by various agencies.

There are a few apex institutions providing funds and capacity building support for microfinance through various MFIs, including SHGs. Under various schemes they provide bulk loans to retail NGO-MFIs and other emerging forms of MFIs such as financial cooperatives, mutually aided cooperative thrift societies (MACTS), and federations of SHGs. A similar approach to NABARD's bank linkage using NGOs/MFIs as intermediaries has also been adopted by other bulk-lending institutions such as the Small Industries Development Bank of India (SIDBI), Friends of Women's World Banking (FWWB), Rashtriya Mahila Kosh (RMK), Housing Development Finance Corporation (HDFC) and Housing and Urban Development Corporation (HUDCO).

SIDBI Foundation for Micro Credit (SFMC)

The SIDBI Foundation for Micro Credit (SFMC) which was set up with the assistance of IFAD and Department for International Development (DFID) in 1999, emerged as a leading microfinance wholesaler in India promoting sustainable MFIs for addressing gaps in the rural credit system. More specifically, SFMC tried to develop a new financial system for microfinance in the country,

- by providing institution building support to MFIs by making them strong, formal, sustainable and responsive, helped in moving them towards commercial sources of finance;
- by encouraging investment in microfinance by the formal financial sector leading to mainstreaming of microfinance;
- by supporting capacity building through reputed technical and management institutes; and
- by facilitating the development of a network of service providers such as Rating Agencies and Technical Support Providers.

SIDBI normally gives loans to MFIs working with different models to on-lend to clients both in urban and rural areas, the most popular ones being the Grameen and SHG model. Among organizations that were given loans by SIDBI to on-lend to SHGs are the Bullock Cart Workers Development Association (BWDA), Sanghamithra Rural Financial Services, Lupin Human Welfare and Research Foundation, Sarvodaya Nano Finance Limited (SNFL), Shramik Bharati, Adhikar, Biswa and Gram Utthan. In course of time, many MFIs who were working with the SHG model, have switched over to the JLG/Grameen model.

As of March 2011, SIDBI had sanctioned ₹ 70.35 billion in loans and disbursed ₹ 65.48 billion to MFIs with a loan outstanding of ₹ 30.50 billion. In addition to this, it has sanctioned ₹ 230 million and disbursed ₹ 190 million in transformation loans to various NGOs to operate microfinance programmes with an appropriate legal entity. Through its MFI partners it had 34 million clients across the country.

Friends of Women's World Banking (FWWB)

As an affiliate of Women's World Banking (WWB), in 1989 Friends of Women's World Banking (FWWB) became a national level wholesaler on-lending to MFIs/community-based MFIs (CBMFIs) in India. In addition to credit support, FWWB provides capacity-building support in terms of trainings, workshops, exposure visits to equip NGOs/MFIs/CBMFIs for management of financial institutions. Also, FWWB provides support to start up MFIs to cover operational deficits. Working in 17 states of India, including Manipur from the North East, FWWB has supported more than 300 institutions with technical assistance and nearly 200 institutions with loan support of approximately ₹ 11.0 billion benefiting 2.6 million women as of March 2010. The loan outstanding as on 31 March 2010 was ₹ 3.75 billion benefitting 1.27 million women borrowers across 117 MFIs in 17 states of India. During the current year, i.e., 2010–11, the lending and investment activities of FWWB have been transferred to a non-banking finance company (NBFC) called Ananya Finance. FWWB affiliates like BWDA, Peoples' Solidarity Association, New Life, Association for Rural Community Development, Rashtriya Gramin Vikas Nidhi (RGVN), Adhikar, Biswa, Gram Utthan, Parivartan, Friends' Association for Rural Reconstruction (FARR) have been given loans by FWWB to on-lend to SHGs. Loans for financing SHGs constitute about 15% of the total portfolio of FWWB.

Rashtriya Mahila Kosh (RMK)

The success of providing microcredit through SHGs encouraged the central government to establish a national level microcredit organization known as the Rashtriya Mahila Kosh (RMK) under the Ministry of Women and Child

Development (MWCD) in 1993, with an initial corpus of ₹ 310 million. Since then RMK has provided loans to NGOs and VAs to on-lend to SHGs at the grass-roots level to help women take up income-generating activities. Till 31 March 2011, RMK had sanctioned ₹ 3.08 billion and disbursed ₹ 2.52 billion to 687,512 women beneficiaries through SHGs. RMK is now being restructured as an NBFC with a corpus of ₹ 5 billion. With the proposed induction of funds and conversion to NBFC, the projected yearly number of beneficiaries and loans at the end of financial year 2015–16 are estimated to be 2,195,000 and ₹ 4.92 billion respectively. Recently, the MWCD has stressed the need to converge schemes and programmes having a focus on formation and promotion of SHGs so as to enable women to have access to microcredit and microfinance. Programmes like National Rural Livelihood Mission (NRLM) of Ministry of Rural Development (MoRD), Swayamsidha of MWCD and similar programmes in other ministries and organizations will be converged to help SHGs develop in a coordinated fashion. In addition, the ministry has also planned training and skill upgradation under schemes/programmes of various ministries for the women beneficiaries of SHGs in order to promote self-employment opportunities and create livelihood options for women.

International Donor Support

The role of international donors has been significant in the growth of microfinance in India and the SBLP. In addition to the contribution of GTZ, SDC and CIDA in terms of providing technical and financial support to NABARD for accelerating the SBLP programme, many bilateral, multilateral agencies and private foundations such as IFAD, World Food Programme (WFP), UNDP, World Bank, DFID, Ford Foundation, SRTT and Humanistisch Instituut voor Ontwikkelingssamenwerking (HIVOS) have contributed to scale up the linkage programme and supported the emergence of many institutional models having SHGs at their base (Ghate, 2006). The contribution of DFID in this regard is worth mentioning. With the support from DFID, the Indian National Microfinance Project was managed by SIDBI from 1999 to 2009 and the Credit and Savings for Household Enterprise (CASHE) programme was managed by CARE India from 1999 to 2006. Two prominent institutions in the SHG sector, viz., ACCESS and APMAS have evolved from the CASHE project. CASHE worked with small SHPIs, SHGs and their federations, while SIDBI initially worked with relatively mature and more viable MFIs for on-lending to SHGs.

Over the years a large number of international donors have supported microfinance (MF) programmes run by NGOs. These donors provided administrative support and grants for capacity building as well as revolving loan funds to NGOs. Several international NGOs, especially charities based on child sponsorship such as ActionAid, OXFAM and Plan International provided funding to the leading NGO promoters for community-based organizations (CBOs) which subsequently made way for SHGs. Plan India, for example, supported promotion of SHGs across all its programmes in India which was helpful in rolling out child-centred community development programmes. Eventually, these SHGs started to function as a strong platform to implement most of the children development programmes like maternal and child health care, children's education, care and immunization, women's empowerment and livelihood promotion. Since these SHGs were recognized by the banks, they received loans under the SBLP. The SHGs also established linkages and mobilized government resources under various schemes to support community development work. These experiences supported by review studies showed that SHGs are not just functioning to support child-centred community development work but also serving its members to meet their financial needs through savings, credit and insurance products that have impact on the household's economic security. Based on this, Plan India initiated the community-managed microfinance institution (CMMFI) model through promotion of SHG-Cluster-Federation structures as an extension of the SHG programme. Besides, Rabobank Foundation has in recent years extended support for the development of cooperative community-managed structures of finance based on SHGs.

Donor support has also generally been available for networks of resource organizations. To address the issues faced by the SHG movement such as quality and sustainability of SHG institutions, shortage of funds for promotion and lending, shortage of quality human resources, inadequate capacity building infrastructure, trainers and material ENABLE was formed in 2007. Currently, the network has seven member organizations—APMAS, CmF, Chaitanya, Indian School of Microfinance for Women (ISMW), Reach India, Sampark and Self-Help Group Promotional Forum (SHGPF), with APMAS as the convener. The combined area of operations of the member organizations is spread across the entire country and the organizations possess expertise and resources to promote member-owned, member-managed and member-controlled people's institutions. Since its inception, ENABLE has been working for strengthening of the SHG movement in the country. The network and member organizations, among others, support national and state-level missions and expert committees, develop resource material and conduct special training and exposure for bankers. ENABLE has been receiving core funding from the Ford Foundation and is in issue-based collaboration with UNDP Solution Exchange, SRTT, DGRV, GIZ and NABARD among others. ENABLE is in the process of expansion by inducting more members and plans to focus on policy advocacy based on high-quality research and capacity building of capacity builders.

The outcome of this concerted effort at SHG promotion and capacity building by a range of players with varied objectives has been the emergence of a large reservoir of SHGs and similar groups of varying capacity and maturity for undertaking a developmental role, particularly in financial intermediation. Since the vast majority of these groups comprise women, they serve to mainstream women's voice and participation in the development agenda. A fair proportion of these SHGs have been able to embark upon bank-linkage and borrow from banks to supplement their own resources for on-lending to their members with women's SHGs contributing up to 90% of SHGs bank-linked. While the SHG system has been designed on the concept of savings as an important financial product for the poor, the linkage programme is basically a credit-driven one. Savings of SHGs were treated by banks as a form of security against the credit given to them but their role in providing an important service for SHGs has only lately been realized by the banks. The outreach and performance of SBLP is discussed in Chapter 3.

The activities and programmes of this wide range of development institutions provide the financial, technical and capacity building support to thousands of NGO promoters currently involved in the SBLP as also the federations that have been developed to strengthen the SHGs and to enable flow of credit and other services to them. All over the country NGOs have been promoting SHGs for savings and credit and other social and economic programmes for the past 20 to 25 years. The leading SHG promoting NGOs are a mixed group that includes pure SHG promoters, NGOs functioning as MF intermediaries, and NGOs that have promoted not-for-profit and for-profit non-banking companies for on-lending grant and borrowed funds to SHGs and SHG-based federations. However, the majority of them act as promoters and facilitators of SHGs. *One of the major issues relating to the functioning of NGOs as MFIs is the absence of an appropriate legal form to assist the NGO to carry out MF activities.* The range of initiatives and institutions developed by 10 leading NGOs to meet this challenge is taken up in Chapter 4.

In recent years, the role of government in SHG promotion has outstripped that of NGOs even as the importance of external donors has declined. While in the initial stages, NGO involvement and partnership was a feature even of bilateral/multilateral-aided government programmes with an SHG component, mega programmes for SHG promotion and support are now being implemented directly by project management units. Along with the substantial number of SHGs promoted over the years by various government departments, a stage has been reached when possibly 75–80% of all SHGs are government-promoted. The context, design of scope of these government programmes, along with the SGSY—and NRLM, its successor—are discussed in Chapter 5.

GROWTH AND PERFORMANCE OF SHG–BANK LINKAGE PROGRAMME

3

The SBLP was the major element of the movement to provide bank credit to unbanked poor households through SHGs in India. Starting with a small number of 620 SHGs linked during the first two years, 1992–93 and 1993–94, SBLP, according to NABARD data, had disbursed credit to over 2.23 million SHGs cumulatively by March 2006 (Table 3.1)[1] and as on 31 March 2011 over 4.78 million[2] SHGs had outstanding loans (Table 3.2). SHGs with savings accounts with banks numbered over 7.46 million as on 31 March 2011. Thus, 97 million families were covered by financial services under the SBLP (NABARD, 2011).[3] Accordingly, SBLP enjoys the status of the leading microfinance programme of the world. Though slow to take off, the growth of SBLP accelerated from 1999 and targets of outreach (such as credit-linking one million SHGs by 2008) were easily exceeded.

Since the launching of the pilot project in 1992, SBLP had given importance to two objectives, viz., outreach and access of the poor to institutional credit.

Three models of bank linkage emerged as follows:

1. SHGs formed by and linked directly to banks (Model I)
2. SHGs formed and facilitated by SHPIs such as NGOs and government departments but linked directly to banks (Model II)
3. Indirect bank linkage or 'bulk lending' where NGOs and other MFIs (like Sanghamithra or Sri Kshetra Dharmasthala Rural Development Project [SKDRDP]) acted as financial intermediaries by borrowing from banks and on-lending to SHGs directly, or through SHG federations (Model III)

---

[1] The last year for which cumulative bank linkage data is available.
[2] This figure is down marginally from 4.85 million SHGs with loans outstanding as on 31 March 2010.
[3] This is under the assumption of 13 members per SHG and 1 SHG member per family for the SHGs having savings accounts with banks.

Table 3.1: Progress of Self-help Group–Bank Linkage Programme (*Amount in* ₹ *Billion*)

Year	No. of SHGs credit linked		Bank loan	
	During the year	Cumulative	During the year	Cumulative
1992–94	620	620	0.1	0.01
1994–95	1,502	2,122	0.02	0.02
1995–96	2,635	4,757	0.04	0.06
1996–97	3,841	8,598	0.06	0.12
1997–98	5,719	14,317	0.12	0.24
1998–99	18,678	32,995	0.33	0.57
1999–00	81,780	114,775	1.36	1.93
2000–01	149,050	263,825	2.88	4.81
2001–02	197,653	461,478	5.45	10.26
2002–03	255,882	717,360	10.22	20.49
2003–04	361,731	1,079,091	18.56	39.05
2004–05	539,365	1,618,456	29.94	68.99
2005–06	620,109	2,238,565	44.99	113.98
2006–07	1,105,749	–	65.70	179.68
2007–08	1,227,770	–	88.49	268.17
2008–09	1,609,586	–	122.54	390.71
2009–10	1,586,822	–	144.53	535.24
2010–11	1,196,134	–	145.48	680.72

Source: Compiled from NABARD Annual Reports and NABARD publications, *Progress of SHG–Bank Linkage in India* and *Status of Microfinance in India*.

Note: From 2006–07 onwards, data on number of SHGs financed by banks and bank loans are inclusive of existing groups receiving repeat loans. Owing to this change, NABARD discontinued the publication of data on a cumulative basis from 2006–07.

The annual progress of the SBLP during the period under review is provided in Table 3.1 and aspects of the growth and performance in subsequent sections. It was originally felt that it would be preferable if NGOs could act as financial intermediaries (Model III above) in order to help ensure the responsible use and repayment of bank loans to SHGs (Harper, 1996). There appeared to be sufficient 'spread' in Model III to allow intermediaries in this long chain to take at least a small margin for their work, and the

Table 3.2: SHG–Bank Linkage Programme—Growth and Performance

(March 2001 to March 2011)

Sl. no.	Indicator	2001	2002	2003	2004	2005	2006	2007	2008	2009	2010	2011
							Physical					
1	Number of SHGs having savings with banks[a]						2,630,510	4,160,584	5,009,794	6,121,147	6,953,250	7,461,946
2	Number of SHGs receiving loans during the year[b]	149,040	197,653	255,882	361,731	539,365	620,109	1,105,749	1,227,770	1,609,586	1,586,822	1,196,134
	of which repeat loans (%)		21	40	47	48	56					
	of which under SGSY (%)							17	20	16	17	20
3	Number of SHGs credit linked with banks[a] (cumulative)	263,825	461,478	717,360	1,079,091	1,618,456	2,238,565					
	of which in southern region (%)	71	69	65	62	58	54					
4	Number of SHGs with outstanding loans[a]							2,894,505	3,625,941	4,224,338	4,851,356	4,786,763
	of which in southern region (%)							53	51	54	53	57
	of which under SGSY (%)							24	25	23	26	27
5	Increase/decrease in no. of SHGs with loan outstanding[a]							686,408	700,968	598,397	627,018	−64,593

Table 3.2 (*Continued*)

Table 3.2 (Continued)

Sl. no.	Indicator	Financial										
		2001	2002	2003	2004	2005	2006	2007	2008	2009	2010	2011
6	Savings of SHGs with banks[a] (₹ billion)	2.88					23.9	35.12	37.85	55.46	61.99	70.16
7	Volume of loans disbursed to SHGs during the year[b] (₹ billion)		5.45	10.22	18.55	29.94	44.99	65.70	88.49	122.54	144.53	145.48
	of which under SGSY (%)							21	21	16	15	17
8	Amount of credit disbursed to SHGs (cumulative)[a] (₹ billion)	4.81	10.26	20.49	39.05	68.99	113.98	179.68	268.17	390.71	535.2	680.72
9	Bank loans outstanding with SHGs[a] (₹ billion)					42.05		123.66	169.99	226.79	280.38	312.21
	of which under SGSY (%)							26	28	26	22	25
10	Incremental loan outstanding[a] (₹ billion)								46.33	56.80	53.59	31.83
11	Average loan disbursed per SHG during the year[b] (₹)	19,256	27,574	39,940	51,281	55,510	72,552	59,417	72,074	76,125	91,081	121,637
12	Average loan outstanding per SHG[a] (₹)								46,834	53,689	57,795	65,224

Source: NABARD (2006, 2007, 2008, 2009, 2010, 2011).
Notes: [a] As on 31 March; [b] During the year ended 31 March.

stage was set for a massive expansion. The combined efforts of the banks, the NGOs and the SHGs themselves thus brought institutional credit to the many millions of people who had earlier failed to benefit from it. However, as the programme spread, a host of SHPIs, especially government agencies, contributed to the large numbers of SHGs that were formed with many of them being linked to banks.

3.1 CREDIT LINKAGE

Though SHG–bank linkage is a savings-led and savings-linked programme, the main thrust of the SBLP has been in the provision of microcredit. According to NABARD data as on 31 March 1996, following the mainstreaming of the pilot programme, the number of SHGs that had been credit linked had risen to 4,757 with an estimated 80,000 members. By March 1999, the cumulative number of SHGs credit-linked had increased nearly sevenfold to almost 33,000, and further nearly eightfold in the next two years with the figure standing at 263,825 by March 2001.

Table 3.2 gives data on the performance of SHG–bank linkage over the period 2001–11. It will be observed that the spectacular early phase of SHG growth in the 1990s was sustained over the next five years, 2001–05, as well with a similar over sixfold increase in the *cumulative number of credit-linked SHGs* taking place (on a substantially higher base figure) by March 2005 to reach nearly 1.62 million. The rate of growth of *cumulative bank loans disbursed* followed a similar pattern, with even higher increases in rates of growth. This involved a doubling every year of the bank loan disbursed to SHGs over three years until 2003–04 and a 75% increase in the following year to reach a cumulative figure of nearly ₹ 69 billion by March 2005. This pattern prevailed despite the increasing size of the base figures on which these growth rates were achieved.

With regard to the *number of SHGs credit-linked annually*, the figure rose from 149,040 during 2000–01 (i.e., year ended on 31 March 2001) to 539,365 during the year 2004–05. The *bank loan disbursed during the year* went up more than 10 times from ₹ 2.87 billion in 2000–01 to ₹ 29.94 billion during 2004–05. Similarly, the *average loan size* per SHG increased from ₹ 19,257 in 2000–01 to over ₹ 55,510 during 2004–05. In the initial years, most of the loans disbursed were new loans but by 2005–06 over half of the loans were repeat loans.

Tables 3.3a and 3.3b give the compound annual growth rates (CAGR) for various physical and financial indicators. It is seen that the cumulative number of SHGs credit-linked to banks during 2001–05 rose by a phenomenal 44% per year. The number of SHGs *credit-linked annually* also increased at an impressive 29% per year. The *cumulative* bank loan

Table 3.3a: Growth Rate (CAGR) of SHG–Bank Linkage (Physical)

Sl. no	Indicator	CAGR (%) 2001–05	CAGR (%) 2006–10	% change 2010–11
1	Number of SHGs having savings with banks	n.a.	21	13
2	Number of SHGs receiving loans during the year	29	21	–25
3	Number of SHGs receiving loans during the year under SGSY	n.a.	9	–10
4	Number of SHGs linked to banks (cumulative)	44	n.a.	n.a.
5	Number of SHGs with loan outstanding	n.a.	14[a]	–1
6	Number of SHGs with loan outstanding under SGSY	n.a.	16[a]	3

Source: As in Table 3.2.
Note: [a]From 2007 to 2010.

Table 3.3b: Growth Rate (CAGR) of SHG–Bank Linkage (Financial)

Sl. no.	Indicator	CAGR (%) 2001–05	CAGR (%) 2006–10	% change 2010–11
1	Outstanding savings of SHGs with banks	n.a.	21	13
2	Bank loan disbursed during the year	59	26	0.7
3	Bank loans disbursed under SGSY	n.a.	12[a]	1.6
4	Bank loans (cumulative)	70	n.a	26
5	Bank loans outstanding with SHGs	n.a.	23[a]	11
6	Bank loans outstanding with SHGs under SGSY	n.a.	18[a]	25

Source: As in Table 3.2.
Note: [a]From 2007 to 2010.

disbursed increased over the same period at more than 70% per year with a CAGR of 59% for volume of bank loans disbursed annually during the five-year period.

In view of changes in the presentation of data on SHGs credit-linked to banks from 2006–07 onwards, it is not possible to have a continuous and complete series on cumulative numbers of SHGs credit-linked and the cumulative bank loans, since NABARD ceased to report this data thereafter. Data are available instead, on number of SHGs with outstanding loans and the amount of bank loan outstanding. The cumulative number of SHGs *credit-linked with banks* as on 31 March 2006 was 2,238,565, while the number of SHGs with *loan outstanding* on 31 March 2007 in the new series was 2,894,505.[4]

The analysis for subsequent years has been carried out in respect of the annual disbursements and numbers of SHGs with outstanding loans. During the period 2006–07 to 2009–10 there was a slowing down of the bank linkage programme from the dizzy heights achieved earlier. Nevertheless, a substantial growth rate continued to be achieved in SHG numbers and disbursements for a few years yet. *SHGs credit-linked during the year* rose from 620,109 in 2005–06 to 1,609,586 by 2008–09 before declining marginally, for the first time to 1,586,822 during 2009–10 and precipitously to 1,196,134 during 2010–11. Thus, during the last couple of years there has been a major deceleration and decline in the growth of SHG–bank linkage. The rate of growth of SHGs credit-linked to banks had increased by nearly 30% during the period 2001–05 and over 37% during 2006–09 but decreased by less than 2% during 2009–10 and as much as about 25% during 2010–11. As a result *the number of SHGs credit-linked during 2010–11 went down to levels lower than those achieved in 2007–08.* The growth rate of SHGs linked to banks was thus already tapering off before the dramatic declines of the past two years. The annual *Microfinance India State of the Sector Report 2006* had already commented on the relative 'stagnation' of SHG–bank linkage even when fairly high growth rates were being registered (Ghate, 2006), possibly in contrast to the even more steep rates of growth of the MFI sector during this period.[5]

In explaining the decline in number of SHGs credit-linked to banks, Srinivasan (2010) drew attention to bank fatigue in lending to SHGs in view of the comparatively small ticket size of SHG loans, the cumbersome procedures and reporting requirements. Other experts suggest that more than this factor, it was due to the saturation of SHG–bank linkage in south

---

[4] Though data on number of SHGs with outstanding loans is not available for the earlier period, a GTZ study for the Parliamentary Standing Committee on Urban and Rural Development estimated (based on a questionnaire sent to all public sector banks, all RRBs and cooperatives in the states of Tamil Nadu, West Bengal, Karnataka, Chhattisgarh and Maharashtra) the cumulative amount of loans as *on 31 March 2005* to be 71.45 billion, and loan outstanding of all banks to SHGs to be 42.05 billion—or that *loan outstanding was 59% of cumulative loans. As on March 2007 and March 2008,* for which data on both indicators is available, *the ratio of loan outstanding to cumulative loans rose sharply to 68% and 76% respectively.*

[5] Srinivasan (2010) further showed that MFIs added significantly to their loan portfolio as compared to SHGs.

India. Also, in most states, the state governments have not been as proactive in promoting bank linkage as in Andhra Pradesh and some of the southern states. As a result the majority of SHGs linked are those under the SGSY programme—the government programme aimed at asset creation through individual and group enterprises and implemented through SHGs in which there is a subsidy and a bank loan component. Unless state governments have well-established and dedicated structures like those of SERP, Bihar Rural Livelihoods Promotion Society (BRLPS) and TRIPTI, it would appear that SHG–bank linkage does not happen automatically. The situation has clearly been aggravated by the microfinance crisis of 2010, which started with Andhra Pradesh but also spread to other states, especially Tamil Nadu and Karnataka. While bankers generally refrained from admitting to a major decline in SHG lending, the freshly released NABARD data for 2010–11 clearly testify to the adverse impact of the crisis not only on lending to MFIs but also on lending to SHGs by the banks.[6] As a result, the number of bank loans disbursed to SHGs during 2010–11 increased by merely 0.7% over the previous year as against annual increases of nearly 60% during 2001–05 and 26% during 2006–10 (Table 3.3b). *Average loan disbursed per SHG* nevertheless continued to increase substantially by 20% in 2009–10 to ₹ 91,712 and again, by as high as 34% to ₹ 121,637 in 2010–11.[7] One inference from this pattern is that banks have concentrated on deepening their portfolio through repeat loans to existing SHGs rather than extend loans to newly eligible SHGs. This is further supported by the widening gap in recent years (particularly large during 2010–11) between the number of SHGs with savings accounts with banks and the number of SHGs with outstanding loans (Table 3.2).

As far as *loans outstanding to SHGs* are concerned, the data from 2007–08 to 2009–10 show an annual increase of nearly 14%. However, during 2010–11 with the steep fall in the disbursement of new loans the number of SHGs with outstanding loans has also declined in absolute terms from 4.85 million to 4.79 million, registering a fall of nearly 1% during 2010–11.

---

[6] Arunachalam (2011) draws attention to the continued unwillingness of banks to lend to SHGs (especially in Andhra Pradesh and Tamil Nadu) following the Andhra Pradesh crisis of 2010 because of the fear that these fresh loans may be used to repay overdue loans to MFIs since SHG members are also members of JLGs formed by the MFIs. However, it appears that repayments to MFIs by their clients have completely stopped and it is unlikely that there will be repayments to MFIs in the near future as well.

[7] There is a kind of inverse relationship between number of loans disbursed and the loan amount. The two years of reduced number of loans disbursed (2009–10 and 2010–11) are associated with significantly larger average loan sizes. The cutback would thus appear to be in the (smaller ticket size) loan component of relatively new SHGs. At the same time during 2006–07, when the number of loans disbursed increased by 78% over the previous year, the average loan size declined by 18%.

This has been an inevitable consequence of the political uncertainty in Andhra Pradesh and other states in respect of microfinance programmes.

The amount of loan outstanding which had registered an annual increase of nearly 23% since March 2007 to reach ₹ 280.38 billion by 31 March 2010 increased by only 11% to ₹ 312.21 billion by 31 March 2011, in view of the nature of the external environment for microfinance lending. Average loan outstanding, however, increased by nearly 13% rising to ₹ 65,224 per SHG on 31 March 2011.

For the period, 2006–07 onwards data on the number of *SHGs with loans outstanding under the SGSY programme* have also been provided in NABARD statistics. While the relative importance of this programme varies across states, its overall share in the number of SHGs with bank accounts which was 24% of total to begin with had improved marginally to 26% by 2009–10 as numbers of SGSY SHGs rose from 687,212 to 1,245,394—an annual growth rate of 16%. However, the share of SGSY SHGs in amount of loans outstanding rose less than in proportion from ₹ 32.73 billion (or 26% of total) in 2006–07 to ₹ 62.51 billion (or 22% of total) in 2009–10. During 2010–11 following the pattern of overall decline there was a (comparatively smaller) reduction of 10% in the *number of loans* disbursed to SGSY groups, and the *loan amount disbursed* under the programme rose by nearly 13% during the year, even as the overall loans disbursed stagnated.

One of the features of SHG–bank linkage has been the disproportionately high share of the southern states. In 2000–01, the share of this region had been as high as around 70% of the cumulative SHGs credit-linked throughout the country. However, over the years it has come down somewhat though it continues to be about 57% in terms of number of SHGs with outstanding loans as on 31 March 2011, up slightly once again from previous years. A fuller discussion of regional shares follows in Section 3.4.

3.2 SHG SAVINGS WITH BANKS

Since March 2006, NABARD data are available on savings of SHGs with different types of banks. The *number of savings accounts of SHGs with banks* increased substantially from a little over 2.6 million to over 6.95 million during the period March 2006 to March 2010 (Table 3.2). This represents a compounded annual growth rate of 21% over this period (Table 3.3a). Notwithstanding the decline in loan accounts the number of savings accounts of SHGs again grew during 2010–11 by 7.3% to reach over 7.46 million by 31 March 2011.

Total SHG savings with banks increased from ₹ 23.9 billion as on 31 March 2006 to nearly ₹ 62.0 billion as on 31 March 2010 (Table 3.2). (These savings figures are over and above the savings retained by the SHGs within the group for internal lending.) During 2010–11, total savings of SHGs with banks further increased to ₹ 70.16 billion—an increase of 13.2% over the previous year's figures (Table 3.3a). Thus, savings linkage continued to grow (though at a reduced rate) even as there was a setback to lending under SBLP during 2010–11. As regards the savings performance for the three-year period, i.e., 2008–10, it is found that though the *average savings balance per SHG in banks* has risen by nearly 20% during 2008–09, there was a marginal decline from ₹ 9,069 to ₹ 8,915 during 2009–10. There was, however, a small increase in per SHG savings with banks during 2010–11 of 5.5% to ₹ 9,403 as on 31 March 2011.[8]

Thus, average SHG savings have hovered around the ₹ 9,000 mark over the past three years. This is approximately one-seventh or less than 15% of the average loan outstanding to SHGs as on March 2011. The savings performance of the SHGs needs to be understood in the context of the limitations of the product that is offered. Easy access to bank linkage for SHGs has increased the quality of savings services offered to their members. This is mainly as a result of the regular savings requirement needed to access bank loans. Nevertheless, the number of SHGs with outstanding bank loans as on 31 March 2011 was less than two-thirds of number of SHGs with savings accounts with banks. At the same time, SHG savings that have been deposited in banks are often unavailable for internal loaning in SHGs due to the insistence of the banks on the provision of margin money or collateral by the SHGs in order to obtain larger loans.

3.3 SHARE OF DIFFERENT BANKS IN FINANCIAL SERVICES

The spectacular increase in the number of SHGs that have been provided with loans from the banking system for on-lending to their members has undoubtedly been facilitated by interest taken by the different types of banks, particularly in the high-growth areas of southern India. While all types of banks have contributed with commercial banks taking the lead, their relative shares in disbursements have undergone variation in recent years.

Loans Disbursed

Details of loans disbursed during the year to SHGs by different types of banks are given in Table 3.4a. Over the years commercial banks have been

---

[8] SHG savings data is as on 31 March of each year which gives only a partial picture of their savings—that of the savings balance on a particular day. Also, the data does not capture SHG funds in the banks in the form of fixed deposits. These savings balances are also not always available to the SHGs for withdrawal as banks often impound savings of SHGs when giving loans to them.

Table 3.4a: Loan Disbursed during the Year by Agency

Agency	Number of SHGs				Loan disbursed during the year (₹ billion)			
	2008	2009	2010	2011	2008	2009	2010	2011
Commercial banks	735,119	1,004,587	977,521	669,741	54.04	80.60	97.80	97.25
Regional rural banks	327,650	405,569	376,797	296,773	26.51	31.93	33.33	31.98
Cooperative banks	165,001	199,430	232,504	229,620	7.93	9.99	13.39	16.26
Total	1,227,770	1,609,586	1,586,822	1,196,134	88.48	122.52	144.53	145.48

Source: NABARD (2008, 2009, 2010, 2011).
Note: During the year ending 31 March.

Table 3.4b: Percentage of Loan Disbursed during the Year by Agency

Agency	Average loan disbursed per SHG (₹)		Percentage share in number of loans disbursed		Percentage share in volume of loans disbursed			
	2010	2011	2010	2011	2008	2009	2010	2011
Commercial banks	100,050	145,199	62	56	61	66	68	67
Regional rural banks	88,461	107,746	24	25	30	26	23	22
Cooperative banks	57,629	70,793	15	19	9	8	9	11
Total	91,081	121,623	100	100	100	100	100	100

Source: As in Table 3.4a.
Note: During the year ending 31 March.

the main source of loans disbursed to SHGs. As far as *number* of loans disbursed to SHGs is concerned, the commercial banks had the lion's share of 62% during 2009–10, followed by RRBs with 22% and cooperative banks with 15%. However, during the year 2010–11 the share of commercial banks in the total number of SHGs declined by over 5% because of the sharp decline in the number of loans disbursed by them. This was made up by the cooperative banks.

The *number of SHGs borrowing during the year* from commercial banks while starting from 735,119 in 2007–08 peaked at a little over one million in 2008–09, but declined marginally in 2009–10 and substantially in 2010–11 coming down sharply to 669,741. The RRBs display a similar picture of rise and decline. It is only the cooperative banks that have sustained an annual increase throughout the period, i.e., from 2008 to 2010 increasing the number of their SHG clients to 232,504 before registering a small decline in 2010–11 to 229,620.

The *total loan amount disbursed* by commercial banks has remained virtually unchanged from the previous year (in fact declined marginally) during 2010–11 at around ₹ 97 billion after registering a steady increase over the previous years. RRB loan disbursements have grown steadily until 2009–10 before declining slightly during 2010–11. It is only cooperative bank lending to SHGs that has shown a sustained increase over the four-year period from 2007–08 to 2010–11.

Despite the decline in the number of fresh loan to SHGs, the *average loan disbursed per SHG* has gone up substantially during 2010–11 (Table 3.4b) for all types of banks. Average commercial bank loans to SHGs are the largest being at ₹ 145,199 in 2010–11—over twice the average size of loans by cooperative banks. As far as share in loan disbursement is concerned, commercial banks continue to provide about two-thirds of the loans during 2010–11. However, the relative share of RRBs has declined somewhat over the years from 30% to 22%. This decline in share has accrued to both the commercial and cooperative banks.

Loans Outstanding

Data on loan outstanding from banks to SHGs is given in Table 3.5a. The *number of SHGs with outstanding loans* from commercial banks was 3,237,263 as on March 2010. This declined to 3,053,472 by March 2011. The corresponding figures for cooperative banks show a similar decline from slightly over half a million SHGs in March 2010 to slightly less than half a million as on March 2011. There was an increase in the number of RRB client SHGs having outstanding loans over this period whose number increased from 1.1 million to over 1.28 million. Amount of loan

Table 3.5a: Loan Outstanding by Agency

Agency	Number of SHGs		Loan outstanding (₹ billion)	
	2010	2011	2010	2011
Commercial banks	3,237,263	3,053,472	201.65	218.83
Regional rural banks	1,103,980	1,281,493	61.44	74.30
Cooperative banks	510,113	451,798	17.29	19.08
Total	4,851,356	4,786,763	280.38	312.21

Source: NABARD (2010, 2011).
Note: As on 31 March.

outstanding however, increased for all the three types of banks at nearly ₹ 219 billion for commercial banks, ₹ 74 billion for RRBs and ₹ 19 billion for cooperative banks.

The *average loan amount outstanding* of commercial banks to SHGs was ₹ 62,290 (Table 3.5b) while that of regional rural banks was ₹ 55,662 and that of cooperative banks ₹ 33,894 with the average total loan outstanding for all banks being ₹ 57,795. The share of commercial banks in *total loan outstanding* was 72% in March 2010 a little higher than their share in the total loans. However, the share of cooperative banks was only 6% as against their share in the number of loan accounts of 11%. A similar position continued to prevail in March 2011.

Table 3.5b: Percentage of Loan Outstanding by Agency

Agency	Average loan outstanding per SHG		Percentage share			
			Number of SHGs		Amount of loans	
	2010	2011	2010	2011	2010	2011
Commercial banks	62,290	71,667	67	64	72	70
Regional rural banks	55,662	57,982	23	27	22	24
Cooperative banks	33,894	42,228	11	9	6	6
Total	57,795	65,223	100	100	100	100

Source: NABARD (2010, 2011).
Note: As on 31 March.

Savings

Data on bank-wise savings position of SHGs are given in Tables 3.6a and 3.6b for the period 2008 to 2011. Though all types of banks registered

Table 3.6a: Agency-wise SHG Savings

Agency	Number of SHGs				Total SHG savings (₹ billion)			
	2008	2009	2010	2011	2008	2009	2C10	2011
Commercial banks	2,810,750	3,549,509	4,052,915	4,323,473	20.77	27.72	36 73	42.30
Regional rural banks	1,386,838	1,628,588	1,820,870	1,983,397	11.66	19.89	12.99	14.35
Cooperative banks	812,206	943,050	1,079,465	1,155,076	5.41	7.82	12.25	13.51
Total	5,009,794	6,121,147	6,953,250	7,461,946	37.84	55.43	61.97	70.16

Source: NABARD (2008, 2009, 2010, 2011).
Note: As on 31 March.

Table 3.6b: Percentage of SHG Savings Accounts in Various Agencies

Agency	Average savings per SHG (in ₹)				Percentage share in savings accounts				Percentage share in total savings with banks			
	2008	2009	2010	2011	2008	2009	2010	2011	2008	2009	2010	2011
Commercial banks	7,392	7,812	9,065	9,784	56	58	58	58	55	50	59	60
Regional rural banks	8,411	12,218	7,136	7,237	28	27	26	27	31	36	21	21
Cooperative banks	6,663	8,302	11,352	11,695	16	15	16	15	14	14	20	19
Total	7,553	9,055	8,912	9,403	100	100	100	100	100	100	100	100

Source: As in Table 3.6a.
Note: As on 31 March.

an increase in the *number of SHGs with savings accounts*, the increase was highest for commercial banks with a 50% increase in the number of accounts during the period 31 March 2008 to 31 March 2011 from a little over 2.8 million to over 4.3 million. RRBs and cooperative banks increased the number of their savings bank accounts of SHGs by about a third each. *Total savings amount of SHGs* with commercial banks and cooperative banks more than doubled over this period. However, savings with RRBs declined substantially after an initial surge during 2008–09.

While *average savings per SHG* in commercial banks went up consistently over this period, that of RRBs displayed volatility, first rising in 2008–09 then falling during 2009–10 and 2010–11 to be substantially lower than the 31 March 2008 level. However, the share of the three types of banks in overall savings accounts did not change much over the period March 2008 to March 2011 with commercial banks having around 58%, RRBs 27% and cooperative banks 15%. As on 31 March 2010, the average savings of SHGs in commercial banks was ₹ 9,065, in RRBs it was ₹ 7,136, and in cooperative banks ₹ 11,352. This increased slightly further by 31 March 2011 to ₹ 9,784 in the case of commercial banks but showed little change for the RRBs and cooperative banks. As far as the percentage share in *total SHG savings with banks*, both commercial banks and cooperative banks registered an improvement (the latter more so) at the expense of RRBs. The share of different banks in savings deposits is positively correlated with the number of SHGs linked by them in a particular year and also to some extent with the amount of loan disbursed. The role of cooperative banks in providing financial services to SHGs needs to be further developed. Indeed, since SHGs are a form of cooperative, cooperative banks are natural potential partners of the SHGs. There is scope for further development of SHG linkage with cooperative banks their and primary agricultural credit societies (PACS). Recent legislation permits SHGs to become members of PACS and avail of financial services from cooperative banks.

Non-performing Assets and Recovery Performance of Banks

Table 3.7a gives the data for non-performing assets (NPAs) for different types of banks as on 31 March 2008, 2009, 2010 and 2011 in respect of their SHG portfolio. It is observed that the overall level of NPAs which was steady at 2.9% in March 2009 and March 2010 has gone up substantially to 4.72% as on 31 March 2011. The share in NPAs of both commercial banks and cooperative banks have increased significantly to nearly 5% and 7% respectively as on 31 March 2011 when compared to the position as on 31 March 2010.

Table 3.7a: Non-performing Assets of Banks and Loans Outstanding to SHGs (*in ₹ Billions*)

Sl. no.	Name of the agency	2008			2009			2010			2011		
		Bank loan outstanding	Amount of NPAs	% of NPAs to total loans outstanding	Bank loan outstanding	Amount of NPAs	% of NPAs to total loans outstanding	Bank loan outstanding	Amount of NPAs	% of NPAs to total loans outstanding	Bank loan outstanding	Amount of NPAs	% of NPAs to total loans outstanding
1	Commercial banks	101.92	2.14	2.1	164.64	3.87	2.4	201.65	5.38	2.7	218.83	10.67	4.88
2	Regional rural bank	38.70	1.73	4.5	42.03	1.78	4.2	61.45	2.18	3.6	74.30	2.73	3.67
3	Cooperative bank	7.47	0.36	4.8	8.94	0.61	6.8	17.29	0.67	3.9	19.08	1.34	7.04
		148.09	4.23	2.9	215.61	6.26	2.9	280.38	8.23	2.9	312.21	14.74	4.72

Source: NABARD (2008, 2009, 2010, 2011).
Note: As on 31 March.

As regards the NPAs of the SGSY component of the SHG loan portfolio of banks (data available in NABARD annual reports) the position is somewhat worse with NPAs consistently over 5% in all the years and over 7% as on 31 March 2011. While the share in NPAs of RRBs and cooperative banks declined during the two-year period from March 2008 to March 2010, that of commercial banks rose to nearly 5% as on 31 March 2010 from 3.7% as on 31 March 2008 and to as much 7.4% as on 31 March 2011.

Table 3.7b gives the agency-wise recovery performance of bank loans to the SHGs for three years from 31 March 2008 to 31 March 2010, the latest period for which data is available. However, the number of reporting banks is different for the three years and the relative size of their portfolio is not provided. Nevertheless, the data shows a less than satisfactory performance. The proportion of banks having more that 95% recovery performance declined from 46.5% in March 2008 to 34.1% in March 2010. Of the commercial banks, between six to eight banks in the three years, or more than one-fourth of total reporting in each year, have less than 80% recovery performance.

At the bottom end about a third of banks show recovery performance of less than 80% in all the years. *About 9% to 10% of all reporting banks, and a similar percentage of RRBs and cooperative banks, show less that 50% recovery performance through the period 2008 to 2010 in respect of their SHG portfolio.*

The recovery performance for loans under the SGSY programme is even more dismal. Nearly half the banks in 2008 and 2010 reported recovery performance of less than 80%, though the figure was slightly lower in 2009. More than 40% of reporting commercial banks too had less than 80% recovery; 12% to 15% of banks reported recovery performance of less than 50%. This could be due to the effect of government subsidies as also poor targeting and poor implementation of the scheme in certain areas. These are discussed further in Chapter 5.

3.4 REGIONAL SPREAD OF BANK LINKAGE

SHGs with Outstanding Loans

Right from the start of the bank linkage programme, the southern states have been predominant in SHG–bank linkage. The share of these states was over 70% in the cumulative number of SHGs credit-linked in the early years of bank linkage but had declined over the years. During the past four years the share of the southern region continues to be in excess of 50% of total *SHGs with outstanding loans* and is found to have increased slightly from

Table 3.7b: Recovery Performance by Agency (All SHGs)

Sl. no.	Name of the agency	No. of banks based on percentage distribution of recovery performance of bank loans to SHGs														
		As on 31 March 2008					As on 31 March 2009					As on 31 March 2010				
		No. of banks reported recovery data	≥ 95%	80–94%	50–79%	< 50%	No. of banks reported recovery data	≥ 95%	80–94%	50–79%	< 50%	No. of banks reported recovery data	≥ 95%	80–94%	50–79%	< 50%
1	Commercial banks (public sector)	25	11	6	8	0	25	6	12	7	0	24	8	10	6	0
2	Commercial banks (private sector)	8	7	0	1	0	7	5	1	0	1	9	6	3	0	0
3	Regional rural bank	70	22	25	17	6	65	12	31	15	7	70	17	28	21	4
4	Cooperative bank	226	113	39	51	23	170	56	58	37	19	199	72	59	43	25
	Total	329	153	70	77	29	267	79	102	59	27	302	103	100	70	29
	Percentage of banks		46.5	21.3	23.4	8.8		29.6	38.2	22.1	10.1		34.1	33.1	23.2	9.6

Source: As in Table 3.7a.

March 2008 to March 2010 and further to 56.6% by March 2011 (Table 3.8). Also, the share of the eastern region which had progressively increased to over 20% continued to improve. West Bengal and Odisha continued to be among the leading states in SHG linkage both in terms of the number of groups with outstanding loans and the outstanding loan amount. There was, however, a significant decline in the share of the western region. With the massive decline in number of fresh disbursements of loans to SHGs particularly in the southern and western states (as also Odisha) during 2010–11, there has been a virtual stagnation or decline in the number of SHGs with outstanding loans as on March 2011 as compared to March 2010.

In examining the share of the different states in the *outstanding loan amount* (Table 3.9), Andhra Pradesh clearly emerges at the top both in terms of the *number of SHG loan accounts* and the *share in outstanding loans*. Its percentage share in the total number of SHGs with outstanding loans was over 30% in March 2010. This increased further to 35% in 2011. A distant second is Tamil Nadu with an 11% to 12% share in total SHGs in at the two points of time under reference closely followed by West Bengal with about a 10.5% share. Other states with substantial number of SHGs having outstanding loan accounts with the banking system are Karnataka, Maharashtra and Odisha though the numbers in the latter two states have come down during in March 2011.

Andhra Pradesh is also the leading state with nearly 43% of the *outstanding loan amount* of banks to SHGs. Again a distant second is Tamil Nadu with around 14% of loans outstanding. Karnataka SHGs have about 7% of loans outstanding. West Bengal and Odisha follow but with around 5% of the SHGs with outstanding loans both in March 2010 and March 2011. There is no significant change in the shares of different states with the exception of Maharashtra which has seen a substantial decline in its share both in the number of SHGs and the amount of loan outstanding.

Bank Loans Disbursed to SHGs during the Year

Table 3.10 gives the data on *number of bank loans disbursed under SHG–bank linkage* during the years 2009–10 and 2010–11 for the leading states. The decline in major states in number of loans disbursed under SHG–bank linkage, especially the southern states, has been nothing short of startling. In fact, there has been a uniform and substantial decline in all regions in the number of loans disbursed to SHGs during 2010–11 as compared to the previous year. Loans disbursed to SHGs in Andhra Pradesh declined to 367,420 during 2010–11 from 564,089 during the year 2009–10. Similarly in Tamil Nadu, the comparative figures were 191,469 during 2010–11 and 259,161 during 2009–10 and for Karnataka the numbers of SHGs receiving loans declined to 90,342 in 2010–11 from 104,151 in the previous year. The most badly affected states were Maharashtra where there was a massive

Table 3.8: Regional Shares in SHG–Bank Linkages

Region	SHGs with loan outstanding 2008		SHGs with loan outstanding 2010		SHGs with loan outstanding 2011	
	No.	% share	No.	% share	No.	% share
Northern	134,783	3.7	152,491	3.1	149,108	3.1
North Eastern	103,424	2.9	133,785	2.8	150,021	3.2
Eastern	753,048	20.8	1,027,570	21.2	1,105,503	23.1
Central	326,763	9	497,922	10.3	358,872	7.4
Western	446,550	12.3	457,476	9.4	316,821	6.6
Southern	1,861,373	51.3	2,582,112	53.2	2,706,408	56.6
Total	**3,625,941**	**100**	**4,851,356**	**100**	**4,786,763**	**100**

Source: NABARD (2008, 2009, 2010, 2011).
Note: As on 31 March.

Table 3.9: Leading States in SHG–Bank Linkage (*Loan Outstanding in ₹ Billion*)

State	As on March 2010				As on March 2011			
	Number	% share	Amount	% share	Number	% share	Amount	% share
Andhra Pradesh	1,471,284	30.3	117.39	41.9	1,693,792	35.4	133.69	42.8
Tamil Nadu	538,867	11.1	40.59	14.5	574,385	12.0	45.26	14.5
West Bengal	507,782	10.5	13.26	4.7	501,284	10.5	14.99	4.8
Maharashtra	384,765	7.9	12.03	4.3	232,835	4.9	10.45	3.3
Odisha	372,646	7.7	15.16	5.4	335,041	7.0	15.79	5.1
Karnataka	300,738	6.2	20.55	7.3	252,613	5.3	22.46	7.2

Source: NABARD (2010, 2011).

Table 3.10: Leading States in SHG–Bank Linkage (*Bank Loans Disbursed in ₹ Billion*)

State	2009–10				2010–11			
	Number	% share	Amount	% share	Number	% share	Amount	% share
Andhra Pradesh	564,089	35.5	67.07	46.4	367,420	30.7	62.09	42.7
Tamil Nadu	259,161	16.3	25.61	17.7	191,469	16.0	25.56	17.6
West Bengal	123,520	7.8	5.34	4.3	131,912	11.0	5.76	4.0
Maharashtra	110,287	7.1	5.13	7.6	63,296	5.3	5.12	3.5
Odisha	117,226	7.4	6.67	4.6	71,843	6.0	5.75	4.0
Karnataka	104,151	6.6	11.30	7.8	90,342	7.6	13.74	9.4
Total	1,586,822	100.0	144.53	100.0	1,196,134	100.0	145.48	100.0

Source: NABARD (2010, 2011).

decline in number of loans disbursed from 110,287 to 63,296 and Odisha where the number of SHGs receiving loans similarly declined from 117,226 in 2009–10 to 71,843 during 2010–11. Two states which appear to have emerged unscathed from this development have been West Bengal and Kerala. Clearly, the microfinance crisis has not been limited to the MFIs alone but has also affected disbursements of bank credit through SHGs. Interestingly, a similar reduction has not been observed in the *volume of loans disbursed* during 2010–11 though these have also either stagnated or declined marginally in almost all states with the exception of Karnataka, among the major states. Apart from factors affecting credit supply at the bank level, there could be two contributory factors on the demand side: (*a*) in states like Andhra Pradesh, virtually every rural woman would already be a member of an SHG, with many members of more than one SHG, and they may have all borrowed; and (*b*) easy access to MFI loans might have dissuaded SHG members from accessing loans from banks.

Share of Priority States

In 2001, NABARD had identified 13 priority states, along with the North East region, for awareness building and identification of NGOs and other partners to promote microfinance. Table 3.11 gives the annual growth rates of the priority states during recent years. During the period 2001 to 2007, in terms of cumulative number of loans the growth *performance in most of the priority states was on par with or better than the all India performance of the SBLP.* The performance of these states thereafter has been mixed and variable thereafter with that of Maharashtra and Uttar Pradesh particularly strong during 2008 to 2010 and that of Gujarat, Uttar Pradesh and Uttarakhand particularly weak. During 2010–11 in the case of most states there has been a decline in the number of SHGs with outstanding loans, with the decline being particularly steep in the case of the earlier lead performers, Maharashtra and Uttar Pradesh. Mention must be made of Bihar, which during 2010–11 registered a growth of over 136% in the number of SHGs with loan outstanding.

3.5 Loans to Savings Ratio for SHGs

Given the fact that the SBLP is a savings-first and savings-led programme, it is inevitable that the number of savings accounts of SHGs is greater than that of the outstanding loan accounts as new SHGs fulfil their mandatory requirements of six months of savings and also the screening process to become eligible for credit linkage. However, the number of savings linked

Table 3.11: Growth Rate in SHG–Bank Linkage of Priority States

Sl. no.	State	CAGR (%) Cumulative no. of SHGs credit linked (2002 to 2007)	CAGR (%) No. of SHGs with loans outstanding (March 2008 to March 2010)	No. of SHGs with loans outstanding (% change between March 2010 and March 2011)
1	Assam	107	10.0	11.1
2	Bihar	62	3.7	136.2
3	Chhattisgarh	49	–5.1	19.0
4	Gujarat	29	–41.4	7.6
5	Himachal Pradesh	33	–8.9	–7.7
6	Jharkhand	44	3.6	13.6
7	Maharashtra	50	73.4	–39.5
8	Madhya Pradesh	44	12.8	–17.1
9	Odisha	50	9.6	–10.1
10	Rajasthan	49	9.8	–6.0
11	Uttar Pradesh	35	42.9	–36.7
12	Uttarakhand	37	–32.0	–37.9
13	West Bengal	48	14.5	–1.3
Total		46	9.4	–13.9
All India Total		36	10.2	–1.3

Source: Progress of SHG–Bank linkage in India 2005–2006, Status of Microfinance in India 2007, 2008, 2009, 2010 and 2011.
Note: As on 31 March.

SHGs (over 7.4 million as of March 2011) seem to be considerably in excess of those SHGs with outstanding loan accounts (4.78 million). While some newly-formed SHGs will be in the pipeline in order to receive their first loan, it also means that a large number of SHGs are not being able to successfully negotiate credit linkage or that some are functioning poorly and thus are ineligible for bank loans. Also, many of the SHGs that are functioning well may not have approached banks for their own reasons—e.g., some have adequate savings and grants provided by NGOs; or alternatively, in some highly deprived areas, SHG members do not have opportunities for investment in viable economic activity.

How much external borrowing are SHGs able to leverage from banks on the strength of their savings? Banks provide a loan or fix a credit limit for SHGs in the form of a multiple of their savings. This could rise progressively in successive cycles to a ratio of 4:1 or higher at the discretion of the bank.

The loan to savings ratio (average bank loan outstanding per SHG/average savings per SHG in banks) serves to illustrate how liberal the banks have been in the provision of credit to SHGs.[9] Different states and regions display varying degrees of development of the SHG–bank relationship in terms of their bank credit to savings ratio for SHGs and the changes in it over time. However, as seen above, *the number of SHGs with outstanding loans was less than two-thirds of the number of SHGs with savings bank balances and SHG savings with banks as on 31 March 2011 were over 22% of the outstanding bank loans.* Table 3.12 gives the ratio of average outstanding loans per SHG to average savings per SHG with banks. The overall credit to bank savings ratio was 6.5:1 as on 31 March 2010. This has gone up slightly to 6.9:1 as on 31 March 2011. The ratio is somewhat higher in the case of the southern states which account for the largest share among different regions. The ratio is particularly high in the North Eastern region and for Bihar among the larger states. Of course, *average savings of SHGs with outstanding loans* would probably be higher than the overall average of both credit-linked and non-credit-linked SHGs and the resultant outstanding loans to savings ratio lower. Reports from many states also suggest that banks are retaining SHGs savings in the form of deposits serving to making the provision of loans by banks more restrictive than suggested by the above data. This pattern raises issues related to savings requirements of banks for SHGs to qualify for loans on the one hand and concerns about the build-up of corpus of savings at the group level on the other, and the need for diversified savings products to be made available to SHG members.[10] Many practitioners and scholars are of the opinion that SHG financial intermediation should be as much about savings as it is about credit. While a large number of SHGs saving with banks appear to be still without access to credit, the comparatively high credit to deposit ratio of the SHGs suggest that the *SBLP is mainly about providing loans to SHG members* rather than a wider range of financial services.

Bank Linkage: Issues and Challenges

One of issues regarding bank linkage relates to the data on the coverage of the programme itself. There are differing views about the accuracy and authenticity of the estimates of bank linkage as conveyed by the data compiled by NABARD. NABARD (2011) itself conveys a sense of the magnitude of SBLP coverage in relation to the rural household population and the population of poor households towards financial inclusion. It

---

[9] Of course, as far as the SHGs are concerned, a fair proportion of their savings could be kept within the group, for which there are no aggregate estimates.

[10] This, in fact, is one of the major proposed changes to be introduced as part of NABARD's SHG 2 initiative, which is discussed in Chapter 9.

Table 3.12: Outstanding Loans to Savings Ratio by Region (*Amount in* ₹)

Sl. no.	State	As on 31 March 2010			As on 31 March 2011		
		Loan outstanding per SHG	Average saving per SHG	Outstanding loans to savings ratio	Loan outstanding per SHG	Average saving per SHG	Outstanding loans to savings ratio
	Northern region						
1	Himachal Pradesh	38,947	6,956	5.6	63,683	6,982	9.1
2	Rajasthan	48,156	6,683	7.2	49,274	6,002	8.2
3	Punjab	66,783	8,099	8.2	70,864	10,716	6.6
4	Haryana	98,136	29,276	3.4	102,364	28,088	3.6
5	Jammu and Kashmir	62,016	41,659	1.5	53,596	6,952	7.7
6	New Delhi	85,629	10,719	8.0	94,152	10,454	9.0
		53,455	**9,723**	**5.5**	**60,559**	**8,814**	**6.9**
	North Eastern region						
7	Assam	48,917	3,371	14.5	46,125	3,344	13.7
8	Meghalaya	41,988	3,056	13.7	43,509	3,531	12.3
9	Mizoram	110,916	4,932	22.5	199,514	3,879	51.4
10	Tripura	66,442	10,641	6.2	49,596	9,895	5.01
11	Sikkim	29,562	5,848	5.1	40,394	6,010	6.7
12	Manipur	42,196	2,018	20.9	44,655	2,331	19.1

No.	State					
13	Nagaland	34,234	5,642	6.1	43,818	3,679	11.8
14	Arunachal Pradesh	33,359	2,569	13.0	30,576	2,632	11.6
		50,340	4,164	12.1	46,344	4,035	11.5

Eastern region

No.	State					
15	Odisha	40,684	7,249	5.6	47,143	6,784	6.9
16	Bihar	67,843	6,064	11.2	40,981	4,374	9.3
17	Jharkhand	45,615	9,345	4.9	44,458	16,279	2.7
18	West Bengal	26,132	9,193	2.8	29,908	12,053	2.5
19	Andaman & Nicobar Islands (UT)	28,428	2,468	11.5	22,886	2,435	9.4
		35,958	8,151	4.4	38,014	9,219	4.1

Central region

No.	State					
20	Madhya Pradesh	57,864	5,696	10.2	59,968	7,590	7.9
21	Chhattisgarh	37,853	6,648	5.7	30,019	7,133	4.3
22	Uttar Pradesh	48,348	6,158	7.9	78,897	7,714	10.2
23	Uttarakhand	60,676	16,297	3.7	57,345	8,952	6.4
		49,453	6,706	7.4	65,912	7,672	8.6

Western region

No.	State					
24	Gujarat	20,440	19,140	1.1	20,853	8,973	2.3
25	Maharashtra	31,274	7,374	4.2	44,874	8,522	5.3
26	Goa	71,698	54,104	1.3	48,667	10,330	4.7
		29,936	9,800	3.1	39,335	8,627	4.1

Table 3.12 (*Continued*)

Table 3.12 (Continued)

Sl. no.	State	As on 31 March 2010			As on 31 March 2011		
		Loan outstanding per SHG	Average saving per SHG	Outstanding loans to savings ratio	Loan outstanding per SHG	Average saving per SHG	Outstanding loans to savings ratio
				Southern region			
27	Andhra Pradesh	79,791	8,668	9.2	78,930	8,920	8.8
28	Karnataka	68,342	11,730	5.8	88,915	17,094	5.2
29	Kerala	39,390	9,527	4.1	88,252	8,542	10.3
30	Pondicherry	113,876	6,525	17.5	127,557	11,009	11.6
31	Tamil Nadu	75,333	10,932	6.9	78,802	10,574	7.5
	Southern region	**73,672**	**9,848**	**7.5**	**80,581**	**10,649**	**7.6**
	All India	**57,795**	**8,915**	**6.5**	**65,224**	**9,403**	**6.9**

Source: NABARD (2010, 2011).
Note: Data for Punjab includes Chandigarh and Kerala includes Lakshadweep.

attempts an estimate of the extent of rural population covered by the SBLP through data on SHGs linked to banks and their membership. Using Census 2011 data, and the norms of the Tendulkar Committee for Rural Poverty as benchmarks for the analysis, it was found that overall *53.4% of total rural households were covered under the SBLP*, subject to correction on account of multiple memberships within the same households and instances of 'urban' households being included as members of SHGs in certain states. The findings appear to be anomalous in so far as *all the southern states and the union territories of Chandigarh, Pondicherry and Andaman and Nicobar Islands had greater than 100% coverage of rural households.* The figure was about five times the number of rural households in Pondicherry and nearly twice their number in Tamil Nadu! On the other hand, in nine states including Bihar, Jharkhand, Madhya Pradesh and Uttar Pradesh, the percentage of rural households covered was less than 20. *If we consider the percentage of* poor *households covered by the SBLP, the estimates yield a figure of nearly 130% for all India and figures as high as over 1000% for Kerala, 765% for Andhra Pradesh and 518% for Tamil Nadu.* This clearly indicates the need for a review of the data on SBLP to ascertain the true position with regard to its outreach.

Fernandez (2007a) had been of the opinion that the SHG–bank linkage data are *underestimates* since they cover the loans for which refinance has been sought from NABARD and could miss out loaning undertaken by banks with their own resources. More likely is an alternative hypothesis that *the credit-linkage data represents an overestimate* of the true picture as multiple agencies involved with SHGs at different levels include such SHGs in their reporting, making for double counting. This is compounded by defunct groups still being shown in the list of SHGs covered. The absence of a uniform reporting procedure or Management Information System (MIS) is also considered to be contributory. One of the sources of confusion has been that every SHG that is given a loan is effectively shown as a newly credit-linked SHG. Besides, it is asserted, that groups which break up or become defunct or cease to take loans from banks continue to be reported as linked by their NGOs and other promoters. An illustration of this is provided by the *Rajasthan Microfinance Report 2007* (CmF, 2008) which states that it may be safe to assume that *only about 70% of the SHGs reported actually exist.* A study undertaken in Bikaner district for all banks found that the actual number of SHGs credit-linked was only 1,755 instead of 2,978 as reported. If this is a wider phenomenon it would seriously put into question the credibility of data of SHGs credit-linked to banks.

The situation in Odisha is similar. The promoting entities in the state can be primarily grouped into three—ICDS offices, Block Development Offices and NGOs. As on March 2011, the total number of savings bank accounts of SHGs in Odisha was estimated to be 521,153 according to NABARD data. However 574,774 women SHGs had been reported as having received credit linkage over the years from banks (as per State Level Bankers' Committee [SLBC] estimates for March 2011). The outreach and credit disbursed figures place Odisha among the states with the highest SHG outreach and credit disbursement in India though no definitive estimate of number of functioning SHGs and their quality are available. Arunachalam (2011)[11] asserts:

> [I]n fact, the correct number of SHGs operational in the country cannot be accurately estimated ... Several stakeholders have also raised questions on whether all linked SHGs are physically (still) present. Much less is known about what happens to older SHGs that have been linked multiple times.

Of course, as has been seen, data on breakdown of number of loans to SHGs between fresh loans and repeat linkages has not been presented by NABARD with effect from 2006–07. However, whatever the situation, no one can deny the fact that the SBLP progressed in India at a great pace due to the massive network of institutions including the commercial banks, RRBs, cooperative banks and NGOs. This got a further boost as several state governments focused on SHG promotion as part of their development process even as GOI adopted the SHG model for implementing SGSY.

Despite the progress and achievements, SBLP faced several challenges with regard to SGSY linkage, quality of SHG lending and its consequences, loan size, indirect competition with the MFIs and the involvement of the NGOs. The pressure of government sponsored programmes for formation of groups and to bring benefits to the BPL families exclusively under SGSY programme tended to split a number of good SHGs. The splitting of the groups also broke the group harmony and encouraged multiple memberships. Both bankers and borrowers seem also to have abused the system in order to realize the benefits of subsidy attached to the SGSY. Under SBLP, banks were expected to finance such SHGs that show certain minimum level of group dynamics, financial management capabilities and behavioural discipline. The government's target approach for forming the groups and linking them with banks, and competition with the MFIs in providing loan fund to the SHGs and their members affected the quality of linkage (Srinivasan, 2009). This may have served to discourage the involvement of commercial banks. The target approach and competition also led to financing of poor quality of groups as shown by various studies.

In addition to this, the relatively small average loan size to the groups and ultimately to the members also created discontent among

---

[11] Available at http://www.moneylife.in/article/microfinance-industry-where-is-the-self-help-group-bank-linkage-model-headed/20381.html#.TpJoSfZPjwc.email (accessed on 8 October 2011).

the SHGs, which prevented them from earning a decent income for sustaining a household (Srinivasan, 2010). Inadequate loans to SHG members encouraged multiple borrowing from informal sources. This in fact prompted the MFIs to finance the SHG members in the JLG mode by constituting them into liability groups and 'centres'. Several MFIs, particularly those pursuing a high growth curve, split up many good SHGs by enticing their members and extending larger loans to the individuals in the SHGs. The JLG methodology gained popularity among MFI clients including SHG members as it provided an opportunity to get a bigger loan for business or other purposes on individual basis. Further, the procedures adopted by the NGOs/MFIs were relatively simple. All the documentation was done by the NGOs/MFIs and more importantly, the loans were served at the door step.

With the success of SBLP, while banks had started emphasizing Model I (SHGs promoted by banks themselves or their agents) and Model II (direct linkage with SHGs promoted by other SHPIs) Model III (NGOs as financial intermediaries) lagged behind for the following reasons:

- Lack of trust of banks on ability of small NGOs to act as financial intermediaries
- Entrance of private banks into microfinance by disbursing loans to big NGOs/MFIs who on-lent the same to small NGOs

Though several leading NGOs did agree to borrow from banks, the move initially was not a great success. Having worked with grant-based programmes and reluctant to resort to coercive methods, they were unable to recover the loans given to SHGs and found themselves in arrears to banks. As a result only about 6% of bank linkages by March 2006 were under Model III. However, NGOs that were prepared to act as financial intermediaries around that time generally switched over to the JLG methodology on being attracted by its good repayment performance. Looking at this business proposition, some of the small and medium NGOs which were earlier involved in nurturing and capacity building of the SHGs in their programmes formed their own MFIs for borrowing from banks and on-lending to the SHGs. This led to a process by which while certain NGOs remained as pure facilitators while other NGOs transformed into MFIs either providing loans through the SHGs or through JLGs or even directly to individuals. (The evolution of SHG-based NGO and community models is documented in Chapter 4.) Nevertheless, on account of SHG promotion and support for SBLP by public sector banks and the implementation of government programmes of SHG promotion and support both in several leading states as also other emerging ones (covered in Chapter 5), SBLP grew uninterruptedly as evidenced above until the recent crisis and the accompanying uncertainty about its future performance.

4

NGOs AND COMMUNITY ORGANIZATIONS AS FINANCIAL INTERMEDIARIES

The innovation of SHG–bank linkage as a means of enabling access of the poor to financial services attracted NGOs as well as national and international donors. Many NGOs started promoting SHGs and facilitating SHG–bank linkage. Some NGOs had viewed SHG promotion as a means to enable access of poor households to the formal banking system. Other NGOs, who had earlier formed SHGs and similar groups as community organizations for supporting livelihoods of the poor and facilitating empowerment of women too came forward to participate in the SBLP. Many NGOs, in addition, promoted activities such as marketing of SHG products, training and technical counselling apart from grant of credits to enable SHGs promoted by them to augment the income of their members.

SHG banking had been channelled through three models of bank linkage (Chapter 3). Of these, Model I related to bank promoted SHGs. Though most NGOs/SHPAs have remained as facilitators (Model II), their size of operations remains quite small as compared to the NGO as financial intermediary (Model III). However, some NGOs realized the potential benefit of direct banking with the poor and their SHGs and migrated to the commercial microfinance or Grameen Model and started accessing large size funds not only from banks, but also from financial institutions like NABARD, SIDBI and international sources. Discussed in this chapter are the major developments in respect of the approach of NGOs adopting Model II and Model III in creating effective structures for financial interme diation over the past 20 years.

The limited credit facilities generally available through the SBLP led many NGOs to design their own microfinance programmes with support from various national and international donors. One major development, which had an impact on SBLP and the SHG movement in the country, was the advent of SHG federations. SHPAs, both NGOs and government programmes, started promoting SHG federations to strengthen the quality of SHGs through the experience of self-governance and social and economic functioning. As a result five broad options emerged for NGOs adopting Model II and Model III, two options involving (*a*) linkage of SHGs and SHG federations with banks; and (*b*) three options involving SHGs/ SHG federations borrowing from various MFIs. These options were:

1. *Direct borrowing from banks by SHGs* under SBLP, with facilitation by the NGOs or the SHG federations
2. NGO-promoted *SHG federations borrowing from banks* and on-lending to SHGs
3. SHGs directly *borrowing from NGO-MFIs* with or without facilitation by SHG federations
4. SHGs directly *borrowing from NGO-promoted company* with or without facilitation by SHG federations
5. SHG federations *borrowing from other MFIs or wholesalers* and on-lending to SHGs

These options or 'models' are discussed in detail in Section 4.2. It should be borne in mind that these are neither watertight categories nor pure models/channels of financial intermediation. In the field there are SHG federations that facilitate SBLP and also act as MFIs by directly lending to SHGs with borrowed funds. Some federations borrow simultaneously from banks as also from NGO-MFIs. NGO-MFIs may be directly involved in financial intermediation and lend to SHGs and individuals or develop a separate in-house MFI to lend to SHGs and their federations. In most of the financial intermediation models that have emerged, the SHG federations have had a role to play. It is instructive, therefore, to appreciate the rationale and benefits of federating SHGs by NGOs and other SHPAs.

4.1 EVOLUTION OF SHG FEDERATIONS

During the past decade or so, federations of SHGs have become an important presence in the rural landscape. The objective of federation building has generally been to scale up the SHG programme and enhance the collective bargaining power of the members with or without a strategy for the withdrawal of the promoting institution.

The rationale behind promoting SHG federations (APMAS, 2007) is

1. to strengthen SHGs,
2. to promote new SHGs of the poor,
3. to provide member SHGs with access to various services,
4. to provide a sense of solidarity among members of different SHGs,
5. to ensure sustainability of SHGs,

6. to facilitate linkages and
7. to empower women.

Nair (2005) has suggested that there are five predominant benefits of federating SHGs:

1. Creation of economies of scale
2. Reduction of transaction costs
3. Reduction in default rates at all levels
4. Provision of value-added services such as special loan products, insurance services, etc.
5. Reduction in the cost of promoting new SHGs

Besides, federations play an important role in SHG capacity building and conflict resolution—both internally and externally.

A few scholars have raised the question whether federations are really required. In the early days of federations, Harper (2003a) circulated '10 commandments' questioning the need for federations of SHGs in financial intermediation. He argued that federations were redundant since India had the largest network of banks in the world and that the SHG itself achieves the necessary bulking up function and reduces transaction costs. Besides, federations could require much hand-holding, add to SHG members' costs of financial access and be prone to political influences. Rajagopalan (2003) too raised the question of the need of federations. She stated that some voluntary development organizations (VDOs), or NGOs, felt that federations usurped the functions of SHGs and of VDOs and that they did a worse job of both. She highlighted the need to protect savings of SHG members and for strong accounting and management information systems for federations. She also drew attention to other conflicting agendas in respect of federations and SHGs, particularly in respect of SHG promotion and SHG bookkeeping. She emphasized the need for strong primaries in the process of federating SHGs as also the positioning of the federation in terms of the rationale behind each tier and the overall structure. She also raised questions about financial accounts and accountability of federations.

For the last decade there has been much debate with regard to the role of federations. Though the debate has not been resolved so far, federations of SHGs have been formed simultaneously with different roles in different contexts. So far, three major roles of federations have been identified: (a) Non-financial support services to SHGs; (b) financial services to SHGs; and (c) Non-credit–related social and economic services (Ghate, 2007). As reported by APMAS (Salomo et al., 2010), *there were 163,852 primary, secondary and tertiary levels of federations across the country. Out of these, a little over 50% of federations were in South India and another 41% in*

East India. Many federations are still in the process of determining an appropriate role as service providers for their member SHGs, which ranges from financial intermediation, livelihood/business support, social services, as well as in systems development. They often perform the role of the promoting institution or as capacity builder and supervisor for the respective next lower tier. But in general, *federations do not have adequate managerial, institutional and financial capacity to provide quality services to their member SHGs.*

Whatever be the case, the SHGs federation model initiated by the NGOs achieved significant scale and widespread acceptance and was also adopted by government programmes. NABARD has also recognized the importance of federations through its policy[1] for supporting federations focusing on non-financial services. NABARD emphasized the need for the organic growth of a federation (evolved based on the felt need of the SHGs) which should become self-managed within three years and not depend upon the promoting institution perpetually. More importantly, *NABARD does not visualize a financial intermediation role for the federation.* While the core idea that poor are capable of savings and creditworthy has been the cornerstone of all such institution-building, the approaches to federating SHGs and their development have varied considerably according to the promoters and in different contexts.

4.2 SHG-BASED FINANCIAL INTERMEDIATION MODELS

To understand the evolution of various models of financial intermediation models involving SHG federations, the structures developed and institutions promoted by 10 leading NGOs working in different states have been studied. These NGOs are PRADAN, DHAN Foundation, MYRADA, Association of Sarva Seva Farms (ASSEFA), Chaitanya, SKDRDP, BWDA, Bharat Integrated Social Welfare Agency (BISWA) and Parivartan. Their organizational particulars such as legal forms, outreach, focus, SHG performance status and the financial and non-financial services provided by them have been given in Appendix 2.

The vision of all the 10 NGOs covered in this study invariably involves the linkage between the informal SHGs and formal or mainstream structures of financial services delivery. Many of these NGOs have been at the forefront of the SHG–bank linkage programme. However, there is a divergence between the long-term paths of SHG development envisaged by the different SHG promoters. A summary of the financial intermediation

---

[1] NABARD circular no. 1058/MCID/2007, dated 14 September 2007.

models promoted by these institutions and discussed in the following sections has been given in Appendix 3.

SHGs and SHG Federations Linked to Banks

Direct SHG–Bank Linkage

This is the basic model in which an SHG, promoted by an NGO or other institution, can access a multiple of its savings in the form of loan funds or a cash credit limit from a bank. The SHG then on-lends the funds to its members. The SHG model is a *savings-led and savings-linked credit* model, with a minimum savings period of six months prior to the availability of bank credit. The quantum of credit available to the SHG from banks starts from twice the level of SHG savings and can increase up to eight times or more of SHG savings in special cases.

The rationale and growing enthusiasm for SHGs among bankers was primarily due to the possibility of externalization of the transaction costs of small loans and assured recoveries through the operation of peer pressure among group members. Loans to SHGs have been available at around 12% per annum on reducing balance from banks. The SHGs on-lend these funds to their members at same bank interest rate of around 12% in some states and 18% to 24% in others; or even more in some cases. Many NGOs also provided a revolving fund grant to SHGs of ₹ 10,000 to ₹ 25,000 to supplement the savings of the SHGs[2] from the grant support received from various national and international donors. This was often recorded as an interest-free loan to the SHG. Though the objective was to provide supplementary resources to kick-start the group's internal lending, the usual practice of most SHGs was to divide the grant among members, instead of using it for credit rotation.

MYRADA, PRADAN and DHAN are the study NGOs committed to direct SHG–bank linkage, the mainstream model of SHG intermediation adopted by thousands of NGOs. The other NGOs covered have developed models involving SHG federations and in-house MFIs and alternative sources of financial services to the SHGs.[3] These are discussed in the following sub-sections. PRADAN, MYRADA and DHAN believe in the social intermediation and capacity building role of the federations on

---

[2] For example, the DWCRA/SGSY and SAPAP projects and several microfinance programmes of NGOs supported by bilateral donors.

[3] PRADAN, DHAN and MYRADA have also promoted federations in village clusters but these are not engaged in financial intermediation. DHAN and MYRADA have also promoted non-profit companies to provide supplementary loans to SHGs.

the one hand, and emphasize bringing the poor into mainstream banking for livelihoods promotion on the other.

To enhance livelihoods on a large scale to empower the rural poor, PRADAN follows a four-pronged approach comprising the following activities: (a) formation and strengthening of SHGs for leveraging institutional finance for promotion of livelihoods; (b) developing locally suitable economic activities to increase family incomes; (c) mobilizing finances from various institutions for livelihood promotion, and (d) setting up mechanisms to sustain livelihoods of poor communities. SHGs take care of bank linkage/supplementary credit and federations look after larger social issues. Livelihood promotion being the important focus, PRADAN believes in multiple institutions for addressing various needs of the poor. Hence PRADAN promotes three sets of institutions: (a) SHG, cluster and federation to address social issues; (b) area-level institutions such as hamlet level *sabha*s, watershed committees where area investments through NREGA, and watershed development are made and (c) producer groups, producer companies/MBTs/cooperatives of agriculture, dairy, tussar, poultry and mushroom cultivation. Though promotion of SHGs is an integral part of the strategy of PRADAN, these institutions are promoted both as an entry point for livelihoods promotion in addition to accessing loans for livelihood purposes both through internal lending and by accessing finance from external sources. PRADAN supports the SHGs in leveraging external finance for various purposes. Also, PRADAN provides support to SHGs in developing mutual trust, democratic decision making and group governance and brings them together to form clusters and federations thus making them capable of taking part in various other livelihood institutions.[4] Often after seeing the operations of SHG clusters and federations in nearby areas, women themselves start forming groups. All clusters and federations have cluster resource persons (CRPs).[5] But clusters and federations are mostly inward looking entities and PRADAN CRPs continue to form new SHGs. PRADAN forms the area plan and priorities are set and new groups formed accordingly.

As a part of a withdrawal strategy PRADAN promoted federations of SHGs such as Sakhi Samiti (Box 4.1) in Alwar district of Rajasthan to provide a platform for the women to come together and gain visibility and bargaining power. SHGs come together to form a cluster at panchayat level and clusters come together to form a federation at block level. Sakhi Samiti in course of time inherited the roles of the promoting institution and provided required services such as auditing, monitoring and facilitation of bank linkage to the SHGs.

[4] Interview with D. Narendranath, Programme Director, PRADAN.
[5] Cluster resource persons (CRPs) are PRADAN employees.

Box 4.1: Sakhi Samiti and Saheli Samiti

Sakhi Samiti a two-tier SHG federation was promoted by PRADAN in Alwar district of Rajasthan to improve women's access to government schemes and enable them to meet emergency financial and/or credit services. After about 10 years PRADAN withdrew its support to the federation. Sakhi Samiti provides non-financial services along with limited financial services. Sakhi Samiti runs with the revenue generated from the SHGs in terms of providing non-financial services such as facilitating bank linkage, bookkeeping and also lending from an associated fund called Sakhi Suvidha to tide over the period of waiting for bank linkage but the sources are insufficient to meet the cost of the operation and hence subsidized from various sources (Ghate, 2007). PRADAN adopted the same strategy for Saheli Samiti a federation of SHGs promoted under the District Poverty Initiative Project (DPIP) programme of the Government of Rajasthan. Saheli Samiti used to promote new SHGs and provide institutional development support to SHGs and clusters, microcredit from its corpus provided by PRADAN, artificial insemination to improve the livestock quality on fee basis, and bookkeeping and MIS to member SHGs through 'computer munshi' software. It also facilitated SHG linkage, training on livelihood enhancement and promotion, linking members/SHGs with the corporate sector/mainstream institutions and other need-based services on fee basis. However, due to difficulties in getting bank loans, the members have not been showing interest in either the SHGs or their federation.

Source: Salomo et al. (2010).

Similarly, DHAN Foundation promoted *nested institutions* under its Kalanjiam Community Banking Programme. The Kalanjiam Community Banking Programme focuses on women in the belief that localized financial institutions owned and controlled by women are an effective strategy to impact on poverty and gender issues. The basic unit of the programme is a Kalanjiam which is an SHG of 15–20 women coming together to save and lend internally. Twenty to twenty-five such Kalanjiams come together to form clusters at the panchayat level called cluster development associations (CDAs) and 200 to 300 Kalanjiams form a federation at block level. *These nested institutions—SHG, cluster and federation—are independent but interdependent structures. The major role of the federations is to provide non-financial services ensuring systems, meetings and performance standards at SHG and CDA level; managing linkage of SHGs with banks, apex financial institutions, government agencies and PRIs, and building the capacity of SHGs and CDAs.* As on March 2011, 31,780 Kalanjiams with 619,439 members, 1,193 CDAs and 122 federations were promoted by DHAN Foundation. The total own fund including savings, reserves and corpus of members as on 31 March 2011 was ₹ 2.554 billion including savings of ₹ 1.987 billion and member loan outstanding was ₹ 3.734 billion. A total of

34 banks and 320 bank branches have been involved in SHG–bank linkage.[6] Life insurance cover has been provided to 576,008 women members and their spouses. Kalanjiam Mutual Movement which is a confederation of Kalanjiam federations has been registered as a mutual trust to represent the interest of the peoples' institutions at the state and national level.

MYRADA also, as a part of its withdrawal strategy, promoted community managed resource centres (CMRCs) for every 100 to 120 *good* SHGs irrespective of promoter and including watershed area groups. The CMRCs also cover Soukhya groups.[7] In fact, 10 to 20 SHGs come together and form a federation (unregistered) and several federations along with the watershed groups and Soukhya groups form the CMRC. One hundred and three CMRCs have been promoted by MYRADA in its project area. *The CMRCs maintain various information relevant to the SHGs, create linkages between SHGs and various government and non-government institutions, provide capacity building, help in conflict resolution, disseminate information on agriculture, health, markets, employment opportunities and organize various training and awareness programmes in collaboration with government and other institutions. CMRCs charge fees to the SHGs for the services they provide along with an annual subscription from the SHGs. CMRCs do not undertake any financial intermediation.* They only provide services for the stabilization and sustainability of the SHGs. The SHG members pay for all the services that the CMRCs extend to them. These CMRCs are bodies managed by a Board comprising elected representatives from the participating organizations at the base. The roles played by MYRADA are mentoring, monitoring and supporting these CMRCs (MYRADA, 2010).

All these three NGOs have federated SHGs to form institutions with different structures and nomenclature but the objectives are same, i.e., facilitating direct SHG–bank linkage and providing non-financial services to strengthen and sustain the SHGs for improving the livelihoods of their members. In view of the challenges faced in directly linking the SHGs to banks, MYRADA and DHAN have promoted non-profit companies as MFIs to ensure the flow of credit to SHGs promoted by them and other agencies. The rationale and coverage of these MFIs is discussed later in this section.

SHG Federations/MACS Linked to Banks

Through participation in SHGs, women could save and get loans for various purposes. However, being small in size, SHGs were somewhat limited in

---

[6] DHAN Foundation, *Annual Report 2011*.

[7] Soukhya Groups are groups of sex workers which focus on health, safe sex without oppression and harassment and later, by their own choice, on alternate livelihoods.

the financial services that they could provide to the members. To bridge the demand and supply gap of bank loans through SHG direct linkage, some of the SHPIs promoted SHG federations and mobilized savings from the SHGs and SHG members and created an own fund for the federation of SHGs. The issues involved in this model are discussed below through the experiences of Chaitanya and GRAM.

Chaitanya

Chaitanya, a not-for-profit organization registered under the Trust Act was one of the organizations which first felt the need for a financial role for federations and started promoting financial federations. It received financial support for federation building from FWWB as far back as 1993 when it promoted the Gramin Mahila Swayamsiddha Sangh (GMSS) (Box 4.2). As on March 2011, Chaitanya had facilitated the formation of 216 clusters and 15 federations of SHGs. These federations have a three-tier structure with SHGs at the primary level, clusters at the secondary level and federation at the apex level.[8] Clusters are collecting points for all transactions and play an active role in social intermediation and in promotion of livelihoods. From 2002 to 2006 clusters were engaged in financial intermediation. Due to the burden of financial operations, clusters stopped financial intermediation and this role of lending to SHGs was taken over by the federations. Federations collect regular savings from their member SHGs on a monthly basis and also receive term deposits from members. The federations provide loans to SHGs at an interest rate of 18% per annum for a period of 12 to 24 months. The SHGs in turn provide loans to their members at the rate of 24% per annum. Federations offer long-term, short-term and emergency loans to their SHG members. Short-term and long-term loans are offered for consumption and livelihood related activities and interest-free loans offered for emergency purposes.

All the 15 federations promoted have also come together to form a 'mahasangh' (confederation) which meets to discuss the technical support that is required by the federations. More importantly, each of the federations allocates 20% of its profits to social activities, 20% for provisioning low-cost loans to the poorest of poor for livelihood initiatives and another 20% for technical support. Chaitanya, along with the federations promoted, has

---

[8] The process of formation is the same for all federations promoted by Chaitanya. SHGs are formed and 15–20 SHGs come together to form clusters; clusters federate to form federations when at least 120–150 SHGs are formed. SHGs and clusters are further added based on the area of operation. GMSS being the oldest federation has a large number of clusters (30) at present. All federations except GMSS are registered as Mutual Benefit Trusts (MBTs).

facilitated the formation of 2,502 SHGs with 36,073 members. Till March 2011, these federations have borrowed ₹ 85 million from various sources out of which ₹ 7 million was borrowed during the financial year 2010–11. During the year 2010–11, federations have disbursed loans amounting to ₹ 92 million to their members. Members had saved ₹ 100 million at SHG level and ₹ 25 million at the federation level as on 31 March 2011. Loan outstanding at SHG level as on 31 March 2011 was approximately ₹ 100 million out of own funds and ₹ 100 million from federation loans with a repayment rate of 95% from SHGs to the federations.

Box 4.2: GMSS: The First SHG Federation of Chaitanya

Gramin Mahila Swayamsiddha Sangh (GMSS), perhaps the first federation of women's groups in India, was promoted in 1991 by Chaitanya. GMSS was registered in 1993 under the Societies Registration Act, 1860 and Bombay Public Trust Act. Since then GMSS has been working with a mission to build institutions which are owned and governed by rural poor women and to ensure their access to efficient financial services. Besides offering financial services, GMSS is also involved in a number of social projects for tackling domestic violence against women through legal counselling and other support services. After starting with a mere 14 SHGs in 1991, GMSS had 527 SHGs as its members in March 2011; its gross loan outstanding to its members was ₹ 46.67 million. State Bank of India and Indian Bank provided loans to GMSS, followed by Bank of Maharashtra and SIDBI. GMSS has also received ₹ 7.5 million from NABARD in October 2010 at 3.5% interest rate for five years. Out of this, ₹ 2.5 million is for capital support and the remaining is for the revolving loan fund. In an effort to develop similar types of federations, GMSS has joined hands with Chaitanya in promotional efforts. GMSS also lends to federations promoted by Chaitanya in other blocks. Loans outstanding to other federations stood at ₹ 21 million as on 31 March 2011.

Source: Information provided by Chaitanya/GMSS.

It is interesting to note that while a few commercial banks have lent to GMSS to on-lend to SHGs, and *despite extending its own lending and equity support to GMSS, NABARD is yet to officially accept a financial role of federations.*

In the case of DHAN Foundation, the supply of loans under the SBLP could not keep pace with the loan demand of the increasing number of groups promoted by it. To meet this challenge and *to increase the quantum of loan available to the SHGs, capture scale economies and to earn much needed revenue to support non-financial services to the groups and clusters through the available 'spread', the federations promoted by DHAN initiated bulk borrowing from banks and financial institutions.* The financial intermediation role of the federation created a competitive environment for the SBLP in certain cases as in Sri Padmavathi Mahila Abhyudaya Society (SPMS),[9] promoted by DHAN. By 2007, cumulatively 25 federations were reported to have leveraged ₹ 240 million from banks and financial institutions as against ₹ 1.34 billion by SHGs through SBLP (Vasimalai and Narender, 2007). Ghate (2007) pointed out that if grant funds were more readily available to finance their non-financial services, federations would more often resist the temptation to get into bulk borrowings.

The examples of Chaitanya and DHAN Foundation clearly show how these organizations over a period of time have changed their policies towards bulk borrowing by the federations promoted by them for livelihoods enhancement of the poor.

Gram Abhyudaya Mandali (GRAM)

Gram Abhyudaya Mandali (GRAM), a leading NGO in Andhra Pradesh, was established in 1980 to promote sustainable organizations among the structurally poor with emphasis on Dalits, women and disabled. Registered under the Societies Registration Act, it has since been working in Adilabad and Nizamabad districts of Andhra Pradesh. From the year 1992, GRAM started promoting SHGs and federated them to form mutually aided cooperative societies (MACS). A total of 20 such MACS came together to form an apex federation called Indur Intideepam MACS Federation (IIMF) under the auspices of GRAM that would support the higher order institutions of SHGs in pursuit of its long-term objective of bringing together large numbers of rural poor and disadvantaged in the area through a process of social mobilization.

IIMF has a three-tier structure with SHGs at the base. The SHGs have been federated at the *mandal* level to form a MACS registered under the MACS Act. As of March 2011, IIMF and its member MACS have promoted 3,623 SHGs with 47,099 members. Each member in the SHG has contributed to the share capital of the MACS located in each mandal and is a direct member of the MACS. The IIMF general body has 20 members, one from each MACS. The board consists of 11 directors, one from each of the first 11 MACS affiliated to IIMF. *On the one hand IIMF sources loans from banks and other financial institutions and on-lends to the MACS, on the other it allows its SHGs to be linked directly with banks.* MACS which also had direct access to loans from the local banks and other financial institutions for the purpose of on-lending to SHGs have stopped external borrowing and IIMF is the only source of funds for MACS. Loans are provided by IIMF to MACS at 15% p.a. and from MACS to SHG members at 21%

---

[9] SPMS was the first SHG federation in the country to be registered, as a society in 1992.

p.a. The SHGs undertake internal lending at 18% to 24% p.a.[10] *While the federation provides a much needed supplementary source of loans for SHGs in addition to the SBLP, the margin of the SHGs, however, is reduced because of the additional layer of intermediary, i.e., MACS* (Srinivasan and Tankha, 2010).[11]

With the support of GRAM, IIMF has set up as a large-scale home-based livelihood programme for women small holders as an entry point to promote producer groups. GRAM has also set up a dairy producer company for collection of milk and marketing of the milk products. MACS borrow from IIMF as usual and provide loans to members for the purchase of milch animals and milk is collected by the producer company. It is a top-down model created by a CBO in its transition from microfinance to livelihoods (ibid.). Apart from this, extensive support services are provided through supply of feed, fodder development and veterinary services. Similar services are being planned in the area of agriculture. A variety of loan products are offered by IIMF which have been developed based on the needs of the SHG members. Crop loans, agricultural investment loans, agriculture allied loans and asset purchase loans are provided by IIMF. Also, GRAM provides support to the SHGs, MACS and their federation in terms of capacity building, training and secondment of staff and provision of external technical expertise.

While IIMF has cumulatively borrowed ₹ 780 million for on-lending to MACS, the SHGs promoted by MACS and IIMF have borrowed ₹ 1.685 billion from banks directly as of March 2011. As of March 2011, the loan outstanding to SHG members through internal lending was ₹ 135 million and from IIMF ₹ 128 million.

However, many other federations of SHGs, where promoted, faced difficulties in leveraging loan funds from banks. In 2006, RBI[12] included registered federations among the agencies eligible to act as business facilitators (BFs) or business correspondents (BCs). Though in many parts of India, banks have realized the potential of federations in facilitating bank linkage and recovery, they have hardly come forward to use federations as BCs/BFs except for a few federations—such as those promoted by DHAN Foundation. NABARD also does not recognize MACS as financial intermediaries because of doubts over their governance and management, their limited assets and the past record of credit cooperatives. Despite these

---

[10] GRAM, personal communication.

[11] The members of the cooperatives promoted by SAMPARK demanded the removal of the additional tier in their respective federations, as the costs increased and profits (shared between the SHGs and the federations) were reduced with the addition of the tier (Premchander et al., 2010).

[12] RBI Circular (RBI/2005-06/288DBOD.No.BL.BC. 58/22.01.001/2005-2006), 25 January 2006.

constraints, due to the credibility of the promoting NGOs, a significant number of MACS are getting loan funds through their respective parent organizations in different states; otherwise, progress in linkage of MACS or SHG federations with banks has been quite discouraging.

SHGs and Federations of SHGs Linked to Various Types of MFIs

Despite the attractions of the SHG–bank linkage model, the considerable reductions in transaction costs both for bankers and borrowers and the further possibilities of 'graduation' of individual borrowers into the banks' regular lending programmes, bankers in many states, especially local bank branch staff, are not always enthusiastic about SBLP and banking with the poor. SHG banking continues to be vulnerable to individual branch managers' whims and fancies. As a result many NGOs and wholesalers favour alternative paths for financial service provision for SHG members. The reasons for this are varied.

NGOs working in the southern states of Tamil Nadu, Karnataka, Andhra Pradesh and Odisha often faced reluctance on the part of bankers to give loans to SHGs promoted by them. Other NGOs were also not happy with the constraint posed by the saving requirement on the credit access of SHGs under SBLP. *A number of leading NGOs across the country including SKDRDP in Karnataka and BISWA in Odisha chose instead to act as or to transform themselves into financial intermediaries under appropriate legal provisions. Others set up independent satellite microfinance organizations under the NGO umbrella to act as intermediaries for SHGs or their federations.* While a few organizations like MYRADA and DHAN Foundation formed 'not-for-profit' MFIs, others such as ASSEFA and BWDA formed 'for-profit' NBFCs to channelize funds directly to SHGs or through their federations. The range of experimentation has been high and the experience of these different models and evidence of their replicability merits greater study and analysis as a sustainable solution to the problem of credit access for poor and excluded families. Discussed below are the features and issues related to the experience of each of the following broad types:

1. SHGs/SHG Federations linked to NGO–MFI intermediaries
2. SHGs/Federations of SHGs linked to in-house 'not-for-profit' companies and NBFCs
3. SHG Federations and MACS linked to wholesalers

SHGs and SHG Federations Linked to NGO–MFI Intermediaries

Over the years this model became quite popular among the NGOs. More specifically, the reduced paper work associated with 'doorstep' lending made this model easier to manage for the financing agencies than the SBLP Model I (SHGs promoted by banks) and Model II (SHGs promoted by NGOs and other SHPIs). SFMC, FWWB and RMK not only provided loan support but also provided capacity building support to the NGOs acting as financial intermediaries. While SFMC tried to develop a new financial system for microfinance in the country, FWWB and RMK provided support to small and new organizations to start microfinance operations through SHGs. A big boost was also provided to NGO–MFIs by the 'partnership model' promoted by ICICI Bank and other private banks. (This model has since been discontinued.)

> The partnership model initiated by ICICI Bank is unique in a sense, it combines both debt as well as mezzanine finance to the MFI in a manner that lets it increase outreach rapidly, while unlocking large amounts of wholesale funds available in the commercial banking sector. (Ananth, 2005)

The most important feature of this model was that, similar to the SHG–bank linkage model, the bank loans were not reflected on the balance sheet of the MFI. *Under this partnership model MFIs received large and easy funds from private banks, often more than their capacity to absorb.* Several NGO–MFIs utilized these funds for lending to the SHGs without proper appraisal and also for bulk lending to other small NGOs and MFIs who were facing problems in leveraging loan funds from public sector banks. *This situation not only resulted in multiple loans being taken by the SHG members but also encouraged small NGOs to enter the microfinance sector without adopting prudent systems and procedures for microfinance operations.* This situation prevailed for about three to four years until 2005–06. It can be seen as contributory to the crises that heralded what many see as the beginning of the end of the microfinance sector. However, some of the organizations which did not believe in commercialized microfinance adopted their own strategy to bring benefits to the poor through a proactive involvement in the credit delivery process as financial intermediaries.

SKDRDP[13] has *continued to act as an independent MFI* over the years. After realizing that the conditions of the poor did not improve merely through charity, SKDRDP started promoting men's SHGs comprising mostly small and marginal farmers. When it was difficult to link those groups to the bank, SKDRDP decided to adopt Model III of SBLP and became quite

---

[13] SKDRDP was conceived by Dr D. Veerendra Heggade, the Dharmadhikari of Shree Kshethra Dharmasthala the holy shrine of Lord Sri Manjunath and set up as a public charitable trust in the year 1991. Its focus was always on charity with the mandate to improve the livelihoods of the people.

successful. SKDRDP is a MFI registered under the Indian Trust Act. It borrows from banks and on-lends to various types of groups.

SKDRDP promotes three different types of groups:

1. Pragati Bandhu Groups (PBGs): These are groups of small and marginal farmers who own lands. The maximum size of the group used to be eight but this has now been relaxed in a few cases. All the members used to be men and farmers. But now women and others who are engaged in petty trade and other non-farm enterprises who happen to be either unmarried, fatherless, widowed or separated are admitted.
2. Jana Vikash Kendra (JVK) groups: The size of the JVK group is 30 to 50. All the members are women (over 40 years of age initially), generally uneducated, under employed rural women from poor sections of the community, including backward castes and tribal people, and women from landless families. In due course of time, with the formation of SHGs (10 to 20 members) by SKDRDP, four to five SHGs were brought together to form a JVK group. The age restriction was dropped and joining JVK by a woman was made voluntary. However, the JVK groups are involved mostly in awareness generation.
3. Women SHGs: 10 to 20 members as per SHG norms.

As of March 2011, SKDRDP has promoted 123,586 groups with a total membership of 1,359,746. Savings are collected from the PBGs and SHGs by SKDRDP, which are used by SKDRDP to give loans to the groups even though it does not have the appropriate legal entity to mobilize savings. With a savings of ₹ 10 per week per member, SKDRDP has been able to mobilize ₹ 3.27 billion in savings from the SHG members as of March 2011. It pays interest at 6.5% per annum to the SHGs on their savings.

SKDRDP has also promoted federations at the village level. The PGBs, SHGs and JVKs in every village organize themselves into one or two federations depending upon the total number of groups in a village. Usually 25 groups form a federation at the village level. By March 2011, SKDRDP had promoted 4,043 primary federations. All these federations are informal advisory bodies and do not have any financial role. They recommend SHGs for loans to SKDRDP. The federations are run by the members of their constituent groups. *SKDRDP does not allow the groups to make their own decisions on any matter related to the loans including rate of interest chargeable to members.* In consultation with the federation, a policy decision is taken and imposed on the SHGs. This clearly shows the top-down approach of SKDRDP that makes the SHGs dependent on it. In fact, SHGs in SKDRDP are used as a channel to provide microfinance and livelihoods promotion services without serious thought to their sustainability. By borrowing from several banks without collateral,[14] SKDRDP has on-lent ₹ 9.515 billion to the SHGs by March 2011 with an outstanding of ₹ 9.57 billion. As of March 2011 loans were given to the SHGs at 9% on flat rate basis[15] with an additional 1% of upfront service charge. *Members are given loans by the SHGs at the same rate they have borrowed from SKDRDP.* Thus, there is no intermediation margin or source of income for SHG. SKDRDP receives subsidized loans for housing and small enterprise from NABARD and D. Devaraj Urs Backward Classes Development Corporation (DBCDC).[16] *The interest subsidy is passed on to the beneficiary.* Loans are based on the savings first principle but not linked to savings and are rationalized; e.g., 1:10 for consumption, 1:20 for Income Generation Activity (IGA) and 1:40 for infrastructure. A three-year-old group is eligible for a loan of ₹ 300,000. As the size of the loan increases the tenor increases, but frequency of repayment remains the same, i.e., weekly. A group is also entitled for multiple loans if it completes three years of association with SKDRDP. No loan is given to C and D grade groups. In case of D grade groups the transactions are frozen and they are not allowed to withdraw their savings. As far as quality of the groups is concerned, 94% of the total groups are in A and B grade; around 4% to 5% in C grade and around 1% in D grade. The repayment rate of the SHGs to SKDRDP stands at as high as 99.97% as on 31 March 2011. This could possibly be attributed in part to the religious ceremony attached to the loan.[17]

BISWA, an MFI registered under the Societies Act is working in 18 states as on March 2011. In addition to microfinance, BISWA works in the areas of health, sanitation, educational and environmental issues. BISWA initiated its microfinance activities in 1996. BISWA's microfinance operations took a major turn when in July 2002 it became a partner NGO of the CASHE project implemented by CARE India. The three and a half years of association with the CARE-CASHE project has given BISWA the capacity to increase

---

[14] SKDRDP borrowings from banks by the Trust are backed by the reputation and resources of the temple. Even the bankers feel that they have given the loan to the God of Dharmasthala, and they are secured by him (Harper et al., 2008).

[15] The rate of interest has been revised w.e.f 1 July 2011 to 10% on flat basis with 1% service charge upfront.

[16] The Karnataka Backward Classes Development Corporation (KBCDC) which was established on 28 October 1977 has been renamed as D. Devaraj Urs Backward Classes Development Corporation (DBCDC) since 28 October 2005.

[17] The repayments remained at a high level, partly because of the group members' reverence for the temple and for Dr Heggade and his wife, who had herself become deeply involved in the women's programme. The groups' financial transactions are carried out in front of a photograph of Dr Heggade and Lord Manjunath, or in front of the Bible for Christians or the Qur'an for Muslims. The first loan to the group is usually disbursed in the presence of a village leader or other respected person, and the cheques are all signed by Dr Heggade and by Mrs Heggade. Before the recipient takes the cheque, a special religious ceremony is held, offering it to God (Harper et al., 2008).

its outreach, scale of financial transactions and infrastructure. BISWA by its philosophy has stuck to the SHG methodology and Model III of SBLP. Due to its credibility, it could leverage loan funds very easily from more than 25 public and private sector banks. As of March 2011, it has promoted 68,962 SHGs (67,859 women's SHGs and 1,103 men's SHGs) covering 1,094,029 members across 18 states. As far as its SHG loan portfolio is concerned, it is mostly concentrated in the state of Odisha and in other states it is not significant. The cumulative loan disbursement of BISWA to SHGs as on 31 March 2011 was ₹ 12 billion with total loan outstanding of ₹ 3.07 billion. Loans are given to SHGs at 19% interest[18] on reducing balance basis to be for passed on to the members. The SHGs do not retain any margin. In addition to this BISWA charges 2.50% of the loan amount as processing fee which is taken upfront while disbursing the loan. BISWA is a micro insurance (MI) agent of a few insurance companies. The insurance premium is deducted while disbursing loans to SHGs.

BISWA does not offer any savings product. However to inculcate the savings habits among the members, BISWA encourages them to save within the SHG. The group members save a fixed amount every month and deposit it in the group's bank account. *The savings of the members are not utilized by the SHGs for internal loaning. In fact, the SHGs are not allowed to withdraw savings from the banks. The savings deposit of the SHGs in the bank acts as some sort of security to obtain loans from BISWA.* SHGs promoted by BISWA have mobilized savings of ₹ 847 million as of March 2011 and deposited them with various banks. This may be one of the reasons why BISWA has been able to leverage loan funds from so many banks. Apart from SHG promotion, BISWA has also promoted federations of SHGs in its operational areas. BISWA federations are an aggregation of around 100 SHGs, consisting of 1,600 to 2,000 members. BISWA has promoted 238 federations of which 122 have been registered under the Mutual Benefit Trust Act. In fact BISWA was planning to have an NBFC like that of ASSEFA's Sarvodaya Nano Finance catering to the MBTs but the idea was dropped. In addition to lending to the SHGs, BISWA used to lend to small NGOs, cooperatives and MFIs and the federations promoted by itself (registered as mutual benefit trusts) acting as a wholesaler by borrowing from various commercial banks. BISWA was one of the largest partners of ICICI Bank under its partnership model.

Federations of SHGs Linked to In-house Not-for-profit Companies and NBFCs

However, many NGOs, who were involved in retail lending to SHGs, started separating out the microfinance component from other activities.

---

[18] From May 2011, BISWA has increased the rate of interest to 24% on reducing balance. In addition to this, BISWA charges 2.50% of the loan amount as processing fee which is taken upfront while disbursing the loan.

Looking at the success of similar ventures across the country, many NGOs created entities designed to separate the microfinance operation from their social agenda in order that a more professional and business-like approach could be adopted.[19] The model became so popular that the NGOs who were earlier carrying out their microfinance operation as 'not-for-profit' entities started having new entities appropriate for microfinance operations. Further *looking at the business opportunities associated with the success of JLGs and trying to pursue a high growth curve, these entities started lending to the SHG members in the JLG mode at their doorstep* (ACCESS Development Services, 2009). *This lending led to the formation of multiple JLGs in an SHG, and also encouraged multiple borrowing by the SHG members from various MFIs. The overall effect of such developments and practices was though the SHGs continued to function and were still necessary to the delivery of financial services their role in financial intermediation was seriously curtailed and undermined.*

As discussed earlier, the limitation on the quantum of loans available through SHG–bank linkage was a major concern of various practitioners regarding the model. This had been particularly so in the southern states where SHG demand for loans was generally higher. Further, the availability of funds from local banks was often determined by the degree of interest shown by the bank manager in the bank linkage programme. In the past there have been many instances of new managers failing to provide loans to SHGs supported earlier by their predecessors. This created uncertainty about availability of the bank linkage facility over time.[20]

Experiencing similar problems in linking its own SHGs, MYRADA which was in the lead in promoting SBLP, decided to have an in-house not-for-profit company, Sanghamithra, to provide financial services to its SHGs. According to MYRADA, the purpose was also to induce an element of competition in the field of rural financial services. *The setting up of Sanghamithra was in response to the apathetic attitude of the bankers to link the SHGs promoted by MYRADA, despite the sustained efforts of NABARD to promote SBLP.* Sanghamithra was conceptualized and promoted by

---

[19] This would also permit them to access funds from a range of microfinance wholesalers and donors supporting only professionally managed and sustainable NGO-MFIs. To cite a few examples, most of the CASHE partners acquired NBFCs or promoted cooperatives registered under the local MACS Act. Sanghamithra was promoted by MYRADA and Swayamshree Micro Credit Services (SMCS) promoted by CYSD. SMCS even started wholesaling to the small NGOs, cooperatives and foundations.

[20] The situation, however, has changed. Following the impressive results over the years and the support for it in the highest banking circles (the RBI had directed banks to make it their corporate strategy) SHG–bank linkage became an acceptable programme. However, though bank managers generally are coming forward to facilitate bank linkage, there continue to be widespread complaints from SHGs and NGO promoters about practices of bank branches that are detrimental to the free flow of loans to SHGs.

MYRADA and incorporated as a 'not-for-profit' company in February 1995 under Section 25 of the Indian Companies Act of 1956. However, it became operational only in 2000. In several areas, *after the banks realized that Sanghamithra had filled the credit gap successfully, they came forward to lend to groups; in such cases Sanghamithra withdrew, but conveyed a clear message that it would re-enter if the banks did not respond adequately in future.* The objective of Sanghamithra was not 'to grow and grow' but to ensure that the SHGs received a line of credit easily and quickly, whatever the source may be. Sanghamithra does not compete with the banks but creates competitive conditions. The SHGs are free—and encouraged by MYRADA—to choose between the banks and Sanghamithra. This helps to ensure that both the banks and Sanghamithra provide quality service at competitive rates (Fernandez, 2007b).

As far as the performance of Sanghamithra is concerned, as of March 2011, Sanghamithra had disbursed ₹ 3.238 billion to 33,960 SHGs to cover 547,335 households with loan outstanding of ₹ 795.44 million to 7,289 groups. In 2010–11, it had disbursed ₹ 688.5 million to 4,070 groups. Irrespective of the duration of the loan, it charges interest of 16% per annum and 15% per annum for general and housing loans respectively on reducing balances. Its financial sustainability ratio was 122.77% during 2010–11 and the operational cost ratio 3.76%. Sanghamithra is providing bridge loans to the SHGs. A question that has been posed is that if bank linkage is any case happening and if credit is accessible to the SHGs then should Sanghamithra continue to exist?[21] Aloysius Fernandez during a personal interview in July 2011 reiterated that the original reason for the formation of Sanghamithra still stood, that it continued to provide competition to the RRBs lending to SHGs and it was not intended to expand to new areas.

As discussed earlier, the federations promoted by DHAN Foundation started bulk borrowing for on-lending to raise resources to finance the non-financial services as per the changed policies of DHAN Foundation. Later on it was decided to centralize the bulk borrowing and *Kalanjiam Development Financial Services (KDFS) came into existence as a section 25 (not-for-profit) company like Sanghamithra* in 2001. Srinivasan and Srinivasan (2009) point out that *the primary objective of KDFS was to establish sustainable financial linkages between SHGs and banks.* KDFS would establish the credit worthiness of a new group before it was linked with banks. The second objective of KDFS was to improve the quality of life and asset base of the people through designing and up-scaling innovative products. A number of financial institutions including SIDBI provided loan support to KDFS. With the formation of KDFS, bulk borrowing by the federations got restricted to specialized purposes like housing. Working in 46 districts across 12 states,

---

[21] Personal interview with Professor M.S. Sriram.

DHAN Foundation facilitates credit linkage of the SHGs through the federation by bulk borrowing through KDFS. As of March 2011, DHAN Foundation had promoted 31,780 SHGs, organized into 1,193 CDAs and 122 federations.[22] KDFS mostly provides loans to the SHGs promoted under its programme. It also provides bulk loan to some of the federations. *The portfolio growth of KDFS is not a robust one as compared to other MFIs since it usually fills a gap left by banks. Further, the SHG client base keeps changing as SHGs after one to two loans from KDFS could possibly go to banks and after availing two or three loans from banks could return to KDFS.* KDFS was able to negotiate the interest rate with banks for its large SHG and tank irrigation programmes and bring down its financial and operational cost enabling it to lend to the SHGs at 12% or 13 % diminishing rate per annum (Srinivasan and Srinivasan, 2009).

From the above, it is possible to understand how Sanghamithra and KDFS have successfully attempted to bridge the gap in loan demand left unfilled by the SBLP. Despite the fact that they are 'not-for-profit' entities, both the institutions under this model have been successful because the parent organizations generally arrange to bear the initial group promotion and capacity building expenses. The degree of replication of this model depends on how far the NGOs can bear the promotional cost of the SHGs. Based on the experience of KDFS, there was a debate in DHAN (ibid.) on whether to set up a for-profit-entity. Sriram (2004) in his study on Sanghamithra points out that,

> … in operating as a section 25 company, there is no element of charity involved. It is just a question whether the interest or service charge levied is reasonable or not. The reasonableness is determined by the context in which the organization is operating. Therefore, strictly speaking it does not matter whether the form of incorporation is actually 'for-profit' or 'not-for-profit'. However, as a matter of general principle, structurally it is necessary to maintain promoters' stake and ensure capital adequacy.

Unlike Sanghamithra and KDFS, there is another popular model in which the SHG federations are linked to an *in-house 'for-profit'* entity. *Sarvodaya Nano Finance Limited (SNFL) is the best example of a 'for-profit' entity that is community-owned.* SNFL is an initiative of ASSEFA having been acquired from BASIX, a leading MFI and livelihoods support organization, and initially managed by BASIX. To overcome the challenges of timely access to microcredit by women, ASSEFA promoted SNFL in 2001. The latter had been given the NBFC license before new regulations for NBFCs in

---

[22] *DHAN Foundation Annual Report*, 2011.

1997 increased the minimum net owned fund requirement from ₹ 2.5 million to ₹ 20 million. *SNF is owned by and lends to Sarvodaya mutual benefit trusts (SMBTs) formed by federated SHGs at block level. With federations of SHGs as SMBTs and the women SHGs as shareholders, it mobilizes resources from mainstream financial institutions for on-lending to women SHGs to meet their credit requirements.* SNFL has a three-tier structure with SNFL at the apex, having the SHGs at the base. *The SHGs are federated into MBTs which serve as intermediaries between the SHGs and SNFL.* As of March 2011, SNFL was working in 23 districts of 5 states and had promoted 30,155 SHGs covering 487,633 members. SNFL has promoted 113 federations in five states and a large number of these federations exist in Tamil Nadu. However, SNFL is currently focusing on 96 federations as the rest of the federations promoted in Bihar, Jharkhand, Madhya Pradesh and Rajasthan have been closed down due to language barrier, lack of enthusiasm among the clients and related issues. As far as the equity structure is concerned, MBTs contribute a part of their surpluses toward the equity of SNFL. Since SNFL does not attract outside equity in order to keep the ownership of the company within the community, the incremental requirement of equity may pose a problem in the future.[23] SNFL gives loans to MBTs to enable them to lend to the SHGs and their members. SNFL's only clients have been the MBTs and the MBTs cannot borrow from any other source. SHGs requiring loans submit an application to the MBTs and after scrutiny and verification the MBTs forward the application form to SNFL. The SNFL loan committee sanctions the loan (Srinivasan and Srinivasan, 2009). During the financial year 2010–11 SNFL has disbursed ₹ 1.115 billion to the member SHGs through the federations. The SHGs had mobilized ₹ 1.284 billion by way of savings with an average of ₹ 42,874 per group as of March 2011. The total loan outstanding at the federation level was ₹ 481 million as on 31 March 2011. SNFL charges interest at the rate of 14% on reducing balance per annum to the federation, whereas the federation charges 12% flat rates to the SHGs and the SHGs charge the same rate to their members for a period of 10 months. At MBT level, 5% of surplus after taxes is used for development activities such as health camps, community marriages, evening schools and dairying. The chairperson of the MBT is the paid employee of SNFL and is termed as Manager, Business Development. The rest of the staff members are employed by the MBTs.

BWDA Finance Limited (BFL) promoted by BWDA is also a similar in-house 'for profit' entity to provide loan support to its promoted SHGs. BWDA operates in Tamil Nadu, Pondicherry and Andaman and Nicobar Islands. In 1988, it started forming SHGs, which got accelerated with the

[23] Personal interview with Mr Selvanathan, General Manager, SNFL.

support of TNWDC under the IFAD project. Initially, it was providing loan support to the SHGs by borrowing from RMK, banks and other financial institutions. Realizing the constraints of the existing legal form for microfinance, BWDA acquired a NBFC through which it started its microfinance operations. In 2003, the process of management and name change were completed and BFL came into existence. BFL is unique in its ownership. The majority of its shares are held by its clients and staff. The remaining are with SIDBI, Centre for Development Education (CDE) and the promoters. Presently BFL mainly undertakes microfinance operations, while BWDA focuses on the development activities like group promotion, awareness programmes, education, health and sanitation as well as vocational training (Arora, 2008). As of March 2011, BWDA had formed 25,459 SHGs (2,497 male groups and 22,967 female groups) with 413,333 members. Total savings mobilized in SHGs were about ₹ 236 million with an average of ₹ 92,383 per group. The total loan outstanding of BFL with the SHGs was about ₹ 105 million with an average loan outstanding of ₹ 42,247 per group. BFL charges 21% interest to the SHGs on reducing balance. The repayment rate continues to be quite good. Even during the recent Andhra Pradesh crisis, the repayment rate was over 96%. BWDA plans to cover 1.5 million members either by SHGs or JLGs by 2015. The SHGs, promoted by BWDA, also directly borrow from banks. About 15,700 SHGs have cumulatively borrowed approximately ₹ 1.55 billion from banks as on 31 March 2011. Over the years, the role of BWDA has changed from a financial intermediary role to formation of SHG and their federations and their capacity building. For its part, as of March 2011, BFL had 1.6 million share holders and it was becoming difficult to manage all of them.[24]

If both the models (SNFL and BFL) are examined, while SNFL is completely community owned, BFL is partly owned by SIDBI, CDE and staff. This sort of arrangement adopted by BFL may never be community-focused. Moreover, BFL has to follow terms and conditions set by SIDBI and CDE. Further, managing a large number of shareholders (as in case of BFL) is a huge challenge, which SNFL does not have. However, unlike SNFL, BFL can attract outside equity to meet the incremental equity requirement of the NBFC. Over the years, the role of the promoting NGOs has changed considerably. In the initial stages the role of promoting institutions was in SHG promotion, building of federations, monitoring and policy formulation. With the emergence of other entities, their roles have become more limited and restricted to fund mobilization for operational sustainability of the microfinance programme along with other developmental activities such as health, sanitation, awareness generation and education.

---

[24] Interview with Dr C. Joslin Thambi, Managing Director, BWDA Finance Ltd and Secretary, BWDA.

In recent years, the outreach and performance of a few MFIs such as Swayam Krushi Sangham (SKS), Spandana, SHARE, Bandhan, Asmitha, BSFL, Action for Social Advancement (ASA), BISWA and Equitas in making a success of microfinance motivated a number of NGOs to promote MFIs in the form of NBFCs for commercial microfinance. Thus, within the ambit of the law of the land, a number of NGOs have promoted and are continuing to look to options to promote NBFCs initially to support their own SHGs and federations and thereafter for wider operations. More specifically, the SIDBI transformation loan has supported a number of organizations to transform themselves into NBFCs.

A common feature in all these models and innovations involving NGO-MFI or in-house 'not-for-profit' or 'for-profit' entities is that the role of the SHG as financial intermediary is effectively eliminated. Loans to SHGs financed from borrowed funds leave little or no margin for SHGs and are invariably passed on to members at the same rate. This creates a dependency relationship with the promoting NGO for the SHGs. SHGs, however, may continue to intermediate own funds and funds directly borrowed from local banks under the SBLP unless such access is specifically disallowed or discouraged by the promoters.

SHG Federations and MACS Linked to Wholesalers

The federations of SHGs discussed thus far have either been linked to the promoting NGO that has taken up the role of the MFI or have accessed funds from other intermediaries, sometimes promoted by the NGO. As such they have continued to be dependent on the NGO for funds for intermediation. However, mature secondary federations have also been able to access funds from MF wholesalers. When registered as societies or trusts, they effectively are converted into MFIs using the same legal forms adopted by the NGO. The costs of operations of these federations cover financial and non-financial activities and are met through interest margins and management fees and contributions. They usually represent a culmination in the development of multi-tier SHG-based community institutions, designed to function independently of the NGO after its phase-out.

As described earlier, DHAN, like its parent PRADAN and MYRADA, has not itself acted as a financial intermediary for its federations. The multi-tier structure of nested community institutions designed by DHAN allowed it to respond to the credit needs of members at the appropriate level—SHG, cluster *Nidhi* or secondary federation. Apart from local bank linkage at SHG and cluster level, the federations promoted by DHAN Foundation accessed loans from apex lending organizations such as SIDBI, RMK, HDFC and HUDCO having fulfilled their creditworthiness criteria. With the emergence of KDFS, direct borrowing by federations from wholesalers was restricted to specialized purposes such as housing, where the lending institutions were themselves wholesaler institutions without branches such as HUDCO, NBFC and National Housing Bank (NHB) (Tankha, 2002; Ghate, 2007).

One of the main supporters of federations has been FWWB, which had taken the initiative to fund this category of institution as well as the MACS where member participation and ownership is assured. Adopting its own rating criteria and deploying financial resources raised in India and abroad (from NABARD and SIDBI among others), it provided funding and capacity building support for SHG federations. The loan support also helped the organizations to leverage larger loans from formal financial institutions. Wherever FWWB felt it is risky to provide loan support to a new federation or cooperative, it provided the same through the promoting institutions, if found to be credible. During the current year, i.e., 2010–11, the lending and investment activities of FWWB have been transferred to an NBFC called Ananya Finance.

Parivartan is an NGO operational in the district of Kalahandi, Odisha. Parivartan was partner of CASHE project between 2000 and 2006. Prior to this, the organization, registered under Societies Registration Act of 1860, had four major projects such as women empowerment through promotion and nurturing of women thrift and credit groups, natural resource management through watershed development, community health care services and rehabilitation of child labourers through establishing special schools. CASHE provided operational grants, technical guidance, capacity building and revolving loan fund support to Parivartan for promoting a client-owned, controlled and managed MFI. Under the project, Parivartan promoted SHGs, built up their financial management capacity and provided loans for different types of livelihoods initiatives. To empower the women through larger collectives and enhance their bargaining power, Parivartan promoted three block-level federations. The federations promoted by Parivartan were of two-tier structure. About 150 to 200 SHGs having a member base of approximately 2,000 members were brought together to form each of the block-level federations. All three federations were registered under the Odisha Self-Help Cooperative (OSHC) Act in 2004. In order to have a client-owned, managed and controlled institution as a part of withdrawal strategy of Parivartan, all the federations (primary cooperatives) came together to form a secondary cooperative called Sanginee Secondary Cooperative (Sanginee) in 2005. Parivartan gradually transferred its portfolio to Sanginee. On account of the inadequate peer pressure in loan repayment, Parivartan changed its strategy from the SHG model to JLG model.[25]

---

[25] In each SHG five to six members were brought together and informal groups (JLGs) were formed. The members of each JLG were reoriented to the principles of joint liability with regard to loan repayment. Interestingly, the JLGs worked better than the SHGs with regard to compulsory participation of the members in the weekly meeting and adequate peer pressure for loan repayment, due to the smaller size of the former.

All the members of the SHGs earlier promoted under the CASHE project were reorganized into JLGs. During six years of microfinance operations of the CASHE project, neither Parivartan nor Sanginee could leverage loan funds from any public sector bank despite a lot of effort. The revolving loan funds (RLFs) provided under CASHE project were the main source of funds for Parivartan to meet the credit demand of SHG members. In the last six years of operation of Sanginee, though it could leverage funds from SIDBI, SMCS and BISWA (which played the role of wholesaler for some time), also could not leverage funds from any public sector banks. In 2009–10, FWWB sanctioned a loan of ₹ 2 million to Sanginee. Sanginee is an example of a federation which depends only upon wholesalers like SIDBI, FWWB, BISWA and SMCS, though it cannot, strictly speaking, call the SHGs as its clients any more. In fact, *Sanginee represents a case of evolution of the SHG model into the JLG model because of the nature of demand for loans, the need for peer pressure on the potential clients, and the limited options available in the form of external funding and legal form for profitable operations.* Indeed, while adopting the cooperative form, it moved away from savings mobilization from SHGs, a critical feature of the cooperatives, for operational considerations.[26] As of March 2011, Sanginee has been able to leverage ₹ 150 million from different wholesalers, with an outstanding of ₹ 306 million. It has promoted 2,635 JLGs with 16,509 women clients. The cumulative loan disbursement as of March 2011 stands at ₹ 173 million with a loan outstanding of ₹ 40 million at the client level. The rate of interest charged to clients is 24% per annum.

4.3 Emerging Structures of Financial Intermediation

As illustrated in the previous section, a wide range of innovations have been attempted by NGOs and federations and community organizations based on SHGs. An amazing variety of possible channels for intermediation result when the different institutional structures created out of SHGs are married with the different types of apex and wholesale organizations and retailers that provide funds for their operations. The progressive liberalization by apex institutions of fund flows to the non-formal sector permits community organizations to access funds even from apex bodies. When the financial intermediation is undertaken by retail MFIs, some regulated and others not, numerous possible channels of finance delivery emerge with funds flowing through various formal and non-formal channels. This is a reflection of the lack of an appropriate regulatory framework for microfinance which in turn

---

[26] However, it again started mobilizing savings from the cooperative members since October 2010.

contributes to the fragility of some of these arrangements. The outcomes resulting from the implementation of the CASHE project implemented by CARE India in Andhra Pradesh, Odisha and West Bengal for seven years provide a good example in support of the above. The project laid the grounds for up-scaling the microfinance sector in the project states. CASHE provided intensive handholding support to 25 NGOs including a few CBOs to develop efficient model to channelize financial services to the poor for the livelihoods improvements and empowerment through SHGs. By the end of the project, several models having SHGs at their base emerged. While a few organizations (promoted by government) continued to operate with the original model, other NGOs experimented with different models in search for an appropriate legal form of the institutions, such as two- or three-tier federations registered under Societies Act; two- or three-tier federations registered under MACS Act; Section 25 companies and NBFCs. While considering the business opportunities, some of the institutions switched over to the JLG mode from SHGs, though a few later moved away from the JLG model and returned to the original SHG-based model.[27] While some NGOs looked at microfinance operations as contributory to livelihoods development, a few entered into the fray as MFIs in a fully business mode based on minimalist credit provision. *Over time a fascinating variety of positive and negative outcomes awaited the innovators in view of the opportunities and constraints posed by the environment for microfinance and the capacity of organizations to engage in or support financial intermediation through SHGs and structures built upon them.* A brief discussion on different models adopted by the CASHE partners and their outcomes in the three states has been given in the Appendix 4.

Like any other peoples' institutions, SHGs and SHG federations prefer to be unregistered or registered with minimum legal compliance requirement or minimum state interventions. For this reason, many federations have registered as societies, trusts, etc., which are not suitable for financial intermediation, especially for mobilization of savings. Liberal cooperative acts proved to be most appropriate legal form for financial intermediation, especially for SHG federations. Andhra Pradesh took the lead in enacting the Andhra Pradesh MACS Act, 1995. This had two main features: (*a*) for the first time members could fully own and control their cooperatives; and (*b*) new cooperatives could be formed in areas where primary agricultural societies were already functioning. Similar legislation has been since enacted[28]

---

[27] For example, Gram Utthan and Adhikar in Odisha.
[28] Bihar Self Supporting Cooperative Societies Act (1996), Karnataka Sauharata Sahakari Act (1997), Madhya Pradesh Swayatta Sahakari Adhiniyam (1999), Chhattisgarh Swayatta Sahakari Adhiniyam (1999), Jammu and Kashmir Self Reliant Cooperative Societies Act (1999), Rajasthan Self Reliant Cooperative Societies Act (2001), Odisha Self Help Cooperative Act (2001), Uttarakhand Self Reliant Cooperative Societies Act (2003).

in Bihar (1996) and extended to Jharkhand, Karnataka (1997), Madhya Pradesh (1999), Chhattisgarh (1999), Jammu and Kashmir (1999), Rajasthan (2001), Odisha (2001) and Uttarakhand (2003). All these parallel cooperative acts are enabling and ensuring autonomous and democratic functioning of cooperatives. However, it is in Andhra Pradesh, where the Cooperative Development Forum (CDF) took the lead in promoting the Act and then in registering its thrift cooperatives under this Act, that this form of cooperative has been pioneered for microfinance. While all these above Acts allows only an individual (not SHG) to be a member of the cooperative, Government of Odisha brought amendments in the membership criteria of the Cooperative Societies Act of 1962—the old act—which provided legal sanction to SHGs for being enrolled as members of a cooperative society for collective economic action.[29]

Thus, *in view of the limitations of the regulatory framework for mobilizing savings by SHG federations registered as societies, a number of NGOs registered their SHG federations under the liberal cooperative act (MACS Act).* Such federations registered under MACS Act became quite common in Andhra Pradesh.[30] Legally, these federations could mobilize savings from members. The mobilized savings and share capital was basically used for on-lending directly to the members of the SHGs. When the credit demand of the members increased and the savings and share capital could not meet the demand, the MACS approached banks for bulk loans. In general banks do not recognize MACS as financial intermediaries. However, some SHG federations registered under the cooperative act have successfully accessed bank loans.

The liberal cooperative acts provided the much needed space for ordinary women and men who were used to acting individually in the financial, commodity, consumer and labour markets, to join together and enter these markets as a force to be reckoned with. Attracted by the provisions in the acts, NGOs in all the states welcomed the new cooperative law in their respective states, and attempted to promote federations of SHGs/cooperatives registered under these acts in the field of savings and credit, without generating much awareness among the members. The MACS/liberal cooperative model was thus widely accepted for microfinance operations by the small and middle level NGOs. Premchander et al. (2010), however, suggest that the cooperative model is not a preferred one for NGOs. They state that promoting institutions (*a*) wish to retain power and control over finances and decision making; (*b*) resist being accountable to women; and (*c*) want to ensure financial sustainability of the promoting institution. Thus, the NGO or the MFI do not prefer the cooperative form, wherein

---

[29] The Odisha Co-operative Societies (Amendment) Bill, 2004.
[30] The MACS legal form has also been adopted by government SHG programmes.

women earn the profits rather than the promoters. While there could be some merit in points (a) and (c), point (b) gives the issue a gender dimension that has not really been raised by other commentators. Many promoting institutions in an attempt to ensure 'professionalism' in federations or MACS tend to depute their own more qualified staff to such organizations. The liberal cooperative acts have been enacted with a view to freeing the institutions registered under them of external controls and making them true agents of their members, managed and controlled by user-members. It is important that promoting institutions do not willingly or unwillingly take over the space that should belong to members. The members of the federation are also generally referred to as clients of such institutions not as owners, managers, controllers and users of the services. As long as members see themselves only as clients, they will not take responsibility for the functioning of the federations/MACS.[31] This has happened in several states, where federations registered under MACS act are engaged in microfinance. Nair and Gandhe (2011) in the course of a study of the GRAM-promoted IIMF MACS in Andhra Pradesh discussed earlier also, point out that building such institutions is complex, time consuming and resource intensive. This becomes more challenging as the poor women have to own and manage the financial institution.

Taking the advantage of the liberal acts, in some of the states a few NGOs started promoting cooperatives with a view to *mobilizing savings* of the community. Rajagopalan (2006) in her study commissioned by CASHE project pointed out that the Odisha government had asked registering authorities to go slow on the registration of credit cooperatives, as some mischievous persons had promoted cooperatives with large areas of operation, and had started mobilizing savings from several people, and now those savings were at risk. This situation continued up to 2009. However, this problem was not faced by genuine organizations.

Srinivasan and Tankha (2010) provide the example of a federation Apni Sahakari Seva Samiti Ltd (ASSSL) registered under the Rajasthan Self Reliant Cooperative Act, which is promoted by Centre for Community Economics and Development Consultants Society (CECOEDECON) in Rajasthan. The cooperative is characterized by two categories of members, viz., provisional and permanent members with regard to ownership and voting rights; the cooperative is thus community represented, but not formally owned by the community of borrowers. Conditions are imposed by the promoting institution upon SHG members becoming permanent members of the cooperative. This has been explained as being on account of

---

[31] The absence of the active interest and involvement in the management of MACS by its members is considered an important reason for the failure of some of the prominent MACS in Andhra Pradesh.

apprehensions of the interference of political elements in the future. It also, in a departure from cooperative principles, relies upon external creditors for loans to finance credit operations.

In some circles the SHG is seen as a kind of cooperative that is a pre-credit union institution. Yet the SHG is not critical to formation of cooperative member-based organizations. While SHG associations have been registered as MACS and NGOs and MF wholesalers are prepared to provide funds to MACS for on lending to their SHG members, some doubts still persist about this model.

First, given the member-owned structure of the MACS, SHGs cannot strictly speaking be its constituents. However, through amendment of the by-laws of the MACS individual members can have a share in the MACS while the representative general body is composed of SHG leaders. Thus, the role of the SHG as a micro-bank is supplanted by the MACS. The SHG becomes a *facilitating institution* rather than a *fund manager* which has the potential to lead to its 'disempowerment'.[32] Second, the MACS do not overcome the SHG weakness of low degree of capitalization and low mobilization of funds. Third, MACS generally continue to be managed and controlled by the NGOs supporting them, as also evidenced by the previous example of ASSSL. The chief functionary is almost invariably an NGO staff member. Finally, like all cooperative structures, the possibility of the exercise of political influence on the control of the MACS cannot be ruled out.

NGO support for MACS follows a similar pattern to that of other federation types, with a planned tapering off of NGO grants and management inputs towards eventual self-sufficiency. However, there are no major instances of NGOs having phased out from involvement from MACS and financial cooperatives promoted by them.

4.4 Conclusions

The SHG–bank linkage model provides the cheapest and most direct source of funds to SHGs. The federations provide a somewhat more costly supplementary or alternative source that is still not fully developed. Indeed, it is the government programmes, especially in Andhra Pradesh, that have given life to the federation and MACS as delivery channels for financial services. These are discussed in greater detail in Chapter 5. In still other

---

[32] Reports from SHGs in Andhra Pradesh also suggest that the role of SHGs had become virtually irrelevant—with loans being decided at higher MACS levels, that meetings were not being held and savings were being collected informally.

structures the mutually reinforcing nature and benefits of financial and social interventions justifies the place of clusters and federations.

This chapter served to set out the rationale for the models adopted by the leading NGOs in an attempt to develop sustainable structures for the delivery of financial and non-financial services through SHGs. In the absence of a suitable regulatory environment for microfinance through community organizations of SHGs, a gap still remains in many areas of unfulfilled needs for credit and other financial services for the poor. Issues regarding the appropriate legal form also remain at the level of the NGO-MFIs and their NBFCs that operate in an unsatisfactory regulatory environment. Over the past several years there have been attempts by government to place microfinance agencies and operations on a sound regulatory footing. However, there have been problems in doing so on account of the periodic crises related to the operations of MFIs. This has carried over to the functioning of SHGs, particularly those in the most affected states. One of the outcomes of the setback to MFI operations has been a revival of interest in SHGs and SHG federations as delivery channels for financial services, with new innovations in the form of various intermediary banks and NBFCs catering to SHGs being promoted. The implications of these and other recent developments for financial intermediation through SHGs and the role of different stakeholders are discussed in Chapter 9.

GOVERNMENT SHG PROGRAMMES

5

Through the 1980s and 1990s, the SHG movement was spearheaded by a few pioneering NGOs and supported by the banking system. The scale of SHG promotion, however, was very small and confined to a few select regions, mainly in the southern parts of India. Subsequently, these SHGs served as a platform for these NGOs to implement various women-centric development programmes for social and economic empowerment and over a period of time, the groups started managing their own savings and credit. The Government of India (GOI) too realized the potential of the SHG model for income and livelihoods generation in alleviating poverty as also to contribute to women's empowerment. The SGSY allowed considerable scope to state governments to scale up NGO innovations in promoting SHGs and linking them to banks under the SBLP. While SGSY partnered with a number of NGOs for promoting and nurturing the SHGs, some of the state governments, again mostly in South India, directly promoted SHGs through district rural development agencies (DRDAs). Some of the externally-aided programmes (funded by IFAD, World Bank and DFID) implemented by the state governments also gave impetus to the scaling up of the SHG model in Tamil Nadu, Andhra Pradesh and Karnataka. Andhra Pradesh was the first state to promote federations of SHGs on a large scale to sustain the SHGs and to provide the much-needed institutional architecture for the poor to access loans as also various entitlements from the state government.

In 1996, the RBI had included financing of SHGs as a mainstream activity of banks under the priority sector lending programmes. From year 2000, state governments started emerging as major SHPIs.[1] They took a keen interest in facilitating SBLP for the poor to access loans to address their consumption and production needs. Gradually, this took the form of a target-oriented approach of promoting SHGs and pressuring the banking system to lend to these SHGs. Since SHG promotion originated under the

---

[1] The terms SHPIs and SHPAs are used interchangeably in the book.

Development of Women and Children in Rural Areas (DWCRA) programme, in many states the Women and Child Development departments were in the forefront of SHG promotion. However, as the SGSY was being implemented through the rural development departments, the DRDAs gradually emerged as the major SHPIs.

By 2005, the state governments in many states had several schemes designed for the welfare of the poor that were delivered through the SHGs and their federations. *Today, SHGs and SHG federations are being used primarily as channels for delivering various state development and welfare schemes. SHGs thus bear many of the responsibilities normally handled by government staff.* Many political parties have also evinced keen interest in the SHGs and included various promises for the SHGs in their election manifesto. SHGs have been used to channelize subsidies and welfare programmes. As a result of this basic SHG principles like self-help, mutual benefit, self-management and self-reliance have been compromised. With increased emphasis on credit and subsidy, there was limited ownership among the SHGs promoted by the state governments resulting in weak group dynamics and high dependence on the promoter. Today more than 75% of the SHGs in India are promoted by the state governments under various schemes and programmes.

In this chapter, various programmes implemented by state governments along with their diversified activities, strategies for poverty reduction and livelihoods development of the poor through community-based institutions have been discussed. A profile of these government programmes is provided in Appendix 5. Features of the federation models adopted by these government programmes along with their products and outreach have been given in Appendix 6.

5.1 INDIRA KRANTHI PATHAM (IKP), ANDHRA PRADESH

Indira Kranthi Patham (IKP)[2] is perhaps the largest donor-assisted poverty alleviation programme in the country. A statewide initiative, it is aimed at

---

[2] Andhra Pradesh District Poverty Initiatives Project (APDPIP), implemented from June 2000 to December 2006 was built on the UNDP-supported SAPAP which was implemented in 700 villages in three districts of Andhra Pradesh and focused on formation and capacity building of women SHGs along with promotion of VOs and federations. Related government development programmes such as education, health and elimination of child labour were implemented through the promoted institutions. APDPIP was implemented in 316 mandals in the six poorest districts of Andhra Pradesh namely Chittoor, Anantpur, Mahabubnagar, Adilabad, Srikakulam and Vijayanagaram. The Andhra Pradesh Rural Poverty Reduction Project (APRPRP) commenced from June 2002 covering 548 backward mandals in 16 districts of Andhra Pradesh. Though the project duration was till September 2008, in the year 2005, the government decided to extend the programme to all the rural areas of the state and initiated the programme called the IKP.

empowering and enabling the rural poor, with a special focus on three million of the poorest households in the state. It has been implemented by Society for the Elimination of Rural Poverty (SERP), set up by the Andhra Pradesh government. With the World Bank's support of a $500 million loan having a significant microfinance component, the project has been implemented in all the 22 districts of Andhra Pradesh. SERP works through a multidimensional poverty alleviation strategy that focuses on building institutions of the poor, leveraging resources through commercial banks, building livelihoods and human development value chains and reducing the risks faced by poor women through social safety nets and entitlements. These activities are undertaken through CBOs such as SHGs, village organizations and *mandal* (sub district) level federations.

Under the programme, SHGs, comprising 10 to 15 members, were formed at the village hamlet level. All the SHGs in a revenue village were brought under the umbrella of a village organization (VO). If the number of SHGs in a village were large (more than 30), two or more VOs were formed at the rate of 20 to 30 SHGs per VO. Two leaders from each SHG formed the executive committee of the VO, of whom five were elected as office bearers. All the VOs in a mandal formed a Mandal Samakhya (MS). Two representatives from each VO formed the executive committee of MS, five of whom were elected as office bearers. All the MS in a district formed a Zilla Samakhya (ZS). One member from each MS had representation in the ZS; among them five were elected as office bearers. By March 2011, 11.1 million poor and the poorest of the poor were organized to form 994,595 SHGs (Table 5.1).

Table 5.1: Progress under IKP as on March 2011

Sl. no.	Particulars	Achievement
1	No. of districts covered	22
2	No. of SHG formed and supported	994,595
3	Village organizations	38,300
4	Total no. of Mandal Samakhyas	1,099
5	Total no. of Zilla Samakhyas	22
6	Total no. of women	11,102,494
7	Total saving of women (₹)	33.831 billion
8	Total corpus of women (₹)	50.705 billion
9	Credit supply from bank (₹)	70.927 billion[a]
10	Pavala Vaddi Incentive to SHGs (₹)	10.995 billion
11	Community Investment Fund to SHGs (₹)	9.307 billion

Source: IKP-SERP, *Monthly Progress Report*, March 2011.
Note: [a]During 2010–11.

These SHGs have been organized into 38,300 VOs and 1,099 MSs. In addition to the above, there are 262 Mandal Vikalangula Sangams, 17 Chenchu MSs, 7 fishermen MSs and 20 Yanadi MSs in the state; 279,161 persons with disabilities have been organized into 30,239 exclusive SHGs, both in the programme and non-programme mandals and forming three ZSs in the state. Under the urban IKP, more than 250,000 SHGs have been promoted in various municipalities of Andhra Pradesh; these urban SHGs are being organized into slum-level federations with the town-level federation as an apex. This structure is part of project design and *the views of the groups on whether VOs and MSs were necessary have not been considered since the project already accepted the requirement of such structure.* All three institutions, viz., SHGs, VOs and MSs, undertake financial intermediation though the sources of loan funds vary. SHGs mobilize savings and rotate them as loans. SHGs also access bank loans to fulfil their members' needs. MSs rotate the Community Investment Fund[3] (CIF) as a revolving fund for lending to the SHGs and may also access bank loans. The CIF has been set up by the project to support the poor and disadvantaged groups and communities to access credit from the project by prioritizing livelihood needs through investments in sub-projects. The cumulative CIF credit to SHGs up to March 2011 was ₹ 9,307 billion and the total number of beneficiaries was 2,673,609.

Through the years savings at SHG level have stagnated at times and, sometimes, even declined. The accumulated savings and corpus of SHG members as on March 2011 were ₹ 33.83 billion and ₹ 50.70 billion respectively. (Though substantial, owing to the relatively small savings requirement even in better-off SHGs and the practice of periodically returning their savings to members by most SHGs, the cumulative saving and corpus of SHGs in the state has not grown as much as expected.)

Each SHG is entitled to a loan of ₹ 50,000 after six months of its formation under SBLP. The second loan of ₹ 100,000 is given only on successful repayment of the first loan. At the time of the third loan of up to ₹ 500,000, the MS guides the SHGs in developing a microcredit plan that incorporates the credit requirement of each household in the group. During financial year 2010–11, ₹ 70.93 billion of bank loans were given to 389,444 SHGs under SBLP. VOs support SHGs through financial intermediation and facilitating bank linkages. The MS takes up financial intermediation in addition to linking SHGs with various government schemes. Some MSs also have received credit from the RMK and from commercial banks for on-lending.

---

[3] Each MS on an average has a community investment fund of ₹ 4.5 million to ₹ 5.0 million. This is an important innovation in the project. As per the original project design by the World Bank the VOs were to be provided grant support in the form of individual loans at 0% for the poor members of the SHGs. The project methodology was subsequently changed and the CIF mechanism was adopted, which positioned the fund at the MS level and revolved it for the purpose of loans to the SHG members.

Realizing the potential of the MS in financial intermediation, the Union Bank of India has started lending to MSs (through cash credit limits) on a pilot basis. It has given ₹ 5 million each to 20 MSs. The State Bank of Hyderabad too has also come forward to give loans to the MSs. Banks are showing much interest in providing bulk loans to MSs as costs are comparatively low. It is notable that at least commercial banks have started providing bulk loans to the federations promoted under the government programme irrespective of the reservations on the part of NABARD and RBI. Bulk loans to MSs are meant to supplement direct bank finance to the SHGs under the SBLP and not supplant it; however the capacity of the MSs to manage finances has to be systematically built up (Srinivasan and Tankha, 2010).

SERP actively promotes bank linkages and tracks repayments of SHG members. As on 31 March 2011, SERP had facilitated the provision of ₹ 70.93 billion of bank loans to 389,444 SHGs. As far as repayment performance of the SHGs is concerned, the status varies from district to district and ranges between 85% and 95%. Banks provide a list of SHGs with overdues to SERP, which is sent to the field for follow-up. With the monthly Core Banking Solution (CBS)[4] data, SERP is in a position to track default SHGs along with their geographical locations on a Geographic Information System (GIS) map based on software developed by Tata Consultancy Services. Using technology the project sends alerts to the field staff. The sub-committees at the VOs send members to overdue SHGs and collect the money. The use of this mechanism has raised the confidence of the banks. However, banks have not come up with any new products and long-term loans are the only loans offered by banks to SHGs. Only one branch of Andhra Bank from Rayavaram has come up with an innovative product, which is a smart card.[5] The product was introduced because of the presence of a large number of SHGs in the area which was often interfering with the other business of the bank branch.

Further, to reduce the financial burden on the SHGs, the government of Andhra Pradesh has introduced the *Pavala Vaddi* scheme with effect from 1 July 2004. In this scheme, there is the provision of an incentive in the form of reimbursement of the interest above 3% per annum on the loans taken by the SHGs. In the last financial year (2010–11), ₹ 5.356 billion was reimbursed to 1,133,269 groups, thus totalling ₹ 11 billion since the inception of the scheme. The government has issued detailed guidelines for e-transfer of the Pavala Vaddi incentive amount to the savings bank accounts of eligible SHGs directly from the core banking system in order to ensure that the Pavala Vaddi incentive reaches the eligible SHGs in time. Srinivasan

---

[4] CBS is the platform where information and communication technology are deployed for the purpose of core banking needs.

[5] The features of the product include a smart card along with provision of a Customer Service Point (CSP) who collects repayment at the villages with the help of a machine. However, this product has not been replicated elsewhere. Currently, women SHGs require home loans, education loans and health loans which are not being provided by the banks.

(2009) pointed out that the loan volumes in Andhra Pradesh were at a high, presumably driven by the low rates of interest. Nevertheless, SERP officials estimate the unmet credit gap at ₹ 40 billion. At the same time *anecdotal evidence suggests that SHG members in turn lend to others and microlending has become the livelihood option at least for some SHG members.*

In the service area of each bank branch two villages are chosen for 'total financial inclusion'. Under it the total credit requirements of a household such as education, housing and debt-swaps are included. SHGs formulate a Micro Credit Plan (MCP) which covers all credit needs of member households.[6] Thus each village receives credit of about ₹ 7.5 million to ₹ 10 million through a saturation approach. As far as bank linkage to meet credit requirements of the SHGs is concerned, it was around ₹ 1.80 billion in 2000 when SERP was formed, in 2010–11 it was ₹ 70 billion and the target for 2011–12 is about ₹ 90 billion. The average per SHG lending has gone up to ₹ 183,000 per SHG and the target of ₹ 90 billion will push that to ₹ 220,000 to ₹ 240,000 per SHG.[7] As a historic breakthrough, an exclusive microfinance bank has been set up in September 2011 to finance the SHGs (see Box 5.1). Equipped with this technology the bank has started providing loans to the

Box 5.1: Stree Nidhi, the State-level Cooperative Microfinance Society

The formation of a microfinance bank—Stree Nidhi has been a milestone in the history of microfinance. Stree Nidhi was launched in Andhra Pradesh on 15 September 2011 as the first cooperative bank in the Indian state to offer women access to microcredit within 48 hours of request. Formed as a joint venture between the government of Andhra Pradesh and the Mandal Mahila Samakhyas (MMSs) of SHGs, the 'bank' is actually an apex cooperative credit society. The bank, which has as its members MMS comprising women's SHGs, has begun operations with ₹ 1 billion equity capital infused by the Andhra Pradesh government. Further, the member MS will provide ₹ 1 million each, totalling over ₹ 1 billion equity contribution by MSs. With over ₹ 2 billion equity capital, Stree Nidhi will mobilize the rest of the required funds in debt from banks and through deposit mobilization. The initial authorized capital of the Bank has been kept at ₹ 5 billion. It has been planned to mobilize ₹ 10 billion of funds in the current financial year (2011–12), which will be increased to ₹ 40 billion by 2014. Stree Nidhi acts as an alternative source of micro-loans for SHGs. It plans to lend its funds to around 10 million female members of the MMS. More specifically, it will be beneficial to SHGs and women, who faced difficulties in getting successive loans from banks. Mr Reddy Subhramanyam, Principal Secretary, Rural Development, Andhra Pradesh said:

---

[6] MCPs are prepared by individual households and their consolidation is done at the SHG level. MCPs plan for investment in asset creation for income generation and household investment needs.

[7] Interview with Mr Rajasekhar, CEO, SERP.

The operations of Stree Nidhi will be handled completely with the aid of technology. The bank started out with four types of loans including funds to meet business requirements, education and health. In order to make the loans cheaper, the administrative costs are planned to be limited to 10% of the net return. The average size of loan is ₹ 15,000 with duration of one year at 13% in monthly repayment mode. The members of MMS, who are from among the same SHG community do the due diligence and assess the need and repaying capacity before sanctioning the loans and get a service charge of 1% commission. Further, on successful repayment of the first loan, the borrowers will be eligible for a nominal 3% interest on subsequent loans. By offering affordable rates, Stree Nidhi hopes to counteract the rampant commercialization of micro-lending that has plagued the state. It is expected that the MFIs in the state will compete with this bank in terms of lowering the rate of interest.

Source: *Microfinance Focus*, 15 September 2011; Sridahar G. Naga, 14 September 2011, *Business Line*; Contify Banking, 24 September 2011.

SHG within 48 hours of the submission of the loan application. IKP's strategy has been to look at credit needs in three categories: viz., (*a*) agricultural allied activities, (*b*) emergency needs such as marriage, accident, health crisis and (*c*) SHG enterprises—SHG Nonfarm Livelihood Project (SNLP) in which 15 sectors are identified where SHGs are already in business, such as handicrafts and fisheries.

The rate of interest applicable at different levels of the intermediation chain varies from scheme to scheme and from source to source as presented in Box 5.2. While an SHG member gets a CIF loan at 12% per annum on reducing balance basis, it is 18% when she gets an RMK loan. For SBLP loans in the case of prompt repayment, the rate of interest is 3%, but from SHG to members, it varies from group to group. As in the case of SBLP, Stree Nidhi proposes to charge a similar subsidized rate of interest to the SHGs.

Box 5.2: IKP—Structure of Interest Rates

CIF	MS to VO—6%, VOs to SHGs—9%, SHG to member—12%
SBLP	Bank to SHG: initially 10% to 12%, on prompt repayment by SHG the interest rate is 3% and the interest difference is credited back to the SHG. Rate from SHG to member differs from group to group
RMK	RMK to MS—9%, MS to VO—12%, VOs to SHGs—12%, SHG to member—18%
Stree Nidhi	13% to SHGs on first loan; on successful repayment, 3% on successive loans

Source: Srinivasan and Tankha (2010); *Microfinance Focus* (2011).

It is not clear how the competition will stand as the SHGs under direct bank linkage pay the lowest interest in comparison to other sources. The most important aspect of IKP is that it has adopted the strategy of convergence of all the government programmes. Each and every government department converges with IKP in executing various development activities for the livelihoods enhancement of the poor.

5.2 MAHALIR THITTAM, TAMIL NADU

The Tamil Nadu Corporation for Development of Women Ltd (TNCDW)[8] was established in 1983 with the prime objectives of bringing about socio-economic development and empowerment of women both in rural and urban areas. In 1989, IFAD assisted a women's development project in five districts after the SHG approach was started in a small way in Dharmapuri district. Later in 1996, the state government launched Mahalir Thittam following the success of the IFAD project. The SHG movement that was initiated with IFAD assistance in Dharmapuri district of Tamil Nadu gradually expanded to all 28 districts of Tamil Nadu through Mahalir Thittam. Mahalir Thittam is based on the SHG approach and is implemented through NGOs and CBOs affiliated to TNCDW. The main activities of Mahalir Thittam are formation of SHGs, training and capacity building of SHGs, formation of SHG federations, providing revolving funds and extending credit linkages to SHGs and youth skill training and placements. In 2006, TNCDW was shifted to the Rural Development and Panchayat Raj department and the Tamil Nadu Vazhndhu Kattuvom Project[9] was launched. This is a community-driven development project for the empowerment of rural poor and improving their livelihoods and is being implemented in 16 districts covering 70 blocks and 2,509 panchayats for a period of six years. Again in 2007 IFAD assisted the Post Tsunami Sustainable Livelihood Project under TNCDW in six districts.

Progress under Mahalir Thittam as on 31 March 2011 is given in Table 5.2. As on 31 March 2011, 7,659,682 women members had been organized into 491,311 SHGs, out of which 68% SHGs we formed in rural

---

[8] Note based on material provided by TNCDW Ltd and India: Completion evaluation of the Tamil Nadu women's development project by IFAD (http://www.ifad.org/evaluation/public_html/eksyst/doc/agreement/phi/tamil.htm).

[9] This is a livelihoods enhancement and empowerment project funded by the World Bank. The project intends to expand horizontally into an additional 46 new blocks (an administrative unit comprising a cluster of villages) spread across 10 new districts, and four additional blocks in existing districts; and to make up a shortfall of funds in the original project implementation area where: (a) the project covered a greater number of villages than originally planned (10% increase) and (b) an increase in the number of identified target population (30% increase) strained the village allocation of resources.

areas. The cumulative savings of SHGs was ₹ 29.73 billion and 447,081 SHGs received ₹ 116.04 billion as revolving fund under SGSY. A total of 21 banks were involved in disbursing credit of ₹ 81.3 billion to SHGs under SGSY, Swaran Jayanti Shahri Rozgar Yojna (SJSRY) and SBLP. In order to encourage bank linkages, the government of Tamil Nadu introduced awards for banks for their outstanding performance in SHG–bank linkage.

Table 5.2: Progress under Mahalir Thittam as on March 2011

Sl. no.	Parameter	Achievement
1	No. of SHGs	491,311
2	No. of SHG members	7,659,682
3	Total savings of SHGs (₹)	29.73 billion
4	No. of SHGs received revolving fund	447,081
5	Credit linkage provided so far (₹)	116.04 billion
6	No. of Habitation-level Forums (HLFs)	11,452
7	No. of Panchayat-level Federations (PLFs) restructured	5,085
8	No. of banks involved	21
9	No. of bank branches involved	6,300
10	Cumulative credit linkage to banks (₹)	81.3 billion
11	No. of NGOs affiliated	447
12	No. of PLFs affiliated	334

Source: TNCDW.

In order to strengthen the SHGs and ensure the sustainability of the movement, SHGs are further federated at the village panchayat, block and district levels. The most important units of Mahalir Thittam are SHGs and the panchayat-level federations (PLFs). Since 2006–07 the Mahalir Thittam has been providing seed money, building the capacities of office bearers and also announcing Manimegalai awards to the best PLFs. Under the programme, existing PLFs were restructured to become more efficient and transparent in their operations and as on 31 March 2011, 5,085 PLFs had been restructured. The government of Tamil Nadu has ordered all the PLFs to be registered under the Tamil Nadu Societies Registration Act, 1975 in order to provide them with a legal status. Also, the government has exempted the PLFs from the purview of Sections 25 and 42 of the Tamil Nadu Societies Registration Act 1975 so as to enable PLFs to take up income generation activities and benefit from them. The PLFs make possible the pooling of strengths and resources of SHGs to bring in economies of scale both in production and marketing. They monitor the performance of the SHGs in a village panchayat and also form and train new SHGs. *On a pilot basis, restructured PLFs have accessed bulk loans from banks and successfully accomplished the role of financial intermediaries to SHGs.*

During 2009–10, 102 PLFs were provided bulk loans totalling ₹ 275.2 million by various banks.

As on 31 March 2011, 447 NGOs[10] and 334 PLFs were associated with the programme. These PLFs[11] facilitate formation of SHGs. SHGs receive required capacity building support from the NGOs/PLFs in social, technical and credit-related areas, as well as in group management and operations. SHGs are rated for credit linkage after six months of their formation by a committee comprising bankers, APOs, NGOs, block level officer and PLF. Eligible SHGs are provided revolving funds and necessary credit support for various economic activities. Required skill building support is provided to them under various programmes. Also, TNCDW provides support in marketing the products locally and also through exhibitions. Mahalir Thittam focuses on organizing women workers and slum dwellers into SHGs for taking up common activities under the National Rural Employment Guarantee Scheme (NREGS).

Under the enterprise development training programme, members from various SHGs, who are interested in taking up economic activities, receive training from reputed institutions. Other than the revolving funds under various schemes and SBLP, SHGs also receive credit from the Tamil Nadu Adi Dravidar Housing and Development Corporation (TAHDCO) which provides financial assistance for projects up to ₹ 0.5 million for SHGs of SC/ST women functioning under the Mahalir Thittam, for starting any viable income-generating economic activities such as dairy farming, vegetable cultivation, hotels and restaurants, provision stores, power loom, leather goods, transport vehicles and trading activities. In order to ensure better coordination between various agencies for promotion of products of SHGs, the Tamil Nadu Welfare Society for SHGs was brought under TNCDW. A permanent marketing complex for SHG products was constructed in Valluvarkottam in Chennai. Also, 90 village *haat*s (three per district) are being constructed at a total cost of ₹ 135 million.

However, there have been a few challenges. One such challenge is the potential competition between PLFs and local/parent NGOs. *Mahalir Thittam intends to groom PLFs as financial intermediaries and they are being trained to act as NGOs/CBOs through whom funds and development programmes can be channelized.* It is understood that instruction from government staff is for PLFs to eventually delink from their parent NGOs. Each PLF has been given seed money and grant by Mahalir Thittam to generate income to cover their cost of operations. Besides, banks are being pressurized into giving loans to PLFs.

---

[10] NGOs undertake formation of SHGs, provide training support and monitor the activities of SHGs. NGOs are remunerated for forming SHGs, monitoring them and also receive incentive for enabling SHGs to access bank credit. NGOs such as MYRADA, Palmyra Workers Development Society (PWDS), OUTREACH and Hand in Hand (HiH) are affiliated to Mahalir Thittam.

[11] Well functioning PLFs, on par with NGO affiliates, support Mahalir Thittam in formation and training of SHGs.

5.3 KUDUMBASHREE, KERALA

Kudumbashree,[12] a programme to eradicate absolute poverty through concerted community action under the leadership of local governments was initiated by the government of Kerala in collaboration with NABARD in 1998. The programme facilitates the organization of the poor, in combining self-help with demand-led convergence of available services and resources in order to holistically tackle the multiple dimensions and manifestations of poverty. Kudumbashree is registered as the State Poverty Eradication Mission (SPEM), a society registered under the Travancore-Cochin Literary, Scientific and Charitable Societies Act 1955. Microcredit, entrepreneurship and empowerment are the three basic components of the initiative. The Kudumbashree is also the nodal agency for implementation of various poverty alleviation programmes implemented by central and state governments and adopts a convergence approach for reducing poverty.

The crux of the Kudumbashree strategy is to create a strong network of neighbourhood groups across all wards of the state, federate the network at the level of the panchayat/municipality/corporation; increase the presence of the poor in *gram sabhas*, enabling women to voice their needs and concerns in the decentralized planning process; create spaces for poor women to interface with local governments through the anti-poverty sub-plan, and women's component plan; and use microfinance as the means of accessing affordable credit through formal financial institutions.

The programme is implemented through three-tier structures with Neighbourhood Groups (NHGs) as the basic tier, Area Development Societies (ADS) as the second tier and Community Development Societies (CDS) as the third tier. Around 10–20 women from economically backward families come together to form NHGs. Members of NHGs elect a president, a secretary and three other volunteers—community health education volunteer, income generation activity volunteer and infrastructure volunteer for undertaking functional responsibilities. Ten to fifteen NHGs come together to form an ADS at the ward level of local government. The general body of ADS consists of president, secretary and three volunteers from member NHGs and the governing body consists of chairperson, vice chairperson, secretary and four members. ADSs are further federated at the panchayat level/municipality (town) level/corporation (city) level to form a CDS, also registered as a society under the Travancore-Cochin Literary Scientific and Charitable Societies Act. The governing body of the CDS consists of vice-chairperson, vice-president, member secretary (ex-officio member) and five elected women representatives and two experienced ex-CDS representatives as ex-officio members. A monitoring and advisory committee is constituted at the municipality level.

---

[12] Means 'prosperity to family' in Malayalam.

Kudumbashree leadership does not see NHGs as SHGs with a microfinance focus. However, NHGs conduct weekly meetings and collect thrift and take up inter-lending. NHGs are linked to banks directly and can access credit under an interest subsidy scheme wherein NHGs can avail loans from banks at 4% interest rate.[13] NHGs receive a matching grant from Kudumbashree. In order to receive the matching grant (10% of savings up to a maximum of ₹ 5,000), NHGs should have passed grading and availed of a bank loan.[14] Withdrawal of savings is not encouraged. NHGs give interest-free loans and some at low rates from 0.5% to 1% per month to the members and the income earned from the interest is either distributed among the members or incorporated into the corpus or used for expenditure for visiting the bank or celebrating festivals by the groups. The by-laws of NHGs restrict the members from withdrawing the savings amount.

The ADSs monitor the performance of NHGs and provide them with appropriate guidance and support in the matters of thrift and credit. Applications of NHGs for availing bank loans or for getting benefits under certain schemes are to be certified by the ADS. The executive committee of the ADS meets once a month and evaluates the performance of NHGs and consolidates the accounts of all NHGs and submits the same to the CDS. The CDS works in close coordination with local self-governing bodies and supports them in identifying poor families for various development activities. CDS evaluates various activities of Kudumbashree and takes corrective steps to improve operations.

NHGs avail loans from various banks and the federated structures support NHGs by facilitating the linkage through active liaison. These community structures are embedded in the local self-government framework, but have an autonomous functional character of their own. Women in these structures work with the local self-government to put forth their needs and also play an important role in implementation of government programmes such as NREGS. The community structure chalks out its plan and integrates it into the Panchayat Development Plan and gets budgetary allocations from the state.[15]

Details of progress under Kudumbashree as on 31 March 2010 are given in Table 5.3. According to latest data made available, as on 31 March 2011, 3,864,293 members were associated with 209,725 NHGs. The cumulative savings of NHGs amounted to ₹ 16.31 billion. A total of 118,711 NHGs

---

[13] Under the interest subsidy scheme, for all those banks who lend to SHGs at 9% or less, interest over and above 4% would be paid to banks by the government of Kerala through Kudumbashree. Seven banks have come forward to participate in the scheme and have been providing credit to NHGs at subsidised rates since January 2010.

[14] In case of NHGs whose members are SCs/STs, availing banks loan is not a prerequisite to avail the matching grant.

[15] Interview with Mr Jagajeevan, Programme Officer, Training and Gender & Organisation, Kudumbashree.

Table 5.3: Progress under Kudumbashree as on 31 March 2010

Sl. no.	Particulars	Achievement
1	No. of gram panchayats covered	999
2	No. of municipalities covered	53
3	No. of corporations covered	5
4	No. of NHGs	0.2 million
5	No. of ADSs	17,486
6	No. of CDSs	1,061
7	No. of families covered	3.74 million
8	Cumulative savings mobilized (₹)	13.75 billion
9	Internal loans disbursed (cumulative in ₹)	39.14 billion
10	No. of NHGs availed bank loan	118,711
11	Bank loan disbursed (cumulative in ₹)	9.94 billion
12	No. of NHGs disbursed with matching grant	64,806
13	Matching grant disbursed (cumulative in ₹)	236.3 million

Source: Annual Administration Report of Kudumbashree 2009–10.

had been linked to banks and the cumulative amount borrowed by them was ₹ 9.94 billion as on 31 March 2011. The total number of CDSs as on 31 March 2011 was 1,061.

Generally, the CDS does not provide financial services directly; rather, it facilitates the linkage between the NHGs and banks. Kudumbashree once experimented with CDS as financial intermediaries but the experiment was not successful and the programme was left with outstanding loans to banks which were paid off through a government loan.[16] In fact, the money that came from CDS was often considered as 'cold money' by the members and hence they did not give importance to its timely repayment. On the other hand, lack of adequate skill to handle financial activities contributed to the failure of the experiment.[17]

Further, Kudumbashree's experience has been that micro plans are not prepared as the communities lack numerical ability and plans are superimposed from above. Kudumbashree tried to address this by restructuring the by-laws, bringing in audit systems and insisting on internal accountability. It promoted the Kudumbashree Accounts and Audit Society (KAAS), as a

---

[16] Under the Bhavanashree scheme which existed till 2005, CDS, used to act as an intermediary for passing on the loans provided by banks to the beneficiaries. However, with the increase in interest rates, the burden of increased interest fell on CDS as it was not passed on to NHGs. Hence in 2010, the government took a loan on behalf of CDS and repaid the bank loan.

[17] Personal Interview with Sarada Muraleedharan, IAS, Executive Director, Kudumbashree, LSG Department, Government of Kerala.

microenterprise wherein 32 KAAS groups comprising 400 members provide the audit services for NHGs. One of the important aspects of Kudumbashree is that the panchayat plays an important supervisory role. The ward member and panchayat president are represented in the Kudumbashree structures and the panchayat president heads the review committee.[18]

Kudumbashree has been particularly successful in involving women members of NHGs along with their family members in implementing other development activities thereby ensuring that they derive additional income for their families. Under Santhawanam, in collaboration with the NGO, Health Action for People (NGO), and SBI, Kudumbashree facilitates identification and monitoring of lifestyle diseases in the community by training educated women from Kudumbashree families in home-based screening for identifying potential risk factors and lifestyle diseases. Also, under 'clean Kerala business', women members of NHGs engage in door-to-door household waste collection and transport to the transit points fixed by the Urban Local Bodies. Kudumbashree supports data entry operations undertaken by poor women and providing work such as digitalizing BPL data and ration cards for the state government.

In order to ensure economic viability of various enterprises, Kudumbashree in association with local self-governments and CDS has launched an initiative called Samagra which ensures scaling up of production activities, product diversification, value addition, improved marketing facilities, research back-up and use of technology to ensure that the products withstand the stiff competition from mainstream markets. Samagra ensures convergence of resources, activities and various government departments thus improving the forward and backward linkages of production. Under this initiative Harithashree, a large-scale project to cultivate and market vegetables; Ksheerashree to improve milk production; a mini apparel park, Madhuram; a large-scale honey production programme; and Naivedyam, a large-scale project to supply bananas to Guruvayur temple has also been taken up.

Kudumbashree also provides support for brand development and communication activities in addition to providing access to various monthly markets in various districts. Also, special marketing events are organized during important festivals like *Onam*. It participates in various national fairs to showcase the produce of its members. Unemployed youth are organized for the management of stalls in these markets. Kudumbashree encourages community marketing of produce to achieve economies of scale.

However, enhancement of livelihoods through self-sustaining cycles of livelihood promotion and tapping the local market has been a great challenge for Kudumbashree. The model needs to be strengthened and replicated. Further, existing policies do not support certain microenterprises

---

[18] Interview with Hemalatha, In Charge, MIS, Kudumbashree.

such as poor farmers' access to various services and bridging the gap in the entire value chain. More specifically, investment in capacity building has emerged as a great challenge for Kudumbashree.

5.4 Mahila Arthik Vikas Mahamandal (MAVIM), Maharashtra

Mahila Arthik Vikas Mahamandal (MAVIM), the State Women's Development Corporation of Maharashtra was established in 1975. The corporation has the objective of bringing about women's empowerment by mobilizing women and building organizations of women, enhancing their capacities and making credit and markets accessible to them. MAVIM implemented the IFAD-assisted Maharashtra Rural Credit Programme (MRCP) through the medium of SHGs from 1994 to 2002 in 12 districts of the state. This programme operated for eight years till 2002. In all 5,321 SHGs were formed in 12 districts and 79,944 women were mobilized through these SHGs.

MAVIM engaged village-level women facilitators called *Sahayogini*s. MAVIM also formed SHGs through its NGO partners, held trainings and special theme camps in the villages to deal with social problems. MAVIM initiated the Tejaswini Maharashtra Rural Women Empowerment Programme, an ambitious livelihood programme to be implemented in all 33 rural districts of Maharashtra assisted by IFAD and the government of Maharashtra, in 2007. The total project cost of ₹ 7.3 billion (Table 5.4). In order to sustain the SHG movement the model of the CMRCs of MYRADA[19] was adopted. The CMRC is a federation of around 200 to 250 SHGs formed in a cluster of around 20 villages. The CMRCs are registered organizations under the Societies Act 1860. The governance and the management of CMRCs are looked after by the SHG members and MAVIM acts as a facilitator.

The overall role of the CMRC is to provide basic primary services to SHGs, i.e., capacity building training to members, bank linkages, grading, and audit of SHGs. CMRCs also provide specialized services to SHGs such as assessing the livelihood needs of SHGs, tapping the required resources through convergence with various government schemes and services and enabling the SHGs to access these services and take up community development programmes. The business plans of CMRCs are being developed under the Tejaswini programme to explore the possibilities of financial sustainability.

---

[19] Chapter 4 discusses CMRCs of MYRADA.

Table 5.4: Progress under the Tejaswini Programme as on July 2011

Sl. no.	Particulars	Achievement
1	No. of districts covered	33
2	No. of blocks	291
3	No. of SHGs formed and supported	58,282
4	Village level committee (VLC)	8,044
5	Total no. of CMRCs formed	299
6	Total no. of CMRCs registered	191
7	Total no. of women	0.75 million
8	Total saving of women (₹)	1.64 billion
9	Credit supply from bank (₹)	3.35 billion
10	Total internal lending of SHG (₹)	4.63 billion

Source: Information provided by MAVIM, October 2011.

With respect to livelihood promotion, the programme is focusing on development of livelihood sub-sectors and is providing skills training to women for developing primary producer groups and producer companies in future. Currently, SHGs are instrumental in setting up grain banks in villages to ensure food security. In some of the villages, land reclamation activities are being taken up by SHGs. In addition, SHGs are taking up various enterprises such as renting out threshers, establishing fertilizer shops, sale of vegetables and groceries, tailoring, laundry, goat farming, flour milling and renting auto-rickshaws.

5.5 MISSION SHAKTI, ODISHA

A structured approach with defined focus on women's empowerment came with the launching of Mission Shakti in 2001 by the state government of Odisha. Unlike other poverty alleviation programmes, this is a movement for women's empowerment. Mission Shakti provided a boost to the microfinance movement in the state, when it was proved that microfinance was a surer means of 'poverty alleviation and women's empowerment'. Mission Shakti, along with a host of other stakeholders such as NABARD, SLBC, commercial banks, RRBs, DCCBs and NGOs played a meaningful role in accelerating SLBP in the state. With the advent of Mission Shakti, initiatives were taken up to form clusters and federations at the panchayat, block and district level. As on 31 March 2011, there were 306,434 SHGs with cumulative savings of ₹ 6.51 billion and cumulative bank loan of ₹ 15.59 billion under the umbrella of Mission Shakti (Table 5.5).

Table 5.5: Progress under Mission Shakti as on 31 March 2011

Sl. no.	Particulars	Achievement
1	No. of districts covered	30
2	No. of blocks	114
3	No. of villages covered under SHGs	44,607
4	Percentage of villages covered under SHGs	87% (44,607 out of 51,302)
5	No. of SHGs formed and supported	306,434
6	No. of federations promoted at panchayat, block and district level	7,940
7	No. of villages covered with credit linked SHGs	42,011
8	Total number of members	3,767,624
9	No. of SHGs credit linked since 01.04.2001	222,501
10	Total saving of women (₹)	6.51 billion
11	Credit supply from bank (₹)	15.59 billion

Source: *Mission Shakti Monthly Progress Report*, March 2011.

The emergence of Mission Shakti created enthusiasm among NGOs but this did not continue for long. Mission Shakti started promoting SHGs through the ICDS machinery. NGOs felt that SHGs promoted by them had been hijacked by the ICDS system. On the other hand, the ICDS staff claimed that SHGs promoted by the NGOs joined Mission Shakti in order to get government benefits. The *anganwadi* workers (AWWs), who were basically responsible for the formation of SHGs, were generally not well-versed with nor properly trained for SHG promotion and management. However, some of the SHGs promoted by the AWWs have been quite proactive and involved in almost all the government programmes. Being the contact point for women in the villages, the AWWs in comparison to the NGOs are better able to bring government programmes to the SHGs. A number of attempts were made by Mission Shakti to bring both NGOs and GOs on to a common platform. In fact, liaison with NGOs would have been ideal for the training and capacity building of the SHGs.[20] The government of Odisha enacted the OSHC Act (the liberal cooperative Act) in 2001. This Act provided a legal status for SHGs, clusters and federations for promoting self-help, self-reliance, mutual aid, autonomous, voluntary, democratic business enterprises, to be owned managed and controlled by women to address issues of economic and social empowerment. Further, the state government in 2004 brought amendments to the old Cooperative Societies

[20] Interview with Usha Padhee, former Director of Mission Shakti.

Act (1962) to enable SHGs to become members of cooperatives, which is not possible in the new act.

Under the umbrella of Mission Shakti, the federation building process was initiated in 2003 in a few districts. However, the process accelerated only in 2008. In Odisha, the block level federations promoted by the district administration in Ganjam district were already engaged in financial intermediation prior to the launch of Mission Shakti.[21] This has proved to be one of the low-cost models of SHG federation, though this model has not been replicated in other blocks/districts of the state. These block-level federations, functioning as societies and without having the appropriate legal entity also mobilize ₹ 100 per SHG per month as monthly contribution and build up their corpus. Each federation has about ₹ 5.0 million to ₹ 7.0 million as its corpus. In addition to the bank loans, this serves as a major source of loans to SHGs. Considering the limited capacity of the ICDS functionaries to manage the federation and the high level skills required for financial management of federations, *Mission Shakti plans to promote block-level federations focusing on non-financial services to its clients, though it had not closed the doors for financial services to SHGs through the federations.*[22]

The Mission Shakti federations have a four-tier structure, viz., SHGs at the village level (Tier-I), cluster or gram panchayat-level federation (Tier-II), block-level federation (Tier-III) and district-level federation (Tier-IV). The clusters are informal bodies but the block and district level federations are registered under the Societies Act. By March 2011, 7,940 clusters and federations had been promoted by the government machinery.[23]

The federations promoted by Mission Shakti are looked upon by SHGs as well as their staff as government institutions owing to their dependence on the latter for grant funds. In fact, the federations promoted by Mission Shakti have not yet made their presence felt as they are relatively new and lack technically qualified human resources, which contributes to their weak performance. A skilled and efficient human resource team to handle the technicalities involved in federation management and the finance and accounts systems is yet to be developed. The executive committes

---

[21] Twenty-three block-level SHG federations registered under the 1860 Societies Act promoted by the administration of Ganjam district of Odisha are undertaking financial intermediation and are linked to and borrowing from banks. Rushikulya Gramya Bank provides loan support to all the 23 federations at 9.5% p.a. In addition to this SBI provides loan support to two SHG federations at 9% p.a. and CCBs to two SHG federations at 9.5% p.a. Two SHGs federations that were borrowing from SBI, have recently declined (March 2011) to borrow when SBI increased the rate of interest from 9% to 14%. Out of the 20,746 SHGs enrolled in 23 federations, 17,791 SHGs have received loans from these 23 block level federations with a cumulative loan amount of ₹ 1.9 billion as of March 2011. There is no other instance of SHG federations linked to banks in other districts of Odisha.

[22] Interview with Usha Padhee, IAS Former Director, Mission Shakti, Government of Odisha.

[23] Mission Shakti Monthly Progress Report, March 2011.

(ECs) of the federations largely depend on the ICDS machinery for fund management. All the federations lack operating systems, procedures and practices (ACCESS, 2009).[24] Most ICDS supervisors, who are responsible for federation strengthening. consider federation work as an additional job and do not take ownership of the programme. Initiatives have also been taken with regard to handholding and capacity building of SHGs and their federations in a few districts by involving NGOs like PRADAN, Lokadrusti, EDII, and BISWA. Mission Shakti has realized the importance of financial literacy for the women in Odisha and organized training of the trainers (ToTs) programmes in the state. In convergence with the State Employment Mission, Mission Shakti has created Shakti Sahayikas, a cadre of skilled women to be used by the federations for SHG bookkeeping, updating records, federation building and marketing. They are expected to be absorbed in the state rural livelihood mission (SRLM) which would require similar human resources.

Mission Shakti has also taken a few livelihoods initiatives in the state—though not on a large scale. Out of 68,977 panchayat tanks that exist in the state, 6,492 have been leased out to the SHGs. A total of 2,137 SHGs are involved in LPG gas distribution under the 'Shakti Gaon Model' of Indian Oil Limited. Two thousand and eleven women SHGs (WSHGs), through Hindusthan Lever Limited (HLL), are acting as 'Shakti Dealers' for selling its products. While 7,820 SHGs are doing retail and selling of kerosene under the public distribution system (PDS), 43,215 SHGs have been brought into the Mid-Day Meal (MDM) programme of the government. Mission Shakti has opened up self employment opportunities for SHGs in KBK district. Raw 'kandul' dal (pigeon pea) of the locality is processed in the dal processing units managed by SHGs and supplied mainly to the government for the MDM programme and Emergency Feeding Programme (EFP) in three districts. Mission Shakti has also tied up with ITC for marketing of incense sticks produced by the SHGs.

However, due to the absence of proper hand-holding and lack of monitoring, the quality of the SHGs in the state is deteriorating by the day. Apart from this, anecdotal evidence from the field suggests that there is unhealthy competition among the SHGs to obtain government benefits. To make the SHG movement a successful one, there is a need for convergence of all the departments.[25] Though a number of bilateral projects such as Western Odisha Livelihoods Programmes (WORLP) implemented by Odisha Watershed Development Mission (OWDM), supported by DFID; Odisha

---

[24] Findings of the assessment of 10 block-level federations commissioned by TRIPTI and conducted by ACCESS Development Services in 2009.

[25] Interview with Pradeep Kumar Jena, IAS, Commissioner cum Secretary, Panchayati Raj Department, Government of Odisha.

Tribal Empowerment and Livelihoods Programme (OTELP), implemented by ST and SC Development Department, supported by DFID and IFAD; and Odisha Forestry Sector Development Project (OFSDP) supported by Japan International Corporation Agency (JICA) have been implemented in the state with SHGs as the base, there has been hardly any convergence with Mission Shakti. It is felt that a clear road map to bring about improvement in livelihoods of the women of Odisha is essential—along with skilled human resources—for Mission Shakti to achieve its goals.

5.6 TARGETED RURAL INITIATIVES FOR POVERTY TERMINATION AND INFRASTRUCTURE (TRIPTI), ODISHA

Targeted Rural Initiatives for Poverty Termination and Infrastructure (TRIPTI), a rural livelihoods project of Government of Odisha was launched on 31 March 2009 with World Bank support of US$84 million for a period of five years (up to March 2014). The project is being implemented in 38 poverty-stricken blocks of 10 coastal districts by Odisha Poverty Reduction Mission (OPRM), a separate society registered by the government of Odisha.

Through this project, TRIPTI is planning to break the vicious cycle of poverty and empowering the rural poor, especially women, economically and socially by

- developing economic organization of the rural poor;
- enabling them to access and negotiate between services and assets from public and private sector agencies and institutions and
- investing in capacity building of public and private service providers.

The TRIPTI project aims to focus on stimulating productive growth in key livelihood sectors and increase the employment generation options in project areas by forming and strengthening SHGs, producer groups and federations along with the provision of community investment funds and project management.

TRIPTI identifies the poor and Extremely Poor and Vulnerable Groups (EPVGs) for effective targeting. It also helps to identify households which are not a part of CBOs like SHGs. TRIPTI's agenda is to promote community-based institutions and strengthen them so that they become the harbinger of development for their own communities. More specifically, TRIPTI works with the SHGs and their federations promoted by Mission Shakti at the gram panchayat (GP) level in the 38 blocks of 10 districts. As of March 2011 TRIPTI had intervened in 4,077 villages in 594 GPs out of 1,020 GPs. Out of 25,698 SHGs promoted by Mission Shakti in 594 GPs, TRIPTI has intervened in 19,077 SHGs and formed 4,927 new SHGs

(Table 5.6). It is attempting to make all the SHGs model institutions by practicing the *Panchasutras*[26] of SHG management. More importantly, the programme is being implemented through a three tier-structure of SHG federations with SHGs at the village level (Tier-I), cluster-level federations (CLF-Tier-II) in between SHGs and gram panchayat-level federations (GPLF-Tier-III). The CLF is the connective link between the SHGs and GPLF. Till March 2011, 1,849 CLFs have been formed by covering 14,241 SHGs. To motivate the rural poor and extreme poor and vulnerable group (EPVG) households to participate equally in the SHGs, the government has decided to support a seed capital of ₹ 15,000 known as Pro-Poor Inclusion Fund (PPIF) to SHGs having five or more poor, EPVG and/or tribal members.

Table 5.6: Progress under TRIPTI as on 31 March 2011

1	No. of districts covered	10
2	No. of blocks	38
3	No. of GPs covered	594 (1,020)
4	No. of villages covered so far	4,077
5	Working with number of Mission Shakti SHGs	19,077 (25,698)
6	No. of new SHGs formed	4,927
7	No. of CLFs formed	1,849
8	No. of SHGs linked to CLF	14,241
9	Total amount of savings by new SHG (₹)	5.68 million
10	Total amount of savings by existing/old SHG	31.8 million
11	No. of SHGs doing internal Lending (old and new)	2,210
12	No. of members doing internal lending (old and new)	103,490
13	Total amount inter-loaned (₹)	15.85 million
14	Amount of Internal Loan outstanding (₹)	14.33 million
15	Total number of members (households) covered	712,342
16	No. of new SHGs credit linked	111
17	Credit supply from bank (to new SHGs) (₹)	2.3 million
18	Amount of savings of new SHGs in bank	1.1 million
19	No. of SHGs received PPIF	236
20	Amount received by SHGs from PPIF (₹)	0.8 million

Source: Government of Odisha (2011a).

---

[26] Panchasutras are five basic principles or pillars of SHG Management prescribed by NABARD. These are regular savings, regular meeting, regular internal loaning, regular repayment and regular bookkeeping.

This amount is provided in two tranches of ₹ 5,000 and ₹ 10,000 to help them start their on-lending activity and to create a group corpus. Eligible SHGs are selected by the CLFs based on certain prefixed indicators on practice of Panchasutras. As on March 2011, 951 SHGs have been given ₹ 4.76 million as the first instalment. Apart from this, each GPLF will also be provided with about ₹ 2.5 million as grant for lending to the SHGs through CLF. When the CLF is an informal structure (federations of 5 to 15 SHGs), the legal structure of the GPLF is yet to be finalized by the project. SHGs in the TRIPTI areas are linked with the banks as usual. So far only 111 out of the 4,927 newly formed SHGs have been linked with banks as of March 2011 with total loans ₹ 2.3 million.

OPRM, the society which is implementing TRIPTI at present, has been re-designated as (NRLM-O)[27] and relaunched in April 2011. The mission ensures sustainable livelihoods through social and financial inclusion for about 0.8 million rural households in the state. TRIPTI has given a lot of importance to the financial literacy of the SHG members by developing training material, and organizing ToTs for its own staff and CRPs.[28] As far as livelihoods innovations are concerned TRIPTI is making concerted efforts in the area of production enhancement by involving SHGs in System of Rice Intensification (SRI).[29]

The progress of TRIPTI is very slow and it has to move at a greater pace during the remaining period for the completion of the project. It needs perhaps to learn from the experience of IKP (SERP) with regard to the convergence of various departments in order to make the project successful.

5.7 Jeevika (Bihar Rural Livelihood Project), Bihar

Bihar Rural Livelihoods Promotion Society (BRLPS) has been implementing a livelihoods programme 'Jeevika' initiated by the state government of Bihar with support from the World Bank. BRLPS through the Bihar Rural Livelihoods Project (BRLP) aims to improve rural livelihood options and works towards social and economic empowerment of the rural poor and women. The BRLP intervenes with the community through four components, viz., (a) institution and capacity building; (b) social development; (c) microfinance; and (d) livelihoods promotion. The project envisages covering 0.5 million families in 4,000 villages of 44 blocks in eight districts.

As far as microfinance initiatives are concerned, the projects target is that 44,100 SHGs of poor households will develop and manage a microfinance

---

[27] Government of Odisha (2011b).
[28] Interview with Subrat Kumar Biswal, Microfinance Specialist, TRIPTI.
[29] Interview with Dr Arabinda Padhee, IAS, Director TRIPTI, Government of Odisha.

portfolio of ₹ 2.86 billion, including cumulative group savings of ₹ 343 million, cumulative interest accrual of ₹ 260 million, cumulative loans from commercial banks of ₹ 514 million and cumulative community investment fund of ₹ 1.74 billion by October 2012. This will be achieved by creating, developing and nurturing microfinance across the hierarchy of self-managed CBOs with SHGs as building blocks. The broader goal of the microfinance intervention through the project is to strengthen the approach of banking with the poor. It aims at creating member-owned, controlled and managed people institutions. More importantly, it has planned to adopt a multi-pronged strategy for ensuring financial flow to the rural economy from mainstream financial institutions and other complementary sources like SHPIs and MFIs. As far as the progress is concerned, 414,086 women have been organized into 31,381 SHGs in 2,043 villages by March 2011. The total savings of these groups is ₹ 187.32 million. However, ₹ 465.42 million has been inter-lent among the members and the repayment rate stands at 72.5%. The repayment rate of internal loans is low because more loans are given for consumption purposes. Out of the total internal loan of ₹ 465.42 million, ₹ 283.65 million (61%) has been given for consumption purposes. Further about 10% of the total SHGs, i.e., 3,145, have been linked to banks as of March 2011 with a cumulative loan amount of ₹ 87.49 million. The total loan outstanding to the bank was ₹ 56.17 million and the repayment rate of bank loan stands at 69.21% (Table 5.7).

Table 5.7: Progress under BRLP as on 31 November 2011

Sl. no.	Particulars	Achievement
1	No. of districts	9
2	No. of blocks	55
3	No. of villages entered	2,717
4	No. of SHGs formed	43,240
5	No. of VOs formed	2,718
6	No. of CLFs formed	4
7	No. of SHG members	504,315
8	Amount of cumulative savings (₹)	195.1 million
9	Total number of members taken loan	367,815
10	Total cumulative amount inter-loaned (₹)	495.4 million
11	Repayment rate of internal loan	85.60%
12	Total number of SHGs credit linked with banks	18,591
13	Amount loaned by banks to SHGs (₹)	756.06 million

Table 5.7 (Continued)

Table 5.7 *(Continued)*

Sl. no.	Particulars	Achievement
14	Loan outstanding with SHGs (₹)	525.8 million
15	Repayment rate of bank loan	93.7%
16	No. of SHGs received CIF	26,793
17	Amount disbursed under CIF (₹)	2,060 million
18	Amount outstanding with SHGs under CIF (₹)	1,412.1 million
19	Repayment rate of CIF	85.8%

Source: *Monthly Progress Report of BRLP*, November 2011.

Under the SHG federation structure 10 to 12 SHGs are brought together to form a VO at the village level. The CLFs are formed by federating all the VOs in about three to five panchayats depending upon the size of the panchayats. As of March 2011, 1,891 VOs and four CLFs have been formed. Though there is the plan to form block-level federations (BLFs), not a single BLF has been formed as of March 2011 since BRLP is largely concentrating on social mobilization and formation of groups and VOs. The Jeevika model design is very similar to IKP, Andhra Pradesh. For the livelihoods improvement of the poorest of the poor, as in SERP, TRIPTI and other programmes, BRLP also provides CIF to the SHGs against microplans through the VOs. Loans are provided by the project to SHGs directly under the agreement that the SHG shall return the amount with 12% interest to the VO and the VO shall return the amount to CLF (as and when it is formed) at 6% interest. Loans are provided from SHGs to members at 24% interest rate. CIF has four components—initial capitalization fund, food security fund, health risk fund and livelihood fund. Currently, SHGs receive loans from the project through the initial capitalization fund. All the other components of CIF are being provided to SHGs exclusively through VOs.[30] As far as CIF is concerned, 14,777 SHGs have been given CIF of ₹ 731.3 million against different microplans developed at the SHG level. With a repayment rate of 67.39%, ₹ 497.6 million CIF is outstanding with the SHGs as of March 2011.

BRLP focuses on enhancing sectoral size and productivity growth in key livelihood areas for employment generation of the poor. This is expected to be achieved by investment in technical assistance, service provision and setting up of market support mechanisms. BRLP has identified a few key areas where the project will intervene. They are—SRI, honey, *makhana*, fishery, poultry, banana, incense stick, Madhubani painting and textiles. Apart from this, Jeevika has a social service fund which will be used in improving access of the poor to preventive and reproductive healthcare,

---

[30] Interview with Mukesh Chandra Saran, State Project Manager, Microfinance, BRLP.

opportunities for primary and secondary education, provision of social risk fund to the VOs for use by the members, and also finance skill development for health, nutrition and gender activities undertaken by the VOs.

5.8 SHG Promotion by the Government of Rajasthan[31]

Under various poverty alleviation programmes implemented by the state government (with support from the central government, World Bank and bilateral donors), the SHG approach has become the key strategy for social mobilization, increasing access of poor to financial services and for livelihoods generation. Promotion of SHGs in Rajasthan is being taken up by five departments of the state with the Department of Women and Child Development (DWCD) as the leading promoter. The SHG programme was initiated by DWCD Rajasthan in 1997–98 and is being implemented in all the 33 districts of the state. AWWs of ICDS have been deployed by DWCD for promotion of SHGs in the state. The DWCD had promoted 196,723 groups in Rajasthan till March, 2010. The total savings of the groups was ₹ 1.07 billion. Compared to this level of savings, only ₹ 619 million has been disbursed by banks as credit during 2009–10, that too to 10% of SHGs. Further, analysis of data provided by DWCD indicates that only 54% SHGs are using their savings to give loans to members. Similarly, the Department of Rural Development, Government of Rajasthan has been promoting SHGs through its three main programmes—SGSY, Watershed Development and DPIP. A total of 209,412 SHGs have been formed under SGSY in Rajasthan till March 2010. Some 18,000 Common Interest Groups (CIGs) were formed, of which nearly half were livestock and dairy groups. Of these, about 4,347 CIGs were linked to the Rajasthan State Dairy Federation for marketing and technical services support. As per the guidelines of the watershed development programmes, promotion of SHGs in the watershed area is one of the strategies. Though 16,783 SHGs have been reported to be formed under the Watershed Development Programme, the focus of the programme is more on water harvesting and land development.

As in other states, in Rajasthan too, data on the exact number of SHGs is not available. The only reference point is the data on bank accounts of SHGs. As on March 2010, a total of 0.217 million SHGs are reported as having bank accounts.[32] Taking the functioning SHGs to be 0.26 million

---

[31] Based on the *Rajasthan Microfinance Report* (Singh and Bhargava, 2010).

[32] However, there are a number of groups that do not have bank accounts. Many SHGs become defunct after some time due to various reasons such as, the promoting organization being unable to regularly visit the group; conflict among group members; and SHG members distributing their accumulated savings among themselves upon failure to link with the bank. Such groups are seldom removed from the list of SHGs reported by the SHPIs.

SHGs and the average membership of SHG as 12, the total outreach of SHGs in Rajasthan would be about 3.12 million members. Annually, about 10% of SHGs in Rajasthan get bank credit and so far about 60% of SHGs have been able to take bank credit. While about ₹ 1.80 billion of SHG savings are in banks, the annual credit from banks to SHGs (including SHGs formed under SGSY) is around ₹ 2.0 billion. SHGs have shown impressive growth in savings and the total savings of all SHGs in the state was about ₹ 4.50 billion by March 2010.

The government of Rajasthan, in collaboration with IFAD and SRTT, is implementing a project titled 'Mitigating Poverty in Western Rajasthan (MPOWER)' for BPL households falling under dry arid zones of the state. A total of 1,040 villages in 245 gram panchayats are being covered during the project. The overall goal of the project is: mitigation of poverty of the target group households through strengthened capacity; improved livelihoods; sustainable enterprises; natural resource management; and increased access to credit and markets. The project, with an estimated investment of ₹ 4.15 billion, will be implemented over a six-year period with the first year of the project being devoted to mobilization and capacity building. The project aims at increasing credit flow to SHGs to the tune of ₹ 1.80 billion. The investment towards institution building will be in the tune of ₹ 20,000 per SHG. The project is expected to impact 87,000 households. The state government has decided to give 50% subsidy on interest to SHGs (from July 2010) who will make prompt repayment. As discussed earlier, in the case of IKP and Kudumbashree, this is intended to help in inculcating a culture of timely repayment and encourage the banks to give more credit to SHGs.

In Rajasthan, the SHGs are often grouped together in clusters to build the social capital of women. Clusters are usually formed by clubbing 10–15 SHGs across two to four villages or a gram panchayat. About 10–20 such clusters aggregate to form federations, functioning mostly at the sub-block level. The federations are mostly registered as societies, or trusts or not-for-profit companies. There are about 312 SHG clusters and 42 SHG federations in Rajasthan as of March 2010. SHG federations in the state have been facilitated by NGOs. Government departments like DWCD and Department for Rural Development (implementing SGSY) are yet to promote any SHG federation.

5.9 STREE SHAKTHI PROGRAMME OF GOVERNMENT OF KARNATAKA

The success of the Swashakti programme initiated by IFAD in the 1990s with World Bank collaboration encouraged the government of Karnataka to

launch a statewide programme called Stree Shakthi[33] based on SHG strategy
in 2000. Under this programme, there are three categories of institutions
promoting SHGs; the government, financial institutions and NGOs. The
promoting institutions play a significant role in the way on how an SHG
develops and functions. Stree Shakthi is an approach through which efforts
are being made by the government with the intention to pool both human
and material resources and empower women in rural areas.

The state has several programmes running through SHGs. The most
significant scheme in terms of funding and outreach is Stree Shakthi,
implemented by the DWCD. It attempts to focus the attention of members
on curbing domestic violence against women, promoting girl child
education, preventing child marriage and empowering women through
savings and microcredit, social awareness, adequate budgetary provision for
training and a grant of ₹ 5,000 per group as revolving fund. The SHGs are
mainly promoted by the DWCD *anganwadi* workers though some NGOs
are also involved. *Anganwadi* workers facilitating group activities and also
monitoring the Stree Shakthi groups are paid special incentives.

By March 2011, 130,000 rural Stree Shakthi groups have been formed
in the state and 1.9 million women members had been organized in these
groups. The SHG members have saved ₹ 9.72 billion over the years. 121,347
SHGs had availed bank loans to the extent of ₹ 11.96 billion and had done
internal lending of ₹ 28.36 billion for taking up various investments and for
other needs.

Stree Shakthi groups are encouraged to save for which *an incentive of
₹ 15,000 is given to groups who have saved above ₹ 75,000 and ₹ 20,000
to those groups who have savings above ₹ 100,000. During 2011–12, 200
groups have received a total incentive of ₹ 4 million. An incentive of 6%
interest subsidy is given to the Stree Shakthi groups which avail loans up to
₹ 100,000.* In addition to the groups formed by DWCD, SHGs formed by
the Departments of Social Welfare, Cooperation and Rural Development and
panchayati raj are also eligible for interest subsidy at 6% for the loan availed
from banks. Till the end of August 2011, ₹ 9.5 million had been released
to 4,370 groups as subsidy for loans availed ranging from ₹ 25,000 to
₹ 100,000.

In order to strengthen Stree Shakthi groups, taluk/block-level societies
are registered in 175 taluks under the Karnataka Societies Registration Act,
1960. Financial assistance of ₹ 30,000 was provided to each society for
strengthening SHGs. Up to the end of August 2011, ₹ 5.25 million had been
released to these societies. To encourage Stree Shakthi groups to take up
income-generating activities and also to provide marketing facilities for the

---

[33] http://dwcdkar.gov.in/index.php?option=com_content&view=article&id=260%3Astree&ca
tid=224%3Aflash&lang=en (accessed on 15 October 2011).

products prepared by these groups, financial assistance of ₹ 16.65 million has been released to construct 17 'taluk bhavans'. Stree Shakthi groups who take up income-generating activities are encouraged with an incentive of ₹ 5,000 per group. Up to the end of August 2011, ₹ 1.79 million was released to 358 groups for taking up for various income-generation activities.

Like the government of Andhra Pradesh, Karnataka had proposed in 2004 to set up a Mahila bank of the Stree Shakthi groups, but RBI[34] had turned down the proposal. Now with the launching of Stree Nidhi in Andhra Pradesh, the government of Karnataka may again try to set up a similar bank.

5.10 SGSY, GOVERNMENT OF INDIA

With the failure of a number of anti-poverty programmes and success of SHGs and its linkage programme, the government of India launched SGSY in 1999 as a key poverty alleviation programme which provided credit and capital subsidy through SHGs as a priority to help BPL populations improve their economic condition. The scheme aimed at encouraging group-based activities (though individuals were also assisted) by providing skill-building support, credit linkages, subsidies and market linkages. Programmes such as IRDP, Training for Rural Youth under Self Employment (TRYSEM), Development of Women and Children in Rural Areas (DWCRA), Supply of Improved Tool Kits to Rural Artisans (SITRA), Million Well Scheme (MWS), etc., were integrated into one single programme of SGSY, which also incorporated the learning accumulated by the implementation of all these programmes. Seventy-five per cent of funds allocated under the scheme are provided by the central government and the remaining by the state governments.

SGSY has been implemented by DRDAs in collaboration with PRIs, banks, line departments and NGOs. For the effective implementation of the programme a Central Level Coordination Committee (CLCC) has been set up. NGOs, CBOs and SHPIs are provided up to ₹ 10,000 per SHG for SHG formation and development. At least 20% of total funds are allocated for development of infrastructure. In order to develop the capacities of SHGs in taking up income-generation activities, SGSY has allocated 10% of its financial allocation for training and skill-building activities. Further, 15% of project funds are allocated to special projects. Under SGSY, a Revolving Fund within the range of ₹ 5,000 to 10,000 is provided to SHGs who have successfully passed the first grading. Also, the scheme provides subsidy for economic activity based on the criteria in Box 5.3.

---

[34] *The Hindu*, RBI rejects plea to convert Stree Shakthi groups into bank, Friday, 29 October 2004.

Box 5.3: Subsidy under SGSY to Different Categories of Target Groups

Category	Subsidy
For all categories	30% of project cost (Up to maximum of ₹ 7,500 per member, to a maximum of ₹ 125,000 per group)
SC, ST and disabled	50% of project cost (Up to maximum ₹ 10,000 per member, to a maximum of ₹ 125,000 per group)
SHGs	50% of project cost (₹ 10,000 subsidy per member, to a maximum of ₹ 125,000 per group)

Source: Adapted from SGSY Guidelines.

Villages for selection of beneficiaries are identified by SGSY committees at the block level and beneficiaries in the villages are selected in the gram sabhas based on the BPL list in the presence of the Mandal Parishad Development Officer (MPDO), the banker and sarpanch. The applications of beneficiaries, selected in the gram sabha, are forwarded to DRDA, which verifies the same, sanctions the subsidy and recommends them to banks.

Though the scheme provides for subsidies for encouraging the poor to take up self-employment, it was observed that there was delay from banks in releasing the loan even after sanction by DRDA. Also, the subsidy component was usually retained by the bankers for acting as a buffer in case of non-payment of the loan component. According to a study taken up by RBI in 2003 in 14 states covering 35 districts, it was found that in 40% to 60% of the cases, non-receipt/delay in receipt of subsidy from DRDA led to delay in release of loans to the beneficiaries. It was also observed that the procedures of banks were cumbersome and owing to poor performance of SHGs, it was difficult to grade them and issue the loans. Also, some of the bank staff did not have sufficient awareness of the scheme. Poor recovery performance of the scheme resulting in NPAs also led to lack of enthusiasm on the part of bankers. Even after release of the loans some of the bankers did not maintain appropriate documentation of the loans and did not inform the beneficiaries about the terms and conditions of the loans, further deteriorating the situation. With respect to sponsoring agencies, DRDA was not able to involve good NGOs for facilitating and nurturing SHGs. Owing to illiteracy and lack of awareness on the part of beneficiaries, they could not complete the loan procedures. Also, lack of appropriate training, prevented them from choosing viable economic activities. Even if they chose a viable activity, owing to delay in release of the loan amount, the activity at times was no longer viable.

Table 5.8 gives the physical progress under the SGSY over the years. Under the scheme, cumulatively 4,019,641 SHGs have been formed, of

Table 5.8: Physical Progress under SGSY since Inception

Year	SHGs formed	Women SHGs formed	% of women SHGs to total SHGs formed	Physical progress—SGSY		SHGs taken up economic activities	SHG Swarozgaris assisted
				No. of SHGs passed Grade I	No. of SHGs passed Grade II		
1999–2000	292,426	176,263	60	125,402	74,234	29,017	347,912
2000–01	223,265	153,285	69	214,011	101,291	26,317	318,803
2001–02	434,387	296,175	68	176,002	54,040	30,575	364,676
2002–03	398,873	221,085	55	189,634	94,754	35,525	414,419
2003–04	392,136	233,136	59	204,987	90,673	50,717	577,532
2004–05	266,230	191,666	72	219,604	105,839	68,102	788,573
2005–06	276,414	213,213	77	210,639	91,920	80,130	873,485
2006–07	246,309	176,712	72	222,029	156,353	137,931	1,472,066
2007–08	306,688	231,670	76	251,163	116,878	181,386	1,154,269
2008–09	563,530	404,972	72	322,322	138,641	114,452	1,470,032
2009–10	320,147	261,620	82	308,366	158,197	203,928	203,928
2010–11	299,236	215,084	72	200,946	184,284	197,939	197,939
Total	4,019,641	2,774,881	69	2,645,105	1,367,104	1,156,020	8,183,634

Source: Website of Ministry of Rural Development, Government of India, and Government of India (2010a).

which 2,645,105 SHGs have passed Grade I and 1,367,104 have passed Grade II, and 1,156,020 SHGs have taken up economic activities as on 31 March 2011. Since 2008–09, dedicated Rural Self Employment and Training Institutes (RSETIs) for promoting skill development have been initiated in each and every district. Also, in order to provide marketing facilities, three village haats are being set up in each district in addition to provision of need-based haats at district and state levels. Table 5.9 provides details of the financial progress of SGSY. The cumulative credit target up to the year 2010–11 was ₹ 394.86 billion of which 64.1% was mobilized and 63.1% disbursed to SHGs. The credit to subsidy ratio was 2:1.

A number of reports, including Tankha et al. (2008) and Patel (2011), have highlighted several shortcomings in the SGSY such as modest scale of programme with a small number of people supported; greater support to farm-based livelihoods than higher productivity activities; insufficient focus on capacity building activities; delay in bank linkages; subsidy-driven nature of the programme with regional imbalances in implementation, etc. (For other weaknesses in design and implementation of SGSY identified by NRLM see Box 5.4.) Being aware of the uneven, slow and in many cases distorted progress of SGSY in different states, the GOI appointed a committee to examine credit related issues under SGSY. The committee in its report (Government of India, 2009) recommended the setting up

Box 5.4: Weaknesses of SGSY

1. The design and implementation mechanisms of SGSY suffer from several weaknesses. The one-off assetization programme focusing on single livelihood activity has not met the multiple livelihood requirements of the poor.
2. Often, the capital investment was provided upfront as a subsidy without adequate investment in social mobilization and group formation.
3. Uneven geographical spread of SHGs, high attrition rates among SHG members and lack of adequate banking sector response have impeded programme performance.
4. Furthermore, several states have not been able to fully invest the funds received under SGSY, indicating a lack of appropriate delivery systems and dedicated efforts towards skill training and building resource absorption capacity among the rural poor.
5. There was considerable mismatch between the capacity of implementing structures and the requirements of the programme.
6. Absence of collective institutions in the form of SHG federations precluded the poor from accessing higher order support services for productivity enhancement, marketing linkages and risk management.

Source: Ministry of Rural Development (2011).

Table 5.9: Financial Details of SGSY (₹ in Billion)

Year	Credit target	Credit mobilized as % of target	Credit disbursed to SHGs as % of credit mobilized	Subsidy disbursed	Subsidy disbursed to SHGs as % of total subsidy disbursed	Total credit + subsidy disbursed	Subsidy + credit disbursed to SHGs as % of total credit +subsidy disbursed	Ratio of credit to subsidy (SHGs)
1999–2000	32.05	32.9	17.7	5.42	23.1	15.98	19.5	1.5
2000–01	32.05	45.5	17.6	7.02	23.9	21.61	19.7	1.5
2001–02	32.01	41.5	23.9	6.66	31.5	19.96	26.5	1.5
2002–03	25.25	46.9	38.8	6.06	46.7	17.90	41.5	1.6
2003–04	21.29	61.2	54.4	7.13	62.3	20.15	57.2	1.6
2004–05	25.08	66.1	62.0	8.59	68.2	25.17	64.1	1.8
2005–06	25.16	72.5	69.9	9.05	74.1	27.28	71.3	1.9
2006–07	28.69	79.9	78.7	9.71	79.4	32.62	78.9	2.3
2007–08	37.44	73.7	75.8	12.89	76.9	40.49	76.1	2.1
2008–09	39.30	89.8	71.2	17.42	66.1	52.72	69.5	2.2
2009–10	44.44	56.4	75.6	10.97	73.5	36.02	74.9	2.3
2010–11	52.11	88.0	77.4	25.19	80.1	71.05	78.3	1.8
Total	394.863	64.5	63.1	126.12	65.2	380.95	63.8	2.0

Source: Website of Ministry of Rural Development, Government of India, and Government of India (2010a).

of the National Rural Livelihoods Mission.[35] The government accepted the recommendations of the Committee and accordingly, SGSY has been restructured as the NRLM to provide greater focus and momentum for poverty reduction and to achieve the Millennium Development Goals (MDGs) by 2015. An ambitious target of mobilizing and building the skills and capacities of nearly 2.8 million SHGs has been set towards this end. A fuller discussion of NRLM follows.

5.11 NATIONAL RURAL LIVELIHOOD MISSION, GOVERNMENT OF INDIA

As mentioned earlier, NRLM (also called Aajeevika Mission) is the restructured SGSY and is proposed to be introduced during 2012. The mission of NRLM is to reduce poverty by enabling the poor households to access gainful self-employment and skilled wage employment opportunities, resulting in appreciable improvement in their livelihoods on a sustainable basis through strong grassroots institutions of the poor. NRLM adopts a three pronged approach—enhancing and expanding existing livelihoods options of the poor, building skills for the job market and nurturing the selfemployed and entrepreneurs.

NRLM plans to support 70 million BPL households across 600 districts, 6,000 blocks, 0.25 million GPs, in 0.6 million villages in the country and facilitate formation of SHGs, SHG federations and other livelihood collectives. Similar to SGSY, financing of NRLM shall be shared between the Centre and state in the ratio of 75:25 except in the North-eastern states where the ratio is 90:10. All the states and union territories of India will transit to NRLM within a year and NRLM shall take up phased implementation and reach all the blocks by the end of the 12th Five-Year Plan (i.e. by year 2017) period.

In addition intensive investments will be made as part of the World Bank-supported National Rural Livelihoods Project (NRLP) in 12 high poverty states[36] accounting for 85% of the rural poor in the country. Even among these 12 states, the intensive livelihood investments would be restricted to 100 districts and 400 blocks. Intensive investments would also be made as part of NRLM through GOI funds in a few districts/blocks. The blocks that are taken up for implementation of NRLM, 'intensive blocks', would have access to trained professional staff and cover a whole range of activities of universal and intense social and financial inclusion, livelihoods, partnerships,

---

[35] The GOI appointed a high-powered committee to examine credit related issues under SGSY. The committee chaired by Professor Radhakrishna in its report submitted in February 2009 had made recommendations for setting up a national level agency for self-employment and a NRLM.

[36] Bihar, Gujarat, Maharashtra, Madhya Pradesh, Odisha, Rajasthan, Tamil Nadu, Uttar Pradesh, Jharkhand, Chhattisgarh, Karnataka and West Bengal.

etc. However, in the remaining blocks or non-intensive blocks, the activities may be limited in scope and intensity. The outlays in these blocks would be limited to the state average allotment for these blocks under SGSY. NRLM would extend long-term dedicated support to them and facilitate the poor in their efforts to get out of poverty. In addition, the poor would be facilitated to achieve increased access to their rights, entitlements and public services, diversified risk and better social indicators of empowerment.

NRLM, which adopts *a demand-driven strategy*, will be implemented in a mission mode wherein the states design livelihood plans of their own within the limits of available funds, with focus on targets, outcomes and time-bound delivery. It also emphasizes on continuous capacity building and monitors poverty outcomes against targets. Government agencies, NGOs, PRIs, banks and related organizations will provide support in mobilizing the poor into various institutions such as SHGs, SHG federations and livelihood collectives to derive economies of scale, linkages, and access to information, credit, technology and markets. Gradually the process of implementation will be taken up by the institutions developed through a bottom-up approach. Various coordination committees set up at the central, state and district level shall ensure smooth coordination between various agencies working with NRLM.

An SHG of 10 to 20 persons in general (5 to 20 persons in difficult areas) is the primary building block of NRLM institutional design. Some of the key elements identified for a successful SHG strategy include,

- self-determined/voluntary group membership;
- promoting homogeneity in group membership (usually comes by default through a self-selecting process);
- encouragement of exclusive membership to women;
- group determined savings and intra-lending norms;
- initial intra-lending from own savings used for smoothing consumption;
- developing social capital for providing support services (like training, bookkeeping, etc.); and
- emphasis on creating federated higher order structures.

NRLM will ensure that at least one woman (preferably) from each poor household becomes a member of an SHG and subsequently both men and women would be organized to address various livelihood issues. More specifically, there will be 100% inclusion of BPL families and SC, ST, minorities and differently-abled persons will constitute 50%, 15% and 3% respectively of the total beneficiaries. The focus would also be on providing rural youth with required training programmes for their self-employment. In addition to SHGs and federations, NRLM will promote livelihoods collectives, producers' cooperatives/companies for livelihoods promotion.

NRLM shall strengthen all existing institutions promoted by NGOs and government in a partnership mode. Also, staff and leaders of existing institutions who have experienced the importance of SHGs in their lives would support the process of formation and nurturing of new institutions.[37]

Figure 5.1 gives the framework for implementation of NRLM. The primary source of financial assistance for the institutions of the poor will be bank credit. NRLM will provide Revolving Fund assistance and capital subsidy fund in the form of seed capital to the institutions of the poor which would strengthen their institutional and financial management capacity and build a good track record to attract the mainstream banks to finance SHGs. For all those SHGs who did not get Revolving Fund support earlier, NRLM shall provide the support with a minimum of ₹ 10,000 to a maximum of ₹ 15,000. Capital subsidy will be provided to SHGs based on their quality. *Making poor the preferred clients of the banking system is core to the NRLM financial inclusion strategy.* Mobilizing bank credit is crucial for accomplishing investment goals under NRLM. The role of banks commences right from the inception of the programme. The banks

Figure 5.1: Framework for Implementation of NRLM

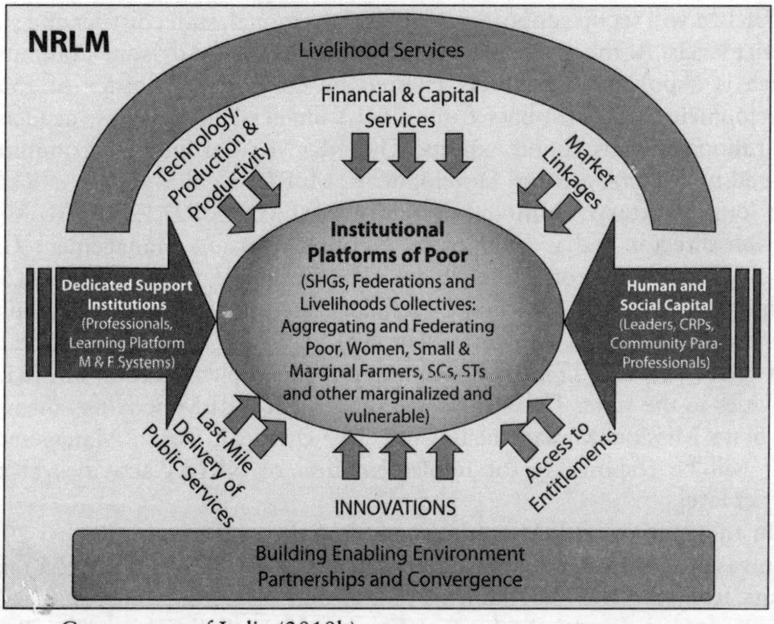

Source: Government of India (2010b).

---

[37] From Ministry of Rural Development, Government of India, NRLM, *Frame Work for Implementation* (22 December 2010) and *Programme Implementation Plan*, 2011.

shall open savings accounts for all programme beneficiaries, SHGs and their federations (unregistered/registered) and facilitate a full range of banking services including savings, credit and remittances. NRLM shall utilize subsidy in a smart way to render the poor bankable. Also, *interest subsidy for interest rates above 7% per annum shall be provided to all the eligible SHGs up to a maximum of ₹ 100,000 per household.* Financial literacy among the poor will be promoted along with universal insurance coverage to poor for life, health and assets by collaborating with various organizations and through convergence with Aam Aadmi Bima Yojana, Jan Shree Bima Yojana, Rashtriya Swasthya Yojana and agriculture and livestock insurance schemes. It shall also strive to provide remittance facilities to the poor. Required infrastructure and marketing facilities for major livelihood needs of the poor will be provided along with establishment of RSETIs in all the districts of the country for providing self employment to rural youth (Government of India, 2010a).

NRLM will focus on convergence with various schemes implemented by government departments such as NREGS and PDS, for enhancing the effectiveness of the programmes by linking with community-based institutions. Also, NGOs and civil society organizations (CSOs) will be brought into partnership for achieving the common agenda of poverty reduction.

NRLM will set up support systems at the national, state, district and sub-district levels. At the national level there is the NRLM Advisory Committee which is a policymaking body chaired by the Union Minister of Rural Development with members from CSOs, financial institutions, academic institutions and livelihood experts. The NRLM Coordination Committee chaired by Secretary, Rural Development, MoRD, would monitor NRLM. The Joint Secretary/Additional Secretary, NRLM, MoRD leads NRLM as mission director and is head of its National Mission Management Unit (NMMU) with a professional team. The Technical Support Cell (TSC) within NMMU will coordinate technical support and multidisciplinary appraisal missions to the states. The SRLM, which will be incorporated as a society, trust or company, will monitor the implementation of NRLM activities in the state. The SRLM will implement NRLM activities through the State Mission Management Unit. The District Mission Management Unit will be responsible for implementation of NRLM activities at the district level.

In an interview with Microfinance India State of the Sector Report 2011 (Srinivasan, 2011), Mr Vijay Kumar stated that the design of NRLM takes inputs from the IKP of Andhra Pradesh and also from other successful projects such as Kudumbashree of Kerala and Mahalir Thittam of Tamil Nadu. It rests on the principle that institutions of the poor are essential and long-term handholding of the poor households is required through them with resource and technical support from sensitive external institutions such as NGOs, government, banks or technical organizations. Sustained financial support is required for SHGs involving five to eight years of nurturing. Other options include reforms of cooperative banks and PACS for providing additional sources of finance to SHGs.

As far as the implementation machinery for NRLM is concerned it is to be a dedicated one but with a role for external professionals and with NGOs and well-managed community-based organizations as partners. A functional relationship with the PRIs would also be enabled so that the peoples' institutions can raise members' issues within the PRI. In building strong institutions of the poor and using these institutions as the nucleus for supporting other activities, is a departure from the SGSY model wherein income-generation activities were prioritized and were not fully effective. NRLM provides a framework for each state to prepare its own state level plans based upon micro-business plans prepared at the household and SHG levels and appraised at intermediary levels. Three streams of different types of livelihoods would be supported under this demand driven planning with agriculture and livestock, micro-enterprises and job-related skills for youth. In this way through building a good ecosystem, the poor could be made partners in economic development.

Patel (2011) suggests that the planning and implementation of NRLM should be integrated with ongoing programmes of health, education, drinking water, sanitation, housing, fuel, transport and communication (instead of NRLM being implemented in isolation) so as to create direct impact on the quality of life of rural households in terms of the Human Development Index (HDI). Learning from past experience, it is expected that NRLM would be able to make greater impact if qualified and skilled human resources are committed, a proper convergence strategy is adopted and a conscious effort is made to partner with competent NGOs and CSOs for handholding support at the grass-roots level. It is also expected that there will not be any need to further redesign poverty alleviation programmes in a new framework, as was done in the past by converting all development programmes to SGSY and subsequently SGSY to NRLM.

The Aajeevika Mission is expected to build on the good work that has been done by the NGOs and the state governments in promoting SHGs, SHG federations and various livelihoods organizations of the poor. Universalization of social mobilization and community organization is a unique feature of NRLM. Partnerships with NGOs and the private sector will be the key to the success of NRLM. Flexibility and context-specific approach would be the cornerstone of the mission. The best practitioners that emerge from the institutions of the poor will lead the development initiatives and these will also become the point of convergence for various development programmes. Innovations to promote sustainable livelihoods would be critical for the success of NRLM.

5.12 Concluding Observations

The state governments have been the major promoters of SHGs and their federations as far as their outreach is concerned. While NGOs have performed their role in piloting the SHG model, it has been proved beyond doubt that promotion of SHGs in all the poorer areas of India and mainstreaming the SHG model in the development intervention is only possible through the state governments. Adoption of SHG institutions by the state and central governments in their projects and programmes of poverty alleviation, women's empowerment and financial inclusion demonstrates the merit of the SHG movement in the country.

All these initiatives (except Mission Shakti) were launched through projects in collaboration with multilateral agencies, but later on mainstreamed by governments when external funding stopped. The governments have scaled up these initiatives, usually through a programmatic approach by setting up separate institutions and funding these initiatives out of the state budget or specific schemes of the central government and through externally funded projects by multilateral agencies. While a few state governments (e.g., Tamil Nadu) have provided scope for the engagement of NGOs for promotion of SHGs and their federations, largely the grassroots institution building is carried out by government machinery (Andhra Pradesh, Kerala, Madhya Pradesh, Odisha, Bihar). As Srinivasan and Tankha (2010) point out the financial services agenda for the federations has been developed by the governments in order to (a) provide competition to MFIs and their high-cost loans; (b) address quality issues in SHG–bank linkages and (c) to ensure sustainability of federations in support of the SHGs.

State governments realized that the SHGs and their federations can play an intermediary role in extending various welfare services. The state governments, especially those implementing externally funded projects have options and large resources, to follow a more target-oriented approach while forming large numbers of SHGs and federations. The agenda set for the federations of delivering the government's poverty alleviation and social security schemes is quite challenging. These SHG federations are effectively seen as agents for delivery of various government services. State governments also disburse subsidies such as seed capital, zero cost revolving funds, interest subsidies, etc., through these structures. Even though the rationale is targeting the poor and vulnerable for poverty reduction, it has served to create a dependency syndrome, undermining the self-reliance of these SHG-based institutions (ibid.). In co-opting these institutions, their legal forms, management, governance as well as products and services are usually decided by the state governments thereby undermining their autonomy. Besides, dependence on staff of government programmes has often resulted in leakages of funds provided to the federations for on-lending. Though the SHG federations have the ability to manage their own institutions, the governments continue to control them. This can result in SHG women members losing interest in the governance and management of their institutions.

A number of donors and government programmes have provided substantial financial resources to community organizations developed by them for a Revolving Fund, which is usually in the form of a non-returnable grant and at zero cost. These grants usually are treated as donated equity and help the federation in the initial stages to augment the loan funds when member contributions in terms of equity and savings are not adequate to meet member demands. The fund also enables the federation leadership and staff initially to build their skills in lending and later to leverage bank loans. Being zero cost funds the grants help lower the average cost of funds and thus enable boosting the profits. However, bureaucratic delays can defeat the purpose of this type of financial support.

In Odisha, a revolving fund of ₹ 2.5 million to each of the BLFs for 170 federations was sanctioned by the government (Mission Shakti) in 2009 to the district administration. However, the district administration has been unwilling to release the funds and are demanding separate accounts be prepared in respect of these funds to be operated by one government officer and the president of the federation. Thus, the fund has remained idle for over two years. On the one hand, the government is not confident about the financial management capacity of the federation, on the other hand the BLFs engaged in financial intermediation do not want to use this money as they have to keep separate accounts. When SHG federations are formed under government programmes, these institutions are inevitably treated by the government as state-owned. Moreover, governments are sceptical about the capacity of the federations in handling large volumes of funds. The termination by the state government of the experiment of financial intermediation by the CDS promoted by Kudumbashree is another example.

IKP has made a very useful innovation in the utilization of the CIF. The CIF is intended to support the microplans of SHGs which are consolidated at the VO level and funded with the contribution of 10% from VO, 50% from CIF and 40% from banks. However, at the field level, such synchronization for creation of assets rarely happens and CIF has been implemented as a standalone credit fund for a variety of purposes, including social needs. Though the donor is the same and the project is more or less similar to IKP and the CIF is intended to support the microplans, TRIPTI and BRLP do not thus far have the system of a contributory funding pattern of the CIF as in Andhra Pradesh. The use of CIF as a standalone credit fund is evident in the TRIPTI project from the disbursement of the first instalment of CIF to 951 SHGs at the rate of ₹ 5,000 per group.

A major criticism of the CIF is that it has crowded out the member ownership through their financial contribution. Neither VOs nor MSs in IKP mobilize member equity or savings. While from a prudential point of view this may be considered appropriate, the project should have ensured a greater financial stake of the SHG members at least in the stronger MSs. CIF could have been designed differently and provided on a matching basis to accompany equity investments by the SHG members in the MS. Creating financial assets of the members could have been the focus rather than pushing more credit. The CIF is administered and largely managed by project staff given the size of the funds—on an average ₹ 7.5 million per MS. Such revolving loan funds have not been managed equally well among the various MSs and the corpus has shrunk due to poor repayments in some MSs. Given the past not-so-positive experience of such revolving funds of several donor projects it has to be seen how the CIF is managed, especially in when the federations are truly autonomous. It is hoped that following and benefiting from the experience of IKP, the Jeevika project in Bihar and TRIPTI in Odisha, will have more positive outcomes.

Federations promoted under government programmes will need to have adequate skills and management capacity to carry out full-fledged financial intermediation and cover their costs. Otherwise, all such institutions will have to depend upon the respective state governments. Further, *this pattern will also affect the willingness and ability of the SHGs to pay for the financial services and affect the sustainability of the federations* promoted under government programmes. By introducing Pavala Vaddi, the government of Andhra Pradesh, and also similar interest subsidies by other state governments like Kerala, Maharashtra and West Bengal,[38] may have encouraged the SHGs to inculcate the habit of prompt repayment, but the long-term implications are yet to be analyzed. This subsidized interest in fact prevents the SHGs from earning a margin and paying for the services which the federations render to the SHGs. Past experience shows that bringing in the culture for payment of services in the groups which are used to subsidies is an uphill task. While state governments can provide interest subsidy for on-time repayment of bank loans, the SHGs and their federations would better be allowed to charge an interest rate that is determined by them that will ensure that the SHGs and their federations have a small margin to meet their costs.

All these government programmes in their projects have given greater importance to credit than other services required for livelihoods development. Except SERP, almost all the projects/programmes have lacked convergence in the efforts of various departments. The implication of the involvement of PRIs in these projects needs to be studied. Only Kerala has systematic

---

[38] Though this system of interest subsidy has not been introduced in Odisha, the state had sent a circular to 100 federations in the initial stages to lend the revolving fund to SHGs at 4% rate of interest. However, after receiving negative feedback from major stakeholders, the rate of interest was enhanced to 10%.

integration of the people's institutions (PIs) and their agenda with the PRIs and their yearly plans and budgets. While PIs are progressively taking up the functions of line-departments, there are no corresponding changes in the functioning of those departments. Without the corresponding changes in the line-departments, the convergence of many departments and institutions is bound to be ineffective.

Though savings is the most important service in the community-based microfinance model, it has not drawn the attention of the state governments. Voluntary savings need to be promoted among the SHG members and, apart from bank, SHG federations could possibly be appropriate institutions to mobilize voluntary savings from SHG members. To ensure safety of the savings, these SHG federations must be registered organizations. While nine states have liberal self-reliant cooperative laws, *there is a need for every state to have a self-reliant cooperative law for SHG federations to be registered and to have a corporate body status*. There has also not been much focus on a self-regulatory system for the SHG institutions which would include financial literacy, SHG audit, annual planning, regular elections at the SHG/federation level for leadership rotation, annual rating of SHGs, awards for best performing SHGs/federations, effective internal control measures and a supervisory system owned, managed and controlled by them.

There is a definite role for the GOI and state governments in facilitating access to microfinance services through SHGs and SHG federations. However, it needs to be undertaken in a professional manner following cooperative principles and through adopting a process-oriented approach aimed at the sustainability of the SHGs and their institutions. With the emergence of the NRLM as a game-changer, it is hoped that the range of issues related to the effectiveness of government SHG programmes will be properly addressed.

6

COST OF PROMOTION OF
SHGs AND SHG FEDERATIONS

The cost of promotion of SHGs has emerged over the years as an important issue for discussion and debate in order to arrive at benchmarks of the expenses necessary to form and maintain an SHG. Even as there was a massive expansion in the number of SHGs around the beginning of this century, the cost of SHG promotion became a particular concern of the donor community, as also of NABARD, in their efforts to ensure the productive and effective use of grants provided by them to NGOs and other SHPAs. As a result the SHPAs came under pressure to demonstrate that these SHGs were sustainable entities for providing financial services. Over the years state governments emerged as the major promoters of SHGs either through departmental initiatives or through large projects and programmes for poverty alleviation such that probably around 75% of SHGs today are government-promoted.

Since the promoters and stakeholders in SHG promotion—NGOs, government agencies, banks and others—have different objectives and varying resources available to them, the nature and purpose of SHGs promoted and the period of support also vary greatly. This has implications for the inputs and costs involved. Most SHGs are also further brought together in some form of association or federation by their promoters, the modalities and structure of which also vary. This necessitates building of capacity at additional levels, along with the attendant costs to ensure the sustained functioning of the federated structures for which external investments are invariably required.

At the same time it is not easy to pin down these costs and it is inevitable that estimates of such costs will vary for different projects and for region-specific and community-specific considerations. In order to undertake a comparative analysis of costs of promotion of SHGs by different SHPIs or agencies, it is necessary that SHGs formed under different approaches are relatively homogeneous and expected to perform similar functions and result in similar outcomes; where exercises are based upon past data, historical costs need to be converted into present values. Since these conditions are not easy to satisfy, it is difficult to compare and pass judgement on the *cost-effectiveness* of SHG promotion by different agencies working in different contexts.

6.1 Issues in Estimation of Costs

Overall, the SHG costs issue is considered from the perspective of the sponsor or donor interested in knowing the amount of investment required to establish sustainable structures for SHG functioning. Thus, they tend to exclude those costs of SHG development that are met by or transferred to the SHG. These include, e.g., costs of account books and record keeping, members' time and meeting expenses incurred by the SHG members. It is, in fact, generally agreed that requiring SHGs to meet such costs, helps to develop the value of autonomy and independence in the groups. Though seen as good practice such a transfer does not bring down costs but only shifts them on to the programme participants; with benefits expected to accrue to SHG members in the form of empowerment through self-reliant functioning.

It is a contested issue as to whether SHG promotion or development cost[1] should be considered to be a charge on the delivery of financial services to and through the group and thereby to be seen through the lens of cost recovery. A widely held view is that SHGs promotion costs should be considered to be part of the financial infrastructure costs for reaching the poor in rural areas and as such these costs should not be imposed upon them. Harper (2002) states that SHG development, or 'promotion' as it is usually called, must at least in the earlier stages of the movement be subsidized. Indeed, it is even argued that SHGs can be seen as a kind of public good[2] that facilitate the delivery of various government programmes apart from bringing about social and political empowerment benefits to the members that go beyond the narrow objectives of financial intermediation.

It is also possible to take the view, like Christen (2006), that the fundamental viability of SHGs as a model for the provision of financial services remains in question because key support and maintenance services have to be provided for the SHG–bank linkage model to remain viable *and their costs recovered*. The question of promotion costs is also linked to the

---

[1] In this chapter the terms 'costs of promotion' or 'promotion costs' and 'development costs' have been used interchangeably and cover both the initial costs of SHG and federation promotion as also the costs of their maintenance over time until a stage is reached when such support can be withdrawn.

[2] http://gulzar05.blogspot.com/2011/04/are-shgs-public-good.html (accessed on 6 October 2011). They are increasingly being used as such in the many government programmes.

sustainability debate. In his study of two SHG federations, Christen (2006) amortizes SHG promotion costs over a three-year period and includes it in the current operating cost calculation. Further, he amortizes the promotion cost of a federation over a five-year period. He asserts that while many in the SHG movement prefer to see this initiative strictly as social mobilization that serves multiple purposes, *the potential of SHGs to cover all their costs, including support functions can only assist in determining the most cost-effective use of the subsidy*. The reason given for this is that the full costs of the system have to be understood in order to decide whether subsidies should be provided and if so in what form and at what level in the delivery structure so that they can have maximum impact in the long run.[3] Proponents of sustainability as a key element in the development of any financial or development system are, like Christen, inclined to include the *cost of promotion as operational cost* in an amortized form while analyzing the sustainability of SHG-based systems.

While one may or may not share the perception that SHG promotion cost constitutes a subsidy that distorts the free play of market forces in determining people's choices, sponsors and donors are interested in knowing the costs of SHG promotion, and with the emergence of SHG federations, the costs of this additional structure as well, in order to decide on their grant-making and financial support to SHPAs to engage in SHG formation.

6.2 SHG Processes and Cost Components

SHG promotion is a process by which SHG members (usually women) are motivated and mobilized to come together for their mutual benefit. This includes, among others, a range of activities including initial surveys and participatory exercises with the community, group formation and the start of thrift activity. It also includes training of SHG leaders and members in relevant areas, dissemination of materials, exposure visits, monitoring and assessing the group capacity to take up larger responsibilities including borrowing from banks. It can also include establishing of higher levels of association at village/cluster level and support for individual and group economic and social activities. These village-level associations are then federated into financial or non-financial structures. Such higher-level institutions may or may not be a necessity; SHGs have shown that they can also operate effectively without them.

As far as federation promotion and development is concerned it too has its own set of processes. Consultations, familiarization and training

---

[3] He proceeds to demonstrate that SHG lending would have to carry higher rates than MFI loans if no subsidy was involved.

workshops and exposure visits are part of this process which culminates in the registration of the federation and the initiation of its financial activities. At the NGO level, staff is prepared for a new form of partnership with community members by working with and for the community-owned federation. In the final phase, as the federation starts functioning, the NGO is required to provide physical and financial support until the federation can meet its costs from its revenues and function sustainably.

The longer period of facilitation required towards forming *financial* federations of SHGs necessitates higher foundation costs in view of the nature of their operations. These processes, from available evidence, are generally planned for and take about five years or until the federations are able to achieve sustainability and independent functioning. This is a longer process and is considered separately from the cost of promoting SHGs themselves.

Thus, it is possible to distinguish between two discrete (or even overlapping) phases in the process of SHG promotion and federation:

1. SHG promotion including development of cluster level organizations
2. Establishment of secondary federation and stabilization of its operations

For the purpose of analysis, cost can be computed in respect of the *initial phase of SHG formation* and development and the following phase of *establishment and stabilization of the federation*. Costs of the *federation* phase can further be divided to distinguish between costs incurred to establish the federation and launch operations and costs of material and financial support until federations are able to operate sustainably. This also enables the presentation of disaggregated data to facilitate further analysis. (This has been done in the case of the ACCESS-Rabobank study findings which are presented in Section 6.5.)

At the NGO/project unit level, the following broad components of direct costs can be readily identified:

1. NGO staff time directly engaged in visits, trainings and provision of support
2. Staff conveyance expenses
3. Training and expenses on capacity building of SHG members, including materials and exposure visits
4. Stationery, cash box and group meeting incidentals

Overhead costs at NGO/unit level include:

1. Office rent and utilities
2. Depreciation on vehicles, furniture, etc.

3. Cost of administration and other support staff, including capacity building

Ideally, a similar set of costs is required to be imputed for expenses incurred centrally by government or donor agencies or intermediaries engaged in the SHG development programme. When added to direct costs, the aggregated figure would represent total costs of SHG promotion.

Estimates of average *total cost* of SHG promotion can be made through imputing the direct costs of activities at the NGO/project level supplemented by a mark up to account for overhead costs at higher levels by support institutions in developing and maintaining the institutional structure of which SHGs form a part. Cost allocation for SHG promotion becomes more complex when staff and other resources are engaged only partially in this activity. There is thus the question of how the staff time of development workers partially engaged in SHG promotion along with other functions is to be estimated and whether and how overhead costs are to be allocated across SHG promotion and activities.[4]

6.3 Review of Studies on Cost of Promotion

There are few, if any, rigorous studies on the cost of promotion of SHGs. The studies that have been undertaken have provided little information on how the total estimates have been arrived at. Nevertheless they have helped to establish some benchmarks for support to SHPIs. Several of these estimates are quite old and only indicative and of academic interest and would have, of course, to be corrected for inflation to make them comparable with present day figures.

Harper (2002) provided some of the early estimates of cost of SHG promotion. He reports that the costs of developing an SHG from scratch to bank linkage were found to range between ₹ 1,350 and ₹ 16,000 according to FWWB (2002). Further, Harper et al. (1998) found that it cost a typical NGO ₹ 8,520 to develop an SHG for linkage while the cost for a bank was ₹ 11,000. He pointed out that costs depend considerably on the previous level of cohesion within the community. Harper also refers to the experiment of microfinance agents of BASIX finance in 1997 and 1998, and finds that it cost ₹ 6,000 to bring SHGs to a stage where they could take loans.

---

[4] It should also be noted that many SHGs have been successfully 'self-promoted'; as village women seeing others benefitting from SHGs have formed and built their own groups without much assistance, apart, perhaps, from some informal advice from neighbours who were members of their own SHGs.

Harper identified five types of SHPIs: (a) NGOs, (b) Banks, (c) VVVs or farmer's clubs, (d) government agencies and (e) self-employed individuals and individual commission agents In addition, there were SHG federations who act as intermediaries between financial institutions and SHGs. Finally, there were a number of SHGs that came up independently and spontaneously without any promoter.

Harper's estimates of cost of the SHG promotion process were as under:

- For five NGOs—₹ 1,200 to ₹ 20,400
- For six banks—₹ 1,200 to ₹ 8,750
- For five VVVs—₹ 400 to ₹ 4,200
- Three government agencies—₹ 200 to ₹ 7,000
- One individual volunteer—₹ 3,300

Harper (2002) took the view that SHG promotion could be viewed as retail marketing channel development or merchandizing. NABARD could be taken to be the manufacturer and banks the channels for the product, financial services for the customers, the rural poor.

Around the same time Tankha (2002) computed estimates of the cost of promotion of SHGs of 10 leading NGOs/projects. The estimates varied from ₹ 4,500 to ₹ 25,000 for different types of SHG initiatives. He distinguished between four types of SHG promotion 'models':

1. Minimalist, focusing only on bank linkage
2. Large project initiatives related to savings and credit and women's empowerment
3. SHG promotion by leading NGOs engaged in livelihoods development
4. SHGs formed by government agencies and local initiatives

Within the 'minimalist' category of SHGs formed for bank linkage, the cost of promotion was estimated at ₹ 4,500 for microfinance agents and estimates of group promotion by local bankers, considering only the cost of time spent by bank staff, were similar.[5] Under a scheme launched in 2001, for banks to appoint suitable individuals for promoting SHGs for bank linkage, payments of ₹ 500–700 per SHG (reimbursed by NABARD) were made to the agents. A similar sum was paid by banks engaging AWWs and school teachers as SHG facilitators. At the time, a number of large projects funded by multilateral and bilateral donors had begun to be implemented which included women's empowerment as a focus area. For one such project, the

---

[5] For example, a study of the Umbley Belu branch of Sahyadri Gramina Bank in Karnataka in 1996–97 (Srinivasan, 2000) estimated a figure of ₹ 3,718 as the average cost of groups promoted by a bank manager in a village over five years.

UNDP–South Asia Poverty Alleviation Project (SAPAP), the cost of SHG promotion was estimated at ₹ 15,000 per SHG and for its successor World Bank DPIP project (Velugu), at ₹ 20,000.

For the two NGOs which were part of the CARE-CREDIT project[6] the estimate, at NGO level, of costs of promotion per SHG was ₹ 15,356 and ₹ 13,726. The average total cost of SHG promotion for other leading NGOs was ₹ 12,100 (PRADAN, Hazaribagh), ₹ 20,575 for Holy Cross Social Service Centre (HCSSC) and ₹ 15,000 to ₹ 25,000 for MYRADA.[7] Outreach had the lowest reported cost among NGOs with a range of ₹ 4,500 to ₹ 6,000 per SHG. Other scattered estimates reported a figure of ₹ 6,000 to ₹ 10,000 as the cost of promotion per SHG for NGOs.

The phenomenon of *Swayambhu* or self-promoted groups had been reported in CARE-India credit project areas as also by ASSEFA which described it as the 'spiral effect'. However, reservations were expressed by other NGOs such as PRADAN and MYRADA about the possibility of lowering the cost of development of such copycat groups. The only savings in costs, it was asserted, was in respect of the initial contact and motivation phase of about three months. For the rest, these groups required to traverse the same ground as other groups with the attendant costs. A relatively new development at that time was the *role of federations in promoting SHGs*. Outreach in Karnataka and Tamil Nadu reported that cluster-level associations (CLAs) formed out of 10–15 SHGs had started promoting new groups in their respective villages. This had brought down the cost of group formation from ₹ 4,500 to ₹ 6,000 for groups promoted by the NGO to ₹ 3,000 per SHG for groups promoted by the CLA.

Following these studies, a consensus emerged around the year 2002 of a figure of *₹ 10,000 per SHG as the cost of promotion by an NGO working towards a wider empowerment agenda for the SHGs that went beyond the narrow objective of bank linkage.* In fact, if we consider the scale of support available to NGOs for SHG promotion at the time, it was quite liberal, with MYRADA and other southern NGOs, receiving funding of ₹ 15,000 to ₹ 18,000[8] from TNCDW and other sources. These NGOs were at the same time characterized by intensive process-oriented facilitation of their SHGs, with MYRADA, e.g., putting SHGs through 14 training sessions covering 23 training modules. OUTREACH had 10 one-day programmes to cover 10 training modules. PRADAN worked with a development support team

---

[6] PRADAN, Ranchi and Nav Bharat Jagriti Kendra (NBJK).
[7] A similar figure of ₹ 17,000 had been reported as the average total cost of SHG promotion for a minimum of 150 groups under DHAN Foundation's *Kalanjiam model* of federating SHGs into a cluster level financial institution and ₹ 12,000 for linking SHGs to banks as part of an integrated development programme (DWCD-CIDA, 2000).
[8] As informed by Aloysius Fernandez during an interview in July 2011.

of relatively highly paid professionals with no lower level field staff. Scales of support provided by other projects and agencies were more or less in line with the estimate of ₹ 10,000 by the Council for Advancement of People's Action and Rural Technology (CAPART), the Swa-shakti programme and the SGSY were ₹ 9,000, ₹ 10,000 and ₹ 10,000 respectively and the CCA programme scale of support was ₹ 8,000. The Ratan Tata Trust similarly provided support for SHG promotion of ₹ 10,000 per SHG to seven NGOs in Rajasthan (CmF, 2008). Other NGOs that did not have access to these funds however managed with much lower levels of financial support for SHG formation.

NABARD, which in 1999 had started supporting SHG promotion by NGOs, RRBs and DCCBs through grants from its microfinance development fund, initially provided only ₹ 2,000 per SHG[9] for NGO promoters and ₹ 1,000 for RRBs and DCCBs. This was based on NABARD's view that this level of support represented the incremental cost of facilitating bank linkage to be incurred by NGOs over and above the expenses undertaken by these SHPAs in routine formation of SHGs. In the years to follow, the leading high-cost NGOs were able to bring down their cost of promotion as well, and MYRADA could successively report lower costs of SHG promotion, coming down to ₹ 6,000 per SHG in 2011.[10]

The cost of promotion of SHG programmes was subsequently examined in a CGAP study, conducted by APMAS which computed the average cost of promotion of SHGs over three years for five promoting institutions.[11] These costs included the costs of social mobilization, which included (a) salaries, allowances and honoraria; (b) costs of books and materials; (c) training costs; (d) capital for entry point activities and imputed cost of 10% for overheads on account of project management. In addition to the direct cost of social mobilization, support costs included (a) staff costs excluding fieldworkers, (b) office administration costs, including meetings, (c) training of executive committee members and staff and an endowment fund for the federation in the case of Mandal Samakhya (CGAP, 2007).[12]

---

[9] The scale of support has over the years risen to ₹ 4,500 over three years at present. The corresponding figure for RRBs and DCCBs is ₹ 2,500 for SHG formation and linkage. In 2003 a scheme for Individual Rural Volunteers was launched which currently provides for ₹ 1,200 per SHG for formation and linkage to such individuals (http://www.nabard.org/microfinance/nabardsupport.asp [accessed on 8 October 2011]).

[10] Aloysius Fernandez, personal interview. While no detailed breakdown is available, the lower cost would appear to be accounted for, among others, by the fact that new groups are now formed by CMRCs and federations in the case of the well-established NGOs.

[11] These were Panagal Mandal Mahila Samakhya, Andhra Pradesh; Sakhi Samiti, Rajasthan; PRADAN, Jharkhand; Chitradurga Grameen Bank, Karnataka; and PANI, Uttar Pradesh.

[12] The cost of forming SHGs and SHG federations was amortized over five years while estimating the profitability and sustainability of the SHG programmes being studied. As in Christen (2006), the study emphasized the need to assess the full cost of the long-term support to maintain the SHG portfolio.

The range of the average total cost of mobilization and support per SHG was US$ 260 or approximately ₹ 12,000 at prices prevailing during the period of the study, i.e., 2003–04. Thus these estimates too were in line with the earlier round of estimates.

Another set of estimates was made by the GTZ-NCAER SHG impact assessment study (NCAER, 2008). The study distinguished between promotion costs and maintenance costs, such that promotion costs were incurred up to the point of bank linkage and maintenance costs thereafter.[13] It provided annual estimates of promotion costs incurred by various types of SHPIs covered by the study. The results showed that the average promotion cost of NGOs at ₹ 8,512 in 2005 was higher than that of banks (₹ 2,957) and where government was the promoter (₹ 3,595). Maintenance cost for the year 2005 was ₹ 1,123 in the case of NGOs and ₹ 964 for banks. In the absence of further information it is not possible to infer the total cost of SHG promotion and maintenance per SHG. However, these estimates too appear to be along the expected lines and levels. The study also pointed to the lack of financial support for continuing maintenance of SHGs with 24% of SHPIs reporting that lack of financial support was a problem faced by them in working with SHGs which they had initially promoted.

6.4 FINANCIAL SUPPORT FOR SHG PROMOTION

During the period of massive expansion of SHG numbers from about year 2000, concerns arose about the quality of SHGs promoted and the adequacy of the support to SHPIs for their promotion. Ghate (2006), taking the promotional cost of SHGs at ₹ 10,000 over the life of the groups, pointed out that to expand the programme at the rate of half a million new groups per year, would require merely ₹ 5 billion,

> which was not much more than ₹ 4 billion a year that was spent by the Central Government on the SGSY programme during the [Tenth Five-Year Plan (2002–07)] on a comparatively small subset of the groups, largely ineffectively and wastefully. This was in addition to the promotional grant to DRDAs at ₹ 10,000 per group.[14]

---

[13] In the study 'promotion' costs included costs incurred by SHPIs on social mobilization, training of animators and SHG members, documentation and linking up SHGs with bank. 'Maintenance costs' were those incurred under different heads such as training, bookkeeping, and social mobilization, for the stability and sustainability of the SHGs. As indicated earlier, in this book, both these costs are being considered to be part of 'costs of promotion' or development costs.

[14] The SGSY programme has a provision for up to ₹ 10,000 per SHG to NGOs for promotion and capacity building. However, this is invariably not utilized for the intended purpose.

He thus suggests that in the context of the scale of development expenditures, the overall social investment requirements of SHG expansion were not very high.

Cumulatively since the inception of SHG–bank linkage programme in February 1992 up to March 2011 NABARD provided ₹ 1.46 billion to 3,953 SHPAs to promote 581,179 SHGs from the Microfinance Development and Equity Fund. This support was provided to a variety of SHPAs like NGOs, cooperative banks, RRBs and farmers clubs and individual rural volunteers. The cumulative average amount released was ₹ 511 million or only about ₹ 1,967 per SHG. Besides, generally NGOs were provided with support from the formation of a limited number of SHGs, usually only 50 to 100 SHGs. However, the scale of support for SHG promotion has been increased substantially in recent years and in November 2011 it stood at ₹ 4,500 per SHG. Though NABARD saw their funding support to the SHPAs as supplementary, most of the NGOs had funding support only from NABARD which meant that many SHGs did not have any support after they linked to banks. As a result many SHGs supported by NABARD were not qualitatively any better than SGSY groups in the absence of necessary capacity building and follow-up support from the NGOs. *There is a need for NABARD and other sponsoring agencies to critically think about their funding for SHG promotion and to consider the stages in the life cycle of SHGs where support is required and the source of that support.* There may be a case for funding by NABARD of a smaller number of NGOs but covering the full cost of promotion of a substantial number of SHGs to be able to have an impact in a particular geographical area.

The SGSY programme also incurred substantial training and capacity building costs of about ₹ 24,000 per SHG as on October 2008 (Salomo et al., 2010), which included the promotional support for SHGs. Among the state governments, Andhra Pradesh invested about ₹ 2,000 per SHG. If the total organization expenses of SERP, Andhra Pradesh are also included their investment could be over ₹ 30,000 per SHG (ibid.). While the leading NGOs are able to get funds from several sources for SHG promotion, other NGOs have to cobble together funds from various development projects and allocate a portion of these for the promotion and strengthening of SHGs and SHG federations. One of the stakeholders that have been slow to contribute to the cost of promotion of SHGs has been the banks. Even though SHGs have the potential to both provide business to banks as well as ensure repayment of loans, only a few banks have some limited schemes for reimbursement of costs of promotion to partner NGOs and to bear a part of the expenses of the SHGs.

6.5 DEVELOPMENT COST OF SHG FEDERATIONS

With the advent of the federations, it became necessary to take a longer view of SHG development and the attendant costs of promotion. Among the important sources of funding for SHGs are NABARD, state governments with funds from the central government and bilateral and multilateral agencies and international and national donors, apart from the banks contributing on a small scale. Though NABARD has announced support for some activities to be undertaken by non-financial federations in 2007, this scheme has not progressed very far.

As demonstrated in Chapters 4 and 5, both NGO and government agencies have seen the federation as a means of facilitating the flow of financial services to SHGs or fulfilling a larger developmental agenda. In any case there has not been much work done on the cost of promotion of federations, especially federations of SHGs designed to undertake financial intermediation. Even major studies on federations undertaken thus far have not developed estimates of costs of promotion. With the renewed interest in SHGs and in federations for financial services as part of the NRLM design renewed interest in cost of promotion of SHG federations is evident. A recent (2010) study conducted by ACCESS Development Services and Rabobank, the only one of its kind, analyzes costs of various types of government and NGO promoted federations towards an understanding of the processes and cost of development of financial federations of SHGs. The methodology and findings of the study are examined below.

ACCESS-Rabobank Study[15]

The study analyzed the development cost[16] of SHG-based federations engaged in financial intermediation as reported by 10 NGO and government promoters. These costs represented the development costs necessary to build a federation structure for sustainable financial operations. The study represents possibly the first time that such a comprehensive exercise has been undertaken towards estimating the level of costs incurred by different development agents in supporting financial federations.

The cost of development of an SHG federation was estimated in terms of the *average total cost of promotion per member SHG*. The *costs incurred at NGO/project level* for promoting and sustaining a federation of SHGs engaged in financial intermediation *until its independent functioning* were estimated. *These costs generally have been incurred or are planned over a period of about five years.*

The study covered 10 federations of different vintages formed by the promoter *at the block or mandal level* (the second or third tier of SHG

---

[15] The findings of this study are reported in Chapter 4 of Srinivasan and Tankha (2010) from which this section is largely drawn.

[16] In this section the terms 'development cost' and 'cost of promotion' have been used interchangeably.

association). Of these three were registered as trusts, one as a society and another is unregistered. The remaining five federations were registered as cooperatives.

Data for the exercise was obtained on a predesigned format covering cost heads at different stages of SHG and federation and stabilization. This was followed up with personal interviews and telephonic discussions with NGO promoters and federation staff. These costs cover three phases of federation formation and support, viz., (a) initial phase of SHG promotion and stabilization; (b) initiation and establishment of the financial federation; and (c) maintenance support for federation operations after start-up. Thus the first phase pertains to SHG formation and maintenance and the latter two phases pertain to federation-related expenses, pre- and post-formation.

For five mature federations historical costs were averaged on an annual basis over the complement of SHGs supported; or alternatively 'modeled' for a five-year period of formation with standardized human resource and other inputs which were imputed at historical prices. For five active promoters cost estimates were developed using current and projected cost data for SHG and federation development into the future.

The estimates related to a period of support usually of five years but going up to six years in two cases and seven years in one case. For the purpose of comparison over time, historical costs were adjusted by the Wholesale Price Index (1993–94 series) to reflect 2009–10 prices and also normalized for a five-year period of support. For ease of calculation, price indices used were for the mid-point of the period for which data was obtained.

The average total historical development cost of the study federations has been estimated at ₹ 19,676 per SHG. When adjusted for price differences in the estimates and normalized for support for a five-year period *the average total promotion cost per SHG for the 10 study federations worked out to ₹ 20,521 per SHG.* Table 6.1 gives estimates of the breakdown of costs of development of an SHG-based financial federation as estimated by the study for 10 leading government and NGOs programmes. The range of average cost of promotion is from ₹ 4,142 to ₹ 45,986, with the government financial coming out as the lowest cost programmes. The PALMA federation with the comparatively high cost includes a revolving fund grant of ₹ 7,000 per SHG. For the rest—the seven NGO federations—have an average cost of SHG federation promotion in the relatively narrow range of ₹ 15,000 to ₹ 26,500 per SHG.

The breakdown of cost of promotion between the SHG social mobilization cost and federation formation and support shows that ₹ 12,098 or 60% of total average cost is accounted for by the federation as against ₹ 8,423 or 40% for the initial social mobilization of the SHG. Further while there is substantial variation in the cost of promotion for the social mobilization phase, the average cost of federation formation and support is relatively even.

Table 6.1: Development Cost of SHG-based Financial Federations (₹ per SHG)

Name of the federation/ promoter	Legal form	Average total five year SHG social mobilization cost at 2009–10 prices (₹) A	Average Total Support Cost for Block/mandal federation cost at 2009–10 prices (₹) B	Average Total Five-year Development Cost at 2009–10 prices (₹) A + B	Loan outstanding per SHG (₹)/Average development cost per SHG (₹) A + B
BMASS, Jagannathprasad (Govt. of Odisha), Odisha	Society	475	3,667	4,142	15.2
Dharmasagar Mandal Samakhya, (SERP) AP	MACS	2,701	10,284	12,984	0.68
Pragathi MACS, (Pragathi Sewa Samiti) AP	MACS	9,204	11,193	20,397	3.07
IIMF, (GRAM) AP	MACS	15,618	4,609	20,227	4.5
Sanginee, (Parivartan) Odisha	Cooperative	3,523	13,577	17,100	1.2
ASSSL,(CECOEDECON) Rajasthan	Cooperative	13,480	10,580	24,060	5.3
Savera, (Ibtada), Rajasthan	Trust	19,160	7,417	26,577	0.7
PALMA, (PWDS) Tamil Nadu	Trust	13,934	32,052	45,986	1.0
Boondh Bachat Sangh, (Shramik Bharati) UP	Trust	3,361	14,944	18,306	0.6
CGMST, (Chaitanya) Maharashtra	Unregistered	2,772	12,661	15,434	0.6
Adjusted Average Total Cost per SHG		**8,423**	**12,098**	**20,521**	

Source: Srinivasan and Tankha (2010).

Table 6.2: Adjusted Estimates of Development Costs of Government and
NGO-promoted Financial Federations

Alternative estimates of federation development costs	Average development cost per SHG (₹)@ 2009–10 prices for five years of support (A) = B + C	Average Cost per SHG for social mobilization (₹) (B)	Average Cost per SHG of federation formation and support (₹) (C)
For 10 study SHG federations	20,521 (100)	8,423 (40)	12,098 (60)
For 8 NGO-promoted SHG federations	23,511 (100)	10,132 (43)	13,379 (57)
For 7 NGO-promoted SHG federations*	20,300 (100)	9,589 (47)	10,711 (53)

Source: Adapted from Srinivasan and Tankha (2010).
Note: *Excluding one outlier value NGO, PALMA federation. Figures in brackets
are percentages of total cost.

Table 6.2 gives alternative development estimates based on the findings
of the ACCESS-Rabobank study. The historical *five-year period average
total promotion cost per SHG for the 10 study federations was ₹ 20,521.*
For eight NGO federations the adjusted average development cost works
out to ₹ 23,511 at 2009–10 prices. *For seven NGO federations (excluding
one outlier value) adjusted average total promotion cost per SHG comes
down to ₹ 20,300.*

Overall, the findings suggest that while the social mobilization costs
were an important part of the costs of promoting a federation, the larger
proportion of costs relate to support for the operations of the federation.
Thus, *53% to 60% of overall costs were accounted for by cost of establishing
and supporting the federation structure in the various estimates while 40%
to 47% of overall costs according to different estimates were incurred for
SHG formation and development.*

A more detailed breakdown of development costs of financial federations
under different heads is given in Appendix 7. Out of the various components
of federation support costs, while other costs such as those for meeting
expenses and training and office premises are important, *staff costs are the
main item of expense for all federations and constitute over 60% of the
development expenses necessary in support of financial federations* of the
eight NGOs. To this may be added the indirect overhead costs at the NGO
level which constitute an additional 18% of total costs incurred during the
federation support phase. Indeed, *a true test of the successful independent
functioning of a federation is how soon it is able to bear the staff costs for its*

operations.[17] The observed pattern has been that promoter-NGOs provide staff and other support to the extent that it enables federations to realize a small surplus.[18] This support is slowly withdrawn as the federation finds its feet and is able to cover an increasing proportion of its costs.[19]

Appendix 8, by way of illustration, gives an activity-based costing of various items of historical expenses incurred in SHG promotion and federation formation in the case of Agni Sahkari Sewa Samiti promoted by CECOEDECON—one of the federations covered by the ACCESS-Rabobank study.

Scale of Operations and Benchmarks

The ACCESS-Rabobank study did not find any relationship between the scale of operations and development cost although a couple of the smaller federations had relatively lower costs of promotion. It considered instead whether federation lending operations were being conducted on a sufficient scale to justify the cost of their formation and support. Estimates of the ratio between loan outstanding per SHG and adjusted costs of SHG and federation development made by the study are also given in Table 6.1. It was observed that *the loan programme had taken off only in the case of three out of 10 federations, viz., Pragathi, IIMF and ASSSL, whereas in the seven other federations loan outstanding after four years and more of operations was not even as high as the adjusted development investment per SHG.* While a couple of the federations were still quite new, the smaller federations had not shown the ability to access and intermediate large funds.

The context, legal form and methodology of SHG and federation formation vary considerably across the different federations selected for study from across the country. However, study data suggests a degree of convergence of cost of federation promotion or development support cost in the range of ₹ 15,000 to ₹ 25,000 per SHG with a mean value of *₹ 20,300 per SHG* for SHGs to be brought together in a federation for financial intermediation and other economic and social activities.

---

[17] Srinivasan and Tankha (2010).

[18] The implication of this pattern of support for federation operations by the SHPA is that any surpluses earned by the federation represent costs incurred by the SHPA in excess of the minimum necessary to sustain the federation in the initial years. Ideally, federation surpluses for the period of support should be deducted from the total cost of federation promotion to yield the *minimum necessary costs of federation support*. However, these have been ignored both because such surpluses are usually small and the practice appears to be reasonable in the interest of stable functioning of the federation.

[19] The analysis of the sustainability of the federations promoted by the 10 SHPAs is presented in Chapter 7. The estimation of benefits accruing to SHGs and their members from federation operations—to compare costs and benefits of federations—is a still larger exercise that has not been attempted by any studies.

Benchmarks suggested in the study on the basis of the data and practices of SHG promotion observed were:

- *Period of support—5 years*
- *Development cost—₹ 20,000 to ₹ 25,000; (a) Social mobilization: ₹ 8,000 to ₹ 10,000; (b) Federation support: ₹ 12,000 to ₹ 15,000.*

When we consider these benchmarks we find that there is virtually no change in the nominal levels of costs that had been estimated a decade ago in the studies of 2001–02! Indeed, ₹ 10,000 was the accepted level of support for an NGO for SHG promotion; and a range of ₹ 15,000 to ₹ 25,000 per SHG was the norm for SHG development to the federation stage. The latest available evidence does not suggest any reason to propose a different level of support a decade later. Clearly there has been a significant decline in the real cost of SHG promotion as evidenced from the ACCESS-Rabobank study and other broader estimates.

Other Recent Cost Estimates

It needs, however, to be clarified that above estimates are essentially based upon historical costs incurred by SHPAs establishing federations that have incurred the full costs of SHG formation and the federation costs thereafter. However, where well-functioning and sustainable federation structures already exist, as in case of the NGOs covered in Chapter 4, additional SHGs could be promoted at a much lower cost; and subsequently integrated into the existing federation structures. Indeed there could be two ways of understanding SHG promotional cost, one based on studies prepared from past data of the NGO promoters and another based on projections of experienced large scale promoters with well-developed decentralized systems and processes for SHG promotion.

Table 6.3 presents recent data on cost of promotion of various federation models with estimated cost per SHG. Data provided by APMAS for various agencies gives the cost break up under different heads of expenses. These represent different types of unpublished estimates which may, however, provide an idea of the relative costs of promotion for different models. The Kalanjiam model of DHAN pertains to the nested institutional structures. The cost of promoting this structure is ₹ 9,640 per SHG. However, if SHG contributions are taken into account the cost doubles. Indeed, the inclusion of SHG costs would reflect the true costs and bring up the cost of promotion to ₹ 20,526. The Kalanjiam federations are non-financial federations.

APMAS estimates for Andhra Pradesh for SHG promotion with secondary level federations works out to ₹ 8,387 per SHG. An estimate from CmF, Rajasthan works out to ₹ 24,000 for three years of promotion expenses. The estimate prepared for NRLM is based upon the assumption of a major

Table 6.3: Cost of SHG and Federation Promotion (₹)

Cost particulars	SHPI or support organization			
	Kalanjiam	APMAS	CMF	NRLM*
Period of promotion	8 yrs	4 yrs	3 yrs	5 yrs
No. of SHGs	240	800	200	,000
No. of Primary-level Federations	1	30	15	252
No. of Secondary-level Federations	1	1	1	5
No. of Block-level Federations				
Salaries	3,085,710	2,558,302	1,600,000	3,762,000
Administration cost	1,840,459	1,535,168	1,000,000	840,000
Capacity Building		2,615,800	2,200,000	78,999,400
Capital Grants to SHGs				
Contributions from SHGs (−)	2,612,657			
Total	2,313,512	6,709,270	4,800,000	83,601,400
Cost per SHG	9,640	8,387	24,000	41,801

Source: APMAS.

Notes: *Cost calculations for Karmnor Block.

Kalanjiam: Mobilizers train the groups; hence, no additional costs on training.

CMF: Information provided by Mr Jaipal Singh, CEO.

NRLM: Capacity building cost includes promotion of livelihood and participatory vulnerability assessment and ranking. Project personnel and hiring resource agency cost for three years has been taken in the salaries.

investment in livelihood promotion and works out to a high ₹ 41,801 from an exercise for a block in Rajasthan. This is still less than half the figure thrown up by the scales of support proposed in the NRLM framework of ₹ 10,000 of promotional grant per SHG and ₹ 75,000 (at ₹ 7,500 per member) of capacity building and skill training support.

If the NRLM estimates are excluded, on account of their large capacity building objectives and costs, the remaining estimates are within a range of ₹ 8,387 to ₹ 24,000 per SHG. These are broadly in line with the estimates of the ACCESS-Rabobank study for promotion of block-level financial federations.

6.6 Concluding Observations

As the SHG movement has grown, SHG development processes too have undergone several changes which have had a bearing on the cost of promotion. First, since the SHG idea is well known throughout the country it has become unnecessary to spend time and resources in motivating women to form groups. Thus, the initial meetings to motivate and mobilize women are not required as they are coming forward willingly to form SHGs after seeing the positive experiences of other groups. Indeed, NGO staff have taken a back seat in SHG promotion as federations and groups themselves help to form new groups. This has an important bearing on the cost of promotion of SHGs. Second, an area of change has been that there is less intensive facilitation of SHGs and their members by SHPAs compared to the early days of the TNCDW and the liberal grant support to NGOs for SHG formation which was in turn necessitated by the higher start up cost of the this new initiative.

Third, a major difference is that NGO functions related to training and capacity building have been taken over by federations and group leaders themselves, thereby making for a reduction in costs. In the past great store was set by imparting bookkeeping skills among SHG members in order that they perform this function themselves. Current practice is more in favour of unpaid or (more usually) paid bookkeepers either from among the NGO or federation staff or relatives of members or persons recruited locally. However, in spite of significant financial costs incurred, the quality of the SHGs is not very good and not much appears to have been done in later years on member education and on financial literacy.

Finally, the evolution of federations too has been speeded up. While in the past SHGs were sometimes federated a decade after formation, in recent years the practice is to prepare for federating SHGs within a year of group formation such that they are able to join a federation within a period of two years or so.

Thus, the resultant changes in the duration and intensity of social facilitation by promoting agencies have affected SHG promotion costs as well to bring about a relative decline in relation to the levels of a decade ago. However, with the institution of the federation taking root, sustained facilitation and investment towards its operation becomes necessary as well.

With the formulation of the NRLM it is inevitable that significant investments are to be made in SHGs and their federations in the future. It is clear that a mechanism will need to be evolved to direct these investments in such a way that self-managed, sustainable and self-reliant SHGs and SHG federations are formed and supported. A step in this direction would be a more rigorous assessment of costs for promotion of SHGs and federations, based upon existing good practices and processes that would cover different regions and contexts.

SUSTAINABILITY OF SHGs 7

The question of the sustainability of SHGs and SHG-based institutions in microfinance has been a major issue engaging practitioners, policymakers and other stakeholders. Within microfinance, sustainability can be viewed at several levels—institutional, group and individual—and can relate to organizational, managerial and financial aspects. However, it is the financial sustainability of MFIs that has become the critical point of focus of mainstream analysis at the expense of the sustainability of the client/borrower. In microfinance the sustainability concept is thus usually applied to the financial intermediary institutions as assessed through various financial performance criteria. Hulme and Mosley (1996), however, distinguished between the 'intended beneficiary' school and the 'intermediary' school wherein the former is more concerned with the impact of microfinance on the intended beneficiary individuals or households and the latter with institutional outreach and institutional sustainability.[1] One of the challenges of microfinance is seen as its ability to sustainably reach the poorest families. This is true of SHG programmes as well. Though the SGSY programme is supposed to target SHGs of BPL households, the identification of BPL households itself has been open to question. *The lack of effectiveness of poverty targeting have not been seriously raised in the Indian microfinance context, even that of SHGs.*[2] There are, of course, differences in the character of SHGs and other microfinance intermediaries such that a differentiated understanding and analysis needs to inform the discussion of sustainability in respect of SHGs.

---

[1] A financially self-sufficient credit operation must cover operating costs (including loan loss reserves), the cost of funds and inflation through revenues in the form of interest charges and fees. The intermediary school thus sets greater store by repayment rates on the presumption that timely repayment of loans by 'rational' borrowers is evidence of adequate returns on their investments.

[2] See Tankha (2009) for a discussion on poverty targeting and mission drift in microfinance in India.

7.1 WHY SUSTAINABILITY?

SHG sustainability needs to be viewed in the context and objectives of their promotion. It is instructive to note that the merits of the SHG as an on-lending group had its roots in the 'flexibility' of the ROSCA and the ASCA, which need not be long-lasting associations. Indeed, successful international programmes of CARE, OXFAM and others usually include the recommendation that these groups should wind up every year, in order to allow those who wish to leave to do so, equitably. It is also important to consider the sustainability of SHGs within the objectives of the SHG programmes. The SBLP itself was conceived as a *supplementary programme to reach the poorest families* unserved by the banking system.[3] However, as suggested in the case of the SGSY above, it is generally accepted that in practice SHGs have not included the poorest families.[4] Thus, even if the sustainability of SHGs and SHG-based programmes was to be established, it would of scant benefit to the excluded 'intended beneficiaries'.

Thus, the sustainability question has multiple dimensions that need to be reconciled in order to judge the appropriateness of different interventions. It also raises the question of the sustainability of the larger financial system as against the narrow focus on a particular intermediary in the supply chain for microfinance.[5] *With multiple layers of financial intermediaries in the banking chain, sustainability is an issue at all levels.* Ensuring an adequate interest spread to cover costs of intermediaries has implications for the cost of borrowing for SHGs and their members. The attractiveness of the SHG as a microbank serving its members arose from the low-cost retailing option it provided through externalization of the transaction costs of banks (in part through transfer of costs to the SHG and its members). In focusing on sustainability of the various intermediaries, the largely supply-led character of modern microfinance does not consider the structure of credit demand, the cost of credit to SHG member-borrowers and the returns to investments financed through microcredit.[6] With SHGs being used in many states as

---

[3] Nanda (2000).

[4] For example, Sinha et al. (2009) through a participatory wealth ranking exercise which was correlated with Objective Wealth Rank categories to enable comparisons across regions, found that of 2,968 SHG members of 214 sample SHGs covered in a study of four states (the Light and Shades study), 51% belonged to the poor and very poor categories with 36% in the former and 15% in the latter. These categories are equivalent to 'below the national poverty line'. Another 32% belonged to the 'borderline' or vulnerable non-poor category.

[5] In the case of SHG models, e.g., it is not the operational self-sufficiency of the SHG (at which level operating costs are minimal) but that of the NGO intermediary or financial federation that is often at issue. Similarly, the viability of bank lending to SHGs is essential to their sustained support for the SBLP.

[6] In fact, as will be seen, many studies focused on viability of SHG lending by banks have pointed to the need to increase the lending rates on their SHG portfolio.

building blocks for primary and secondary federations, financial and non-financial, to access loan funds and for the delivery of non-financial services, the financial and organizational sustainability of the SHG federations comes into question as well.

In the Indian rural context, the role of SHGs in recent years can be seen as one of facilitating 'financial inclusion' by banks. In this connection the targets for financial inclusion and implementation of the RBI's BF/BC model[7] has acquired relevance for the future role of SHGs. The chief feature of this model is that NGOs and federations and other BCs operate as agents of banks rather than financial intermediaries. This model emerged around the time of the demise of the 'partnership' model of ICICI Bank in 2006 which had similarly used MFIs as agents to undertake 'off-balance sheet lending'. (The differences between these two agent models and that of the NGO as MFI [Model III of SBLP] are illustrated in Appendix 9.) The use of BCs and BFs can *on the one hand extend the outreach of banks so that more individuals can have their own bank accounts, and there is less need for the SHG to intermediate between a rural woman and a bank. On the other hand, SHG federations (or even SHG functionaries) can themselves be BCs, which would give them a role as a link between their SHG members and banks, but would also reduce the need for them to be involved themselves in financial intermediation.* This is likely to have a bearing on the nature of future role of SHGs in serving families that had earlier been excluded from the reach of the banking system.

7.2 ORGANIZATIONAL AND FINANCIAL SUSTAINABILITY

SBLP had been promoted as a *savings first* and *savings-led* model. It is instructive to examine the growth path of an SHG formed under bank linkage. An SHG of 15 members, with a modest saving contribution of ₹ 30 per member per month can after one year save ₹ 5,400 and be able to raise an initial bank loan of around ₹ 10,800. With the accumulation of savings and internal rotation and the progressively increased leveraging of bank funds, this can increase rapidly. Thus with a savings fund of about ₹ 50,000 after five years,[8] the SHG could be eligible for a loan of eight times this

---

[7] RBI has permitted banks to use the services of NGOs, MFIs, SHG functionaries and other civil society organizations as intermediaries in providing financial and banking services through the use of BF and BC Models vide Circular of 25 January 2006 (list of organizations subsequently revised vide RBI circular dated 28 September 2010) with the objective of ensuring greater financial inclusion and increasing the outreach of the banking sector. Tankha (2006b) provides details of the challenges and potential of this model.

[8] If the interest margin some SHGs take is added, this sum can grow much bigger, and faster.

amount or ₹ 400,000.[9] However, few SHGs, except in a certain areas have been able to achieve such levels of borrowing from the financial system. A contributory factor could be the single loan policy of banks. Banks provide a relatively large two- or three-year loan to SHGs which have no access to another loan, even smaller- or short-term, in the interim period.

Despite the importance of savings in the SHG model, it is the savings service that is least developed. There are invariably no savings products other than the compulsory weekly/biweekly/monthly contribution and open access to savings is not available. Profits of SHG operations are only shared as bonus or interest on savings in some SHGs. Exit rules are unclear (hence the argument for annual closure) but usually result in loss of claims over share of separating members in accumulated profits of the SHG. Even where comprehensive rules exist, such as in Andhra Pradesh, due to factors and practices such as lack of motivation to increase mandatory savings, a tendency of distributing accumulated surplus among members, repayment of bank loans from internal funds, idle internal funds (including those deposited in banks), the growth of internal resources of SHGs (even in older groups), has been slow or even negative.

The viability or sustainability of SHGs in financial terms is generally not an issue. SHG income through interest charges and fines, for absence and late attendance of meetings, though small is matched by an extremely low cost of operations limited to maintenance of books of accounts and payment of an honorarium to the local accountant. Typically, borrowings are at around 12% per annum under the bank linkage scheme and on-lending to members at 2% per month. SHGs are, of course, free to charge whatever they wish while on-lending to members from their bank loans—part of their original empowerment agenda.[10] Indeed, well functioning SHGs are able to use part of their profits for buying services of accountants, teachers, paravets and so on from their own funds for social and economic services and contributions are raised for other one-off activities.

The organizational sustainability of SHGs is more open to question. Little research has been done on the internal dynamics of SHGs, and the access of relatively poor members to loans. Experience suggests that even after a period of three to five years (the time usually taken for SHGs to achieve the experience and maturity required to function as an independent financial entity), SHGs in many regions are not equipped to engage directly with banks and other agencies.[11]

---

[9] The constraint of the link between savings and credit for bank lending has since been lifted and banks are free to lend at their discretion in excess of eight times the SHG savings.

[10] SHGs may charge a higher rate (3% to 5% per month) on the mainly consumption and emergency loans provided by them from their own funds, especially in the initial years, in order also to build their capital.

[11] There are reports, also of the vulnerable stage of 'group fatigue', two to three years after the formation of an SHG, when the initial enthusiasm of group functioning wears off and renewed motivation of SHG members is necessary.

The sustainability of SHGs is clearly related to the 'quality' of groups promoted. Investments by leading SHPAs in intensive training and capacity building undertaken at group level at various stages towards SHG quality may in turn contribute to higher costs of promotion. NGOs and banks have accordingly devised assessment criteria for appraisal and periodic evaluations of group performance and sustainability.[12] Assessment indicators include frequency and attendance of meetings, volume of savings, rotation of own savings, development of financial skills and quality of leadership.

The longer-term prospect for SHGs linked to banks is unclear. The leading NGOs covered in the study have phased out from some areas after having linked the SHGs which they have formed to banks while others have promoted federations or other MFIs. There is, however, unease about the ability of SHGs to continue to directly access funds from the banking system and to move along a growth path out of poverty. The logical path for members of SHGs linked to banks should be to graduate to (larger) individual savings accounts and loans under the bank's normal lending programme, as is consistent with the move towards financial inclusion and no-frills accounts. This does not appear to be happening, both on account of the absence of a vision at promoter and bank level as well as infrastructural and other constraints operative on the absorption of credit by the SHG member households. *Many bankers also seem content to keep their SHGs at a modest level, rather than to encourage their members to use them as a 'ladder' to individual banking.*

The wide spectrum of emerging models of SHG-based institutions reflects the efforts of SHPAs and other stakeholders in addressing the challenge of sustainability. The multiple constraints and opportunities that determine the types of institutions promoted include: (*a*) the legal and regulatory provisions in the states of operation; (*b*) the origins of the programmes and the broader vision for the community; (*c*) the capacity of SHPAs to support community microfinance institutions; (*d*) poverty contexts and social conditions in different areas and (*e*) the availability of the physical and financial infrastructure and external support.

In the rest of this chapter the question of SHG sustainability in the Indian context is considered at three levels. In the first instance the evidence of the quality and performance of SHGs and SHG structures that have been promoted by the leading NGOs and government under various development programmes is reviewed. At a second level, the viability of lending by banks to SHGs under SBLP is analyzed and the innovations and measures that are required to expand the provision of financial services by banks through SHGs. At a third level the sustainability of institutional innovations in

---

[12] NABARD has developed rating criteria for appraisal of groups for bank linkage, as have various banks. MYRADA, for example, used very detailed criteria for evaluation of group performance, guidelines for financing its SAGs and guidelines for an evaluation to decide if NGO involvement could be phased out.

the form of federations is examined; as also the prospects they hold as an appropriate infrastructure for financial services delivery, particularly to poor households.

7.3 Quality and Performance of SHGs and SHG Federations

One of the overriding concerns as the SHG movement has grown has been the quality of the groups promoted. There is a general consensus that the quality of groups promoted has been on the decline especially with the rise of state agencies and programmes as the principal promoters. NABARD had developed the 'critical rating index' to be used by banks to ascertain the quality of SHGs towards their suitability for savings and credit linkage. Other agencies, including Sa-dhan, the association of community finance institutions, developed various indices to assess SHG quality though the parameters considered related largely to regularity of meetings and savings contributions and the internal credit rotation performance. Over the years APMAS has been at the forefront in the conduct of studies in Andhra Pradesh and other states to assess the quality of the SHGs and as an advocate of the need to focus on SHG quality and performance. APMAS (2005) (see Box 7.1) reports the findings of a study of 400 SHGs in eight districts of Andhra Pradesh. It graded the groups into A, B and C quality based on NABARD's critical rating index and found that the proportion of groups in the sample was 66% A grade, 26% B grade and 8% C grade. Further, the quality of groups tended to deteriorate after a few years, recovering again in years 7–8, and then deteriorating once again thereafter. However, group quality tended to improve with repeat loans. The proportion of A grade groups was as much as 91% in groups that had received three loans.

Box 7.1: APMAS

APMAS, working for poverty reduction since its foundation in 2001, is a unique resource organization with a vision of a 'Sustainable Self Help Movement in India'. Originally established with the aim of providing technical support and consultancy services to different stakeholders in the SHG sector in the state of Andhra Pradesh, APMAS, for the past years, has been working on a larger scale. APMAS's mission is to support the development of a sustainable financial system in India, and to open up access to secure microfinance products to members of SHGs. APMAS is contributing to quality assessment, capacity building, and by promoting sector-own control and external auditing and ratings of CBMFIs with the aim of securing a longterm quality for these institutions. In addition, it is active in research, and livelihood promotion. APMAS provides its services to SHGs, SHG Federations, SHPAs, civil society organizations and the government. It is an important link between individual institutions and other stakeholders. APMAS is also collaborating closely with NABARD.

Source: Adapted from Salomo et al. (2010).

A study of quality issues of SHGs in Rajasthan conducted by the CmF and APMAS (2006) found that the overall quality of groups was low and that there were startling inter-district and intra-promoter variations across the groups. The study was carried out in five districts of Rajasthan covering a sample of 202 SHGs. It found that only 59% of members borrowed, of whom 17% were group leaders and that the sample groups were by and large functioning around loans, and to access the subsidies available under the SGSY. Savings were found to be only nominal in most groups. Since two-thirds of the groups were organized by government functionaries, there was danger of the target-oriented approach overtaking the question of quality. The mushrooming of groups, particularly under the aegis of government is a phenomenon to be found in other states as well, e.g., the rapid expansion of SHGs in the state of Odisha.

In assessing the performance of SHG federations and their constituent SHGs, APMAS developed a rating tool called GRADES[13] for quality assessment. APMAS (2007) reports that it undertook the assessment of over 400 SHG federations in Andhra Pradesh, Odisha, Tamil Nadu, Maharashtra, Madhya Pradesh, Gujarat and Rajasthan. One of the findings was that while governance improves with the age of federations, it begins to slip again after a period of four years or more. In terms of financial resources available for lending to member SHGs, only 11 out of 83 federations (13%) assessed during 2003 to 2005 had more than ₹ 20,000 of funds available for lending to member SHGs. Further, a high proportion of idle funds were found both at SHG and federation level. Asset quality measured in terms of portfolio at risk (PAR) showed that while there was 90% repayment of loans from banks and other financial institutions by SHGs, they gave second priority to federation loans. PAR greater than 90 days was more than 5% in 72% of the federations and more than 25% in 42% of federations. The internal repayment rate was higher than 95% only in 22% of federations and lower than 80% in 45% of federations.

Internal control systems and MIS were found to be not up to the mark in most cases with flow of information from the federation to the SHG being minimal as compared to information flow from the SHG to the federation. In terms of efficiency and profitability, operating cost ratio against loans outstanding was found to be high at an average of 12.5% of loan outstanding on account of low internal fund mobilization, poor portfolio quality management and high defaults among others. While 65% of federations showed greater than 100% operational self-sufficiency, only 21% were found to be financially self-sufficient. Overall *it was found that federations that were doing only financial intermediation became*

---

[13] GRADES represents the following six key areas of federation assessment: (*a*) governance and strategy, (*b*) resources, (*c*) assets quality, (*d*) design of systems and implementation, (*e*) efficiency and profitability, and (*f*) services to SHGs in addition to SHG performance.

operationally self-sufficient within four to five years while federations doing financial and social intermediation had problems becoming financially self-sufficient even after five years. The profitability of federations was linked to the quantum and quality of the loan portfolio.

A related study of SHG performance in respect of 320 SHGs that were members of the 83 federations studied above provides an assessment of the performance of SHGs according to certain well-established parameters. While savings contributions were regular in over 90% for SHGs, the APMAS study showed that on an average, regularity and attendance for meetings for the sample SHGs was less than 60% and members' participation in decisions and awareness less than 50%. Similarly, the quality of bookkeeping was a cause for concern in over half of the SHGs studied. Loan amounts per member were relatively small at a little over ₹ 5,000 and portfolio at risk was over 33%. The external repayment rate averaged over 88%. The study concluded that the *attention and focus on federations was impacting SHG quality* with the awareness level of SHGs about federations remaining low and the attention being paid to operational and financial sustainability resulting in the social service functions receding into the background. This finding could be important in the overall measurement of whether SHG federations are or are not beneficial to the groups and their members.

One of the major issues that has emerged over the years has been the use of subsidies under SHG bank linkage to reduce the interest burden on the SHG borrower-members. Under Andhra Pradesh government's Pavala Vaddi scheme (an interest subsidy scheme for bank loans to SHGs introduced in 2004),[14] SHG members receive loans at a rate of 3% per annum. Banks receive a subsidy from the state government, representing the difference between their rate of lending to the SHGs and the specified rate, which is passed on to the SHGs upon satisfactory repayment. Other states such as Karnataka, Kerala, West Bengal and Maharashtra too have such subsidized interest schemes. This could also have been a major source of capital formation for the SHGs; but government has insisted that the 3% is to be effective end user interest rate, leaving the SHG with a gross margin of interest subsidy to cover administrative expenses, loan losses and profits. The government brought in this policy to mainstream SHGs and to inculcate a habit of on-time repayment.

One of the consequences of this pattern of lending as reported from Andhra Pradesh is that in view of the availability of loans at such low

---

[14] Under the Pavala Vaddi scheme ₹ 5.4 billion were reimbursed to 1.1 million groups (rural and urban) in Andhra Pradesh during the fiscal year 2010–11 (SERP, 2011). The SGSY programme, had earlier provided SHGs with loans-cum-subsidies as well as a capacity building grant.

interest rates, SHG members tend to distribute the bank loan equally such that no member is denied the benefit of the subsidy. Further, SHG members undertake micro-moneylending with the funds and this has become a source of income for some of them. They presumably compete with local moneylenders when they do this, but this was hardly the purpose of the SHG movement when it was originally started.

The principle of Pavala Vaddi is being further extended to loans being provided by the recently formed state-level cooperative Stree Nidhi, as also under provisions of the NRLM. However, there is some disquiet among microfinance practitioners and stakeholders on the long-term effects of such subsidized rates of interest. In certain sections there is a view that these interest rates distort the market and create an uneven field for different microfinance agencies—an example of which is provided by the on-lending by SHG members of their loans from banks. Further, the subsidized funds are detrimental to the SHGs own savings and internal rotation of funds at higher rates of interest. SHGs are understood to have limited the build-up of their savings for intermediation and are inclined to distribute their accumulated corpus at frequent intervals. This brings into question the fundamental role of SHGs as *micro-banks*, intermediating own and borrowed funds on a long-term and sustainable basis. Instead, their position becomes one of *user groups*, essentially in existence for channelling government loans and other development services from government agencies.

7.4 SUSTAINABILITY OF SBLP: EVIDENCE FROM STUDIES

Viability of SHG Lending by Banks

SHG–bank linkage was envisaged as a means of reducing the transaction costs of both banks and borrowers in the delivery of credit. However, there still does not appear to be a conviction among bankers to support the view that lending through SHGs is viable for the different types of banks in the formal financial system. Indeed, the reluctance of banks to lend to SHGs in certain areas is attributed to the fact that SHG lending is not a demonstrably profitable enterprise as compared to other components of their portfolio. Even in areas where bank linkage is well-developed there are reports of dissatisfaction with the bankers' attitude to the SHGs. In a recent report from Andhra Pradesh, Seibel (2011) notes that the quality of customer service from banks to SHGs has declined. There are delays in the disbursement of loans to SHGs, sometimes delivered beyond planting time, reductions in loan amounts irrespective of eligibility, delays in entering transactions in SHG passbooks, and delays in providing financial reports to SHGs which are needed when SHGs are audited. There are also complaints by SHGs that banks have been slow in opening new SHG accounts on grounds of staff shortage. At the same time there are reports that under target-driven pressure some banks try to sell high-cost insurance to SHG members and to persuade them to open bank accounts, while in other cases members find it difficult to open savings accounts.

Has lending by banks to SHGs been a profitable activity that covers the transaction costs incurred by them in servicing the relatively small sized loans to this new rural clientele? Are banks justified in entertaining apprehensions in lending to SHGs? Over the years a few studies have been undertaken that address these issues. An analysis and review of the major studies addressing the subject of viability of bank lending through SHGs is given below.

An early study by Puhazhendi (1995) had concluded that intermediation by NGOs and SHGs significantly reduced the transaction costs of both banks and borrowers. Subsequently, several other studies provided similar results. A later study by Srinivasan and Satish (2000) attempted to (a) assess the impact of linking SHGs on the transaction and risk costs of bank branches, and (b) quantify the cost of credit delivery under five models of bank lending. The study covered eight branches, four each of RRBs and commercial banks, in four states. The study concluded that lending to SHGs by bank branches was not just an exercise in social and economic empowerment, but was a profitable business proposition. They suggested that lending through SHGs was a major and profitable new market for many banks, particularly those with large, underutilized rural networks. In fact *lending to SHGs through NGOs emerged as the cheapest means of financing the rural poor*, with a total transaction cost (comprising cost of lending, cost of funds, cost of mobilizing deposits and default risks) at branch level of 9.83% in the case of lending to NGOs and 13.07% in the case of lending directly to SHGs. The default risk was negligible in the case of lending to SHGs and NGOs.

Moreover, the total cost of rural lending, i.e., the transaction cost of the bank plus the cost to intermediaries like NGOs and SHGs was 16% where the NGO was acting as financial intermediary, 18% where the bank lent directly to SHGs and nearly 22% when the bank was lending to individuals. They recommended that the cost incurred by NGOs in group formation should be reimbursed by the banks in the form of a service charge conditional upon good repayment performance of the loans by the groups. To cover this, the banks could charge a higher interest on the bank loans to the SHGs.

Similarly, Seibel and Dave (2002) *concluded that SHG banking was more profitable as compared to other competing products for the clientele of a rural bank branch*. Their study covered seven units of three banks and was conducted in October 2002. They applied average cost analysis for each product and marginal cost analysis in respect of personnel costs of SHG banking because of existing idle capacities. They found that non-performing loans (NPLs) to SHGs were zero per cent. In contrast, consolidated non-performing loan ratios ranged from 2.6% to 18%. The returns on average assets of SHG banking ranged from 1.4% to 7.5% by average cost analysis and 4.6% to 11.8% by marginal cost analysis, as compared to −1.7% to 2.3% for the consolidated portfolio. Operational self-sufficiency of SHG banking ranged from 110% to 165% by average cost analysis and 142% to 286% by marginal cost analysis.

SHG banking was found to be a robust financial product, which performed well in both healthy and distressed financial institutions. In terms of all measures used, the profitability of SHG banking was positive throughout all units studied despite low interest rates charged by banks. The profitability of SHG banking significantly exceeded the profitability of the respective units—bank, branch or cooperative society—using average cost analysis and exceeded the profitability of the respective units *by a wide margin* using marginal cost analysis. SHG banking outperformed other products, e.g., cash credit and agricultural term loans, by a wide margin. Besides SHG banking was found to have indirect commercial effects on banking activity as well as intangible social benefits at various levels for women and in the community.

An M-CRIL study of five branches of RRBs, of which four were engaged in SHG–bank linkage, however, *showed that all the bank branches irrespective of SHG promotion mechanisms were making substantial losses on this product* (M-CRIL, 2003). They estimated that SHG portfolio yield was 12.5% to 13% and the operating cost was 19%. The effort expended on SHG lending neither translated into substantial outreach nor was a useful source of income for the banks. The exposure of SHG loans in the sample RRBs ranged from 2% to 17% of the total average balances for the year. This showed little evidence also of economies of scale in SHG lending. A reason for this was the high level of scrutiny in the appraisal of SHG loans, even repeat loans, along with the accompanying costs. These findings were thus contrary to the findings of earlier studies.

A set of studies undertaken by the GTZ-NABARD Rural Finance Programme also examined the viability of SHG lending through banks and MFI.[15] Ramakrishna and Meissner (2007) provided a comparative analysis of these four studies and synthesized their findings, which pertain to four types of lending institutions, namely, RRB branch, MFI, a PACS and a commercial bank (CB) branch. The GTZ studies examined the transaction costs of credit allocation: (*a*) cost of obtaining information, handling, monitoring

---

[15] These were Meissner (2006a, 2006b, 2006c) and Tankha and Meissner (2007).

and enforcing the loan (or information cost), and (*b*) risk cost incurred due to loan losses. In order to ensure the financial viability of the financial intermediary, its intermediation spread should be sufficient to cover its transaction cost, as also the opportunity cost of capital. In addition to transaction costs, the group methodology of linkage banking also involves costs related to group formation and guidance or social investment costs. The studies examined the hypothesis that linkage banking was a profitable business for banks and that the initial social investments of banks could be paid off in time.

In the case of a branch of an *RRB* based in Rajasthan, with 7% share of SHG loans in the total loan outstanding of the branch, the overall SHG lending operations were found to be viable and sustainable once a certain amount of loan per SHG was reached. The study was restricted to one operational year only. *SHG lending was found to be more time and cost intensive than normal lending but had better repayment performance* (which in turn justified relatively lower loan loss provisioning). The bank management saw SHGs as a long-term investment even though follow-up promoting measures were lacking. One of the spillover effects reported was that SHGs helped the branch manager to recover loans that had already been written off.

The *MFI* studied was an NGO in Odisha in the process of transformation to an NBFC. The study was confined to two single branches of the MFI and the cost structure of one operational year only. Field staff cost and overhead cost of SHG lending at the MFI were the major cost drivers. The social investment cost at the MFI was relatively high compared to other institutions analyzed. *The intermediation margin of 8% to 9% could be considered to be sufficient for operations* though with a relatively high nominal rate of interest of 18% per annum. This in turn could be justified in view of the high cost of funds.

The *cooperative institution* studied *was a leading DCCB of* West Bengal *along with one of its affiliated PACS*. As per estimates, the effective operating income from SHG business of the DCCB branch (including overhead) and its affiliated PACS was not sufficient to cover the total operating expenses during financial year 2004–05. A reason for this was the nominal intermediation margin which the institutions chose to take, at DCCB level (1% per annum) and at PACS level (2.5% per annum). SHG lending at the PACS level was also slightly loss making after amortization of social investment cost. A major cost driver influencing results was the overhead costs, which were considerable. *Though this model had high staff costs there was a corresponding reduction in risk of SHG lending. However, if one were to take into account the returns on locked-in savings of SHGs, the PACS would make a small profit.*

In the study of *commercial bank* viability, the SHG operations and transaction costs of SHG business of one branch of a commercial bank and its attached central processing cell (CPC) were covered. The CPC had been formed to support bank branches in the opening and servicing of SHG accounts. The CPC acted as a kind of internal business facilitator and business correspondent in its dealings with the branch. It was found that the net operating income after taking into account total operating expenditure and loan loss provisioning as per the bank's criteria was –10.4% of average deposits for deposit mobilization and –8.9% of average loan outstanding for lending operations. If promotional costs payable as incentives to the NGO promoter of SHGs were taken into account, the net income declined further. Positive income flows during the year under study, i.e., financial year 2005–06 accrued only by including one-time bonuses, resulting from incentives given to the branch under the bank's Transfer Price Mechanism. These were not likely to be sustained as SHG business would develop.

However, a multi-period analysis over a six-year period in the form of a business model for the bank's expanding SHG business showed that to ensure viability of SHG business there was a case for a higher rate of interest to be charged by the bank. *By revising the lending rates to SHGs, at least to the benchmark prime-lending rate (BPLR)[16] the innovation would be viable.* Besides the existing low interest rate would only serve to perpetuate the 'social-banking' attitude of staff. The CPC model has since been extended by the State Bank of India to several parts of the country.

Overall, *the GTZ studies, though limited in that they analyzed single branches and banks, provided some evidence that SHG lending was potentially viable for each of the types of banks studied.* The studies pointed to the fact that the major portion of transaction costs was made up of staff costs and overhead costs. While in the case of MFIs, compensation packages were productivity-linked, this was not the case in government run banks. Transaction costs were the same regardless of the size of the loan and it was only by increasing the loan volume and the numbers of SHGs catered to, that SHG lending could help to generate sufficient returns. The studies also highlighted the possibilities of cross-selling financial products such as microinsurance, savings and remittance products. The SHG business was potentially profitable if the intermediation margin was sufficient, and there was no evidence that SHG members objected to paying slightly higher rates to banks. This margin depended on the cost structure of the institutions, which varied from 3% in a PACS and a commercial bank, 6% in a RRB and 15% in a young MFI.

---

[16] The then existing BPLR became ineffectual since much lending by banks, including to SHGs, was undertaken at sub-BPLR rates. In the interests of greater transparency of bank lending rates, with effect from 1 April 2010 the new 'base rate system' was introduced and banks were free to choose their own base rates for lending. These rates are calculated on the basis of various elements of cost.

Two characteristics of crucial importance that emerged from the studies were that revenue depended on loan volumes, especially loan outstanding and that transaction costs were almost the same regardless of the size of the loan and that this has to be factored in while pricing small loans. One of the factors contributing to the lack of enthusiasm on the part of banks to lend to SHGs has been the inability, by and large, of per group volumes to increase over the years. The average membership of SHGs is around 13 and as low as 10 in new groups being formed under different programmes. This in turn increases costs to bankers and while lowering the size of the transaction such that the average loan outstanding per SHG is smaller than the outstanding average per agricultural loan account (Srinivasan, 2011).

While the SHG portfolio of most bank branches has been generally quite small in relation to their total portfolio, several notable instances of bank branches that devoted much innovation, investment and a large share of their portfolio for the SHG clientele have been documented. *The case of Oriental Bank of Commerce, Rudrapur, UP; Pandya Grama Bank, Tamil Nadu; and Bidar Central Cooperative Bank and its PACSs in Karnataka are documented instances where banks and their branches engaged in viable SHG lending in the early years of SHG–bank linkage.* In recent years Indian Bank has opened dedicated branches designated as Microsate Branches catering exclusively to SHG clients in urban and progressively in rural areas. In addition to providing loans, they also started providing skill development trainings to take up IGAs or link them with training organizations. Based on the success of the original branch in Chennai these have expanded to other areas. All the 41 such Microsate branches are profit-making.[17]

With the additional pressure of meeting the objectives and targets of financial inclusion further innovations within and outside the SBLP framework have been initiated by various public sector and private banks. These include Internet kiosks and other doorstep banking initiatives and the use of BCs and BFs. SBI had covered approximately 28,000 SHG groups and 154,000 SHG members with 'tiny cards' for individuals by 31 March 2011. Using authorized signatories and finger print validation technology the cards are operable with BCs/CSPs/PoS devices near their place of residence. Its kiosk banking initiative uses internet-enabled personal computers (PCs) with biometric validation. Many other banks, such as Indian Bank, Indian Overseas Bank, Bank of Baroda and United Bank of India too have introduced Smart Card Banking through BCs as per the guidelines of RBI and Andhra Bank has piloted doorstep banking for SHG members in four branches in Andhra Pradesh. Bank of Baroda's Micro Loan Factories at Raebareli and Sultanpur in UP have a mobile van with facilities and all

---

[17] Based on interviews with Mr M.S. Sundara Rajan and Mr Selvam Veeraghavan, Indian Bank, Chennai.

stationeries/documents related to SHG financing. It is managed by officers who are duly authorized to sanction and disburse loans up to ₹ 25,000 to SHGs on the spot and at their doorstep.[18] Some of the MFIs promoted by the NGOs have begun to operate as BCs, e.g., KDFS which has been operating as a BC of SBI since 2009. While the possibilities of the latter route has not been fully realized as yet, experiments with the deployment of both SHGs as well as their higher level associations such as village/cluster organizations and secondary federations at block level as BCs and BFs are under way.

On the matter of interest rates to be charged by various financial agencies, Usha Thorat, former Deputy Governor, RBI, expressed the opinion that by lending at 15% to 18% per annum banks should be able to regard microfinance business as a viable one which can be scaled up in a relatively short period of time.[19] She suggested that *banks can actually lend at much lower rates to individuals than SHGs or MFIs* as they can reduce the transaction cost through the use of BCs to provide doorstep services to customers. Given these new innovations as also the use of information technology towards financial inclusion the comparative costs and viability of bank lending to the poor and excluded through various channels, including that of SHGs, will need further examination.

7.5 SUSTAINABILITY STUDIES OF SHGs AND SHG PROMOTERS

In the previous section the transaction cost and sustainability dimensions were examined from the point of view of the banks engaged in the business of lending to SHGs. For some time, right from the days of the IRDP loans, attention has been drawn to the transaction costs incurred by individual rural borrowers, and subsequently by SHG members in their dealing with the banks. While the agency of the SHG permitted the banks to reduce their transaction costs, could it be that it was resulting in an unacceptably high burden on the SHG members?

A study conducted by Karduck and Seibel (2004) considered whether SHG banking was profitable at the expense of SHGs, i.e., whether banks had transferred the transaction costs to the SHGs and their members, such that they have to bear a high cost of access to finance. The study covered 78 SHGs with a total membership of 1,160 in four districts of Karnataka.

---

[18] As per information provided in respective annual reports for 2010–11. Besides, under the Janashree Bima Yojana of Life Insurance Corporation of India group life insurance cover is provided to all women members of SHGs credit linked to banks wherein the premium is subsidized by GOI.
[19] Usha Thorat, Director Centre for Advanced Financial Research and Learning (CAFRAL), Valedictory Address at International Network of Alternative Financial Institutions (INAFI) Conference, 23 June 2011, Hyderabad.

Transaction costs of SHG members were split into two: (a) real costs of SHGs incurred in rupees and (b) opportunity costs. Real costs of SHGs mainly included transportation costs of office bearers, remuneration of external book writers and auditors, loan documentation, stationery and photos. Real costs of members included mainly costs of photos, transportation costs and fees for no objection certificates.

The study opined that *opportunity costs of both office bearers and SHGs members were largely fictitious since there was no income foregone*, except in rare cases, and opportunity costs were more than offset with intangible benefits such as self-confidence and familiarity with financial matters. Social mobilization costs and maintenance costs of groups were not included. It was found that real costs were 0.62% of loans outstanding and opportunity costs were 0.60% of loans outstanding. Transaction costs tended to be an absolute amount, which did not vary by the size of the loans, and thus decreased as SHG loans increased. By the time loans outstanding reached ₹ 200,000, usually by three years or so, transaction costs of SHGs became negligible. Thus, over time the *transaction costs of SHGs were negligible and were more than offset by the intangible 'empowerment' and other benefits that accrued to office bearers and individual members.*

The question of transaction costs incurred by SHG members in accessing bank loans is a contentious one. Of course there is the additional issue of commissions, bribes and 'speed money' that might also have to be paid in order to receive loans. While the real costs incurred in visits to distant bank branches and documentation are legitimate costs of SHG–bank linkage, it is not clear whether the opportunity cost of the time of SHG members undertaking SHG functions and interfacing with banks for their loan processing and other requirements can reasonably be accepted as true costs. (Indeed, it is possible to argue that time spent in frequent group meetings and other group obligations are also costs being incurred by SHG members which are invariably not taken into account.) However, there is a palpable asymmetry in the valuation of the labour-time of SHG members when it comes to the time taken in interface with banks as against the imputation for labour in pursuing their own productive enterprises.

Many analysts are quick to impute the opportunity cost of labour in terms of work opportunities foregone by poor SHG members while assessing transaction costs of SHG members in their dealings with the bank. However, often the same analysts are equally quick to justify high rates of interest payable by poor microfinance clients on their borrowings by suggesting that returns to their enterprises are substantial. This result is obtained by asserting that the *opportunity cost of labour in such households is zero* or near zero, especially for women, because of the absence of opportunities for in-home self-employment (Mor, 2006).

The inflated returns to income-generating activities of microenterprises of poor households (such as buffalo and small animal rearing) that are computed by ignoring household labour costs have also served to justified the high rates of interest payable by such households borrowing from MFIs and even through SHGs. Indeed, if an imputation to the labour of poor households for such enterprises is made using any reasonable norms, many of these enterprises would be found to yield negative profits. A failure to cost a poor household's own (idle) labour input in such activities can *yield positive (but flawed) returns to the household—even* as *returns to the enterprise may be negative* if labour inputs are also taken into account. (One research inquiry into this anomaly artlessly posed the question, could it be that women do not price their own labour when they think about profits?) That poor households may undertake such activities through self-exploitation in anticipation of small supplements to family income does not justify what amounts to an expropriation of the returns to their labour through high interest rates.

Indeed, *the thrust of several studies on the viability of lending to SHGs makes the case for higher interest rates by banks to be charged to SHGs.* In another exercise, Christen and Ivatury (2007) examined the sustainability of four reputed SHG promoters: (*a*) Oriental Bank of Commerce, New Delhi; (*b*) Sarvodaya Nanofinance Limited, Tamil Nadu; (*c*) DHAN Foundation, Tamil Nadu and (*d*) Microcredit Foundation of India, Tamil Nadu. Based on field visits, interviews and financial results of the programme, they examined the sustainability of SHG lending. They estimated the total costs of providing support services and computed whether operating income was enough to cover these. Overhead costs of banks were not considered because SHG lending was only a tiny proportion of branch operations. However, cost of forming SHGs and SHG associations was amortized over five years. Subsidized funds were not included in operating income. Thus income, costs and assets for each programme were constructed. The indicators revealed that on average the four SHG programmes covered all the costs of providing support services to SHGs and two of the programmes covered all of their costs. The most efficient programme was that of the bank branch of Oriental Bank of Commerce at Rudrapur. When the performance of the four SHG programmes was compared with benchmarks from other groups of microfinance providers such as Grameen style MFIs, leading MFIs, and other SHG MFIs, the study programmes compared highly favourably. They also compared favourably with international benchmarks. The study, nevertheless, made out a case for banks charging SHGs higher rates of interest to protect the quality of SHG lending.

CGAP carried out *an analysis of SHG level performance* of 150 SHGs from five well-functioning SHG programmes. *The findings were largely positive and suggested that the SHG model could work sustainably as compared to other microfinance programmes.* Based upon the study it was found that the SHGs reached poor and excluded groups though they did not fully match the financial needs of their members. Savings mobilization was low with only a limited number of SHGs offering voluntary savings. As regards the financial sustainability of SHGs, it was found that income from their loan portfolios was high and operating expenses low, which enabled the study SHGs to be profitable even after adjusting for loan loss provision and promotion and monitoring costs amortized over three years. Unadjusted returns to SHGs in the five programmes averaged 13%. However, *after provisioning for loan losses, all the SHG models were still profitable, averaging 9% returns.* Further, after amortizing promotion costs,[20] returns on assets were wiped out on the average though they were still positive for three out of five programmes, and only marginally negative for another.

As far as SHG portfolio quality is concerned, PAR greater than 30 days was an average of 25%, and ranged from 8% to 53%. PAR greater than 90 days was not much different at an average of 24%. Generally the levels of loan delinquency were much higher than for other types of microcredit programmes, and *high level of late repayments in SHGs did not always translate into defaults.*

Sinha et al. (2009) explored the question of SHG sustainability in terms of certain financial indicators in a study which covered 214 SHGs in four states. A high degree of equitable functioning was observed in the SHGs studied in respect to access of loans and their distribution among SHG members. SHG leaders were not cornering a disproportionately large amount of the loans. Further, half the sample groups were operating at a profit with a good return on assets of 6.5% and a return on internal capital of 11%. However in only one third of the SHGs was the return on members' capital higher than the rate of inflation. *Around 45% of groups had defaults, which were more than one year old, which was affecting the income of the group. However, there were other positive features having a bearing on the sustainability of the groups.* For instance, the proportion of broken groups was relatively low at 7%.

The findings related to sustainability of SHG in the above studies thus stresses that SHGs may not measure up to the highest standards in terms of financial performance expected of and achieved by microfinance retailers and other intermediaries. However, SHG loans were generally repaid by members and that *rigorous criteria for assessing portfolio quality may not be very appropriate in the case of financial intermediaries like SHGs.*

---

[20] Whether such cost allocation is appropriate, given that SHG formation constitutes an investment in the social and financial infrastructure, has been discussed in Chapter 6.

7.6 SHG Federations and Sustainable Financial Services

One of the major innovations in the development of SHGs in India has been the formation of federations with various and multiple objectives. In this section the question of the sustainability of financial federations in enhancing the flow of financial and non-financial services to their constituent SHGs is examined. Ghate (2007) makes a case for SHG federations as a cost-effective means of enhancing the sustainability of the SBLP and individual SHG quality. He indicates that where federations have become strong it has been possible for them to act as channels of financial services—including bridge financing. Finally, he expresses the view that federations offer the prospect of empowerment benefits, and that these benefits are the major factor in encouraging promoters to form federations rather than merely acting as aggregators of services. Many of the federations have been multi-purpose federations catering to both financial and non-financial needs of member SHGs.

Ghate (2007) also states that anecdotal evidence suggests that once federations get into the business of accessing bulk funds, *the preoccupation with sustainability can lead to the neglect of non-financial services*. Besides equipping federations with the financial skills to manage large funds was and is a challenging task. Indeed, DHAN Foundation moved away from bulk borrowing for its federations and set up the centralized Section 25 company, KDFS, as has been discussed in Chapter 4. *Many federation promoters, after toying with the idea of financial federations, restricted their activities and have facilitated direct linkages through the banks*. Bulk funding had come to the federations mainly from private banks whose role since the two Andhra crises, however, has considerably diminished.

In an early study of the emerging SHG federations, Nair (2005) found that two leading federations had become self-sustaining on the basis of the fee they charged their members. In another paper, Christen (2006) reviewed the issue of financial sustainability of federations as part of a superstructure to provide long-term support to SHGs. In his analysis (based on data from Nair's study on sustainability of SHGs), of two community-level financial systems (CLFs) Christen added the operational costs at the SHG, federation and apex levels to the financial costs at the SHG level to get the total costs for the CLF and on comparison with total SHG level income *confirmed that the two CLFs were sustainable*. However, if the CLFs were to provide for loan loss expenses and amortize the expenses of promoting SHGs and their federations, the systems are not sustainable. Christen thus came to the conclusion that if all subsidies were accounted for, *a sustainable federated SHG model may be more expensive than the MFO model for reaching the same target group*. He thus made out a case for higher interest rates to be charged from SHGs.

Srinivasan and Tankha (2010) in a study of 10 financial federations in six states[21] (two government and eight NGO-promoted federations) noted that the sustainability of financial federations depends on four key factors: (a) the strength of the SHGs which are the building blocks of federation—the quality argument—since SHG quality will contribute to determining the capacity of the federations formed out of them; (b) sound governance and efficient systems to build the capacity of the federation; (c) the policy environment that supports and provides the flow of finance and quality manpower towards sustainability; and (d) the viability of federation operations—which is in the final analysis based upon the ability of SHGs to pay for the financial services provided by it. The criteria adopted for measuring the financial viability of federations were similar to that of other MFIs, viz., operational self-sufficiency, the ability to meet all administrative costs and loan losses from operating income. The study found that *all federations, except one newly launched federation, had excellent portfolio quality and had reported operational self sufficiency.* These were self-reported figures without adjustment for loan losses and subsidies. However, *in several smaller and newer federations they did not take into account contributions of staff, office space and other inputs and services provided by the promoting organization.* The study found that the five cooperative organizations were advantageously placed in relation to other legal forms of federation in view of their ability to mobilize savings as an inexpensive source of capital for operations, as well as to build equity in order to access external funding.

Srinivasan and Tankha (2010) also suggest that in the absence of both savings as a source of funds and an appropriate legal framework that would allow the federation to mobilize savings, the financial viability of federations of SHGs would be severely constrained. A small federation operating, say, at the block level, on a 6% spread between funds mobilized at 12% per annum and lending at no more than 18% per annum would need to have a portfolio in the range of ₹ 10 to ₹ 20 million under which cost recovery would be possible. It is also debatable whether federations, given that many of them have weak management, should be allowed to take their SHG members' savings. It might be more secure for the federations to act as BCs and channel members' savings to regulated banks.

Besides this, at higher levels of operation, diseconomies of scale in the form of constraints on the capabilities of federation managers invariably set in necessitating large investments in systems and personnel. While in some states there may be adequate demand for loans from SHGs to permit this scale of operation, in other geographical areas credit absorption through this channel may not sustain this threshold portfolio level. Federations in

---

[21] Andhra Pradesh, Tamil Nadu, Maharashtra, Odisha, Rajasthan and Uttar Pradesh.

these areas could be hard pressed to achieve scale and viability by seeking external loans. It is also argued that as far as ownership, governance and management factors are concerned, it is important to understand the culture of CBOs and before SHGs are called upon to federate and sufficient time and process inputs need to be provided towards clear governance structures. The boards of SHG federations often are led by the promoters' representatives and the ownership of SHG members and the community is often not evident. At the same time, the limited capabilities of board members from the community can pose a constraint to the functioning of federations, affecting institutional and organizational sustainability.[22]

Srinivasan (2010) notes that the emergence of state-sponsored federations in different states has been a cause of concern for banks because of the pressure on the part of the state governments to extend loans to these institutions. He indicates that the typical loan exposure to a Mandal Samakhya in Andhra Pradesh would be around ₹ 25 million. In Tamil Nadu where the panchayat-level federations have been promoted as financial intermediaries bank loan of ₹ 5 million has been proposed. Given the limited capacity of these federations and the inadequate human resources, lending to thousands of such federations could be fraught with serious risks. There is need to provide both support to such SHG-based institutions as well as lay down norms for their functioning for them to be effective and sustainable.

Srinivasan (2010) further states that when the state enters the scene, such as in Andhra Pradesh, it brings problems such as subsidies, poor quality groups and ghost groups and the creation of a dependency among SHGs. Besides unsuitable staff, low levels of training and lack of accountability are present. At the same time state officials are unwilling to provide autonomy to the groups and their federations with development benefits being provided as 'charity' through a hierarchical system. The result of this is a lack of ownership of the programme by the SHGs with its attendant problems such as high defaults, equal division of loans, multiple borrowing, proxy loans and irregular meetings. Though the Velugu/IKP project has been able to deepen bank linkage, it has been at the expense of positive group dynamics and has resulted in dependence on project staff. Besides, in Tamil Nadu, the formation of panchayat level federations has created a wedge between the federation and the NGO promoters. The banks are also not convinced of the ability of small village-level federations to handle financial operations running into millions of rupees and there is need for RBI and NABARD to come up with clear policies and to support federations with financial and professional skills so that they can play an appropriate intermediation role.

---

[22] This can, of course, stem from the failure of the promoter to build the management capacities of the board.

As NGO-promoted federations evolve, the nature and type of support from promoters may need to change. The case of GRAM and IIMF (Chapter 4) provides an instance of this changing relationship. After GRAM promoted federations in the form of the mandal MACS, the need was felt to bring them together under an umbrella federation and thus IIMF was promoted and was allowed to develop linkages with banks and donors while GRAM withdrew from providing active support. At the same time, IIMF utilized the services of GRAM to train grass-roots leaders for better governance and subsequently in business partnership to promote livelihoods through a dairy initiative. Most of the NGOs covered in the present study have undergone some form of transformation in their role after they have promoted federations of various types. However, they do not withdraw from supporting the federations completely, and continue to operate various development programmes for member SHGs of the federations promoted by them.

Thus the sustainability of federations, in an organizational and institutional sense, is greatly facilitated by the NGO promoters. One of the early instances of exit by a promoter from involvement with the federation promoted by it was provided by PRADAN in the case of Sakhi Samiti in Alwar district. The premature exit of PRADAN meant that Sakhi Samiti, even while providing bookkeeping and other services to member SHGs, was not able to recover its costs fully to finance its support activities. There were also reports of resistance from SHGs to pay the fees for federation services and for federation staff to be seen as essentially parasitical in realizing fees for their role in facilitating SHG–bank linkage.

This provided a valuable lesson of the consequences of premature withdrawal of NGO support. MYRADA which promoted CMRCs (which were not strictly federations), to provide fee-based services to SHGs were able over the years to more or less fully disengage from the SHGs through systematically paving the way for a greater role and responsibility for the CMRCs. This has been an exceptional case. Still other NGOs such as Chaitanya, and possibly DHAN Foundation, while striving for the financial and organizational sustainability of federations promoted by them, do not appear to envisage a withdrawal from active involvement with the federations.[23]

As noted by Salomo et al. (2010), many such pioneer institutions as MYRADA, DHAN Foundation and People's Education and Development Organisation (PEDO) argue that if federations cover their operational costs

---

[23] During discussions Sudha Kothari, Director and Kalpana Pant, Deputy Director, Chaitanya suggested that decentralization by the SHPA is important but some central control is equally important. Chaitanya realized that independent functioning of federations is important is used by them to strengthen their bargaining position vis-à-vis banks and other agencies.

through their own microfinance operations, their accountability towards their member organizations could be jeopardized. However, if members make direct contributions, they will develop an ownership stake in the federations and will more closely monitor the quality of their services. Also in the case of financial intermediation by federations, the dependency of federations on professional staff or on the promoters would be higher and they would tend to neglect normal SHG–bank linkage.

As far as government-promoted federations are concerned, the tendency is to use federations for the delivery of programmes instead of promoting a structure built upon the needs of the various SHGs and community-based initiatives. Thus these federations are used as part of the delivery system for various development services rather than have their independent reasons for existence. The IKP in Andhra Pradesh has a financial intermediation role for mandal samkhyas, which are provided with substantial grant funds, and which in turn are sought to be supplemented with external loans. (However, in the case of Kudumbashree, the move to use the CDSs as financial intermediaries was not successful.) It is not evident as yet whether the necessary capacity exists with the mandal samakhyas to undertake sustainable financial intermediation even though much investment and effort has been expended to develop this capacity. Besides, the role of federations has to be built not only upon their sustainable functioning in terms of efficiency and profitability indicators but the larger developmental agenda of women's empowerment and enhancing the choices and access of the poor to a range of financial and non-financial services.

The role of external financial institutions and banks in support of financial federations has been critical to the expansion of their role in support of SHGs. The financial support provided by banks in extending on-lending funds has been rather mixed. Some of the mature federations have been able to access loans from private sector banks. Still others have acquired loans from the public sector bank branches, while yet others have been able to access funds from wholesalers such as SIDBI, RMK and FWWB.

Indeed the pattern of acceptability of federations with various external financial institutions varies from state to state. The federations which had mobilized loans under the 'partnership model' nearly a decade ago later faced a credit crunch nearly a decade ago when the model was abandoned by the private sector banks. The interest of public sector banks has been consistently lukewarm, except in the case of federations that have evolved to borrowing through the legal form of the NBFC. Even in Andhra Pradesh, the state with the largest number of financial federations, until recently the government-promoted federations and NGO-promoted federations had both not been successful in mobilizing credit from public sector banks. Corporate status is becoming necessary to enable federations to access bank funds. However, in several cases, especially in Tamil Nadu, the credibility of the parent NGO promoter has meant that even the not-for-profit Section 25 company format has been able to attract bank funding. Also, some funders are beginning to recognize that there is a space for smaller MFIs, like federations based upon the cooperative format. Nevertheless *the viability of financial federations is generally at risk unless they operate as MFIs and satisfy the appraisal and rating norms of the lending institutions. This, given the limited educational qualifications and capabilities of the board and management of the federations, is a tall order.*

Salomo et al. (2010) suggest that while SHG–bank linkage has contributed to the development of the SHG network in the country, no genuine role has been envisaged for federations. Even formally registered federations at the block level are not directly involved in the SBLP and its promotional activities. It recommends that the SBLP properly integrate federations as it would be advantageous for all stakeholders. Thus the effectiveness and efficiency of the linkage programme could be improved by channelling loans through federations instead of directly dealing with each SHG. From the point of view of SHGs, it would improve their bargaining position and improve transparency and risk management. The report also sets out the idea of *sector-owned promotion*, especially for the financial cooperative federations based upon SHGs (see Box 7.2). It emphasizes the scope for spreading the self-help idea and extension of SHG networks through the exchange of experience and mutual support with the help of secondary and

Box 7.2: Sector Own Control

APMAS, in collaboration with SERP and DGRV, Germany, initiated a pilot on Sector Own Control (SOC) also called Swayam Niyantrana Udyamam (SNU) in Telugu. As of July 2011 the pilot project area is the Kamareddy Cluster in Nizamabad district, Andhra Pradesh. The cluster comprises six sub-district level federations made up of 172 primary federations, and 6,084 SHGs. The overall objective of self regulation for SHGs and SHG federations is to ensure that SHG members set their own agenda and manage and control the processes, so that the SHG system sustainably works for the benefit of SHG members. The pilot developed and tested systems and processes of SOC in the framework of the SBLP of NABARD. The focus of capacity building is to train SHG members as bookkeepers, auditors and facilitators to implement the bookkeeping and financial reporting of SHGs and federations; and building the capacity of women to manage, govern and control their SHGs and the federation system. It helps to improve financial literacy among SHG members, ensures legal compliance to the MACS Act. It includes conduct of the annual general body meeting, elections by secret ballot and annual planning to improve transparency and accountability at all levels. The core modules have been prepared in English and Telugu and are being translated into four other Indian languages.

Source: APMAS.

tertiary institutions and a range of other promotional activities through the collaboration between SHG structures and networks.

Regarding the financial service function of federations, the report suggests that the long-term solution would be to establish financial service federations as full-fledged retail banks or MFIs. (This is of course debatable given the large numbers of financial institutions which already exist; it can be argued instead that it would be more effective to devote more effort to reviving and renewing the existing member-owned institutions, such as PACS and DCCBs.) However, in the initial stages it would be more practical for federations to act towards only intermediating the financial products of different external providers for SHGs and their members. Nevertheless, the report emphasizes that the financial service function is the central element of the federating process—to be based mainly on the sector's own financial resources (savings, share capital, deposits) but to also include external financing. Towards this end there is need for coordination between different stakeholders not merely in support of SHGs but also the specific requirements of federations and SHG structures.

In regard to the different roles of *SHG federations*, at an SHG Round-table in September 2011[24] T. Vijay Kumar, MoRD, suggested that since mainstream institutions were moving away from SHGs, federations had emerged as *important community-based institutions to offer choices to the poor*. While starting as bridge financing entities, they evolved and started lending according to microcredit plans in Andhra Pradesh and Kerala, thus enabling the banks to provide loans independent of the savings linkage. The most important role played by them has been that of a force multiplier and their work on social issues, apart from providing bargaining power to the SHGs. At the same time Vipin Sharma, ACCESS, felt that *if federations were to be the base of NRLM, there is need to define standards and see what kind of investment is required to promote federations* for financial intermediation. Though federations can respond to the needs of their members more effectively than banks, they require longer-term hand holding support. Besides, apart from the extensive network of support structures and institutions required for this purpose there is the *threat of politicization of district level federations*. In any event federations need to be regulated, and require equity investment and display good governance. Since federations have neither professional staff nor collateral, it is difficult for them to get credit ratings and bank loans. It is important, however, to persuade bankers to judge these organizations on their mission and financial track record. One of the reasons why federations had failed in the past was that federation members did not have clarity about their role. This had

---

[24] ACCESS Development Services, 2011.

not been discussed with them had any capacity building been undertaken for them, since federations were often formed without conducting any needs assessment. With the involvement of professionals, the power of decision-making would also tend to shift into their own hands rather than the members. While such involvement was necessary in the early stages of federations an exit role had to be planned for the promoters as well.

A new source of funds for financial federations has come up in the southern region which can serve to offset the lukewarm attitude of most bankers towards federations. To boost the growth of the microfinance sector, Karnataka Agriculture Development Finance Company Limited (KADFC) was restructured into an MFI called NABARD Financial Services Limited (NABFINS) in 2007. NABARD is the major stakeholder of NABFINS, while the Government of Karnataka, Canara Bank, Federal Bank and Dhana Lakshmi Bank are the other stakeholders. The main aim of NABFINS is to support sustainable on farm and off farm livelihoods of the poor. NABFINS extends loans to individuals, SHGs and JLGs through BCs but also to second-level institutions such as SHG Federations, producers groups, small and medium enterprises, Producers' Companies, MACS, Souharda and other cooperative societies, trusts, societies or other organizations that support production, aggregation, marketing and related activities in various sectors for supporting the poor. Currently NABFINs is focusing on lending to SHGs in Karnataka, Andhra Pradesh and Tamil Nadu. During 2010–11, it disbursed ₹ 512 million of loans in 22 districts.

7.7 Concluding Observations

The quality of SHGs promoted under various government and NGO programmes, with some notable exceptions, appears to be less than satisfactory and can be traced to inadequate capacity building inputs towards self-management. This in turn could be affected by limited funding for maintenance of SHGs for NGO initiatives. Innovations like SOC are designed to provide capacity building and fee-based services to SHGs that could serve to consolidate and strengthen the SHG movement.

Similarly, the supposed reluctance of banks to lend to SHGs, or to impose various conditions and charges, is not fully borne out by the data on SBLP and the corporate level support for SBLP in the case of most public sector banks. Commercial banks also are seen to be taking important new initiatives for financial inclusion, through and outside the SHG channel. As far as RRBs and cooperative banks are concerned, SHGs should form their natural clientele. The evidence of viability studies suggest that transaction costs of banks need not be a factor inhibiting lending to SHGs on a sustainable basis. Indeed, the opportunities provided by the BC/BF model, which some banks are already utilizing, could allow for both the provision of essential savings services and other financial products to SHGs, and even to individual clients, through SHG federations (and even SHG functionaries) acting as BCs in a more cost-effective manner.

As far as SHG federations are concerned, the situation, appears to have changed during 2011 even as the microfinance sector in India was affected by a crisis situation. A role for financial federations is increasingly being accepted particularly as a supplementary source of funds to bank linkage over and above SBLP especially since the long-term nature of loans under the latter preclude the possibility of additional borrowing by SHGs for emergencies or other legitimate needs. There is a clear place for financial federations in the NRLM framework. A dedicated institution in support of SHG federations has come up in the form of the Stree Nidhi, which is an apex cooperative credit society formed as a joint venture between the Government of Andhra Pradesh and the MMS of SHGs of the states (as discussed in Chapter 5). Chaitanya's GMST (Chapter 4) was also financed by the local branch of Bank of Maharashtra after the bank had satisfied itself regarding its transactions with the leaders of the federations. GMST has received loans from SIDBI and Indian Bank and has even *received revolving fund loan assistance from NABARD—a first for an SHG federation.* Besides, with the promising performance of NABFINS and the possibility of the launch of similar initiatives in other states, the outlook for sustained flow of funds to SHGs and their federations through alternative channels appears more positive than has been the case in the past.

EVIDENCE OF IMPACT

8

In view of the importance of SHGs in rural microfinance and financial inclusion it becomes necessary to ascertain the impact of the SHG programmes on the borrower-members of the SHGs. The success of any development programme lies in its ability to effect a desired transformation in the lives and livelihoods of the target groups it aims to benefit. Impact assessment is of interest to donors concerned about the results of the interventions that they have sponsored. It is also of importance to the practitioners in their endeavour to find out what works and what does not and to refine the scope and nature of their products and processes. The range of impact assessment objectives in microfinance is thus delineated on a continuum marked by two poles of 'proving impact' and 'improving practice' (Hulme, 2000). Donors, academics and policymakers are more concerned with the former as it represents objectivity, accuracy and analytical rigour. The latter is more subjective and process-related and directed at in-depth learning of practitioners and field staff.

8.1 ISSUES IN IMPACT ASSESSMENT

A whole host of reviews and evaluations have been done that pose as impact assessments of development interventions. The critical evidence of impact, however, pertains to *sustained net benefits* to families or participants covered by the programmes being assessed. Other agents can also be benefited positively or negatively. These benefits may be *intended* or *unintended* as the effect of programme activities depends on various shifting local or broader forces. While impact assessment is largely concerned with the member-beneficiary or household, or client-level impact, impact evaluation can be and is extended to other levels of aggregation such as enterprise, community and institutional levels. *This chapter is primarily concerned with the assessment of impact at the level of the SHG members and their households.*

The *attribution* of impact, however, presents a major problem. It is difficult to establish a causal relationship between interventions and activities of a particular project and changes observed in relevant variables representing levels of benefits realized by the participants. It is particularly problematic to attribute benefits to a component of the programme in the case of integrated interventions. This is the case, e.g., with SHG microfinance programmes simultaneously implemented with other economic and social development initiatives. Besides, external changes in the infrastructure or environment in the project area may influence the factors mediating and facilitating impact. Thus, several methodological weaknesses remain that prevent a rigorous assessment of beneficiary-level impact. State of the art methodology of impact assessment is favouring randomized controlled trials (RCTs) to better ascertain the impact on an experimental group of project beneficiaries. The benefit of RCT is that it can eliminate the problem of selection bias in impact assessment (Odell, 2010). Such trials have been conducted in respect of client-based microfinance programmes.[1] It is, however, open to question whether these tools are appropriate for assessing the effectiveness of financial services delivered through SHGs. This is because it is difficult to deny the control group the 'treatment' indefinitely in the interests of studying longer-term impact. Also, such trials are very expensive, have to be planned in advance and cannot be used in the case of ongoing programmes. Finally, programme design involving RCTs may not be acceptable in many development circles.

As far as microfinance in India is concerned, credible impact studies are virtually non-existent even among the best-practice NGOs. Programme MIS is by and large not geared to providing impact data. Instead the evidence of impact is usually pieced together on the basis of unstructured enquiries as part of mid-term reviews and evaluations using case studies or focus group discussions. The reporting of impact has not addressed a major question regarding the separation of effects of different elements of the integrated package of development interventions. Even in a few studies undertaken by NABARD and at its instance using the 'before-after project' analysis, the effect of running government development programmes is not taken into account.[2] In some other studies, however, a comparison is made between benefits realized by the group of intended beneficiaries and another similarly placed group not covered by the project. This eliminates to an extent the

---

[1] A celebrated study used RCT evaluation to study the effect on borrowing by establishing a new branch of the MFI Spandana in Hyderabad (Banerjee et al., 2009). It showed that over 15 to 18 months microfinance had a positive effect in enabling households to create and expand businesses but did not impact social empowerment indicators. The authors acknowledge that over a longer period, the results might be different.

[2] Many SHG members have usually simultaneously benefited from subsidized government programmes for the poor, such as housing, irrigation, health and sanitation, etc.

problem of causality, though elements of selection bias remain. However, apart from carefully executed randomized control trials, the ethics of which are debatable and which are not feasible for studying long-term impact, it is possible to question the robustness of virtually any impact assessment exercise. These limitations exist in the case of studies on SHG–bank linkage that are covered in Section 8.2.

Finally, it can be argued that the perceptions of and relative weightage given to different types of benefits need to be determined by the target group of a programme rather than implementing agencies or external observers. This has resulted in the growing importance of participatory methods of impact assessment through focus group discussions and other exercises towards participatory learning and action (PLA) methods. These have indeed been undertaken by some of the leading NGOs promoting SHGs. This is also the basis for a proposed shift in emphasis to continuous monitoring of impact instead of major one-off evaluations towards the conclusion of projects. However, the subjectivity of its conceptualization and the data used for assessing impact constitute problem areas with this approach, besides the fact that variables covered vary from case to case preventing wider comparison.

As observed above, donor requirements and support are largely responsible for studies being undertaken to prove impact. As donor support to NGOs for SHG promotion has declined in over years, so have the number of impact studies undertaken. Besides, the state governments that have been playing a major role in the SHG movement have not conducted such studies. As a result, virtually no major impact studies have been undertaken in recent years. Section 8.2 gives the findings of a few major studies undertaken thus far to assess the impact of SHG banking on the lives of SHG members.

8.2 FINDINGS OF IMPACT EVALUATION STUDIES ON SBLP

A few studies undertaken by NABARD provided the first evidence of impact of the SBLP. The NABARD impact evaluation of SHGs covered by the programme (Puhazhendi and Satyasai, 2000) was the first of its kind. The study covered the changes in socio-economic conditions of 560 members of 223 SHGs in 11 states before and after (spanning a three-year period) their association with the SHG. The reference year of the study was 1999. In terms of economic impact the findings of the study were:

1. Average value of assets per household (including livestock and consumer durables) rose by 72.3% to ₹ 11,793 during the three-year period.

2. Average net income per household from income-generating activities where loan amounts were deployed, increased from ₹ 20,177 prior to group formation to ₹ 26,889.
3. Household employment increased by 17% from 320 to 375 days between the pre- and post-SHG period.
4. Average household saving increased threefold from ₹ 460 during the pre-SHG period to ₹ 1,444 in the post-SHG.
5. Similarly, average borrowings nearly doubled from ₹ 4,282 during the pre-SHG period to ₹ 8,341 in the post-SHG period.
6. Borrowing for IGAs increased from 50% to 70%. It was estimated that 112 households or 47.8% of the poor had crossed the poverty line.

The number of SHG members living below the poverty line declined from about 42% to about 22% in the post-SHG situation. The only unexpected finding was that *326 households out of the sample of 560 covered by the study (58.2%) were already above the poverty line in the pre-SHG situation.* This raised the serious question as to whether the SHGs really covered mainly poor families.

Another significant finding was that a *standard of living index of sample households comprising of socio-economic parameters rose for both economic and social parameters.* However, the *impact was more pronounced on social aspects rather than economic aspects.* Further, social impact was found to be stronger in the case of groups promoted by NGOs than in groups promoted by banks.

Other positive impacts experienced by SHG members related to increase in self-worth, communication skills, and desire to protest social evils, improved response to problem situations and a decrease in family violence. A consistently increased access to various amenities such as water, health and sanitation, schools and markets was also indicated, though it is hardly clear how this could be ascribed to loans accessed by some members of SHGs.

Soon after, another NABARD study conducted in 2001–02 (Puhazhendi and Badatya, 2002) attempted to assess the impact of microfinance channelled through the SBLP in eastern areas (Odisha, Jharkhand and Chhattisgarh). The study was based on primary data collected from 115 members in 60 SHGs. It compared the socio-economic conditions of the SHG members in the pre- and post-SHG situation to quantify the impact.

The study reported an increase in household savings for the SHG members after they formed the group. The average loan per member in the post-SHG situation was 123% more than in the pre-SHG situation and the dependence on moneylenders and other informal sources at higher interest rates was significantly reduced. Consumption loans were replaced by production-oriented loans in the post-SHG situation. About 45% of the

SHG members registered an increase in assets between the pre- and post-SHG situations. The average annual net income per sample household was 23% more than in the pre-SHG situation. Similarly, employment per sample household increased by 34%—from 303 person days to 405 person days between the pre- and post-SHG situations. Finally, there was a significant improvement in social empowerment of members in terms of self-confidence and their involvement in decision-making, as also improved mobility.

It was also observed that NGO promoted groups performed better than bank promoted groups in targeting weaker sections and in economic performance. The performance of older groups was better than recently formed groups suggesting that sustainability of SHGs was well established. Out of total loans received by SHG members, 72% were used for income-generating purposes and 28% for consumption purposes. The share of BPL households in the SHGs reduced from 88% to 75% after group formation.

A study by MYRADA on women's empowerment of SHG members was undertaken in 2002 for NABARD in the four southern region states, viz., Tamil Nadu, Andhra Pradesh, Kerala and Karnataka (MYRADA, 2002). In all, 190 members from 13 SHGs were interviewed covering four professionally managed NGOs (DHAN, Rashtriya Sewa Samithi [RASS], Changanassery Social Service Society [CHASS] and MYRADA), one selected from each state. The components of 'empowerment' in the context of an SHG member were defined in terms of (a) her influence over the family's economic resources and her participation in its economic decision-making; (b) the influence made by her on her own development as an individual; (c) her power over local polity and participation in socio-political decision-making; (d) her influence over other decisions pertaining to general welfare of the family; (e) increased interactions with other members of the group/community; and (f) improvement in technical and managerial skills.

Comparisons were made across selected groups which were composed of those over three years and under one year of age. More members in the older groups reported a positive influence on their share in the family income than in the new ones. The average share of earning SHG members in the family income was also higher in the older SHGs at 74% as against 50% for the newer groups. Eighty-nine per cent of members interviewed in the old group stated that their financial position had improved as against 71% in the new groups. Other findings suggested that there was a positive influence on other empowerment-related parameters such as dealing with people and institutions and confidence in travelling alone. There was also a higher awareness of health and hygiene. A higher proportion of old group members decided on matters pertaining to family welfare than the new group members. Similarly, a higher proportion of old group members also had acquired managerial skills necessary for the efficient operation of SHGs.

Hannover (2005) reviewed the findings of the three NABARD studies discussed above. He examined how the linkage banking impact chain by enabling improved access of SHG members to microfinance services, capacity building and empowerment processes could produce outcomes directly or indirectly impacting on elements of MDGs 1 to 6 (Box 8.1).

Box 8.1: Indicators of Impact on MDGs

MDGs	Indicators/proxy indicators of impact
MDG 1: Eradicate extreme poverty and hunger	(a) Diversification of financial products for SHGs; (b) increase in financial, productive and physical capital; (c) decreased dependence on moneylenders; (d) increase in income and diversification of income sources; (e) reduction in incidence of poverty; (f) improvement in nutrition; (g) increased take-up by women of causes of poverty, e.g., dowry system, alcohol abuse and others and (h) increase in number of self-organized micro forums of SHGs
MDG 2: Achieve universal primary education	(a) Change in enrolment rates of boys and girls in primary and secondary schools and (b) change in proportion of pupils reaching Grade 5 in primary education
MDG 3: Promote gender equality and empower women	(a) Increase in ratio of girls to boys in primary and secondary schools; (b) increased ability to influence decision-making in their households by female SHG members; (c) increased ability to participate in public issues on village level by female SHG members and (d) increase in the number of politically active women in the village
MDGs 4–6: Reduce child mortality, improve maternal health and combat HIV/AIDS, malaria and other diseases	(a) Increased use of curative health measures by SHG households; (b) increased use of preventive health measures, e.g., hygiene and immunization by SHG households and (c) increased demand for financial services (e.g., health insurance by members of SHGs)

Source: Adapted from Hannover (2005).

On analysis it was found that the main impact of SBLP according to the results of the NABARD studies was on indicators related to MDG 1, such as increased use of financial products and increased financial capital, reduced dependence on moneylenders and increased income that brought about the observed reduction in incidence of poverty. The data from the studies also suggested that more financial resources were spent on nutrition in the post-SHG situation. Causes of poverty were also addressed as indicated by a high share of members protesting against social evils.

The impact studies could not, however, provide information of impact on indicators related to MDG 2. As far as MDG 3 was concerned there were clear indications from all impact studies that members of SHGs, nearly all women, were substantially empowered. Their improved self-confidence, status in the families and communication abilities had an increased influence in decision-making in their households. The other indicators could not be assessed with the information available. Similarly, with MDGs 4 to 6, while the data suggested that in the post-SHG situation the health-care system was better utilized and that SHGs contributed to health awareness, impact on health indicators could not be fully assessed through the studies.

The largest and most comprehensive study to assess the impact and sustainability of SBLP on the socio-economic conditions of the individual members was undertaken by the NCAER. The study was conducted in six states, viz., Andhra Pradesh, Karnataka, Maharashtra, Odisha, Uttar Pradesh and Assam (NCAER, 2008). The reference year of the study was January to December 2006. In order to assess the impact of the SBLP the 'before and after' approach was primarily followed. The study covered 961 SHGs and 4,791 SHG members. The overall findings of the study suggested that the SBLP had significantly improved access to financial services of the rural poor and had considerable positive impact on the socio-economic conditions and reduction in poverty of SHG members and their households. The SBLP also reportedly empowered women members substantially and contributed to increased self-confidence and positive behavioural changes in the post-SHG period as compared to the pre-SHG period. Some of the major findings of the study were:

1. Net household income increased at 6.1% per year between the pre-SHG and post-SHG periods with livestock activity registering the highest growth at 11.2%.
2. Household consumption expenditure on food and non-food items increased annually at 5.1% and 5.4% respectively.
3. Annual expenditure per household on education and health increased at 5.6% and 5.5% respectively.
4. Average total savings per household increased significantly when compared to the base level with both physical and financial savings registering over 14% annual growth rates.
5. Net change in the value of consumer durable assets was ₹ 4,329 between the pre- and post-SHG periods.
6. Annual growth rate of assets was a high 9.9%.
7. On the average, each household borrowed an amount of ₹ 14,640 in the post-SHG period as compared to ₹ 5,384 in the pre-SHG situation.
8. More than 60% of the households indicated an increase in the ownership of productive assets in the post-SHG situation as compared to the pre-SHG situation.

9. The number of households reporting that they had taken loans was 93%, which was double the percentage during the pre-SHG situation.
10. The share of households living below the poverty line reduced from 58.3% in the pre-SHG situation to 33% in the post-SHG situation.
11. Ninety-two per cent of households reported that social empowerment of women had increased after membership in SHGs over a period of time. The share of women members reporting significant improvement in their self-confidence levels had gone up in the post-SHG period for all indicators.
12. More than 70% of women respondents reported improvements in their ability to face health problems and financial crises and 21% a significant improvement in their control over money with respect to buying of consumer durable assets.
13. As compared to the pre-SHG period showing greater participation in the public sphere, 49.4% of households had approached government officials to solve problems in the post-SHG period.

In addition the findings from case studies undertaken revealed that membership and participation in the group were socially and, to a reasonable extent, economically empowering. There were success stories of group enterprises as well, but these were not very remarkable.

As discussed earlier, it is possible to query the methodology of such quantitative surveys that use before–after comparisons. Also, the attribution of impact to a particular intervention has been seen to be a difficult proposition. As Swain and Varghese (2008) have noted, 'that by computing impact through a percentage difference of the means of members' variables pre- and post-SHG membership does not account for changes in observable characteristics nor broad economic changes through a control group due to the absence of appropriate corrections for selection bias'.

Swain and Varghese (2008) themselves evaluate the impact on a long-term impact parameter, namely asset creation, by comparing the impact *on current borrowers vis-à-vis future self-selected borrowers*. The data was collected from two representative districts in five different states (Andhra Pradesh, Tamil Nadu, Odisha, Uttar Pradesh and Maharashtra) in India for 2003. The sample consisted of 604 respondents from old SHGs, 186 from new SHGs and 52 non-members. Recall data for the year 2000 was also collected. They found that longer membership duration in SHGs positively impacted asset creation for all types of assets. However, they did not find any impact on short-term variables such as total current income. The impact on asset accumulation arose from the savings requirement of the programme and the income diversification made possible by accumulation of livestock.

In a subsequent paper, Swain and Varghese (2011), provide a detailed critique of the NCAER impact study (and the earlier NABARD studies) and the limitations of adopting the pre–post methodology and the use of recall data as well as the specific weaknesses related to estimation of impact in the NCAER study by covering only mature SHGs. They offer alternatives for more precise identification of impact and they recommend the use of pipeline methodology (by using self-selected SHG members from new SHGs still awaiting loans) for the control group. They also recommend the collection of panel data for SHGs for more rigorous impact assessment. As such the positive findings of both the NABARD studies and the NCAER study in respect of the SBLP have to be viewed with some caution.

8.3 Findings of Other Impact Assessments

Over the years several other studies examined the impact on the SHG members of various programmes. While these studies may also not pass as rigorous a test as the studies discussed earlier, some of them do use baseline data or adopt the pipeline method. The methodology and findings of a few major impact assessment studies are discussed below.

The mid-term assessment of the CASHE programme, which started in 1999, reported the findings of the impact of microfinance on the poor and women, bringing together the results of three studies in West Bengal, Odisha and Andhra Pradesh in 2003 (CASHE, 2006). The key strategy of CASHE was to build social capital by mobilizing women into SHGs and supporting these SHGs into becoming community-based microfinance institutions. With the support of the CASHE programme, 26 local organizations were transformed into operationally and financially sustainable microfinance organizations. In the case of Odisha and West Bengal, control groups of non-members or newly joined members were used for comparison. In the case of Andhra Pradesh, however, baseline data was available.

All three states reported increases in incomes of the households of the poor women members. In Odisha, the experimental group earned 15% more than the control group, in Andhra Pradesh the mid-term income was 20% higher than the baseline and in West Bengal, the experimental group's income was 53% higher than the control group. In all states, the difference in average annual household expenditure between the experimental and control group (or baseline) was about one-third (31% in Odisha, 32% in West Bengal and 38% in Andhra Pradesh). Expenditure in all three states on food, health, education and shelter was higher with the exception of West Bengal, where expenditures on health were found to be very low. For every type of asset, land, durables, and livestock, West Bengal and Andhra Pradesh registered an increase by comparison. In Odisha as well, for all three types of assets, other than mechanized agricultural equipment, the data indicates that the experimental group had a higher average value per household than the control group. Given these findings it could be generally said that SHG members increased their assets as a result of the CASHE programme.

A study was conducted by DHAN Foundation to examine the impact of the Kalanjiam Community Banking Programme (DHAN Foundation, 2004).[3] The study covered a total of 240 Kalanjiam members and 60 respondents from control groups. It was conducted in 31 blocks of Tamil Nadu where the project had existed for more than three years. Some of the major findings of the study were:

1. Average loan from the kalanjiam by a member increased along with the age of membership.
2. Significant reduction was observed in the debt burden of members to other informal sources and the rate of interest paid by them on such borrowing.
3. Savings of members increased significantly for kalanjiams of three to five years of age.
4. There was an increase in family income after the intervention of kalanjiams, being nearly 30% since the time of joining for members in the three- to five-year-old group category and 27% for members in the more than five years category.
5. Nearly a third of kalanjiam members reported an improvement in their access to food. However, 60% reported that they were already having sufficient food before joining the kalanjiam.
6. In comparing the empowerment status of kalanjiam women with that of the control group, findings showed the programme had empowered a considerable proportion of women and that the members showed progress in vital aspects of their life such as controlling husbands' habits, increased contribution of husbands to household work and in taking independent decisions regarding health, education and purchase and sale of assets and durable consumer goods.
7. More than 80% of kalanjiam members stated that they had developed skills to solve issues at family, kalanjiam and village levels after becoming members.
8. Finally, women living in rural areas started visiting banks and other public offices and showed increased involvement in public activities.

An impact assessment of the SHG programme of the PEDO was carried out in 2006 by the CmF, Jaipur (CmF, 2006). The study was conducted in three blocks of Dungarpur and 205 families were surveyed with 36 families acting as a control group. Members who had recently joined the programme

---

[3] The Kalanjiam project envisages empowering women by providing access to microfinance and stabilizing the livelihoods of the poor through promoting primary groups of women in village/slum neighbourhoods popularly called 'kalanjiams', which are further federated at panchayat and development block level.

in the same areas acted as the control sample. There was evidence of increased household income as also food security, which was much greater for the sample clients. In addition, it was found that in the sample group, 7.6% of women took their own decisions and 45.1% were involved in the decision-making process in their family, whereas in the control group, only 3.8% women took independent decisions and only 10.4% were involved in family decision-making. Awareness of and access to various government organizations and NGOs was significantly higher for sample women as compared to the control sample, even though in absolute terms it was still very low.

Another later study undertaken by SRTT reviewed the broad impacts of groups promoted by Kalanjiam, DHAN Foundation (Sriram, 2010). The Kalanjiam movement reaches its community banking programme through direct action but also by linking groups to mainstream banking, government and NGOs. The study looked at the overall differences in SHGs at different levels of maturity, while controlling for broad parameters of socio-economic zones and agro-climatic conditions in mature, young and new locations and locations where larger societal impacts were expected to be seen. Cross-sectional data were collected from 878 households in randomly selected groups. Without attributing causality it was found that:

1. Cash income per capita and per household were both higher in groups that had been in existence longer.
2. Generally locations with mature groups showed significantly better indicators than relatively new locations.
3. Though the role of moneylender had not diminished the households were able to negotiate better interest rates from this source.
4. A larger number of households in mature locations tended to have a larger portfolio of assets. The mature groups borrowed a smaller amount for survival-based purposes and a higher proportion towards working capital and asset purchase. Thus as compared to new locations, groups in mature locations were borrowing more for income augmenting purposes.

An evaluation of impact of SAGs promoted by MYRADA was conducted in 2009 (APMAS-MYRADA, 2009) to assess the quality, financial performance and impact of SHGs. The study covered 60 SHGs of ages varying from 8 to 20 years, with an average age of 10 years. Long-term changes reported by members at group, community and household level as a result of group activity were as follows:

At *SAG* level:

1. Adequate credit available
2. A large SHG common fund
3. Greater solidarity and greater respect from bankers

4. Linkages with other agencies and government departments
5. Lower dependence on promoting and external agencies

At the *community* level:

1. Good relations with the *gram panchayat* and educational institutions and campaigns
2. Reduction in interest rates of moneylenders from 5% to 2% per month—even becoming on par with that of SHGs
3. Attitudinal change in gender relations with men also being motivated with the performance of women's SAGs

At the *household* level:

1. Out of a sample of 120 SHG members, 94% moved to higher categories in wealth ranking.
2. Ninety-eight per cent of members were able to access three meals a day, ensuring food security for the families of SHG members.
3. As regards occupational mobility, while agriculture remained the mainstay, households depending on jobs increased from 5% to 21% and several households started new economic activity.
4. Benefits to household members accrued in multiple ways such as new and greater employment, higher education and improvement in health status, improvement in livestock and ability to conduct life cycle ceremonies.
5. Fifty per cent of households improved their housing and 23% purchased gold. Others reported savings in formal and informal institutions.
6. Nearly half of SHG member households purchased milch animals and about 15% of households purchased motorcycles, taxis, auto rickshaws and cycles.
7. As far as women's empowerment was concerned, self-confidence of SHG members, family support, access to family income, access to food, control on resources and assets, mobility of SHG members and an overall change in women's role had come about. In addition to traditional roles women acquired new activities and new roles such that a vast majority of women SHG members felt that there was a higher workload on them. However, women benefitted greatly through the massive reduction in gender disparity in various forms, and were also able to carve out a place for themselves in community and political activity.

The results support the view of MYRADA that only sustained participation in the SHG and repeated access to loans can bring about a major impact on the lives of the SHG members.

A large study by Deininger and Liu (2009) assessed the economic impacts of a longer-term exposure over two and a half to three years (2003–04 to 2005–06) to the World Bank–supported DPIP that promoted and strengthened SHGs in Andhra Pradesh. Based upon two rounds of data for a panel of 2,400 households, the authors used methodologies such as propensity score matching, double differences and pipeline comparisons to assess the economic impacts of this programme, which promoted and strengthened SHGs groups. *The analysis found that longer-term exposure to the programme had positive impacts on consumption, nutritional intake and asset accumulation.* This study had perhaps the most rigorous methodology and robust findings.

A recent NABARD study (Guha, 2010) on impact evaluation of SHGs assessed the impact of microenterprises on the livelihoods of SHG members taking up IGAs. The study assessed the impact of microenterprises or IGAs taken up by SHG members on their livelihoods. The reference year of the study was 2005–06 and it was conducted in Andhra Pradesh, Gujarat, Jammu and Kashmir and Himachal Pradesh. It covered 155 SHGs and 632 members of these SHGs. The study concluded that SBLP had brought positive socio-economic changes in the lives of the SHG members. The study found that the income of the members increased by 25% from the pre-SHG to the post-SHG situation in Andhra Pradesh, 38% in Gujarat and 81% in Jammu and Kashmir. Around 70% of households stated that the value of assets owned by them increased in the post-SHG joining period. Out of 632 members covered under the study 149 members had set up 30 different types of microenterprises and 158 members had taken up 31 different types of IGAs. Some of the SHG members had become active members of local committees like water committees and the gram sabha and joined ICDS as AWWs.

Findings of more recent studies on SHGs sponsored by NABARD in 2010–11 in Tamil Nadu (by Gandhigram Rural Institute in Karnataka) in the states of Rajasthan, Gujarat, Madhya Pradesh and Himachal Pradesh (Institute for Development Studies, Jaipur) and in Maharashtra (Centre for Study of Social Science, Pune)[4] were as follows:

1. SHGs have helped reduced dependence on local moneylenders.
2. Loans to individual members ranged from ₹ 10,000–20,000 in the majority of cases.

---

[4] As reported in Srinivasan (2011).

3. Bankers continue to take a long time to provide the first loan to SHGs.
4. The training given by SHPIs did not completely meet the skill requirements of members for taking up suitable IGAs.
5. Loans given by banks, which were linked to savings, were much lower than the actual requirements.
6. Asset creation out of SHG loans was seen in about 28% of cases while in other cases loans were used for consumption or purchase of utility items and household goods.
7. Competition among various SHPIs resulted in multiple memberships of SHG members.

8.4 Women's Empowerment

As evidenced from the earlier sections, apart from economic benefits through participation in SHG programmes, empowerment has another major domain of impact for women members and which has been largely positive. The constituency of women was compulsively involved in the consensus built around microfinance as a tool for poverty reduction in the 1990s since it held the promise of economic and social empowerment as well as contributing to eroding inegalitarian structures of patriarchy. Apart from the findings reported in the earlier sections, many studies have attempted to focus specifically on women's empowerment and gender relations. In the SHG context, a few major studies provide valuable insights into the functioning of SHGs and outcomes in relation to the gender and power relations being experienced by women SHG members. These studies add a further dimension to the understanding of SHG processes and impact.

An important contribution in this area has been that of Burra et al. (2005) which conceptualized empowerment of women in terms of their physical, economic, socio-cultural and political space, and asserted that expanding control and access and control over each element is central to their empowerment. They concluded that that there was no linear link between microcredit, poverty and empowerment. They reported findings of six studies of NGO and quasi-interventions including those by DHAN Foundation, Lokadrusti, Odisha, Swayam Shikshan Prayog, Maharashtra, and UNDP-SAPAP project, Andhra Pradesh, based upon SHGs or savings and credit groups. The case studies revealed that there were many elements to each space and that empowerment impact was better when access to more elements of each space was expanded. Thus, the four promoters above through a combination microcredit, grain banks, watershed programmes and women's own banks had a greater impact that those organizations that had focused only on microfinance.

As in other studies, it was found that women members pointed to improved access to economic resources and basic needs, increased mobility and greater control over income generated. However, there were limitations in that the interventions and impact were circumscribed by the poverty and gender sensitivity of the microfinance strategies of the intermediary organizations. Further, there were limitations to how much microfinance could achieve by way of impact on gender inequalities and poverty in terms of reaching the ultra-poor. Finally, the initial state of gender relations in a household, which may vary across households, mediated the outcomes of participation in microcredit programmes and on empowerment and gender impact.

The EDA-APMAS Light and Shades study (EDA Rural Systems, 2006) was based on a primary survey of 214 SHGs in 108 villages in 9 districts of four states, two southern (Andhra Pradesh and Karnataka) and two northern (Odisha and Rajasthan). The sample of the study was based on four years or older women's SHGs, mostly linked with banks before March 2000. It was not an impact study but was based instead on focus group discussions and semi-structured and individual interviews in an attempt to collect insights into the functioning of women's SHGs on their social role, their outreach and sustainability. Selected findings of the study are given below:

1. SHG members reflected a diverse membership covering different social and economic categories, with 51% of poor members as determined by an objective household wealth ranking.
2. While the proportion of very poor women members was lower for older SHGs, even after seven years of membership, half the members were still poor, including 13% very poor.
3. The dropout rate among members was moderate at less than 10% of overall membership. It was highest for the very poor. The main reasons were financial constraints and migration for employment.
4. SHG membership contributed to women's election to PRIs but more important than SHG support was the fact that members had political leanings and activities before joining SHGs.
5. Higher incidence of actions of social justice by women in Andhra Pradesh (25% of sample SHGs) reflected the actions of government and NGOs in that state. The incidence was lower in the other states.
6. Under one-third of SHGs had been involved in a range of community actions, usually one-off instances. One out of five SHGs attempted group enterprises of which under half appeared to be viable, though with relatively low earnings. Government contracts under the PDS and the midday meal scheme were found generally to be unviable for the SHG women members.
7. A high degree of equitable functioning was observed in respect of access to loans and their distribution among members and SHG leaders did not, beyond reasonable limits, corner a high proportion of the loans.

8. Eighteen per cent of the sample SHGs gave loans to non-members, suggesting that credit was being pushed on to SHGs without assessing their absorption capacity.

Nirantar (2007) examined the *impact on women members joining SHGs*. Processes were primarily seen in the context of capacity building, literacy and its relationship with power. The survey included 2,750 SHGs from 16 states of which 1,650 SHGs were formed under government programmes and 1,100 SHGs were formed under NGOs. Key findings of the study were as follows:

1. Very limited efforts were made on the part of sponsoring agencies to provide literacy training to SHG members.
2. Forty-seven per cent of groups formed under government programmes had not received any kind of capacity building input during the past two years and only 19% had received inputs on income generation and livelihoods.
3. Less than 50% of groups studied had made any kind of linkages with the panchayat and only 36% of groups had taken up any social issue in the past two years.
4. Only 11% of groups formed under government programmes had taken up issues such as domestic violence.
5. Fifty-eight per cent of the groups had not received any loans even though more than 90% of the groups were depositing their savings.
6. Most of the larger loans were given to leaders of the groups.
7. Literacy emerged as the single most important determinant of leadership in the groups, with 69% of the women in leadership roles being literate.
8. Group leaders had much greater opportunity to receive capacity building inputs and access resources coming to the groups.
9. Forty-six per cent of the large loans were availed of by group leaders although they constituted only 13% of the total membership. This suggests that literacy creates access to leadership, which in turn leads to access to other opportunities, thereby creating access to power within SHGs.

While many of the findings of the two studies were common the Nirantar study provided less positive results as compared to the Light and Shades Study especially in respect of the degree of equity of access both to loans and training opportunities between members. In contrast to some of the other studies, the Nirantar study generally contained reservations about the degree and equity of the positive impact experienced by the women SHG members.

However, many smaller studies conducted by SHG promoters and researchers at the state or district level show that SHG programmes result in significant women's empowerment, along lines reported in the studies discussed earlier. From among the larger studies, Swain and Wallentin (2007) estimated the mean level of women's empowerment for the years 2003 and 2000 (recall data) while measuring the impact of the SHG programme. Their study was based on data collected from five different states in India for 1,000 households, both SHG and non-SHG. Using quasi-experimental sampling design, one thousand households both SHG and non-SHG were surveyed. Their analysis showed that there was *a significant increase in women's empowerment of the SHG members* group while no significant change was observed on the average for the control group members. The results also suggested that *additional services like training, awareness raising and other activities were an important determinant of the degree of impact.*

8.5 Conclusions

Notwithstanding the shortcomings of the study methodologies and the limited scope of some of the studies these reviews and evaluations of SHG-based microfinance programmes suggest that participation in SHGs has had the following positive impacts:

- Helped promote the savings habit and increased the savings of SHG members.
- Improved their access to credit from mainstream financing agencies.
- Reduced the dependence on moneylenders through availability of credit at lower rates.
- Increased the use of loans for IGAs.
- Yielded moderate economic benefits in the form of higher household incomes and food security and in asset holdings.
- Contributed to increased household employment and poverty reduction.
- Resulted in empowerment benefits to women, who through the experience of self-management of the SHG acquired self-confidence and voice in the household and in the community.

Studies and anecdotal evidence, field impressions and communications and reports from organizations also suggest:

- Contrary to the vision of SHG development, SHG membership is quite broad-based and members do not generally constitute the poorest.

- There is greater evidence of social empowerment rather than significant and consistent economic impact, except in the case of families involved in small business.

A selection of case studies illustrating household-level outcomes across a cross section of regions and activities drawn from various promoters and sources is given in Appendix 10.

Generally speaking, impact evaluations of SHGs and SHG federations have been sporadic undertakings rather than part of any comprehensive impact monitoring exercise. It is fairly clear that impact assessment in microfinance, more especially of SHGs and federated structures based on them, is still undeveloped. It would appear that pressure is not felt by NGO facilitators or banks to undertake impact monitoring and assessment unless directed to do so by donors or for studies undertaken by NABARD, with the necessary funds being provided for the exercise.

Besides, with the SHG acting as a financial intermediary, transactions between the SHG and its members are not usually recorded at higher levels. As a result loan tracking as also tracking the stream of benefits accruing at the individual or family level is not possible. As SHGs relinquish some of their functions to cluster and higher-level federations, the roles and responsibilities, MIS requirements and training to assess programme effectiveness need to be planned at different levels. This will help to generate impact information at the appropriate level both for 'proving impact' as well as 'improving practice' of microbanking through SHGs.

There have been considerable numbers of more rigorous attempts to evaluate the impact of MFI's on their clients, as opposed to that of SHGs, both in India and internationally, perhaps because they have attracted large amounts of foreign aid and investment, whereas SHGs have mainly been financed by existing banks, and although the total amounts are substantial they are quite small in the context of most banks' total operations. It is difficult to compare the SHG impact evaluations that have been referred to in this chapter, and the larger numbers of MFI impact studies, and it would probably be impossible to compare both in one study, partly because so many women are both members of SHGs and clients of MFIs, but in general the impression seems to be that the overall impact of SHG membership is more positive than for MFI clients.

FUTURE DIRECTIONS

9

As we complete two decades of SBLP it is time to take stock of where SHGs stand in their role as financial intermediaries. What is the learning from the experience of SBLP? Are SHGs fulfilling the role expected of them? What are the strengths and weakness of the SHG movement as it has grown and evolved? What new opportunities and challenges have emerged? Do SHGs have to be positioned differently now?

9.1 SHG MODEL OF FINANCIAL INTERMEDIATION: STRENGTHS AND WEAKNESSES

One of the fascinating aspects of SHG development in India is that a host of players have promoted SHGs for a wide range of purposes, in varied contexts and with different levels of available resources. While some elements may be common to all or most SHGs, their character and purpose can be quite different making for exceptional diversity in their approaches and outcomes. The one important common element has been that of regular thrift by SHG members. This has enabled, along with other requirements, a large, even predominant, number of SHGs to go on to be linked to banks. It is, however, necessary to distinguish between regular thrift as an end in itself, and as a qualification for loans and the rather large number of SHGs which are not borrowing would appear to confirm this point. SHGs are best seen not only as a route to loans, but as a route to financial inclusion which would also cover access to services for savings, insurance, pensions and remittances. An increasingly large proportion of SHGs are being federated with others for some common goals and activities. The purpose for which SHGs were formed and priorities in their agenda included a range of economic and social objectives. Indeed, the concept of self-help and self-reliance led to the formation of other SHG-like groups of village women and men, taking different forms and shapes, under various projects and by NGO promoters. For some NGOs, SHGs were but one of a set of small group 'types' that could be drawn upon for development activity. Several such NGOs considered an excessive preoccupation with financial matters as limited and detrimental to a broader vision encompassing livelihoods of the poor. For other promoters the 'affinity' required for successful SHGs could be supplanted by shared economic activity or occupation as the defining criterion for people coming together. With the confines of SHGs with the objective of financial intermediation, though initial savings was a prerequisite, the emphasis was clearly on provision of credit. Without it being proclaimed, the SBLP represented an innovation which, at least to begin with unlike the ongoing IRDP, did not involve explicit grants or capital or subsidies to member-clients.[1] *Over time, it emerged that all SHGs were not coming together merely for credit or only for credit.* Accordingly, SHPAs, particularly NGOs, experimented with different approaches with some degree of success. Apart from its diversity, as the SHG movement expanded it contributed to the development infrastructure creating immense possibilities of its utilization in both financial and non-financial activities.

The effect of this type of development has been that SHGs have contributed to the needs of their membership in different ways in different areas with no particular 'model' predominating. While the demand for credit has generally driven SHG formation and development, it is also been the case that SHGs have come together for savings and for group enterprise (see case studies in Appendix 10) and also for collective action in the social sphere. However, this phenomenon has its flip side too. Even today there is no common understanding among stakeholders regarding the critical interventions necessary in the lifecycle of an SHG. NABARD is mainly concerned till the SHG gets its first credit linkage with the bank. The banks would prefer to have SHPI involvement for assistance in recoveries. NGOs like MYRADA and DHAN, which are concerned with the holistic development of the poor, see the need for longer-term interventions, institutional development and empowerment. The MoRD in pursuing the NRLM seems to see the SHG as a virtually independent, extended arm of the mainstream banking institutions, which would play an important role in livelihood strengthening and development.

Equally, given the varied context and experience, it is difficult to pin down elements of 'good practice' among SHGs or any kind of minimum requirements for their sound functioning. In the early days, great store was set by rotation of leadership, bookkeeping skills among members and frequency of meetings. Over time these requirements have ceased to be

---

[1] It is not entirely coincidental that it was introduced not long after the major loan waiver of 1990 which served to seriously undermine the morale of bankers and around the time of the economic reforms of 1991 which ushered in the era of liberalization.

non-negotiable. This has not necessarily meant that SHGs invariably provide useful services to their members, or opportunities for activities and actions for mutual benefit. Indeed, there are misgivings about the true numbers of active SHGs due to unreliable data and the absence of data on repeat loans and fate of SHGs linked in earlier years (as discussed in Chapter 3). Besides, *practitioners and researchers assess that not more than a third of SHGs nationwide would be of good quality in that they are functioning as intended and where members' savings are secure.* This must raise questions about the investment cost incurred to build the SHG infrastructure—more so since SHGs need not necessarily be a permanent institutional form.

In addition to concern about the quality and cost of SHG promotion, several issue discussed elsewhere continue to be of importance. First, the risks posed to the democratic functioning of SHGs (and even SHG federations) by local elites, especially in view of the increasing importance of SHGs both as a political force and as a channel for government benefits. This is exacerbated by lack of awareness among members of the state of SHG affairs and accounts, non-replacement of leaders and cornering of loans and other benefits by the SHG leadership of a few members. Where SHPI monitoring and influence are strong, and where federated structures have been put in place the situation is somewhat better. However, as also discussed in Chapter 4, overall, the independence and role of SHGs as financial intermediaries is undermined both in federated structures and where they are dependent on NGO- or NBFC-MFIs for loans.

In the context of the competition and tension between the MFI and SHG models, Aloysius Prakash Fernandez poses the question of whether the last mile is controlled by the NBFC or the SHG. Unlike the staff of the MFIs, SAGs (good ones) provide the space at the last mile to cope with diversity and to customize products. They also have a built-in insurance (savings, fines, etc.) which provide a cushion that helps to overcome unexpected external and internal situations which affect cash flow of the member. However, it requires investment to build good groups through institutional capacity building towards their empowerment. Fernandez and Girija Srinivasan, independent consultant favour linking SHGs through NBFCs since banks are unable to drive SBLP for a variety of reasons. These include staff constraints and the consolidation of RRBs making them bigger and more profit-oriented, such that they do not find small loans viable. For this reason, all major SHPIs have an MFI of their own—MYRADA, DHAN, Hand in Hand, BWDA, SKDRDP—and now the government of Andhra Pradesh.

Another angle to SHGs as financial intermediaries is that their absorption power is limited—that in most regions beyond immediate consumption requirements there are limits to the absorption of credit by SHGs and after two or three loan cycles. Further, with their limited capacity to handle larger loans, SHGs may experience a phenomenon similar to that of the Peter

Principle wherein SHGs 'rise to the level of their own incompetence', i.e., borrow and return loans from banks until they are unable or unwilling to do so. This level could vary for different SHGs. The important empirical question is whether constraints exist on the supply side on the part of the banking system or on the demand side or both.

Much blame has been laid at the door of the banks for their failure to extend the outreach of their SHG operations. According to Sitaramachandra Machiraju, World Bank,[2] the banking sector in the poorest states is characterized by few banking outlets which are understaffed to take the transaction load (the age profile is also turning adverse) and their business outlook does not cover local area development. This coexists with misaligned incentives in the rural banking sector. As a result there is an institutional void in the last mile financial service delivery. Mutuals like SHG Federations, corporate/NGO BCs, NABFINS, etc., can effectively fill this void in the last mile, if targeted investments are made in institutional innovations and alternate business models for priming and catalyzing the formal financial sector in the high poverty areas. SHGs can fill the critical gap of co-creating and delivering financial services with a range of BCs and customer service points (CSPs) with interoperable systems. This emphasizes the continued relevance and role of SHGs in financial intermediation.

9.2 SHG Banking: Taking Stock

Some practitioners believe that the golden period of SBLP was from 1995 to 2000 when it helped recover from the old loan waiver shock of 1990 and pure SHG bank linkage brought about a new discipline with good repayments.[3] With the reformulated anti-poverty programme SGSY, from about year 2000 government programmes took the lead in SHG development. Around that time the first instances of 'poaching' of NGO groups by government agencies to fulfil their targets were reported.[4] Though NABARD was involved in SGSY it was not able to counter the effects of the SGSY model. Interestingly, though SGSY itself was a bank linkage programme, but with a back-ended subsidy, tension came about between the policymakers of the SBLP and the SGSY on the subsidy issue. It became clear that there was need for convergence between the two programmes with differences to be

---

[2] Personal communication.
[3] Personal interview with D. Narendranath.
[4] Notably in Andhra Pradesh, but also elsewhere, it was natural for existing SHG members to be attracted to the benefits on offer from the SGSY and to become members of multiple groups. Related to this was the issue of excluding non-BPL members from SHGs which broke many preexisting groups.

resolved at higher levels. This did not happen, and the disconnect between the two programmes continues to this day. (While the SGSY has not been implemented on the same scale as the IRDP, in several states such as Assam, Madhya Pradesh, and Bihar the strength of the SHGs promoted under SGSY is considerably in excess of the SBLP SHGs.)

Around the year 2000 the innovation of SHG federations, first supported among wholesalers by FWWB, provided the platform for sustainable SHG operations and the SHG federation model was adopted by many SHPAs as also by government promoters. *The role of federations continues to be a contested one which places the some state governments and NABARD in different camps.* As discussed in Chapters 5 and 7 there is a clear role for federations as financial intermediaries (at different levels, primary and secondary) under government programmes in Andhra Pradesh and Tamil Nadu and other states. NABARD officials have, however, raised questions about federations as suitable financial intermediaries both on account of their limited capacity as well as the possibility of political or elite capture. More recently, as discussed in Chapter 7, *the possibilities of technology in reducing transaction costs and enabling banking through BCs and BFs*[5] *may provide alternatives to federations as intermediaries in delivering microcredit and wider financial services.* NABARD, however, has provided selected support to a federation promoted by Chaitanya and also supports a replication of the IKP model from Andhra Pradesh in Uttar Pradesh by Rajiv Gandhi Mahila Vikas Pariyojana (RGMVP).

Mention has been made of the fact that NABARD's promotion of the SHG model moved down from top gear around 2003–04 by which time the target of a million SHGs set for 2008 had been achieved. With the emergence of private banks (particularly ICICI Bank) in support of MFIs, big and small, through the 'partnership model'[6] a significant increase in the credit flow to MFIs was made possible. Apart from attracting all kinds of MFIs this also led NABARD through its newly designated Microfinance Development and Equity Fund in 2007–08 to start providing capital support to MFIs, including start-ups[7] as part of a new thrust in favour of JLG the model. SIDBI's transformation loan contributed to making MFIs out of many NGOs which resulted in their focusing more on commercialized delivery of microcredit rather than the wider development agenda. The managed funds from ICICI Bank caused the NGO-MFI sector to grow at an unsustainable pace with the bank giving loans on its books to clients whom they knew nothing

---

[5] These could, of course, also be SHG federations registered as societies, trusts or cooperatives, or even, as per RBI circular dated 28 September 2010, the SHG functionaries themselves.

[6] Illustrated in Appendix 9.

[7] Forty MFIs had been sanctioned capital support by NABARD to the extent of ₹ 274 million by March 2011 (NABARD, 2011).

about. This model was discontinued peremptorily since it did not meet RBI's newly introduced Know Your Customer (KYC) norms. This was quite disastrous for the sector as a whole, as well as for SHGs and their members who were clients of various MFIs.[8] It also affected the several leading NGOs (Chapter 4) which had opted for the partnership model through in-house NBFCs in seeking larger loans for their SHGs. This aggressive lending had its repercussions in the form of the Andhra crisis of 2006 which left a lasting negative impact on both microfinance and SHG clients.

Notwithstanding this setback the way was paved for the growth of MFIs, which not only outstripped the growth[9] of SHGs but became a serious factor affecting SHG lending and SHG repayment. In their quest for exponential growth the NBFC MFIs are widely reported and accepted to have split well-functioning SHGs to form JLGs[10] and SHG members buckled under the pressure of MFIs that offered multiple loans. With weekly repayment obligations to MFIs and their use of coercive practices, women found it difficult to repay their loans to SHGs, resulting in SHGs defaulting to banks. For banks too, lending to MFIs was an easier route to fulfil the targets of priority sector lending.

The 2010 Andhra crisis brought the two channels of flow of credit in serious confrontation. Measures undertaken against MFIs in the wake of suicides by borrowers through the enactment of a contentious ordinance severely restrained the freedom of the MFIs to operate in Andhra Pradesh. This in turn led to charges being laid at the door of the state government that it was acting maliciously in order to favour the clients of its SHG programmes. The crisis had emerged because of problems being exacerbated by many MFI practices including multiple lending that also involved SHG members who were borrowing from MFIs. As a result, SHG members were also debarred from being members of more than one SHG. While *MFI lending* came to a grinding halt as a result, particularly in Andhra Pradesh, the effect has also been felt on *bank lending* not only to MFIs which was more or less suspended in all the major states (and is only recovering sporadically at the time of writing) but also *lending to SHGs* which declined substantially—as discussed in Chapter 3. As with the withdrawal of the partnership model this development also affected several of those NGO-promoted MFIs lending to SHGs referred to in Chapter 4.

---

[8] M.S. Sriram, personal interview.

[9] Estimates of the client outreach of SHGs and MFIs show that while SHG clients (borrowers with outstanding accounts) grew from 38 million in 2006–07 to 62.5 million during 2010–11, MFI clients increased in number from 10 million to 31.4 million during the same period (Srinivasan, 2011).

[10] Aloysius Fernandez, in a personal interview, was also of the opinion that the crisis was because of the manner in which the MFIs formed the JLGs. The phenomenon of MFIs 'riding' on preexisting SHGs and state governments expressing discomfort at such 'poaching' has also been referred to in Reddy (2011).

The situation in Andhra Pradesh has become the marker by which to the judge the condition and the future both of microfinance as a whole as well as the SHG programme since the developments here have far-reaching effects spreading to other major states as well. Despite the fact that MFI lending has come to a standstill, according to one leading stakeholder,[11] the current situation of government-supported SHGs, especially in Andhra Pradesh, is a major source of concern as well. Weekly meetings are monotonous and routine and are not utilized as a forum to discuss social issues. In many cases, meetings are over in a few minutes after the collection of savings contributions. This situation stems from the failure of capacity builders to create a sense of ownership among SHG members and appropriate systems and processes. As far as annual planning in SHGs and federations and preparation of microcredit plans is concerned, these too are done in a routine rather than a holistic manner. *Though microcredit plans are attached to SHG loan applications, these are disregarded by bankers,* who decide the loan amount adopting their own criteria and in many cases encourage the equal distribution of bank loans among SHG members. This compromises the larger empowerment agenda of SHGs. In addition to this, bankers often indulge in practices such as impounding SHG savings, retaining a portion of the SHG loan as fixed deposit, introducing hindrances in savings withdrawal and forcibly selling insurance to SHG members. Undesirable practices of the banking system also include the transfer of funds from the SHG savings account into its loan account upon sanction of the bank loan without informing the SHG members. In areas where 'total financial inclusion'[12] has been implemented in Andhra Pradesh, there is data to support that defaults by SHGs have gone up. These practices have been reported in various studies conducted by APMAS. Finally, the government's practice of providing interest subsidy, though well-intentioned, has proved to be detrimental to the accumulation of SHG savings and retained surpluses as a source of funds for the credit requirements of SHG members.

While banks have lent large sums to SHGs it would appear that these have not been adequate and that there is a need to also look at innovations in the SHG–bank linkage *model* since the inability of *banks to adequately respond to the credit needs of the SHGs,* has allowed the ingress of MFIs into SHGs. The loan tenure has become a major issue for groups because loans are generally being given by banks for a period of two to three years, though cash credit limits (CCLs) are now also becoming more common. This has meant that no fresh loans can be taken by SHGs for a long time until the previous loan is cleared. There has also been an absence of innovation by banks in terms of products for the poor. In addition to these

---

[11] Personal interview with C.S. Reddy, CEO, APMAS.
[12] Described in Chapter 5.

shortcomings, there is the *overburdening of SHGs in Andhra Pradesh by their being given responsibilities in multiple overlapping projects and government programmes and even being mobilized by force to join political meetings.* The result has been an insensitivity of the needs and aspirations of SHG women with groups being formed more for the ease of implementation of government projects.

Reddy Subrahmanyam[13] feels there is a need to develop more appropriate credit institutions that are owned by the community and work for the poor. With the growth of SBLP tapering off radical measures need to be taken by the state governments. There was the need to bring in a different focus and new enthusiasm. The traditional way in which things were done may not work any longer particularly when SHG members were becoming economically better off. When the next generation of SHGs is organized, initiatives like the replication of the Anand dairy model would be attempted. The interest subsidy provided by the Andhra Pradesh government covered about 900,000 loan accounts which were getting about ₹ 5.5 billion, i.e., ₹ 5,000 per group or ₹ 500 per person for building the repayment culture. B. Rajsekhar[14] while admitting to some of the problems related to sharing out of loans and the ineffectiveness of microcredit plans in Andhra Pradesh suggested that these were relatively few instances in nearly a million SHGs in the state. He stated that the confidence of bankers in SHG lending was being built up with measures such as bank mithras, mobile technology and GIS mapping of defaulting SHGs by which repayments of banks can be assured. In fact, SERP had let it be known to bankers that repayment of SHG loans was the responsibility of SERP, the state government implementation agency. This had increased the confidence of the banks in lending to SHGs and they were also coming forward to lend to the MSs.

9.3 NABARD AND THE BANKING SYSTEM

A lot of the criticism, merited and unmerited, is levelled at NABARD for the limited support received by SHGs from the banking system. However, it needs to be stated upfront that SBLP was visualized as supplementary to the efforts of the banks to reach the rural poor and to meet credit needs for consumption and/or involvement in small-time IGAs. The urban poor were not on the radar of NABARD and SBLP was introduced only with limited objectives and expectations. The thinking was that an individual requiring a large loan should approach the bank branch and show his/her credit history with the SHG to obtain additional credit.

---

[13] Personal interview.
[14] Personal interview.

At the time of the launch of SBLP no clear ideas existed about how the programme would evolve. The question of graduation of borrowers to other mainstream bank products and programmes was not seriously examined. Mr Y.C. Nanda, former Chairman of NABARD at the time of the rapid expansion phase of SHGs at the turn of the century, admits to *a major error of judgment regarding the SBLP through target-chasing in NABARD, which resulted in increasingly less attention being paid to the qualitative aspects.*[15] He observes that bank linkage is process-oriented work, which requires painstaking effort, as part of the strategy to build groups and replace traditional collateral by group liability. The transfer of certain functions/jobs by banks to the SHGs (sanctioning, monitoring and recovery of individual loans) required the building of skills of SHG members and creating conditions for the SHG to ensure financial discipline. Forming SHGs hurriedly towards fulfilment of targets under SGSY and also by NGOs as an add-on activity through small grants from NABARD resulted in poor quality groups.[16] Right from the start, SHPAs have questioned the level and the basis of NABARD scales of support for SHG promotion. A large number of SHPAs that rely on NABARD have no other source of funds for SHG promotion and are unable to leverage the balance amount from other sources. The quality and sustainability of the SHGs thus promoted becomes seriously compromised.

As the SHGs have accessed larger loans, going up to ₹ 500,000 and more, the loans being availed in turn by individual borrowers became too large for the principle of mutual help and collective liability to sustain. Accordingly, *the need is being increasingly felt for 'graduation' of SHG members to individual loans or to smaller joint liability models.* While there was some discussion about this issue in the past nothing has been done so far. This remains as an area on which further work needs to be done.

Sudha Kothari and Kalpana Pant[17] were of the view that NABARD has not done much over the last 20 years and is not playing a pivotal function

---

[15] In a candid interview with ACCESS Development Services for the Microfinance Summit 2011 (similar to the admission by RBI Governor Y.V. Reddy of his mistake in trusting NBFC-MFIs [Reddy, 2011]), Y.C. Nanda states about the SBLP:

I feel I made serious errors of judgment as MD/Chairman of NABARD regarding this programme which are responsible for the programme's failure to exploit the full potential of this great mobilisation effort. I hope NABARD would modify the programme and the earlier mistakes (mainly my mistakes) would be rectified.

[16] The grants sanctioned by NABARD were intended originally to cover the extra out-of-pocket costs that NGOs might incur in promoting an SHG in a community where they were working anyway. The notion of the NGO as specialist SHPI only came along later.

[17] Personal interview.

in the design and implementation of NRLM either. According to them, NABARD has virtually handed over the whole SHG model to the banks on a platter without any innovative measures of its own. Nor did NABARD and banks invest in building MIS structures and software for federations. NABARD needs to consider possibilities of models which are differ from monolithic structures. NABARD did, however, roll out one of the largest public sector training programmes for bankers and NGOs, and it helped to establish vast numbers of SHGs.

A major stakeholder in SBLP which does not have the same visibility in the discourse is the banking sector. It is clear by now that *there is support for SBLP among the public sector banks at the corporate level*, and as far as the RRBs and the cooperative banks are concerned, they are even more natural partners of SHGs. *It is now possible for informal groups like SHGs to become members of the primary agricultural credit societies and to become customers of cooperative banks.* The performance of cooperative banks in SBLP is picking up only now and commercial banks remain the most active promoters of SBLP. It is disquieting to find the long list of complaints that have been placed at the door of the banks. It would seem that the sensitization of bank managers to serving this class of clientele, which has been ongoing process for decades, needs to be further strengthened such that SHG needs can be fulfilled by the banks as planned. Another issue pertaining to banks is their reluctance to bear the costs of the infrastructure for financial services that needs to be built for lending through SHGs. While some banks have come forward to pay fees and commissions to agents and other SHPAs, this is far from a universal phenomenon. Another area of disquiet in respect of banks is the lack of innovative products on offer to SHGs and their failure to respond to the financial needs, particularly in regards to savings products. Finally, the reluctance of banks to lend to SHG federations has meant that this channel has not been able to develop as an additional source of funds for SHGs. Banks, however, will be required to play their role in financing the federations and SHGs under the NRLM. One of the recent developments in respect of the SHG programme in Andhra Pradesh has been the formation of the SHGs' own 'bank' after being unable to meet their diversified credit needs from the banking system. While the banks had been happy to provide high-ticket loans to the large MFIs, they had been lukewarm towards federations. Even now, most banks have appointed BCs and BFs and piloted technological innovations as part of the financial inclusion agenda but mainly through bypassing SHGs to serve individual clients.[18] Meeting targets for opening no-frills accounts, may have led to banks ignoring 'real' accounts such as millions of SHG

---

[18] The opening of millions of 'no-frills savings accounts' for the families excluded from banking services that has been the hallmark of this initiative has been much criticized as studies showed that only a small percentage of these accounts were operative.

members have opened with the banks to which they were 'linked'. Banks need to be persuaded to be more positive in similarly supporting SBLP as part of the financial inclusion agenda—support for which has been somewhat uneven across regions, banking agencies and as between different public sectors banks.

9.4 STAKEHOLDER VIEWS ON NEXT PHASE OF SHG DEVELOPMENT

The discussions at a Round Table organized by ACCESS Development Services in collaboration with the NRLM on the next phase of development of the SHG model on 29 September 2011 (ACCESS Development Services, 2011) to assess and explore future strategies to give momentum to the SHG programme to reach and impact the poor reflected the considered opinions of a wide range of stakeholders. The feedback from the Round Table suggested that SHGs were *in need of investment in institutional capacity building and phased expansion.* Many felt that the *in-built subsidy component in national schemes such as the SGSY had diluted the main objectives of the model, since it clashed with the concept of SHGs as self-reliant units.* The *limitations of the SBLP that were identified principally related to the lack of innovation in policy.* It was felt that the *model lost its original focus of forming groups of the poorest for collective action* and social empowerment. Some of the areas that needed attention included provision of savings products for the poor and to address *problems of developing last mile connectivity to enable access to financial services. Since the basic premise of the SHG model is being diluted, building institutions of the poor under the NRLM would be a major challenge.* The role of NABARD in SHG development covered various financial capacity building and group formation aspects but there have been suggestions that, at the same time, there was *little policy innovation* after the success of the initial years while there was need for continuous review and revitalization. The *SBLP was undoubtedly credit-focused.* There have been doubts also whether SHGs have really reached the poorest and whether SHGs narrowly focused on credit can help the poorest break out of poverty. There were also concerns that the *savings function had not been adequately developed* under the SBLP and that beyond a point SHGs were not equipped to handle large loans.

There was a consensus among stakeholders that *sustained handholding and capacity building of SHGs and SHG-based institutions was required* and the failure to provide this has been a factor responsible for the mixed results and outcomes that are observed. The mistake was to imagine that support was needed only until SHGs were 'linked' and that then they would not need any help thereafter. There are several outstanding concerns also about the quality of groups that have been promoted and of the phenomenon of group fatigue and also of banker fatigue in catering to these small-sized clients. *The phenomenon of equal distribution of loans among group members has also emerged as an issue, which effectively questions the role of SHGs in financial intermediation.*

As far as NABARD was concerned, though it had provided good support to the SBLP, there was the *absence of a long-term vision.* There was a concern also that the way money is allocated for SHG promotion, the space for NGOs is shrinking with the government, corporates and banks competing with them and the policy environment also becoming hostile for charitable societies. The Round Table also noted the emergence of federations as higher-level institutions based on SHGs and the role taken up by them as financial intermediaries, service providers and livelihood promoters, with second-generation organizations taking up the formation of producer companies. Related to this was the need to invest in strong systems such as internal audit mechanisms and sound MIS for SHG and their federations. This would have to be undertaken at various levels in the form of investment in a cadre of local resource persons in building capacities of federation board and staff members and also of community resource centres at district or state levels. There was need also to *consider bulk lending to federations or to creatively use them as BCs for viable financial services delivery.* An important issue in this context was that whether the ownership of the SHG based interventions lies more with the promoting agencies, government agencies or apex agencies or with these unregistered cooperatives themselves. Some of the proposals from round table participants to make the SBLP effective were as follows:

1. *Policy changes*

   • It was felt that with the advent of the NRLM, NABARD as the originator of the bank linkage programme needs to align as an institution with the NRLM. NABARD should have a policy for SHG and federation promotion linking both together. Federations take up to eight years to emerge as sustainable self-managed institutions and will require long-term assistance.

   • NRLM is an unconventional programme, which requires large-scale investment of about ₹ 100,000 per target household over 10 years, and the financial structure of the country should be geared for this.

   • The financial inclusion agenda of the government needs to be merged with SBLP to form the banking architecture required to implement NRLM. For this product development, investment in technology and strong MIS for SHGs would be required with financial education as a pre-requisite. Banks should be convinced that lending to SHGs is a value proposition, rather than an anti-poverty scheme.

- There is a need to build the capabilities of SHPAs. Region-specific policies for SBLP are required according to the geographical context. Cost of promotion to form new SHGs of ₹ 7,500 per SHG that is proposed under the NRLM does not take into account the differential investment required for capacity building of existing SHGs.
- The implementation of NRLM requires a large number of community professionals. It is necessary to think about the large-scale investment required to build this human and social capital.
- The BC model should be adjusted for it to be viable and adaptable throughout the country and customized to the needs of the clients.

2. *Institutional arrangements necessary for making SBLP effective*

- Banks could support SHG federations promoted by SHPAs to help attract professionals and capacity building institutions for SHG promotion. PACS could emerge as an important institutional arrangement for bank linkage following their success in West Bengal.
- Indian Postal Service can be involved in provision of financial services to SHGs lending. Mobile banking could be promoted for servicing remote and inaccessible villages.

9.5 THE NRLM FACTOR

The IKP in Andhra Pradesh has been the model for the NRLM which is set to be introduced in 12 states. A discussion on the framework of the NRLM has been carried out in Chapter 5. The implementation of this programme has the potential to change the entire complexion of the SHG movement as it stands in the country. Through the medium of SHGs and their federations, it seeks to drive a 'demand-driven', long-term programme for livelihood development of the target population of the poor. Several questions, large and small, can be raised in regard to the NRLM framework and implementation plan. As far as the SBLP is concerned, banks are likely to be drawn in to finance the credit plans prepared at different levels on an unprecedented scale under the NRLM. There appears to be little scope for NABARD to exercise leadership in respect of the modalities of the involvement of the banks in the NRLM. Several issues have emerged related to the NRLM approach and the manner in which it involves SHGs and their promoters. A cross section of views of leading NGO figures, government officials and consultants are discussed below.[19]

Aloysius P. Fernandez of MYRADA asks whether the government is best placed to build institutions. According to him, focus on skills training is good but the NRLM should not be implemented like NREGA in a top down

---

[19] Based on personal interviews with the author.

fashion. Problems lie in lack of clarity on who will take the lead and drive the programme in terms of conceptualization rather than implementation. Another question is whether federations should act as financial intermediaries.

D. Narendranath of PRADAN is of the view that Andhra Pradesh is a leading example of a state that has taken over the work of NGOs successfully and this is a model which should be upheld and emulated. If a group conforms to the norms set, then NRLM should cover this group even if it is formed by an NGO, and make NGOs their partners. PRADAN is advocating for at least 25% to 30% of blocks to be given to NGOs and provide equal opportunity to them in implementation. Government has presently entrusted 10% of blocks to NGOs under the framework of NRLM.

Girish Sohani of BAIF comments that NRLM has incorporated a very strong Andhra Pradesh influence that the starting point is SHGs, but he has several reservations on this and feels that *there are groups other than SHGs*, which could be the starting point. In earlier years there was no interaction between NGOs and government and NGOs were interacting with donor agencies for implementation of programmes. However, this is changing with government coming up with innovative programmes such as NRLM. Though most path-breaking work happens outside standard government programmes, for achieving scale there is no option but to seek government support. Innovation can be locally driven and should happen outside government. Government is needed to ensure the material possibility of achieving scale, along with the necessary resource allocation. Ultimately, an urgent transformation is needed in the way government delivers through the line departments.

Reddy Subrahmanyam, government of Andhra Pradesh, while discussing the impact of the NRLM on Andhra Pradesh believes that it would not change things very much excepting that some women from Andhra Pradesh would find employment in other states as trainers. Other issues which would need to be looked at include additional resource flows into the sector and the impact of provisions such as increased involvement of PRIs in the delivery system. Though traditionally PRIs in Andhra Pradesh have been weak, and there have been few attempts to strengthen them based on the underlying fear that PRIs today represent interests of better-off sections. It is felt that and given a chance they will put down SHGs, since any organization of poor is a threat to them. Even in NREGA, the role of PRIs is 'theoretical' and they have been kept at an arm's length.

Sudha Kothari and Kalpana Pant, Chaitanya, believe that the project design of NRLM is very practical; however, there are issues in implementation, beginning with the fact that preparation of the plan for NRLM is outsourced, which compromises the flexibility of the project.

Usha Padhee, Former Director, Mission Shakti is of the opinion that within NRLM, there are potential problems related to the scale of implementation and the coordination required of different departments.

There is need for convergence in implementation but the different departments are unable to grasp this reality.

C.S. Reddy of APMAS stresses that NRLM must partner with NGOs in SHG development and national banks should provide supplementary finance to SHGs. With an NGO-intensive approach (10% of the blocks) there is greater emphasis on the livelihoods aspect, including agriculture and allied services. A non-intensive approach is being designed, based on recommendations of a working group, where there is discussion on implementing NRLM in more blocks across the country and where they are looking at SHGs as institutions of the poor rather than just as starting points in the NRLM framework. NRLM also focuses on job creation—10 million jobs and 6 million enterprises are to be created along with emphasis on mobilization and institution building. *NRLM in essence emphasizes livelihood organizations rather than federations and SHGs models.* NRLM will identify a set of NGOs with multistate presence and the working group will work towards empowering NGOs and giving them an implementation role. An innovation fund and social fund is needed within NRLM to promote programme convergence.

Hans Dieter Seibel is of the opinion that SHG village organizations (licensed as MACS and similar forms) have the potential of turning into viable and sustainable local organizations with 'financial and non-financial services' within the NRLM framework.

M.S. Sriram, Independent Consultant, offers the view that NRLM is a bottom up demand-driven project. He points out that there is a design flaw in NRLM. There is an imbalance created by the amount of resources that will rest in the federation (if it is financial) and the type of personnel that the federation will employ. This would mean that employees will not be accountable. He believes that investing resources in upper tier institutions does not work unless it is done in missionary mode such as the Amul or MYRADA model. Sriram himself was sceptical about whether NRLM policy can be reshaped, since terms of reference are given at the outset. Belonging to a cooperative background, he expressed reservations about the federation structure and multi-tiered organizations.

The major questions and concerns raised above relate to the space for NGOs in the NRLM strategy, the nature of SHGs and the multi-tier institutional structure being promoted and on the financial role for federations, apart from implementation issues. A few more specific questions also arise relating to the experience of the IKP and its place as a model for the NRLM.

1. The experience of implementing IKP in Andhra Pradesh has not been entirely successful and a large number of issues have been raised about the programme. It is open to question whether the design would be appropriate for other states where the infrastructure and human

resource capacity for delivering the programme will also have to be built.

2. More fundamentally, is not an excessive burden being placed upon SHGs and their members in carrying such a large development agenda? Are SHGs and institutions of the poor appropriate agencies to build a framework for an even larger agenda of livelihoods promotion? Though SHG members may use their SHG loans and savings as part of their household management strategies, for 'consumption', cash flow smoothing, and also livelihoods, it would be incorrect to think of SHGs as primarily a livelihood device.

3. Other stakeholders such as banks and NGOs and even IKP project staff have pointed to the downsides of providing interest subsidy through SHGs on their functioning? What is the rationale of the interest and capital subsidy structure and is it sustainable?

4. The NRLM design is supposed to be demand-driven—however, it seems that there are problems in preparing and effectively financing household level and SHG level microcredit plans in both Andhra Pradesh and Kerala?

5. What will be the role of the panchayats—will it not create room for politicization of the programme and sidetracking of the benefits?

6. What is the rationale for the using SHG federations as financial intermediaries? Does it have the support of the banking system? How is sustainable functioning of the SHG federation structure in providing financial and non-financial services to be ensured in an environment of subsidies?

7. What is the future of SHG development outside the NRLM fold by NGOs and other agencies—will NRLM take away the space for other promising initiatives?

No doubt there are answers to some of these questions and for other they will have to be found as the NRLM gets under way with its agenda for the SHGs.

9.6 Strategy for the Future

With the passage of two decades of SBLP, NABARD is revisiting its approach in order to prepare a strategy for the future. In view of the many issues that had been raised in respect of the role of NABARD, it is imperative that it take up a set of fresh policy initiatives to re-energize the SBLP. NABARD continues to support SHG promotion from the MDEF, along with a host of other capacity-building measures for the SBLP. NABARD has already started another channel for the disbursements of loans to SHGs and their federations, through BCs in the form of NABFINS. NABFINS is confined to a few southern states but with the idea of such a subsidiary taking root it could expand to other regions as well. However, some basic policy decisions to give shape to SBLP are needed.

As far as revisiting the design and content of SBLP is concerned, Malcolm Harper in a note to NABARD dated 23 March 2011 outlined the steps required to launch a Version 2 of SBLP. Harper notes that basic principles of SHGs needs not change but those changes that are necessary should be 'hard-wired' into the new design. Harper mainly emphasised SHGs as a way of savings, individual 'no frills' accounts for SHG members and the need for members to be able to access the full range of financial products. Besides, he highlighted the need for banks to see SHG banking as a business proposition and the need to provide indefinite support to SHGs.

He outlined certain general principles which included (a) a focus on developing strong new groups and improving existing ones, rather than on ever more 'sidelines' such as enterprise training, or federations or other institutional structures; (b) redesign of existing training modules in the current context; (c) the need to select and roll out simple systems of records for SHGs from the best existing systems; and (d) to create appropriate agencies in a given area where there may be no effective NGO-SHPIs or other existing agencies.

Most of these suggestions are unexceptionable though some of them, such as voluntary savings, may not be easy to implement as part of an SHG 2 initiative, since SHGs are unregistered associations which are not even audited.

NABARD's own views on SHG 2 also favour some of these steps though a clear policy statement has yet to be formulated. In an interview with the Microfinance India State of the Sector Report, 2011 (Srinivasan, 2011), Dr Prakash Bakshi, Chairman, NABARD highlighted the fact that *though the SBLP was for the banks a way of reducing their transaction cost and risk cost, today there are other means of reducing transaction costs with the help of technology* and the introduction of BCs also has a huge potential. He indicated that new elements of *the reworked model called SHG 2* were (a) voluntary savings, apart from compulsory savings; (b) widening the livelihood opportunities, including those in services sector; and (c) graduating select members of groups with entrepreneurial potential into JLGs to enable them to borrow larger amounts. With more intensive capacity building, the groups would perform even better. *NABARD intends to link a million groups each year—SHGs and JLGs—over the next five years, apart from improving the quality and efficiency of existing SHGs.* It was also intended to use BCs of banks that are serving 73,000 large villages as self-help promoting individuals and transaction points for the SHGs. Using BCs as SHPIs and experienced SHG members to promote other

SHGs, groups could be linked through BCs to bank branches, through new ways of compensating the mobilizers and appropriate incentives at all levels.

With the amendment of the Co-operative Law, PACS should be able to link with SHGs. It would also be possible for them to handle SHG savings with proper capacity building. Computerization of PACS can make deposit taking easier. Technology is a key enabler with the potential to reduce the cost of services to rural areas. Bakshi also suggested that *delivering financial services through SHG federations may not be necessary and that the latter could better focus on capacity building for livelihoods activities than undertaking financial intermediation.*

Suran (2011) sets out some of NABARD's ideas for repositioning SHGs as part of the SHG 2 initiative. These encompass four areas: (*a*) product design and positioning, (*b*) partner selection and training support, (*c*) opportunities for convergence and (*d*) enabling livelihoods. Principal among these is a greater focus on savings, especially voluntary savings for individuals, diversified credit products to permit financing of emergent needs and introduction of other financial products such as insurance, pensions and remittances. In addition, within a wider financial inclusion space, it envisages greater role for ICT-enabled monitoring and bookkeeping, mandatory audits and self-ratings by SHGs. It seeks more flexible functioning of SHGs in the form of profit-sharing and the enabling of SHG members who are economically active or have the risk appetite for entrepreneurial activity to come together in the form of JLGs to access enhanced bank loans, coupled with various training inputs. Towards this end, it proposes the use of SHG mentors in villages as BCs and BFs operating on behalf of local banks to undertake a range of intermediation functions on behalf of them. These BCs and BFs could include selected SHG members or SHGs themselves. Finally, it contemplates different approaches in high-income and low-income states and convergence with government programmes, especially the livelihoods-oriented NRLM.

NABARD has sought inputs from members of the microfinance community, through the discussion group of UNDP's Solution Exchange, with a view to develop new savings products for SHG members. This has elicited a mixed response with some contributors supporting such a practice and sharing their own innovations and experiences, but with others pointing to the risky nature of informal savings practices, especially since most SHGs do not have financial literacy and strong internal processes of audit and control. On balance, *development of savings products for SHGs members makes sense only if savings services are linked with banks through the use of BCs* which could be SHG federations. Otherwise, a voluntary saving corpus maintained with the SHGs is likely to expose the savings of less privileged members at risk. The discussion appears to point in the favour of an emerging role for BCs and BFs in further developing the banking relationship between SHGs and their members on the one hand and the banking system on the other.

A longer wish list of specific policy and institutional development measures have been already set out in Section 9.3. Besides, there is a need also, as mentioned in Section 9.2, to find means for the successful graduation of large scale borrowers so that SHG loan and individual loans do not reach unacceptably high levels. Here, the idea of forming JLGs of enterprising members out of existing SHG members, to be provided with larger loans appears to be an unnecessary elaboration (going beyond simple graduation) which is fraught with potential problems and dangers as well.[20] Besides, a target-driven approach of 800,000 SHGs and 200,000 JLGs per year—as part of NABARD plans for a major expansion of SHGs to be promoted and bank-linked—suggests that past lessons have not been learned. Further, there does not appear to be any link between these targets and the coverage under NRLM, which will itself thrown up additional demands and responsibilities on the banking system. NABARD, like Harper, does not have much faith in financial federations. However, it may need to support the NRLM in this regard. Perhaps *the use of SHG federations as BCs could enable the flow of funds to the SHGs through this channel* without their undertaking a financial intermediation role—though there is as yet not much evidence of BCs having made an impact in the supply of credit to SHGs. The promise and potential of such agents for SHG banking is seen to be more in terms of promoting small savings through performing a 'doorstep banking' function.

Finally and importantly, the question of convergence between the SBLP and the government's poverty alleviation programme is an old one, which has remained unresolved in the past. With the NRLM having taken the necessary steps to ground a comprehensive strategy for the livelihoods development of the poor, there appears to be little space for NABARD to pursue a strategy in respect of its financial services component independent of the positioning of the NRLM. Indeed, NRLM, financial inclusion, SBLP, like IRDP and so on before them, all generally tend to operate in silos, to guard their 'turf', rather than to realize that they are all merely facets of one aim—to help poor people. The ball appears to be very much in the court of NABARD to finalize a strategy for reviving the SHG movement in the context of the policy space that exists at the present time and the opportunities for innovation available through the use of technology. However, more

---

[20] For example, whether the small Grameen-type group 'joint liability' principle could be extended to large individual loans as well.

important than any specific policy measures that are planned for the SBLP, *it is necessary for NABARD and MoRD, other ministries, and state governments and concerned government agencies implementing the NRLM make a common cause for the larger development objective of strengthening livelihoods of poor people and alleviating poverty.* It is then only that banking on SHGs will truly fulfil its mission.

APPENDICES

Appendix 1: Important RBI/NABARD Circulars Regarding SHG–Bank Linkage

1. RBI Circular dated 24 July 1991 advised commercial banks that studies had brought out that SHGs have the potential to bring together the formal banking structure and the rural poor for mutual benefit and that NABARD is launching a pilot project to cover about 500 Self-Help Groups (SHGs) promoted by Non-Governmental Organizations (NGOs). The selected SHGs,

   (a) should be in existence for at least six months;
   (b) should have actively promoted the savings habit;
   (c) could be formal (registered) or informal (unregistered) and
   (d) membership of the group could be between 10 and 25 persons.

   The banks were advised to actively participate in the pilot project.
2. NABARD Circular dated 26 February 1992 gave details of the pilot project, the objectives of which were,

   (a) to evolve supplementary credit strategies for meeting the credit needs of the poor;
   (b) to build mutual trust and confidence between the bankers and the rural poor and
   (c) to encourage banking activity, both on the thrift as well as credit sides.

   The main criteria for group selection were that the group should have been in active existence for at least six months, it should have successfully undertaken savings and credit operations from its own resources and should be maintaining proper accounts/records.

Appendix 1 (Continued)

Appendix 1 *(Continued)*

The size of the group was to be *10 to 20 members though larger groups could also be considered for bank linkage.*[1] The banker was expected to provide credit in bulk directly to the group, which may be informal or formal (i.e., registered). The group in turn would undertake on-lending to the members. The proportion of savings to loan could vary from 1:1 to 1:4 depending on the assessment of the SHG by the bank. Banks could finance such SHGs through the Voluntary Agency (VA) or Self-Help Promoting Institution (SHPI) that had promoted the SHG, if it were willing to borrow from the bank and the bank was also prepared to lend to the VA/SHPI.

3. RBI Circular 4 January 1993 allowed SHGs, registered or unregistered, to open Savings Bank Accounts with banks and RRBs.
4. NABARD Circulars of 29 May 1993 and 12 June 1993 respectively extend the linkage programme pilot to cooperative banks and RRBs as well.
5. In September 1993 NABARD decided to extend on a pilot basis, refinance support to banks for providing credit support to VAs/NGOs which act as financial intermediaries for meeting the credit requirements of individuals or small groups.

NABARD vide Circular dated 19 October 1994 informed banks that Section 11(2) of the Companies Act forbids any company, association or partnership consisting of more than 20 persons for the purpose of carrying on any business unless it is registered as a company under the Companies Act. In view of the above, it would be advisable to have SHGs with not more than 20 persons for the linkage activities.

6. RBI Circular dated 2 April 1996 and NABARD Circulars dated 1 October 1996 and 7 October 1996 to Commercial banks/RRBs and cooperatives respectively as follow up of recommendations of Working Group on NGOs and SHGs, advised that:

   (a) SHG lending was to be treated as normal mainstream lending activity of banks.
   (b) There would be a separate segment for SHG financing under priority sector.
   (c) SHG lending was to be included in the Service Area Plans of banks.
   (d) SHGs were to be allowed to open Savings Bank accounts with banks regardless of whether availing credit or not.

---

[1] See also NABARD's subsequent Circular dated 19 October 1994 below, which limits the size of SHG membership.

(e) The defaults by a few members of SHGs and/or their family members to the financing bank should not ordinarily come in the way of financing SHGs per se by banks provided the SHG is not in default to it. However, the bank loan may not be utilized by the SHG for financing a defaulter member to the bank.

7. NABARD Circular of 21 February 1997 indicated that banks are reportedly insisting on keeping group savings of SHGs in savings bank accounts or in fixed deposits with their branches as collateral for providing loans to SHGs. Since this practice deprives the SHGs of their savings otherwise available to them for loaning to their members, banks were advised to take a pragmatic view in the matter and issue suitable instructions to their branches.

8. RBI Circular dated 10 February 1998 extended opening of savings bank accounts in the name of SHGs to all SHGs.

9. NABARD Circular dated 28 February 2000 advised banks to develop norms for identification of SHGs for the purpose of lending.

Source: Compiled from RBI and NABARD websites.

Appendix 2: Organization Profile of Study NGOs

#	Particulars	MYRADA/Sanghamithra, Karnataka	PRADAN, Rajasthan and other states	DHAN/federations of Kalanjiams/KDFS, Tamil Nadu	GRAM/IIMF, Andhra Pradesh	Chaitanya/GMSS/other federations promoted by Chaitanya, Maharashtra	SKDRDP, Karnataka	ASSEFA/SNFL, Tamil Nadu	BWDA/BFL, Tamil Nadu	BISWA/CMPL/BMPL, Odisha	Parivartan/Sanginee, Odisha
1	Year of data	March 2010	March 2011	March 2011	March 2011	March 2011	March 2011	March 2011	March 2011	March 2011	March 2011
2	Legal form	Society/not for profit section-25 company	Society	Charitable trust/charitable trusts or societies/not for profit section-25 company	Society/MACS	Charitable trust/society/MBT	Charitable trust	Society/NBFC	Society/NBFC	Society/NBFC/NBFC	Society/co-op
3	Area of operations—states/districts	20 backward and drought prone districts of Karnataka, Andhra Pradesh and Tamil Nadu (as on January 2010)	152 blocks of 51 districts across 8 states	54 districts of 12 states	Adilabad and Nizamabad districts of Andhra Pradesh	7 districts of Maharashtra as on March 2011 and 18 districts of Maharashtra as on July 2011	11 districts of Karnataka	5 states/23 districts	3 states/11 districts	18 states	8 blocks in 1 district of Odisha
4	Year of start of SHG promotion	1984	1987	1990	1994	1991	1982	1980	1992	1996	2000

	5 Year of start of MF operations	6 MF methodology followed by SHPA	7 Total no. of SHGs promoted	8 Total no. of members	9 Cumulative no. of SHGs linked to banks
	1996 (through Sanghamithra which is an independent legal entity)	Primary focus is on SHG-bank linkage. Promoted NBFC Sanghamithra	SAGs—12,050; Soukhya groups—512; Watershed groups—538 (as on January 2010)	n.a.	n.a.
	Not applicable	Link SHG, cluster, federation and producer cooperative type institutions with banks	14,285	More than 198,000	4,286
	1990	Providing credit through federations and also Kalanjiam Development Financial Services (KDFS)	31,780	619,439	n.a.
	2002	Lends through IIMF to MACS who further on-lend to SHGs	3,623	47,099	13,480
	1991	Lends through SHG federations and also to SHGs	2,502	36,073	n.a.
	1996	On-lend to SHGs; facilitated by SHG federations	123,586	1,359,746	123,586
	1991	Lends through SMBTs	30,155	487,633	n.a.
	1999	On-lend to SHGs, promote SHG–bank linkage and promoted NBFC to lend to SHGs	25,459	463,073	15,699 (tentative)
	1996	NGO-MFI which on-lends to SHGs	68,962	1,094,029	n.a.
	2005	On-lends to individuals through SHG/JLGs	2,635	16,509	198

Appendix 2 *(Continued)*

#	Particulars	MYRADA/Sanghamithra, Karnataka	PRADAN, Rajasthan and other states	DHAN/federations of Kalanjiams/KDFS, Tamil Nadu	GRAM/IIMF, Andhra Pradesh	Chaitanya/GMSS/other federations promoted by Chaitanya, Maharashtra	SKDRDP, Karnataka	ASSEFA/SNFL, Tamil Nadu	BWDA/BFL, Tamil Nadu	BISWA/CMPL/BMPL, Odisha	Parivartan/Sanginee, Odisha
10	Cumulative amount borrowed by SHGs directly from banks (₹ millions)	n.a.	n.a.	13,580	1,685	n.a.	650	n.a.	1,549.7 (tentative)	n.a.	0.17
11	No. of SHG federations promoted	103 CMRCs and 108 federations (as on January 2010)	39	1,193 CDA, 122 federations	20 MACS and 1 IIMF	15 block-level federations, 216 village-level clusters	4,043	113	436	238 two-tier federations out of which 122 have been registered as MBTs. Loans to Federations discontinued	3 primary and 1 secondary federation
12	Cumulative amount borrowed by SHG federations directly from banks and other sources (₹ millions)	Not applicable	Not applicable	n.a.	780	85	Not applicable	920	Not applicable	Nil	47

#	Description										
13	Loan provided to SHGs by the organization/ or organization promoted NBFC/ federation during 2010–11 (₹ millions)	Sanghamithra loans to SHGs promoted by MYRADA and others. 688.5	Not applicable	n.a.	93.7	91.88	9,520	1,120	1,420	3,091	67.3
14	No. of MF field staff	MYRADA 231 (January 2010) and Sanghamithra 132 (March 2011)	n.a.	n.a.	86	130	3,759	901	686	2,965	32
15	Total savings of SHGs to date (₹ millions)	n.a.	410 (approx.)	1,986.6	Internal savings n.a., savings with federation 54.8	100 (approx.) internal savings and 24.7 in federation	3,270	1,280	2,350	847	2.3
16	Loan outstanding (₹ millions)	Sanghamithra 795.4	200 (approx.)	3,734.2	Internal lending—134.7; from banks—284.5; from federation—128.3	105 approximately through internal lending and 99.9 through federation	9,570	480	1,050	3,070	42.5615

Appendix 2 *(Continued)*

Appendix 2 (*Continued*)

#	Particulars	MYRADA/Sanghamithra, Karnataka	PRADAN Rajasthan and other states	DHAN/federations of Kalanjiams/KDFS, Tamil Nadu	GRAM/IIMF, Andhra Pradesh	Chaitanya/GMSS/other federations promoted by Chaitanya, Maharashtra	SKDRDP, Karnataka	ASSEFA/SNFL, Tamil Nadu	BWDA/BFL, Tamil Nadu	BISWA/CMPL/BMPL, Odisha	Parivartan/Sarginee, Odisha
17	Current SHG repayment rate (% per annum)	n.a.	n.a.	n.a.	MACS to IIMF—94	95 to SHG federation	100	96.86	96.26	99 (to BISWA)	90 (bank linkage); 98 to SHG federations
18	Rate of interest paid by SHGs (% per annum)	Sanghamithra 16 for general purpose loans and 15 for housing loans on declining basis	Not applicable	n.a.	IIMF to MACS 15, MACS to SHG members—21	18 to federation (on reducing balance)	9 flat up to June 2011 and 10 flat w.e.f. July 2011	23.8 reducing for 10 months tenure	21 (on reducing balance)	24 (on reducing balance) w.e.f 1 May 2011	24 (on reducing balance)
19	Range of groups internal lending (% per annum)	n.a.	n.a.	n.a.	18 to 24 (lending rate for SHG savings on reducing balance)	24 (on reducing balance)	10 flat	24 (on reducing balance)	8 to 36 (on reducing balance)	19 reducing balance from SHGs to members on loans. SHGs do not inter-lend savings	n.a.
20	No. of SHGs and members covered by insurance products	n.a.	n.a.	Life insurance—576,008 (members and spouses)	16,000 (all members who have taken loan)	LIC Janshree policy—962 groups and 2,290 members	Sampoorna Suraksha (Health insurance)—	Sarvodaya social security scheme offered by SMBTs	Nil	526,745	1,715 groups and 13,544 members, type of insurance—life insurance coverage

21	Other financial and non financial services provided by the organization	MYRADA along with independent entities promoted provide support in education, micro watersheds, networking, participatory water management, public private	Livelihood intervention, networking with various government and non-government institutions, strengthening of gram sabhas, support in MIS through computer munshi	Development of small tanks, ICT for developing poor, development management through TATA-DHAN academy, restoration and livelihood activities in Tsunami-	Health insurance—14,215 family members spouses)	Promoted women's dairy producer company, Bulk Cooling Milk Units established, support services provided for supply of feed, fodder development, veterinary services, etc.	Health: OPD by doctor appointed by federation, health camps, kitchen garden, livelihood—Vermi compost, Horticulture, craft classes. Social: cluster-level social programmes,	Deepti Arogya Nidhi—community-based health insurance programme—piloted in 2 blocks with 2 federations; 5,700 members	House construction in flood-affected areas, pension to destitute, Sujananidhi scholarship for students, SRI, sanitation, gobar gas, solar units, community infrastructure,	4.60 lakh families; 17 lakh members; Jeevan Madhur—4 lakh policies	Health and eye camps, support for dairy industry, evening classes for drop out students from government schools, community marriages	Capacity building support, formal educational program with three schools, three colleges, non-formal education—summer school, health and sanitation, relief and	Elementary education, primary health care, safe drinking water, livelihood enhancement, water management, Swadhar—a rehabilitation home, renewable energy	Skill development and livelihood promotion, training on financial literacy and organizing legal literacy camps, awareness creation on cooperative principles, rights, entitlements,

Appendix 2 (Continued)

#	Particulars	MYRADA/ Sanghamithra, Karnataka	PRADAN Rajasthan and other states	DHAN/federations of Kalanjiams/ KDFS, Tamil Nadu	GRAM/IIMF, Andhra Pradesh	Chaitanya/ GMSS/other federations promoted by Chaitanya, Maharashtra	SKDRDP, Karnataka	ASSEFA/ SNFL, Tamil Nadu	BWDA/BFL, Tamil Nadu	BISWA/CMPL/ BMPL, Odisha	Parivartan/ Sarginee, Odisha
		partnerships, governance in gram sabhas and panchayats, capacity building, microfinance		affected areas, rain fed farming development programme, social security through people's mutuals and convergence with government programmes		legal counselling centres	primary education, training programmes for women, business correspondent		rehabilitation, etc.		gender and legal issues

Source: Data submitted for this study, annual reports and websites of respective organizations.
Note: n.a.: not available

APPENDIX 3: SUMMARY OF SHG-BASED FINANCIAL INTERMEDIATION MODELS PROMOTED BY LEADING NGOS

#	Name of NGO/ state	Brief statement of vision/mission	SHG model type	Particulars of federation/ financial intermediation model	Sources of external loan funds for SHG on-lending	Terms of loans to SHGs	Remarks
1	MYRADA, Karnataka	**Mission:** 'Building institutions of the poor and marginalized which are appropriate to the resource to be managed and objective to be achieved.'	SHG–bank linkage and credit linkage through NBFC promoted by MYRADA	100–120 SAGs, Watershed Area Groups and Soukhya groups form Community Managed Resource Centres (CMRCs). CMRCs are non financial federations focusing on various developmental issues including livelihoods.	Loans and grants from MYRADA, banks, Sanghamithra, DRDA/Women's Development Corporation, others. Sanghamithra borrows funds from NABARD (MFEDF and RFA), SIDBI and various commercial banks at 3.5% to 11.25% per annum.	**SAGs:** 1. From various RRBs, co-op. and commercial banks at around 12% per annum. 2. At 15 to 16% p.a. from Sanghamithra	CMRC charges fee for the member groups and provides services such as credit linkage, capacity building, auditing, conflict resolution, etc. SAGs also form federations which are unregistered bodies formed to help the SAGs to collect data and sort out any problems related to loans and repayments.

Appendix 3 *(Continued)*

Appendix 3 (*Continued*)

#	Name of NGO/ state	Brief statement of vision/mission	SHG model type	Particulars of federation/ financial intermediation model	Sources of external loan funds for SHG on-lending	Terms of loans to SHGs	Remarks
2	PRADAN, Jharkhand	**Vision:** PRADAN seeks to enable poor rural families to live a life of dignity.	SHG–bank linkage	SHG-village SHG forum-federation at cluster level which takes up nonfinancial activities.	Direct bank linkage and linkage through SGSY for SHGs. Members from SHGs who take up common activity are organized into producer groups which are registered as an MBT which accesses funds from various banks, other financial institutions. MBTs further federate to form Producer companies which also access credit from various	SHGs are linked to various RRBs, cooperatives and commercial banks at around 12% per annum. Also, SHGs are linked to banks under SGSY.	Promotes three sets of institutions— SHG, cluster, federation being the first one to address social issues, area-level institutions such as hamlet level sabhas, watershed committees as second set and producer groups, producer companies/ MBTs/ cooperatives of agriculture, diary, tussar, poultry, mushrooms etc. as the third set of organizations.

| 3 | DHAN Foundation, Tamil Nadu | Building people and institutions for development innovations and scaling up to enable the poor communities for poverty reduction and self-reliance | Nested institutions | 15–20 women form SHGs called Kalanjiams, 15–20 such Kalanjiams come together to form clusters at village level and 200–250 Kalanjiams form federations. All federations | banks such as ICICI, DCB, HDFC and financial institutions/trusts such as IFMR trust and NABARD under various programs. Local commercial sources and Regional Rural banks. For special needs such as housing they access loans from SIDBI and HDFC | **Kalanjiams:** From KDFS to federations 12%, from federations to Kalanjiams 15% and from Kalanjiams to members 15% to 18% | All the institutions—SHG, cluster and federation—are independent but interdependent structures. Clusters support Kalanjiams in providing |

Appendix 3 *(Continued)*

#	Name of NGO/ state	Brief statement of vision/mission	SHG model type	Particulars of federation/ financial intermediation model	Sources of external loan funds for SHG on-lending	Terms of loans to SHGs	Remarks
				have been registered as Kalanjiam mutual movement as mutual trust to represent peoples institutions at various levels.	through their federations. For bridge loans, they access finance from Kalanjiam Development Financial services (KDFC).		accounting services, auditing services and conflict resolution support. In order to provide support in terms of bridge loans, KDFS was promoted which not only provides credit support to Kalanjiams but for all other groups promoted by Dhan foundation for various purposes.

| 4 | Chaitanya, Maharashtra | A gender just, equitable and self reliant society where women have access to and control over financial and other sources. | SHG-cluster-federation model | Three tier structures with SHGs at the primary level, clusters at the secondary level and federation at the apex level. | Bank linkage + loans from SHG federation GMSS: GMSS which is the oldest federation of Chaitanya borrows from banks, SIDBI, FWWB and on-lends to SHGs and other federations too. Recently, one of the new federations has been linked to Ananya. | SHGs: SHGs receive loans from banks at 12% and from federation at 18%. | Other than loans, federations provide the following services: 1. Health— OPD by doctor appointed by federation, health camps 2. Training and necessary inputs for kitchen garden, Vermi compost pits, Horticulture, stitching classes for stitching bags. 3. Legal counseling centers through Jankars who are trained village women (literate/ illiterate) who act as paralegal workers. |

Appendix 3 (*Continued*)

Appendix 3 (Continued)

#	Name of NGO/ state	Brief statement of vision/mission	SHG model type	Particulars of federation/ financial intermediation model	Sources of external loan funds for SHG on-lending	Terms of loans to SHGs	Remarks
5	GRAM	Promote sustainable organizations among the structurally poor with emphasis on Dalits, Women and Disabled	SHG-MACS-IIMF	GRAM has promoted SHGs which were later organized into MACS. 20 such MACS from Adilabad and Nizamabad districts have come together to form IIMF	**IIMF:** receives funding support in terms of grant from NOVIB and loans from ABN AMRO bank, Axis bank, BASIX, BELLWETHER MF fund, Corporation bank, FWWB, HDFC bank, IOB, SIDBI, Manaveeya holding, Matha milk federation at 11% to 12.65%	**SHGs:** receive loans directly from banks or from MACS which receive loans from IIMF Loans from banks at 3% interest rate under paavala vaddi. IIMF lends to MACS at 15% which on-lends to members at 21%. Groups are lent at 18% to 24%.	A women dairy producer company is promoted under the guidance of GRAM; Bulk Milk Cooling Units are established at 10 locations covering all MACS operational area. Support services are provided in the areas of supply of feed, fodder development, veterinary services, etc.

| 6 | Sri Kshetra Dharmasthala Rural Development Project, Karnataka | **Vision:** Empowering the rural poor, minority groups and women to achieve progress through sustainable farming, creation of rural infrastructure, entrepreneurship, spiritualism and networking | SHG–bank linkage. SKDRDP acts as business correspondent. SKDRDP also takes loans from banks and lends them to various SHGs promoted. | Village level federations consist of SHGs and farmers groups as members. Federations are promoted for social purposes. Appraisal of loan applications from SHGs for receiving loans from SKDRDP, recovery of bad debts, capacity building are the functions of federations | Federation does not act as financial intermediary. SKDRDP acts as financial intermediary and receives loans from banks for further lending to SHGs. Loans are taken by the organization from various banks at 12% to 12.5%. | SHGs receive loans from banks at 8% to 12%. SKDRDP provides loans at 10% per annum flat and SHGs are expected to pass on to members without retaining any margin. | SKDRDP is presently working with 1,313,042 families SKDRDP that received subsidized loans for housing and small enterprise from NABARD and DBCDC. The interest subsidy was passed on to the beneficiary. SKDRDP also acts as Business Correspondent for SBI. |

Appendix 3 (*Continued*)

#	Name of NGO/ state	Brief statement of vision/mission	SHG model type	Particulars of federation/ financial intermediation model	Sources of external loan funds for SHG on-lending	Terms of loans to SHGs	Remarks
7	ASSEFA group, Tamil Nadu	To establish self-reliant village communities	1. Two community owned MFIs (NBFCs): (*a*) Sarvodaya Nanofinance (SNF) (*b*) Sarva Jana Seva Kosh (SJSK). 2. Other ASSEFA companies for housing and dairying lend to SHGs. 3. Direct linkage of SHGs with banks.	1. SNF is an NBFC owned by mutual benefit trusts formed of SHGs. 2. SJSK acts as fund manager for accumulated revolving funds of village groups (nidhi foundations).	Bank linkage + other financial institutions (both private and public), government agencies	1. SNF borrows at 8%–11.5% p.a. from different sources, lends to MBTs at 12%, MBTs to SHGs at 15%, SHG to members at 18%. 2. Nidhis pay a service fee of 2% of their funds managed by the SJSK.	1. (*a*) ASSEFA promoted women's SHGs under IFAD-TNWDC project have been constituted into registered block level mutual benefit trusts (MBTs) (200–250 SHGs each). (*b*) SHGs contribute for MBT to subscribe to share capital of SNF. MBT is entitled to borrow six times its share holding in SNF, which it on-lends to SHGs.

8	BWDA/ Tamil Nadu	'A poverty free, prosperous, equitable and sustainable society'		SHGs directly access loans from banks as well as from BWDA.	BWDA promoted federations (SHGs-Panchayat Level Federation-Cluster Level Federation-Block Level Federation) under Mahalir Thittam. The federations do exist but are not so active.	Banks, BWDA Finance Limited Accessing funds from SIDBI, FWWB, Ananya, various commercial banks, Manaveeya Holdings	SHGs are provided credit at 15%/21% (on reducing balance). SHGs inter lend at 36% for the first two years and from thereafter charge 18% to 24%	BWDA has gradually transferred its portfolio to BFL and as on 31 March 2008, loan outstanding of BCL is 99% of total outstanding of BWDA and BFL put together.

(c) Promotional activities including formation of new groups are carried out by MBT. (d) SNF borrows from wholesalers including SIDBI, HDFC, Rabobank. 2. SJSK acts as fund manager for accumulated revolving fund of communities built up through donor grants.

Appendix 3 (*Continued*)

#	Name of NGO/ state	Brief statement of vision/mission	SHG model type	Particulars of federation/ financial intermediation model	Sources of external loan funds for SHG on-lending	Terms of loans to SHGs	Remarks
9	BISWA	**Vision:** 'Just and equitable society with greater emphasis on spirituality, compassion and peace on earth.'	Thrift and credit SHGs linked to banks and NGO promoted NBFCs for credit	SHGs (100–150) were federated earlier as MBTs and also acted as financial intermediaries. But these federations are not currently active.	Credible Securities and Finance Pvt. Ltd and BMPL (BISWA Microfinance Private Limited) both are NBFCs promoted by BISWA.	BISWA lends to SHGs at 19% reducing balance. SHGs also receive loans through two of the NBFCs floated by BISWA	BISWA provides lending to SHGs by itself and also through two NBFCs promoted. The only source of credit to SHGs is through these organizations. SHGs do not take up inter lending as their savings amount is deposited into

						banks and used as a security by BISWA to take loans from various banks for providing credit to SHGs. Also, SHGs are not allowed to take loans from banks.
10	Sanginee	**Vision:** To usher in a just social and economic order in which there will be equality of opportunity to all regardless of race, sex, caste or religion and in which socio-economic justice will prevail.	SHGs formed earlier were transformed to JLGs and five JLGs form a centre and around 25 centres form primary cooperative.	Women are organized into Joint Liability Groups and JLGs are organized into various centres	Sanginee Secondary Cooperative Limited **Sanginee:** Received loans from BISWA, CSFPL, BASIX, Ananya, SMCS, SIDBI at 12% to 16%	**SHGs:** Bank loans at prevailing interest rates and from Sanginee at 24%	Under DFID program SHGs were formed during 1996 by Parivartan which also provided credit support to these SHGs. SHGs were federated to form primary cooperatives

Appendix 3 (Continued)

#	Name of NGO/ state	Brief statement of vision/mission	SHG model type	Particulars of federation/ financial intermediation model	Sources of external loan funds for SHG on-lending	Terms of loans to SHGs	Remarks
							and three such primary cooperatives formed Sanginee which is secondary level cooperative. Sanginee took over the credit portfolio of Parivartan.

APPENDIX 4: SHG-BASED FINANCIAL INTERMEDIATION MODELS AND THEIR EVOLUTION: THE EXPERIENCE OF CASHE NGO PARTNERS

Started in 1999, CASHE was a poverty-focused seven-year project designed to address the fundamental problem of low incomes of poor women and their limited control over that income. It was implemented by CARE in three states, Andhra Pradesh, Odisha and West Bengal with support from Department for International Development (DFID) of Government of the United Kingdom. The goal of CASHE was to increase significantly the incomes and economic security of one million poor rural women and their households by increasing the availability of a wide range of microfinance services to them. CASHE had a three-tier prolonged strategy through alliances which facilitate significant scale-up (Government, NGOs).

- Targeting households and microentrepreneurs with financial and business development
- Making institutions sustainable through capacity building and linkages with mainstream financial institutions
- Networking and advocacy (providing an enabling environment for effective mF delivery.

CASHE provided intensive handholding support to 25 NGO-MFIs including a few community based microfinance organizations as a part of its Tier-I strategy. Operational grant, revolving loan fund and technical support were provided to each partner organization to build them up as Microfinance Institutions. As a part of its Tier-II strategy, CASHE trained thousands of trainers with a variety of technical inputs in SHG promotion activities, bank linkages process and SHG rating. CASHE partnered with RRBs and Commercial banks in three states with the objective of accelerating the SHG-bank linkages programme. Setting up of microfinance resource centres in different states to build up the capacity of SHG federations and small and middle level NGOs for effective delivery of MF services was one of the major activities under Tier-II. At the Tier-III level, CASHE was involved in creating an enabling environment at the state level for microfinance operations by popularizing the liberal cooperative acts and organizing microfinance conventions in all the three states.

The seven year project concluded on 31 December 2006 and was successful in terms of outreach, impact and innovations in promoting various models of microfinance institutions. At the end of the project, partners had strong Governing Boards, skilled staff, computerized MIS, quality groups, higher average loan sizes and appropriate insurance coverage. By the end of the project 40,245 SHGs and 109 primary and secondary federations covering 545,575 households were formed in three states. As far as savings was concerned, ₹ 943 million was mobilized from the SHGs with a loan outstanding of ₹ 1.2 billion. The total credit flow from bank to SHGs was ₹ 1.36 billion. In addition to this, revolving loan support of ₹ 151 million was also given to the SHGs through the partner organizations by the end of the project. However, *after the completion of the project, driven by market considerations, many of these partner organizations revisited their mission and vision. As a result the paths taken by them and their results were very varied.*

In Andhra Pradesh, all the partner organizations registered under the Societies Act had adopted the SHG model for delivery of the microfinance services. Pragathi Seva Samithi (PSS) formed 35 cluster level federations in Warangal and confederated them into a district level federation. At the time of completion of the CASHE project it was able to meet about 90% of the operational cost from the revenues earned. The district-level federation along with the cluster federations grew in terms of outreach, portfolio and operational sustainability. However, over time PSS transformed itself into an NBFC and got diverted from its focus on strengthening SHG federations. Modern Architects for Rural India (MARI), Warangal formed 22 Cluster-level federations in Warangal and confederated them into a district level federation called Sanghatitha. At the time of withdrawal of the CASHE project, it was able to meet almost 80% of its operational costs. For a year after separation from the promoting organization, it made good surpluses and was able to mobilize loan funds from HDFC, Maanaveeya Holdings, etc. But later due to weak management and non-adherence to the prudential systems and procedures developed during the CASHE project, it started to experience operational losses, poor portfolio quality and non-availability of funds for on-lending.

Also in Andhra Pradesh, Social Education and Voluntary Action (SEVA), Warangal had become a legal entity under Section 25 not-for-profit company for microfinance operations. At the end of the CASHE project it withdrew and allowed the federation to manage by itself. SEVA through its Section 25 status provided loan funds from banks and financial institutions to the federation. However, in course of time it could not leverage loans from the financial market because of low capital adequacy. Also, it could not attract equity investments because of its section 25 'not-for-profit' company status. Finally, it had to close the Section 25 company and restart its microfinance operation through the earlier legal form as a society This did not succeed as expected. Navajyothi, another NGO had promoted four *mandal*-level federations with village organizations to support social intermediation. All these mandal federations were operational at the time of the end of the CASHE Project and were managing their operations with their own funds and SHG–bank linkages. But they could not meet the market demand and achieve the required growth. Only two federations are operational at present; the other two federations have closed down their operations. A contributory factor has been that Navajyothi never wanted to adopt a businesslike approach to expand its microfinance portfolio. On the other hand, People's Action for Creative Education (PEACE), Nalgonda adhered to its community-based model and promoted eight federations. It continued to work as a community-focused institution. Without leveraging loans from the financial market as a matter of principle, it has been able to sustain its federations through grant funds. In contrast, Aadarsha Welfare Society (AWS), Mahbubnagar and Krushi, Karimnagar totally discontinued the SHG model and adopted JLG/Grameen method by the end of CASHE project. They started NBFCs for their microfinance operations. Krushi envisaged expanding its NBFC operations but failed to mobilize funds from financial institutions. Krushi thus closed down its microfinance operation due to heavy losses, whereas AWS is running a successful NBFC.

In Odisha, out of the eight CASHE project partners, BMASS Jagannath Prasad, BMASS Sorada and BMASS Hinjlicutt were three block-level SHG federations that had been promoted by the Ganjam district administration and registered under the 1860 Societies Act. In fact, the district administration promoted 24 such BMASSs. CASHE partnered with these three federations to build their capacity. From the inception of the federations till the end of the CASHE project and thereafter they continued lending to SHGs through the same legal form. As March 2011, they were lending to SHGs at 12% by borrowing loan funds from banks at 9.5%. All these federations are more than 100% operationally self-sufficient. Since their inception these federations have been collecting monthly savings (in the name of monthly contribution) from the SHGs but never attempted to transform themselves into an appropriate legal form to collect savings. On the other hand, Samabaya Limited (SMSL), Cuttack, a federation of SHGs registered under the Odisha Self-Help Cooperative (OSHC) Act and promoted by Swayanshree, another CASHE partner, is a new generation cooperative. Before registering under the OSHC Act, it was a federation of SHGs registered under the Societies Act. The federation was meeting the loan demand of its member clients organized into SHGs from the savings mobilized from the members. Since the 1860 Societies Act was not the appropriate legal form to mobilize savings, it got registered under OSHC Act in 2006 and slowly transferred the portfolio from the societies to the cooperative. While SMSL undertakes financial activities, Swayanshree provides non-financial services to the SHG members. In view of its credibility, SBI lent ₹ 3 million to SMSL on 'cash credit' basis. No other bank prior to this or subsequently (except SIDBI) has sanctioned any loans to federations in Odisha. Under the influence of some MFIs, Swayanshree also experimented with JLGs but had a very poor experience.

Parivartan, an NGO in Kalahandi promoted SHG cooperatives under its microfinance programme and ultimately formed an apex cooperative,

Sanginee Secondary Cooperative, registered under the Orissa Self help Cooperative Act 2001. Sanginee changed the financial services delivery from the SHG mode to the JLG mode. Except for loan support from wholesalers like SIDBI, FWWB, SMCS, and BISWA, it has not been able to mobilize loan funds from any of the public sector and private sector banks. Similarly, Mahashakti Foundation, Kalahandi is the outcome of the microfinance programme of the NGO, FARR, Kalahandi. By the end of CASHE project, FARR promoted SHG federations registered under the new liberal cooperative act and confederated them into an apex institution registered under the Indian Trust Act. Like Sanginee promoted by Parivartan, Mahashakti Foundation also changed its delivery model from SHG mode to JLG mode. It started operations through savings mobilized in the cooperatives and on-lending to the members of the same cooperatives through the JLG mode. With its professional staff and operations it could attract and borrow from a number of microfinance wholesalers in due course of time. Recently, Mahashakti Foundation has also acquired NBFC status but its operations are yet to start. BISWA, Sambalpur (mentioned above) and Gram Utthan, Kendrapara still continue to on-lend to the SHGs they have promoted by borrowing from various financial institutions. Also, both the organizations have acted as wholesalers to smaller NGOs and MFIs in the state. While public sector banks are quite comfortable lending to BISWA and the BMASSs, they are only recently opening up to lending to the other MFIs. After more than 10 years of operations, State Bank of India has lent only ₹ 3 million to Swayanshree. Central Bank of India sanctioned ₹ 102.8 million to Gram Utthan but has disbursed only ₹ 72.8 million thus far. No public sector bank has supported Sanginee Secondary Cooperative or Mahashakti Foundation. To seek an appropriate legal entity, Gram Utthan and Mahashakti Foundation acquired NBFCs to run their microfinance operations and BISWA has acquired two NBFCs. In the case of BISWA, the transfer of portfolio to the respective NBFC has been slow; others are yet to start in full in the absence of skilled and qualified staff.

The situation has been somewhat different in West Bengal. There were nine CASHE partners and all of them had adopted the SHG model. Except Bagnan Mahila Bikash Cooperative Credit Society Limited (BMBCCSL), the rest of the organizations were registered under the Societies Act and were undertaking microfinance operations along lines of Model III of SBLP. Except those of Uttar Banga Tarai Mahila Samity (UBTMS), the federations promoted by other partner organizations are informal bodies and not involved in any financial intermediation. Kenduadihi Bikash Society (KBS) and Swanirbhar are the two organizations that have not promoted any SHG federations. A few organizations like Sreema Mahila Samity (SMS), Kajala Janakalyan Samity (KJS) and Swanirbhar could leverage loan funds from public and private sector banks. In all the organizations, loans were given by these NGO-MFIs to SHGs who in turn on-lent to the SHG members. However, *after the conclusion of the CASHE project, almost all the organizations have adopted the methodology of individual lending*. While SHGs continue to exist and meetings are held regularly, loans are given to individual members directly by the organization and the peer pressure applied by the SHGs helps repayment in case of delinquency. SMS continued its microfinance operations with the same legal form, i.e., society. Due to the credibility gained by partnering with the CASHE project it could leverage loan funds from banks—₹ 250 million from State Bank of India and ₹ 30 million from the United Bank of India. It could also leverage ₹ 10 million from NABARD. It retains its SHGs but lending to SHG members has been changed from group methodology to individual lending method. It has also promoted a federation of SHGs but the role of the federation is restricted to social intermediation only. Similarly, BMBCCSL continues its original block-level SHG federation model registered under the Cooperative Society Act. It provides saving and credit services to individuals, both members of SHGs and non-members. As on 31 October 2011, BMBCCL had 22,363 individual clients. It provides a variety of saving products and loans for a number of purposes. As the cooperative retained the SHGs savings, there is no internal lending in the SHGs. It is not interested in accessing external loan funds even though it is apparently not able to meet all credit needs of members.

The above experiences illustrate the many paths along which CASHE partner NGOs and their SHGs and SHG-based associations evolved after being confronted by the pressures and possibilities of the market; and adopted a wide range of innovations to provide financial services to the poor. *Most of these innovations involved the undermining or bypassing of SHGs as financial intermediaries as had been originally envisaged*. Thus, for better or worse, the original SHG model that NGOs started with has over the years undergone many changes and several alternative modes of financial services delivery to SHG members have since evolved.

APPENDIX 5: PROFILE OF LEADING SHG-BASED GOVERNMENT PROGRAMMES

#	Particulars	SERP—Andhra Pradesh	Mahalir Thittam—Tamil Nadu	Kudumbashsree—Kerala	MAVIM—Maharashtra	Mission Shakti—Odisha	TRIPTI	BRLP—Bihar
1	Year of data	March 2011	March 2011	March 2011	July 2011	March 2011	March 2011	March 2011
2	Promoter	Government of Andhra Pradesh	Government of Tamil Nadu through Tamil Nadu Corporation for Development of Women Ltd.	Government of Kerala through 'State Poverty Eradication Mission' (SPEM)	State Women Development Corporation of Maharashtra	Mahila Vikas Samabaya Nigam/Women's Development Corporation, Odisha	Orissa Poverty Reduction Mission (OPRM)	Bihar Rural Livelihoods Promotion Society (BRLPS)
3	Legal form	Society	Corporation	Society	Company	Cooperative	Society	Society
4	Area of operations—states/districts	22 districts of Andhra Pradesh	32 districts of Tamil Nadu	14 districts of Kerala	291 blocks in all (33) districts of Maharashtra	30 districts of Orissa	38 blocks of 10 districts of Orissa	8 districts of Bihar
5	Year of start of SHG promotion	2000	1989	1998	1994	2001	2009	2007
6	Year of start of microfinance (MF) operations	n.a.	1989	1998	Not applicable	n.a	n.a	n.a
7	MF methodology followed by SHPA	SHG–bank linkage and lending through federations promoted	Promote bank linkages in partnership with NGOs and CBOs and also promote loans to SHGs through PLFs	Promote NHG–Bank Linkage; Also promoted Federation–Bank Linkage (though stopped now)	SHG–bank linkage	SHG–bank linkage, lending through Block level SHG federations (only in Ganjam district)	SHG–bank linkage	SHG–bank linkage and lending through Cluster level federations and VOs promoted

8	Total SHGs promoted	994,595	491,311	209,725 (NHGs)	58,282	306,434	24004(19377 SHGs of Mission Shakti+4927 SHGs formed by TRIPTI)	31,381
9	Total members	11,102,494	7,659,682	3,864,293	755,000	3,767,624	712,342	412,086
10	Cumulative no. of SHGs linked to banks	389,444	447,081	16,869	n.a.	222,501	111 out of 4927 newly formed SHGs	3,145
11	Cumulative amount borrowed by SHGs directly from banks (₹ millions)	70,927	116,038.3	2,914.2	3,350	15,587.5	2.3	87.49
12	Number of SHG federations promoted	38,300 VOs, 1,099 MS, 22 ZS	5,085	1,061 (CDS)	299 (CMRCs)	7,940 GP, block- and district-level federations	1,849 CLFs	Around 1,891 VOs and 4 CLFs
13	Total savings of SHGs to date (₹ millions)	33,830	29,730	16,310	1,636.9	6,513.9	37.48 (new+old SHGs)	187.3

Appendix 5 (*Continued*)

Appendix 5 (Continued)

#	Particulars	SERP—Andhra Pradesh	Mahalir Thittam—Tamil Nadu	Kudumbashsree—Kerala	MAVIM—Maharashtra	Mission Shakti—Odisha	TRIPTI	BRLP—Bihar
14	Other financial and non financial services provided by the organization/ programme	• Building strong/ sustainable institutions of the poor • Sustainable livelihoods • Community-managed sustainable agriculture • Livestock and poultry development • Access to social safety nets and entitlements • Disability welfare • Capacity building	• Capacity building of SHGs • Formation of Panchayat Level Federations • Capacity building of SHGs • Marketing support and products exhibitions • Convergence with government departments • Skill training and placement of youth	• Capacity building of community leaders • Facilitating action plans for CDS • Financial Literacy Campaigns • Micro Enterprise promotion and support • Yuvashree (programme for generating jobs) • Crisis Management Fund • Solid Waste Management • Promotion of collective farming • Implementation of NREGS • Implementation of Ashraya (rehabilitation of destitute families) • Holistic child development	• Strengthening the SHGs, VLCs and CMRCs • Capacity building for upgrading the skill of women • Convergence with line departments • Gender integration • Promotion of drudgery reduction activities • Training and support for taking up income generation activities	• Support in SHG-bank linkage • Convergence with government programmes with respect to women and child • Support in income generation activities—skill development and marketing support • Support in working against social evils • Providing awareness in health, hygiene and sanitation • Capacity Building support	• Financing Micro Investment Plans • Skill development and jobs for rural youth • Innovations on livelihood enhancement and promotion	• Capacity Building support • Social development • Livelihood promotion

Sources: Data submitted for this study, annual reports and websites of respective organizations.
Note: n.a.: not available.

APPENDIX 6: FEDERATION PROMOTION DETAILS—GOVERNMENT ORGANIZATIONS

#	Name of NGO/state	Brief statement of vision/mission	SHG model type	Particulars of federation model	Sources of external loan funds for SHG on-lending	Terms of loans to SHGs	Remarks
1	SERP, Andhra Pradesh	**Vision:** Every poorest of poor family in the rural areas of the state comes out of poverty with increased and sustainable livelihood opportunities, established with intensive handholding support in a phased manner.	Promote SHG–bank linkages directly and through SHG federations.	SHGs–Village Organization–Mandal Samakhya (block-level federation)–Zilla Samakhya (district-level federation)	**Mandal Samakhya:** CIF is a grant to Mandal Samakhya which is lent to VOs at 6%. Bank loans to Mandal Samakhyas at prevailing rates.	**SHGs:** Receive loans from banks both at 8% to 12% and also at 3% back end subsidy under pavala vaddi scheme. Receive loans from Mandal Samakhya through VO at 12%. Since Sep 2011, receiving loans from Stree Nidhi at 13% interest rate in the first year.	A host of services including building strong/sustainable institutions of the poor, sustainable livelihoods, community managed sustainable agriculture, livestock and poultry development, access to social safety nets and entitlements, disability welfare and capacity building are provided by SERP through CBOs.

Stree Nidhi, a microfinance bank has been established as joint venture of government and MSs. |

Appendix 6 *(Continued)*

#	Name of NGO/state	Brief statement of vision/mission	SHG model type	Particulars of federation model	Sources of external loan funds for SHG on-lending	Terms of loans to SHGs	Remarks
2	TNCDW (Mahalir Thittam), Tamil Nadu	**Vision:** To build strong and self reliant SHG federations at the village panchayat, block and district levels throughout the State.	SHGs consist of 12–20 BPL women members in the age group of 18–60 years residing in the same area.	Village level SHG federations—Panchayat Level Federations registered as societies under Tamil Nadu Society's Registration Act of 1975.	Bank Loans, SEED Money. On a pilot basis, restructured PLFs accessed bulk loans from banks and successfully accomplished the role of financial intermediaries to SHGs. Hence during 2009–10, 102 PLFs have been provided bulk loan of ₹ 275.2 millions by various Banks.	Receive loans from banks at applicable rates.	PLF is promoted for SHG monitoring, SHG strengthening, economies of scale in production and marketing provides collective strength to the SHGs and acts as a platform to fight against problems commonly faced by the members. Since 2006–07, government is providing seed money to the PLFs. Representatives of PLF included in credit rating team to rate SHGs for credit linkage, in committee to oversee payments under NREGA. Also, well functioning PLFs associated with Mahalir Thittam for formation of SHGs on par with other NGOs.

		Mission	Model	Structure	Financial intermediation	SHG loans	Activities
3	Kudumbashree (Kerala)	**Mission:** To eradicate absolute poverty through concerted community action under the leadership of local governments, by facilitating organization of the poor for combining self-help with demand-led convergence of available services and resources to tackle the multiple dimensions and manifestations of poverty, holistically.	Neighbourhood groups (NHGs)—Groups of 10–20 women from the same neighbourhood form the foundation of the structure.	Three-tier model with Neighbourhood Groups (NHGs) form the basic tier, Area Development societies as the second tier and Community Development Societies (CDS) as the third tier.	Not applicable. CDSs did take up financial intermediation role in implementation of Bhavanashree but were not successful in the role and hence currently are not taking up financial intermediation.	**SHGs** receive loans from banks. Also, interest subsidy of 5% is provided by the government for loans taken from 7 banks which came forward to lend at 9% (before subsidy).	NHGs avail loans from various banks and, CDS provides bank linkage coordination, Information dissemination, Community network strengthening, Facilitating income-generating activity, identification of poor for other development programs, Legal literacy activities, Facilitation of Centrally Sponsored Schemes.
4	MAVIM	**Mission:** To bring about gender justice and equality for women, investing in human capital	SHG–bank linkage model	200–250 SHGs form Community Managed Resource Centre (CMRC) in a cluster of around 20 villages.	Not Applicable	**SHGs** take loan from banks at prevailing interest rates. Also, Maharashtra	CMRCs, registered under Society's Act 1860 and provide capacity building training to members, bank

Appendix 6 (*Continued*)

Appendix 6 (Continued)

#	Name of NGO/state	Brief statement of vision/mission	SHG model type	Particulars of federation model	Sources of external loan funds for SHG on-lending	Terms of loans to SHGs	Remarks
		and the capacity building of women, thus making them economically and socially empowered and enabling them to access sustainable livelihoods.'				government provides subsidized loans to SHGs under which SHGs can avail bank loan at 4% interest rate (back ended).	linkages, gradation, and audit of SHGs, assess the livelihood needs of SHGs, tapping the required resources through convergence with various government schemes and services and enabling the SHGs to access them and take up community development programmers. CMRCs charge fees from SHGs for the services provided.
5	Mission Shakti	Mission statement: Help construct a self reliant gender just society which is conscious of socio-economic issues, with	SHG–bank linkage and linkage of SHGs with Block Level Federations	Four tier structure with SHGs at the village level, cluster level federation, Block Level Federations and district level Federations.	23 federations receive loan from banks at 9%–9.5%, other federations are yet to start financial	SHGs: Receive loans from banks at prevailing rates and from federations at 12% reducing balance (in Ganjam district)	The clusters are informal bodies but the block and district level federations are registered under the Societies Act.

No.	Objective	SHG formation	Federation structure	Revolving fund	Bank loans	Project provides assistance
	cooperative spirit where women are skilled to undertake their choice of activities without hindrances or dependence.			intermediation; 170 federations received revolving fund from government and they are yet to disburse it to SHGs.	Bank loans at applicable interest rates	Project provides assistance for livelihood initiatives of poor through by developing CBOs, strengthens them, enhances the skills and capacities of poor and promotes transparent governance and social accountability.
6	TRIPTI aims at enhancing the socio-economic status of the poor, especially women and disadvantaged groups	SHG–bank linkage. Forms own SHGs and also associated with SHGs formed under Mission Shakti	SHGs at the village level (Tier-1), Cluster level federations (CLF-Tier-II) in between SHGs and Gram Panchayat level Federations (GPLF-Tier-III)	Not Applicable		
7	**Objective:** To enhance the social and economic empowerment of the rural poor by creating self managed community	SHGs formed by members of poor households for promotion of savings and credit	SHGs (12–15) federate to form VO and cluster level federation by federating the VOs in about 3 to 5 Panchayats.	Not Applicable (only source is CIF)	Bank loans at applicable interest rates and loans from project to SHGs at 12% interest.	There are no block level federations so far. The CBO framework is not yet complete and hence loans are provided by project to SHGs directly under the agreement that

TRIPTI (row 6): Bank loans at applicable interest rates

Appendix 6 (*Continued*)

Appendix 6 (Continued)

#	Name of NGO/state	Brief statement of vision/mission	SHG model type	Particulars of federation model	Sources of external loan funds for SHG on-lending	Terms of loans to SHGs	Remarks
		institutions of participating households, enhancing income through sustainable livelihoods and increasing access to social protection and food security					SHG shall return the amount with 12% interest to VO and VO shall return the amount to CLF (as and when it is formed) at 6% interest. Loans are provided from SHGs to members at 24% interest rate. CIF has four components—initial capitalization fund, food security fund, health risk fund and livelihood fund. Currently, SHGs are receiving loans from project through initial capitalization fund and all the other components of CIF are being provided to SHGs exclusively through VOs.

Note: n.a.: not available.

Name of the federation	BMASS, Jagannath-prasad Average cost per SHG (₹)	Dharmasagar Mandal Samakhya Average cost per SHG (₹)	PMSS Average cost per SHG (₹)	IIMF Average cost per SHG (₹)	Sanginee Average cost per SHG (₹)	ASSSL Average cost per SHG (₹)	Savera Average cost per SHG (₹)	PALMA Average cost per SHG (₹)	Boondh Bachat Sangh Average cost per SHG (₹)	CGMST Average cost per SHG (₹)	Average total cost (unadjusted) (all federations)	Average total cost for NGO federations (unadjusted) (i.e., except BMASS and Dharmasagar)
Cost of Social Mobilization and SHG Development												
1. Salaries and Honoraria	0	1,405	3,651	8,830	2,335	10,685	12,575	1,473	1,144	698	4,280	5,174
2. Cost of Books and Materials	0	233	982	79	116	463	303	663	906	166	391	460
3. Training Costs	401	1,000	2,639	4,230	145	1,751	1,454	1,621	1,187	1,263	1,569	1,786
4. Capital for entry point activities of SHGs and VOs/clusters	0	0	0	0	0	0	0	0	0	645	65	81
A. Average Social Mobilization Cost per SHG	401 (11)	2,638 (21)	7,272 (42)	13,139 (56)	2,596 (14)	12,900 (61)	14,332 (46)	3,757 (8)	3,237 (19)	2,772 (19)	6,305 (32)	7,501 (33)

Appendix 7 (Continued)

Appendix 7 (Continued)

Name of the federation	BMASS, Jagannathprasad Average cost per SHG (₹)	Dharmasagar Mandal Samakhya Average cost per SHG (₹)	PMSS Average cost per SHG (₹)	IIMF Average cost per SHG (₹)	Sanginee Average cost per SHG (₹)	ASSSL Average cost per SHG (₹)	Savera Average cost per SHG (₹)	PALMA Average cost per SHG (₹)	Boondh Bachat Sangh Average cost per SHG (₹)	CGMST Average cost per SHG (₹)	Average total cost (unadjusted) (all federations)	Average total cost for NGO federations (unadjusted) (i.e., except BMASS and Dharmasagar)
Support Costs for Project/Block/Mandal level Federation												
1. Initial dialogues on federation formation and other events	443	2	4,834	0	0	917	236	1,332	188	79	803	948
2. Federation staff costs	1,794	1,133	184	3,420	12,903	3,379	4,002	15,573	8,865	387	5,164	6,089
3. Office rent and other costs	337	0	74	484	178	1,370	346	1,298	1,522	3,412	902	1,085
4. Honoraria and Meeting Expenses	294	778	3,225	411	397	784	176	779	611	5,175	1,263	1,445
5. Training of EC members	237	22	1,167	0	56	799	116	91	233	61	278	315
6. Provision of RLF/Endowment Fund	0	8,333	0	0	0	726	0	7,267	0	0	1,633	999
B. Average Support cost for block/mandal federation per SHG	3,105 (89)	10,268 (79)	9,484 (49)	4,315 (26)	13,533 (81)	7,975 (28)	4,876 (27)	26,340 (64)	11,419 (65)	9,114 (60)	10,042 (51)	10,882 (48)

Overheads - Project management at NGO/district federation/PMU level												
(a) Social Mobilization SHGS/VOs	0	62	898	3,371	926	0	3,765	8,617	0	0	1,764	2,197
(b) Support to Federation for operations	0	15	458	729	45	2,150	3,604	2,124	2,971	3,548	1,564	1,954
C. Average NGO/project/PMU level overheads per SHG	0 (0)	77 (1.5)	1,356 (9)	4,100 (18)	971 (6)	2,150 (11)	7,369 (29)	10,741 (27)	2,971 (16)	3,548 (21)	3,328 (17)	4,151 (18)
D. Average total development cost per SHG (A + B + C)	3,505 (100)	12,984 (100)	18,113 (100)	21,556 (100)	17,100 (100)	23,025 (100)	26,577 (100)	40,837 (100)	17,627 (100)	15,434 (100)	19,676 (100)	22,533 (100)

Source: Srinivasan and Tankha (2010).

Note: Values in brackets are percentages of Average Costs per SHG to Average Total Costs per SHG for each federation

@ Not adjusted for years of support

APPENDIX 8: APNI SEHKARI SEWA SAMITI: ACTIVITY-BASED COSTS OF DEVELOPMENT AND SUPPORT FOR SHGS AND FEDERATIONS (₹ PER SHG)

Particulars of activity/cost item	Total 2002–03 to 2007–08	Remarks
1. Stationery	500	Costs met by SHGs from 2004–05 onwards
2. Formation visit	3,000	Formation visits (first meeting—choupal with three staff + 3 visits—one staff + 12 visits to monthly meeting (two meetings covered per day)— ₹ 250 × 6 person days, i.e, ₹ 1,500 *plus* 250 × 6 person days for meetings, i.e., ₹ 1,500, total ₹ 3,000 @ ₹ 250 per day with travel and extras
3. Leadership training at village for all SHG members	400	Two-day training (2 staff plus travel + food and other meeting expenses)—per village average 3 SHGs, ₹ 1,200, i.e., ₹ 400 per SHG.
4. Block-level training for all SHG leaders—residential	600	3 staff facilitators—cost salary, travel, food, stay ₹ 6,000 for 10 SHGs, i.e., ₹ 600 per SHG
5. EDP training group leaders—at block level	900	Year 2 (2003–04) EDP training group leaders—at block level—inc. resource persons @ ₹ 1,000 per day, total expenses ₹ 9,000 for 10 SHGs, i.e., ₹ 900 per SHG
6. Attending meetings/ bookkeeping	7,500	Attending meetings/ bookkeeping—12 visits per SHG—2 SHGs per day—12 day @ ₹ 250, i.e., ₹ 1,500 per SHG per year (also third year and onwards)
A. Social mobilization, SHG formation and support cost per SHG (total items 1 to 6)	12,900	

Particulars of activity/cost item	Total 2002–03 to 2007–08	Remarks
7. Exposure visit for federation leaders	300	Exposure Visit for federation leaders—to leading NGO, other SHGs by bus, e.g., MYRADA (₹ 100,000) for 2 federations (350 SHGs)—₹ 300 per SHG
8. Exposure visit for mature SHG leaders to SEWA, PEDO, etc.	225	Exposure visit for mature SHG leaders—SEWA, Ahmedabad, PEDO, etc.—50 persons— ₹ 75,000, i.e., ₹ 225 per SHG
9. Workshop for discussion on mode of federation	150	Two two-day workshops for discussion on mode of federation 30 participants—₹ 25,000 each, ₹ 50,000 or ₹ 150 per SHG
10. Study on federation mode	150	Study on federation mode— ₹ 50,000–₹ 150 per SHG
11. Registration fee	0	Registration fee—nil for cooperatives
12. Intensive one year of meetings at block level	1,100	Year 3 and onwards: Intensive one year of meetings at block level—on credit linkage and federation formation—one SHG leader per group—12 meetings— ₹ 40,000–₹ 1,100 per SHG
13. Executive committee meetings of federation—monthly	600	Executive committee meetings of federation—monthly—travel and meeting expenses—₹ 100,000 per 350 SHGs—Total ₹ 300 per SHG over two years
14. Orientation and inputs of NGO staff	2,000	Orientation and inputs of NGO staff—including training outside at BIRD, Lucknow and abroad— approx. ₹ 150,000 to ₹ 200,000 per year—₹ 500 per year per SHG (covers all annual NGO technical support and overheads)
15. Federation office rent	400	Federation Office Rent—₹ 12,000 per federation—₹ 100 per SHG—4 years

Appendix 8 *(Continued)*

Appendix 8 *(Continued)*

Particulars of activity/cost item	Total 2002–03 to 2007–08	Remarks
16. Federation office utilities	400	Federation Office Utilities— ₹ 12,000 per federation—₹ 100 per SHG—4 years
17. Human Resources	3,600	Human Resource—1 Accountant and 1 Office Attendant per federation—year 2004–05 and 2007–08 (on account of expansion) ₹ 180,000, i.e., ₹ 1,800 per SHG (at time of grant availability from RMK and SIDBI)
18. Furniture and fittings	200	Furniture and fittings/Computer— ₹ 100,000 per federation—twice; ₹ 100 per SHG in *2004–05* and ₹ 100 per SHG in *2007–08*
19. Revolving loan fund	1,000	
B. Cost of Federation Formation and Support per SHG (total items 7 to 19)	**10,125**	
C. Average Total Cost per SHG	**23,025**	

Source: Srinivasan and Tankha (2010).

APPENDIX 9: MODELS OF BANK LENDING TO SHGS/JLGS

Figure A9.1: SHG–Bank Linkage, ICICI Partnership Model and RBI's Business
Correspondent Model

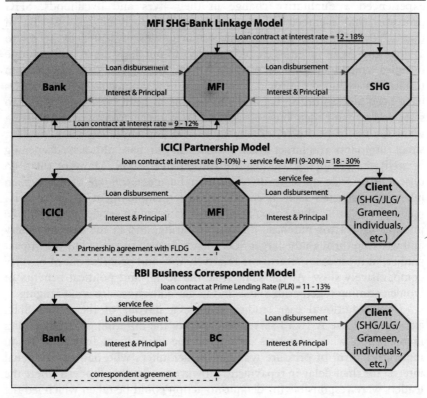

Source: Tankha (2006b).

Notes: 1. Panel 1 illustrates the variant of the SHG–bank linkage model where
            NGO-MFIs act as financial intermediaries. Panels 2 and 3 illustrate two
            types of business correspondent models: (*a*) partnership model as earlier
            implemented by ICICI bank (since discontinued); and (*b*) as envisaged
            by the Reserve Bank of India vide its 25 January 2006 guidelines. Dotted
            lines in panels 2 and 3 show the pass-through character of bank loans
            in partnership and BC models where NGO-MFIs and other business
            correspondents effectively act at bank agents or 'microfinance service
            providers' rather than financial intermediary institutions.
         2. Interest rates are indicative and not necessarily currently prevalent rates.

APPENDIX 10: SHG CASE STUDIES

An analysis of the outcomes and impact of SHG functioning is incomplete without an account of the real-life stories of SHGs members who experienced a qualitative change in their lives and livelihoods. SHG processes and membership are widely accepted to be empowering in themselves. However, the economic opportunities presented by access to savings and credit facilities enable members to purchase assets and generate incomes which had not been possible before. The first 12 case studies from 6 states are included to provide examples of how women members of SHGs have been able to utilize big and small loans to fulfil family needs and to start and expand their businesses. The cases range from women utilizing loans for major health crises, education and household expenses, poultry, small ruminants and larger milch animals, to purchase of house, deepening of well, sharecropping, trading and productive assets. Many of them go on either to scale up or to diversify their businesses. Some of the women microentrepreneurs have been able to offer employment to other SHG members. In still other cases, the focus has been on group activity made possible by tractor purchase for custom hiring; and in the case of fishery and weaving through the larger SGSY loan. As also suggested by the impact studies, in most cases returns are relatively low and progress out of poverty comparatively slow. At the same time the social and political benefits of women coming together in SHGs and larger collectives are wide-ranging.

Three additional case studies provide a flavour of the varied SHG experience. Case A.10.13 serves to illustrate the differing group dynamics in operation when members default on the bank loan. In Rajasthan an innovative form of pressure was put on defaulters who had to pay penal interest for their delay in repayment. However, in Andhra Pradesh where the leaders were responsible for default no action could be taken which led the SHG to become defunct. When it was revived it was on the condition that all members would equally share the loans.

The last two case studies illustrate experiences from tribal areas. In these areas due to the absence of opportunities for investment in enterprises on a large scale, loan demand and off-take is limited. Yet the SHG has been used as a means for strengthening preexisting institutions and as a means of food security. The grain bank is a popular initiative undertaken under SHG management, which in turn has led to SHGs managing the public distribution system in certain areas. Case A.10.14 provides an experience of grain banking from Maharashtra. Indeed, NABARD launched grain banking pilots in Odisha and Chhattisgarh and a pilot project in Kalahandi district Odisha for SHGs to save in grain and use the grain stock for loan eligibility. Finally, Case A.10.15 an SHG experience, also from Kalahandi district in Odisha, illustrates the counter-intuitive, but rational, behaviour of SHGs and their promoter and the fact that there are development challenges that SHGs microfinance cannot address.

A.10.1 Tamil Nadu

From Wage Earner to Entrepreneur

Panjavarnam hails from a small village, Alagapuri in Natham Taluk, Dindigul district, Tamil Nadu. Her husband works as a wage labourer in a coconut warehouse located in Parali village. Panjavarnam contracts mango and coconut trees as a business in addition to running a thatch making business as a permanent venture. Her husband's role is limited to managing family affairs, whereas she is the main breadwinner in her family.

Panjavarnam started the first SHG in the village in 1987 without any external support. After joining Kalasam, she formed five Kalasam groups on her own. This helped her to become Ward member in the panchayat board without any competition. As Ward member, she has been involved in development efforts such as bringing drinking water connections to all the streets in the village, building a cement platform for processing grains as well as a road facility.

She joined Muthalamman Kalasam in 1999 and availed loans to meet her family needs like education, household expenses, jewellery and to start her business. The first loan that she got from Kalasam was used for redeeming her jewels and to close her external high-cost debts. She managed her family finances professionally and started a thatch making business. The Kalasam loan helped her to become a self-made entrepreneur. She provides employment to two to three persons on an average in the business. She invested ₹ 30,000 for mango tree contracting and earned ₹ 13,375 as profit from the business. She also invested ₹ 6,000 for coconut tree contracting. She earned ₹ 8,500 as profit from coconut sales alone in addition to the supply of the tree thatches. With her increased income she leased mango and coconut orchards.

Muthalamman Kalasam is functioning well under her leadership. It has linked itself with Mahakalasam (federation) and the local commercial bank branch. The group has availed four loans worth of ₹ 195,000 from Mahakalasam and the Indian Overseas Bank.

Adapted from
'The Role of SHG Federation in the Promotion of Livelihoods and
Community Enterprises: A Case of Mahakalasam'
—Indian School of Livelihood Promotion

A.10.2 Andhra Pradesh

Investment in Microenterprise

Padmavati Devi of Garla Mandal in Khammam District of Andhra Pradesh belongs to a very poor family. With a meagre income, it was very difficult for her husband to meet the expenditure of family. Padmavati was, however, playing multiple roles in the family like wife, daughter and provider. She thought of doing some work as a provider. The first problem before her was how to do a business without money. Through one of her friends she came to know that in her village there was an SHG called Gram Samakhya that provides loans to the members of SHGs. She thought of investing in a grinding mill in the village. Therefore, she became a member of the Gram Samakhya and approached her group leader for a loan. The group leader placed her application before the Mahila Mandal Samakhya. She could convince the Mahila Mandal Samakhya. She got a loan of ₹ 25, 000 from Rashtriya Mahila Kosh through the Mandal Samakhya. She decided to go for two grinding mills—for chillies and rice. The total cost of these mills was ₹ 30,000. To meet the full cost of the mills she also borrowed ₹ 5,000 from one of the members of the SHG. With this she started two grinding mills in the village. She now earns ₹ 2,000 per month. Out of this ₹ 1,500 is being used to repayment of the loan and the remaining amount of ₹ 500 is being used to supplement her monthly expenditure. She says that her family and other group members of Gram Samakhya are happy to have easy microcredit assistance from RMK.

Adapted from Department for Rural Development Website

A.10.3 Odisha

Mukta Uplifts Her Family

Mukta lives in a remote tribal village in Odisha. The major source of livelihood for the family is sharecropping (paddy cultivation) and daily wage earning on construction sites. The income from sharecropping was not enough to meet their basic needs. Seasonally, the family collected minor forest produce like Sal leaves to make leaf plates, which helped them earn an extra ₹ 500 per month. Mukta and her husband needed to borrow money from moneylenders at a very high rate of interest.

When CYSD-Plan initiated operations in Baliposi village in 1999, the situation analysis showed that exploitation by moneylenders was a priority area requiring intervention. The idea was to develop a platform not just for mobilizing savings and recycling them to meet the credit needs of the members but also to develop social cohesion among women.

After a series of capacity building inputs on leadership, group management, recording keeping and entrepreneurship development and learning visits to other SHGs, the women's group started participating in the village development committee and playing a crucial role in village development activities. Mukta became one of the active members of the Maa Gojabayani SHG initiated by CYSD-Plan. Mukta, along with other group members, started by saving ₹ 5 every month. Mukta availed a loan of ₹ 2,000 from the group to buy two goats and two ducks as an additional source of income for her family. Within two years, Mukta had 10 goats and 15 ducks. Once the goats matured, she sold them, earning ₹ 5,000 from two goats and five ducks. Mukta repaid the loan to the group.

After some time, she took another loan of ₹ 10,000 from the group and invested ₹ 20,000 which she had saved from rearing goats and ducks to set up a tent house business. She purchased chairs, cooking utensils, lights and sound systems and engaged her son to manage the unit. Earlier the villagers used to depend on others outside their village for such needs. Her son managed the business well and Mukta repaid the loan. Mukta became an active member of the group and always made repayments on time. Once the tent house business was established, Mukta took a third loan from the group and bought a trolley rickshaw for her husband. As a result all the members of Mukta's household were engaged in regular employment and could make timely repayment of the loan. The family had a regular income and was financially secure. Her thatched house has been replaced with a newly built house with a tiled roof and she has purchased one acre of cultivable agricultural land which is a permanent asset for her and her family. The Maa Gojabayani SHG is now linked with a bank and additional credit is available for members. Like Mukta, other members of the group have also started individual enterprises. Mukta has become a role model in the area and is now confident enough to motivate other villagers to work together for their own development. The case study demonstrates how aspiration and conviction of an individual play a significant role in progressive utilization of credit for improvement of the household economy.

Adapted from material provided by Plan India

A.10.4 Odisha

Housewife to Successful Entrepreneur

Gangadevi Sahu aged 43 years belongs to Nua Kamasaragada village in Odisha. Surrounded by hills and jungles, the village is situated 110 km from Berhampur—the silk city of Odisha. Gangadevi's husband works in a bakery for a monthly income of ₹ 3,000. After taking care of his own expenses, he can barely manage to send ₹ 500 to ₹ 1,000 per month to his family.

Gangadevi suggested to her husband to leave his job and start a bakery in her village. As Secretary of Maa Saraswati WSHG, it was Gangadevi's responsibility to create employment opportunities for herself and other SHG members in the village. Initially her husband was reluctant to start an enterprise on his own. Motivated by his wife and SHG members, he decided to start a bakery in the village with support of Gangadevi and other SHG members. As they did not have capital to start a bakery, Gangadevi took a loan of ₹ 10,000 from the Jagannathprasad Mahila Sanchayika Sangha SHG federation. After facing initial problems in running the business, things began to change and the business started flowing with Gangadevi's constant encouragement and support for her husband's efforts to improve the quality and variety of the bakery products.

To further extend the business enterprise, Gangadevi availed of four more loans from the federation. Her bakery has today grown to produce and sell a large variety of products like buns, biscuits and cakes. At the same time, by employing four other SHG members besides her husband she also generated income for them. The four SHG members earn ₹ 1,200 to ₹ 1,500 per month and the people of Nua Kamasaragada have benefited from a variety of affordable baked goods. The family income of Gangadevi has gone up from ₹ 12,000 to ₹ 14,000 a month. Gangadevi then undertook training in mushroom cultivation and has recently started a mushroom cultivation unit that has helped to diversify her source of income as well as provide employment to other members of her SHG.

Adapted from Block Mahila Sanchayika Sangh, Jagannathprasad

A.10.5 Rajasthan

Life transformation through SHG

SabitaBen is a resident of Simalwara Road which is 5 km away from Kankradara Gram Panchayat in Simalwara block of Dungarpur district in Rajasthan. She became a member of an SHG in her village. Initially the members started with small savings. Soon enough they realized the importance of savings and began increasing. Today SabitaBen has a cumulative saving of ₹ 6,756 against her name in the SHG account. She has undergone various training programmes organized by PEDO such as SHG leader's orientation, camp on SHG functioning, training on credit planning, institutional arrangements and cluster management.

The first loan taken by SabitaBen was used to purchase a house, while subsequent loans were taken for livelihood activities. SabitaBen also took a loan of ₹ 10,000 to buy a buffalo. The buffalo has been yielding 4 litres of milk every day for the last 10 months and SabitaBen has earned a net income of ₹ 9,600 by selling the milk. The 5 kg ghee produced from the milk earns her another ₹ 2,000. Sabita also sold organic manure at ₹ 2,000 per tractor load. Thus her total income from the buffalo earned her ₹ 13,600 over a period of 10 months. SabitaBen also availed a loan of ₹ 10,000 for deepening her well. SabitaBen then decided to cultivate high-value fruits and vegetables for which there was a readymade local demand in the village. The farm produce also served the needs of her family and has ensured nutritional security for them.

The SHG intervention has enabled SabitaBen to generate savings and initiate a range of livelihood activities. She was motivated and guided by the SHG in all her initiatives. Her self-image has improved radically as she is viewed with respect by her husband and the village community as the main livelihood earner.

Adapted from Jan Shiksha Evam Vikas Sangathan,
People's Education and Development Organization (PEDO)

A.10.6 Uttar Pradesh

Livelihood Enhancement through Self-help

Dilawarpur was a village that typified rural poverty. Most poor households eked out an existence from farming; others relied on labour on the richer families' fields while still others found employment outside the village. In these cases, the poor borrow money from the local moneylenders at 10% interest, and failure to return the loan would result in the male members of the family becoming bonded labour for the *sahukar*.

All this began to change when RGMVP first started motivating the women to join SHGs. Shiv Swayam Sahayata Samooh was formed on 18 November 2005. Initially, its 16 members began by saving ₹ 20 per month which was later increased to ₹ 40 per month. A cash credit limit of ₹ 25,000 was cleared by Grameen Bank where the SHG had its account. The members of the SHG took small loans from the amount for their needs. The turning point came when the National Dairy Development Board (NDDB) set up a Bulk Milk Cooler (BMC). RGMVP began encouraging and motivating the members of Shiv Swayam Sahayata Samooh to invest in milch cattle. One member borrowed ₹ 10,000 initially for purchasing a buffalo and then took another loan of ₹ 15,000 for another buffalo after returning the first loan. A total of 7 members took a loan of ₹ 105,000 to purchase buffaloes or cows. Almost all of the group's members are engaged in the dairy business and earn between ₹ 150 to ₹ 250 per day from this activity. The women have received three days of training from experts at RGMVP on the best practices of dairy work and are now adept at ensuring that their milk has the right fat content to get a good rate per litre.

The milk collected at the village is sent to the NDDB's BMC. At the BMC, each lot of milk is weighed and tested for fat content. The rate is decided on the basis of the fat content and the weight, and is ₹ 16 per litre on average for buffalo milk and ₹ 14 per litre on average for cow's milk. Before the advent of the BMC, the women used to get a rate of ₹ 10 per litre for both cow and buffalo milk.

The lives of the members of the Shiv Swayam Sahayata Samooh have seen a marked and steady improvement over the past two years as a result of income generation and livelihood enhancement due to dairy activities.

Adapted from Rajiv Gandhi Mahila Vikas Pariyojona Website/
Case Studies

A.10.7 Tamil Nadu

Women SHGs Show Bankers the Way

M. Latha, barely 27 years old, has not let her village background and limited education come in the way of handling the intricacies involved in getting a loan of ₹ 300,000 from a nationalized bank in her village, Perumanur, about 10 km from Salem town in Tamil Nadu. The bank on its part closely observes the saving pattern of the SHG and decides to lend only when savings range from ₹ 10 to even ₹ 50 a week per member. It identifies an NGO that works with the group, monitoring its meetings, keeping the accounts and training the members on all aspects of micro credit. Once a group has saved ₹ 40,000 to ₹ 50,000 the bank moves in to provide three to four times the amount as loan.

Latha is the leader of a 20-member SHG in Salem district, where the Indian Bank hopes to disburse, by the end of the financial year, loans of ₹ 60 million to about 1,200 SHGs. With ₹ 300,000 her group has bought a tractor and is renting out its services for a range of activities from ploughing of fields to transporting of sand, bricks and other construction material. On an average, the group is able to rent out the tractor for about 20 days a month at ₹ 300 an hour. From the profits, the SHG has already repaid ₹ 152,000 of the amount lent by Indian Bank at 12% interest.

While her husband works as a daily wage labourer, Latha handles the group's finances, which include the personal savings of its members and the repayment of loan from the profits earned through the tractor. The less advantaged members of her group are employed, four or five at a time, in loading and unloading construction material. The group pays each worker a daily wage of ₹ 50. So for these women, it is a double income.

Adapted from Self-Help Group success stories—NABARD Website

A.10.8 Andhra Pradesh

Success Story of a Bangle Trader

Satyavati lives in Peravali village, a mandal in West Godavari District of Andhra Pradesh. Her husband owns one and a half acres of land, but apart from cultivating, he has no other employment. Satyavati sells bangles, plastic toys and other simple gift items in village markets. She buys ₹ 2,000 worth of stock at one time and can usually sell these items in a fortnight or one month. Since she normally sells her goods for double the cost price she earns about ₹ 2,000 a month.

Satyavati had heard about various government schemes but could not access any scheme where credit from financial institutions was linked. She could not take a bank loan as she does not have any property in her name as security against the loan. She borrowed working capital form the local moneylenders at a very high rate of interest up to 36% in a year.

Satyavati was very happy when she heard that the DWCRA scheme had been introduced in the district and a group of women were coming together as an SHG as their savings entitled them to ₹ 25, 000 as revolving fund from DRDA. She suggested to 14 of her friends in the neighbourhood who were in the same business to form an SHG so that they could avail revolving fund under DWCRA scheme. The members of the group started meeting regularly once in a month and deposited ₹ 450 in their joint account opened in Andhra Bank. After three months, members decided to prioritize their needs and two of the members borrowed ₹ 500 each from the group.

Within four years the group had saved ₹ 21,600 and built a corpus of ₹ 54,000. The group has earned more than ₹ 3,000 from interest on loans. The women members have taken 32 loans ranging from ₹ 200 to ₹ 3,500. Satisfied with the discipline of the women, Andhra Bank extended a credit of ₹ 75,000 to the group under the SHG Scheme of NABARD. Each member who earned ₹ 300 to ₹ 400 per month is now able to earn ₹ 1,500 to ₹ 2,000 by expanding their business activity. The group has thus set an example for many more women in the village to come together as SHGs.

Adapted from Department of Rural Development, Government of Andhra Pradesh Website

A.10.9 Assam

Success Stories of Two SGSY SHGs

The Milan SHG was formed under the guidance of Nowboicha Development Block in Assam during 2002–03. The group passed the first grading test in

2002–03 after which a sum of ₹ 25,000 was provided as revolving fund in 2003. During 2004–05 the SHG passed the second grading test as a result of which the Co-op Apex Bank, North Lakhimpur sanctioned an amount of ₹ 2.50 lakh. A subsidy amount of ₹ 60,000 was released to the SHG in the first phase.

A common fishery tank of area measuring about one hectare was constructed at a convenient spot in the village. The members of the group have since been rearing fingerlings and fish seeds along with fish and selling them in the local market as well as outside the state in Arunachal Pradesh. Till date the group has earned more than ₹ 1 lakh. The SHG has already repaid the bank ₹ 35,000.

The Biswajyoti Mahila SHG, Kalita Gaon was formed under the guidance of Telahi Dev. The group passed the first grading test in 2005–06. A sum of ₹ 25,000 was provided to the SHG as revolving fund in March 2006. During 2005–06 the SHG passed the second grading test after which the Bank of Baroda, Bormuria Tiniali, North Lakhimpur sanctioned an amount of ₹ 250,000 against their weaving activity.

The group now weaves different types of cloth such as *mekhela, sadar, gamusa, endisadar* and sells their products in the local market as well at the different SHG *melas* held from time to time in the state and at district level.

Adapted from Department of Rural Development,
Government of Assam Website

A.10.10 Odisha

The Catalyst Within: Women's SHG Transforms a Community

In Majhi Sahi, a hamlet in Jhatiada village in Rasgobindpur block of Mayurbhanj district, Odisha that has a predominantly scheduled caste population, a WSHG has made a mark in the face of male apathy to look beyond everyday realities. The Majhis are an economically weak community whose primary occupations comprise wage labour and Sal leaf collection. Most men folk are addicted to country liquor and shirk all household responsibilities.

When Unnayan, already involved in livelihood and woman empowerment issues in the area, launched its unique programme, Mahila Shanti Sena (Woman Peace Corps), among the women of the community and explained the merits of forming a SHG, the response was lukewarm. The challenge was accepted by Gayatri Behera who was already impressed by the work of other SHGs in nearby villages. She took the mantle of the leader and tried to motivate other women. Through counselling and hard work, she formed Balukeswari Swayam Sahayak Gosthi, an SHG comprising 17 women.

Each member of the group has been able to save ₹ 25 per month. They have accumulated ₹ 30,325 (member's monthly savings and interest generated from the internal credit). The group also procured a bank loan of ₹ 18,000 that was used for share cropping in summer. The SHG members participated in training programmes on SHG concepts and management, gender, etc., conducted by Unnayan which has built their capacity.

Since there was an earning from the group activities SHG members now have a say in domestic decision-making. Earlier women were victims of domestic violence which has now been substantially reduced. They have also been able to put pressure on their male folk against consumption of liquor. The training and exposure have made the group members aware about health, good hygiene practices and education of children.

Most importantly the Majhi community that was earlier treated as outcasts and untouchables has come to be accepted by neighbours as a force that has helped solve problems in the village.

Adapted from case study prepared by Bhanu Prasad Panigrahi
for Unnayan

A.10.11 Andhra Pradesh

Ideal Women's Self-help Group (WSHG)

Sailaja is fully aware of the harmful effects of environmental pollution. She has started a bag manufacturing unit for her livelihood and shaped the unit as an environment-friendly one. She has undertaken the jute bag manufacture as a cottage industry in Shadnagar town of Mahabubnagar district.

Sailaja, a member of an SHG in the town, took a loan amount of ₹ 100,000 from Andhra Pradesh Grameena Vikas Bank and started making different varieties of jute bags which are harmless and ecological. Sailaja has employed 11 more SHG women in the process thus helping them for their livelihood.

She sells the bags in the neighbouring villages of Gadwal. All the women are earning ₹ 3,000 per month after paying the bank the monthly loan instalment of ₹ 5,000. Sailaja has set up her stall in the exhibition at the ongoing Bharat Nirman Public Information Campaign in Gadwal.

Adapted from Press Information Bureau,
Government of India, Hyderabad

A.10.12 Tamil Nadu

SHG Helps Meet Health Expenses

Sahin Banu has been a member of Kathambam Kalanjiam for the past eight years. Born and brought up in Erode, she came to Salem after marriage.

She is the mother of two school-going girls. She was forced to procure loans to meet her household expenses from moneylenders who charged her exorbitant rates of interest. She then joined Kalanjiam and was able to get credit support to meet her needs.

'I also suffered from severe stomachache and frequently visited the doctor,' she recalls. Her problem was diagnosed as a cyst in the uterus for which she had to undergo surgery that would cost ₹ 60,000.

'Kalanjiam came to my help at that time.' Given that she already had ₹ 10,000 as savings in her group, she was immediately given a loan of ₹ 40,000 from the group and could have her operation. 'Now I am well and paying back the money to the group,' says Sahin Banu.

Adapted from DHAN Foundation Website

A.10.13 Group Dynamics: Default of Loan

Rajasthan: Collective Action against a Defaulter

Five years ago, an SHG group in Madri village, Rajasthan had borrowed ₹ 50,000 from the bank. Ten members divided it equally between themselves. The monthly instalment to the bank was ₹ 1,700. Each member was supposed to pay ₹ 300 for 20 months. There was a penalty of ₹ 5 per month for late repayment. However, most members were late and only six had repaid by the 33rd month. These members then decided to start holding meetings at the place of those members who had not repaid. That member would then have to bear the expenses for their refreshments during the meeting. One of the members quickly paid up soon after this decision out of embarrassment. Five years from loan disbursement, the bank sent a notice to the group. Two women were still to pay. The group finally made full payment after the notice and the two defaulters were made to pay ₹ 2,500 each to cover the extra interest that the group had to bear due to late repayment.

Andhra Pradesh: No Action in Case of Default

Indira Podupu Sangam, an SHG from Nellepalli village in Chittoor district, Andhra Pradesh was formed in the year 1998 with 15 members promoted by a rural branch of the SV Grameen Bank. Within the group, eight of the members belong to two closely related families, and were relatively well off (borderline). The other members were not related, and were from borderline and poor families.

In 2000, the group got its first bank loan of ₹ 30,000. The two group leaders borrowed over half of this between them (one with ₹ 11,000, the other ₹ 6,000) and the balance amount of ₹ 13,000 was shared by the other members. The leaders did not repay their loans. Others in the group who were related to the leaders would not put any pressure on them to repay.

The other members questioned this, stopped depositing their savings and dropped out in 2001.

The group eventually stopped meeting—although the savings remained in the group account—and were partially adjusted against the bank loan. With government schemes increasingly being linked to the SHGs, 10 members (mostly related to each other) decided in 2004 to revive the group, this time on the understanding that they would divide equally whatever may be the loan amount. The group got a bank loan of ₹ 20,000 which was divided equally.

Adapted from SHG Light and Shades study (Sinha et al. [2009])

A.10.14 Maharashtra

Tribal Village Prospers through Grain-Bank

About 30 km from Shirpur block at Post Chakdu, Dhule district is a village situated just off the Shirpur Shahada Road. MAVIM mobilized SHGs of women in the village. The women in this small tribal village have successfully implemented this experiment.

The SHGs were taken to Waghshepa village in Nandurbar district for an exposure visit. They studied the grain-bank model implemented in that village in 2003 which led to the Durga Mata bachat gat in 2004. As the first step of the scheme, all members of the SHG collected one kg of grain each. Ten women initially collected 150 kg of grain. After this, the collected grain was safely stored. It was distributed among the members as per their need. When the harvest was over, the borrowers returned the grains with interest, that is, women members who had borrowed 15 kg returned 17½ kg of grain in repayment. Thus, eventually the SHG had a collection of 6 quintals of 'capital grain' and 82 kg of 'interest grain'. This collection gradually progressed year after year. Today, the SHG has a collection of 27 quintals of grain.

The members come together on a pre-decided day and dry this grain in the sun. The neem leaves that are found in ample quantity in the village are also dried during this time. After this, the dried grain and the dry neem leaves are stored together in a silo. The silo is sealed. This is one of the best ways to seal and store the grain. The SHGs thus not only succeeded in their experiment by fulfilling the needs of their members, but also helped other families in the village to become self-sufficient in their food grain needs. The village was able to rid itself of ruthless moneylenders. All this was possible due to the SHGs. More importantly, a PDS shop has been sanctioned to the Durga Mata SHG. The village has successfully traversed the path towards self-reliance with SHGs as their vehicle.

Adapted from material provided by Mahila Arthik
Vikas Mahamandal (MAVIM)

A.10.15 Odisha

Who Needs to Borrow from SHGs?

The Khond tribals of Thuamul Rampur block of Kalahandi district live in a part of Odisha that is known for both its food scarcity and starvation deaths as well as the breeding ground of *Plasmodium falciparum*, the deadly celebral malaria parasite. A reasonably assured water supply, grants from the Integrated Tribal Development Agency (ITDA) and agricultural extension programmes of a leading NGO of Odisha have helped the former practitioners of shifting cultivation to harvest a variety of fruits, vegetables and medicinal plants to enhance their incomes and living standards. Nevertheless, the four-month lean season from May to August continues to be a period of economic stress and scarcity.

In one hamlet the women of this community have been organized into four SHGs. They contribute ₹ 10 per month per head by way of savings. Their entire small monthly savings collection is religiously deposited in the local bank branch. Thus the Manikeswari SHG has built up an accumulated fund of ₹ 16,930.

The SHG with the encouragement of the promoting NGO, engages in the trading of niger seed (*alsi*) for which ₹ 7,000 was withdrawn from its bank account to buy the village produce of this crop and sell it at 25% profit over a three-month period. This translates into a small income of about ₹ 125 per member.

One would have expected that during the lean season that followed the SHGs would have been flooded with demands from their own members for consumption loans. However, no other withdrawals had been made from the group fund since the formation of the SHG. The reasons for the absence of SHG loaning are not far to seek. The ITDA and the NGO have created a grain bank which is managed each year in turn by a different SHG and is functioning effectively. The grain bank idea is based on the villagers' own coping mechanisms of the not too distant past. The Targeted Public Distribution System too provides highly subsidized grain. The small cash commitments of the secluded community are met through new sources of cash income from high-value crops. The villagers resort to the consumption of 'fallback foods' such as the controversial mango kernels at times of food scarcity. In any event the members do not borrow from the SHG or withdraw of their unutilized cash savings to fulfil their food requirements.

SHGs themselves are not keen to lend to individual members at times of scarcity. This is supported by the NGO—for fear of losses due to the inability of members to repay their loans. All this makes for a failure to rotate SHG funds which lie idle for nine months in the year in the low-yielding savings account with the local bank. At the same time it gives an idea of the alternative survival strategies, other than taking recourse to cash borrowings, adopted by the poor in times of scarcity along with some support from development agencies. As for endemic malaria in the district which has led to the deaths of many NGO personnel and villagers, it is a sombre reminder of the fact that many challenges of development cannot be addressed by microfinance.

Adapted from Tankha (2006a)

REFERENCES

ACCESS Development Services. (2009). 'A Study of SHG Federations in Odisha', commissioned by TRIPTI, Government of Odisha (unpublished).
———. (2011). *The Self Help Group Programme Beyond Two Decades ROUND TABLE*, Microfinance India Summit, New Delhi, 29 September.
Ananth, Bindu. (2005). 'Financing Microfinance—the ICICI Bank Partnership Model', *Small Enterprise Development*, 16 (1): 57–65.
APMAS. (2005). *A Study on Self-Help Group (SHG)-Bank Linkage in Andhra Pradesh*, Andhra Pradesh Mahila Abhivruddhi Society, Hyderabad.
———. (2007). *SHG Federations in India: A Perspective*, Andhra Pradesh Mahila Abhivruddhi Society, Hyderabad.
APMAS-MYRADA. (2009). *An Evaluation of Self-Help Affinity Groups Promoted by MYRADA*, Andhra Pradesh Mahila Abhivruddhi Society, Hyderabad, August. Available at http://www.apmas.org/pdf/Myrada%20-%20APMAS.pdf (accessed on 21 October 2011).
Arora, Sukhwinder. (2008). *Bullock-cart Workers' Association and BWDA Finance Limited: Leveraging Partnership for Growth*, Micro Save—market led solutions for financial services.
Arunachalam, Ramesh S. (2011). *The Journey of Indian Microfinance: Lessons for the Future*, Aapti Publications, Chennai.
Banerjee, A., E. Duflo, R. Glennerster and C. Kinnan. (2009). 'The Miracle of Microfinance: Evidence from a Randomized Evaluation', IFMR Research Working Paper Series No. 31, Centre for Microfinance, October. Available at http://economics.mit.edu/files/4162 (accessed on 20 October 2011).
BRLP. (2011). *Annual Administration Report of BRLP*, Bihar Rural Livelihood Project, March.
Bouman, F. (1995). 'Rotating and Accumulating Savings and Credit Associations: A Development Perspective', *World Development*, 23 (30): 371–84.
Burra, Neera, Joy Deshmukh-Ranadive and Ranjani K. Murthy (eds). (2005). *Microcredit, Poverty and Empowerment: Linking the Triad*, SAGE Publications, New Delhi.
CASHE. (2006). *The Impact of Microfinance on the Poor and Women: A Mid Term Assessment of CASHE Programme*, Credit and Savings for Household Enterprise, Cooperative for Assistance and Relief Everywhere-India, New Delhi.

CGAP. (2007). *Sustainability of Self-help Groups in India: Two Analyses*, Occasional Paper No. 12, Washington D.C., August.

Christen, Robert Peck. (2006). 'Microfinance and Sustainability: International Experiences and Lessons for India'. In *Towards a Sustainable Microfinance Outreach in India: Experiences and Perspectives*, NABARD–GTZ–SDC, Mumbai–New Delhi, March, pp. 43–68.

Christen, Robert Peck and Gautam Ivatury. (2007). 'Sustainability of Self-Help Groups in India: Two Analyses', Occasional Paper No 12, Part II, Consultative Group to Assist the Poor (CGAP), Washington D.C., August.

CmF. (2006). *PEDO's SHG Programme Impact Assessment*, Center for Microfinance, Jaipur.

———. (2008). *Rajasthan Microfinance Report 2007*, Jaipur. Available at http://www.srtt.org/institutional_grants/pdf/rajasthan_microfinance_report_2007.pdf (accessed on 13 October 2011).

CmF and APMAS. (2006). *Quality Issues of SHGs in Rajasthan*, Center for Microfinance, Jaipur.

Contify Banking. (2011). 'Andhra State's Women Co-op Bank Stree Nidhi to Offer 11 Bln Loans in 1 Year at 13% Interest', 24 September.

Deininger, Klaus and Yanyan Liu. (2009). 'Longer–term Economic Impacts of Self-Help Groups in India', Policy Research Working Paper 4886, The World Bank Development Research Group, Sustainable Rural and Urban Development Team, March.

Department of Women and Child Development, Government of Karnataka. (2011). 'Stree Shakthi', http://dwcdkar.gov.in/index.php?option=com_content&view=article&id=260%3Astree&catid=224%3Aflash&lang=en (accessed on 15 October 2011).

DHAN Foundation. (2004). *Impact of Kalanjiam Community Banking Programme*, DHAN Foundation, Madurai, November.

DGRV-APMAS. (2010). *A Study of SHG Federation Structures in India: Core Elements for Achieving Sustainability*, APMAS, Hyderabad, December.

DWCD-CIDA. (2000). 'Best Practices in Group Dynamics and Micro-credit'. Proceedings of a workshop organized by Department of Women and Child Development, Government of India, and Gender Equality Fund, CIDA.

EDA Rural Systems. (2006). *Self Help Groups in India: A Study of the Lights and Shades*, EDA Rural Systems, Gurgaon.

Fernandez, Aloysius Prakash. (1992). *The MYRADA Experience—Alternate Management Systems for Savings and Credit of the Rural Poor*, MYRADA, Bangalore.

———. (2003). *Putting Institutions First—Even in Microfinance* (2nd revised edition), MYRADA, Bangalore, February.

———. (2007a). 'History and Spread of the Self-help Affinity Group Movement in India: The Role Played by IFAD', Occasional Paper 3, IFAD Asia and Pacific Division, July.

———. (2007b). 'Why Sanghamithra Is Different?', Rural Management System Series, Paper 54, MYRADA, Bangalore.

FWWB. (2002). 'Indian Self-Help Groups and Bangladesh Grameen Bank Groups: A Comparative Analysis', Discussion Paper, Friends of Women's World Banking, Ahmedabad.

Ghate, Prabhu. (2006). *Microfinance in India: A State of the Sector Report, 2006*, ACCESS Development Services, New Delhi.

———. (2007). *Microfinance in India, A State of the Sector Report, 2007*, Access Development Services, New Delhi.

Government of India. (2008). *Report of the Committee on Financial Inclusion*, Chairperson C. Rangarajan, January. Available at http://www.nabard. org/pdf/report_financial/Full%20Report.pdf (accessed on 30 November 2011).

———. (2009). *Report of the Committee on Credit Related Issues under SGSY*, Ministry of Rural Development.

———. (2010a). *Annual Report*, Ministry of Rural Development.

———. (2010b). *NRLM—Frame Work for Implementation*, Ministry of Rural Development, 22 December 2010.

———. (2011). *NRLM—Project Implementation Plan*, Ministry of Rural Development.

Government of Odisha. (2011a). *TRIPTI Quarterly Progress Report*, Targeted Rural Initiatives for Poverty Termination and Infrastructure, January to March, Department of Panchayati Raj.

———. (2011b). *TRIPTI VARTA* (bi-lingual newsletter of Targeted Rural Initiatives for Poverty Termination and Infrastructure), III (I, August). Available at http://www.odishapanchayat.gov.in/English/Pdf/Tripti_ AUGNews.pdf (accessed on 15 November 2011).

Government of Tamil Nadu. (2010). *Policy Note—2010–2011*, Rural Development and Panchayati Raj Department.

GTZ-NABARD. (2006). 'Management Information System (MIS) SHG-Bank Linkage Programme' (final draft), GTZ Rural Finance Programme India, New Delhi and NABARD Mumbai, March.

Guha, Sampati. (2010). *Microfinance for Micro Enterprises: An Impact Evaluation of Self Help Groups*, NABARD, Mumbai.

Hannover, Wolfgang. (2005). *Impact of Microfinance Linkage Banking in India on the Millennium Development Goals (MDG)*, NABARD–GTZ, Mumbai–New Delhi, May.

Harper, Malcolm. (1996). 'Self Help Groups: Some Outstanding Issues from India', *Small Enterprise Development*, 7 (2): 36–41.

———. (2002). 'Promotion of Self Help Groups under the SHG Bank Linkage Programme in India', paper presented at the Seminar on SHG–Bank Linkage Programme, New Delhi, 25 and 26 November, NABARD, Mumbai.

———. (2003a). 'Do We Really Need SHG Federations?', personal communication for the National Workshop on SHG Federations on 20 and 21 June 2003.

———. (2003b). *Practical Microfinance*, Vistaar Publications, New Delhi.

Harper, Malcolm, D.S.K. Rao and Ashis Kumar Sahu. (2008). *Development, Divinity and Dharma: The Role of Religion in Microfinance Institutions*, Practical Action Publishing, Rugby, United Kingdom.

Harper, Malcolm, Ezekiel Esipisu, A.K. Mohanty and D.S.K. Rao. (1998). *The New Middlewomen—Profitable Banking through On-Lending Groups*, Oxford & IBH Publishing Co. Pvt Ltd, New Delhi.

Hulme, David. (2000). 'Impact Assessment Methodologies for Microfinance: Theory, Experience and Better Practice', *World Development*, 28 (1): 79–98.

Hulme, David and Paul Mosley. (1996). *Finance Against Poverty*, Vols 1 and 2, Routledge, London and New York.

Isern, Jennifer, L.B. Prakash, Anuradha Pillai and Syed Hashmi. (2007). 'Sustainability of Self-Help Groups in India: Two Analyses', Occasional Paper No. 12, Part I, Consultative Group to Assist the Poor (CGAP), August.

Karduck, Stefan and Hans Dieter Seibel. (2004). *Transaction Costs of Self-Help Groups: A Study of NABARD's SHG Banking Programme in India*, Gesellschaft für Technische Zusammenarbeit, New Delhi. Available at http://www.microfinancegateway.org/gm/document-1.9.24993/33.pdf

Kropp, E.W. and B.S. Suran. (2002). *Linking Banks and (Financial) Self Help Groups in India—An Assessment*, National Bank for Agriculture and Rural Development (NABARD), Mumbai.

Kropp, E.W., M.T. Marx, B. Pramod, B.R. Quinones and H.D. Seibel. (1989). *Linking Self-help Groups and Banks in Developing Countries*, Eschborn, Gesellschaft für Technische Zusammenarbeit, Bangkok, APRACA, Rossdorf, TZ-Verlag.

Mahila Vikas Samabaya Nigam. (2011). *Mission Shakti Monthly Progress Report, 2011*, Mahila Vikas Samabaya Nigam.

M-CRIL. (2003). *The Outreach/Viability Conundrum: Can India's Regional Rural Banks Really Serve Low-Income Clients?* Micro-Credit Ratings International Limited, Gurgaon, February. Available at http://www.m-cril.com/pdf/M-CRIL-RRB-report-2003.pdf (accessed on 26 October 2011).

Meissner, Jan. (2006a). *Viability Analysis of SHG Lending in a Regional Rural Bank Branch*, GTZ–NABARD, New Delhi–Mumbai, February (with the support of Klaus Maurer).

———. (2006b). *Viability Analysis of SHG Lending in a Microfinance Institution*, GTZ–NABARD, New Delhi–Mumbai, October.

———. (2006c). *Viability Analysis of SHG Lending in a District Central Co-operative Bank Branch and Its Affiliated Primary Agriculture Co-operative Credit Society*, GTZ–NABARD, New Delhi–Mumbai, November.

Microfinance Focus. (2011). 'AP Govt's Microfinance Bank to Begin Lending at 13% Interest', 15 September.

Mor, Nachiket. (2006). *Some Thoughts on Access to Markets as a Strategy to Address Poverty*, Institute for Financial Management and Research, Centre of Development Finance Working Paper Series, October.

MoRD. (2011). *Programme Implementation Plan, National Rural Livelihoods Mission*. Ministry of Rural Development, New Delhi.

MYRADA. (2002). *Impact of Self Help Groups (Group Processes) on the Social/ Empowerment Status of Women Members in Southern India*, NABARD, Mumbai.

———. (2010). *MYRADA: An Agency Profile, Past, Present and Future.* MYRADA, Bangalore, January.

Nair, Ajai. (2005). 'Sustainability of Microfinance Self Help Groups in India: Would Federating Help?', World Bank Policy Research Working Paper 3516, February. Available at http://www-wds.worldbank.org/external/ default/WDSContentServer/IW3P/IB/2005/03/06/000090341_2005030610 3912/Rendered/PDF/wps3516.pdf (accessed on 27 October 2011).

NABARD. (1989). *Studies on Self-Help Groups of the Rural Poor*, National Bank for Agriculture and Rural Development, Mumbai.

———. (1995). *Reserve Bank of India's Working Group on Non-Governmental Organisations and Self-Help Groups: Report*, National Bank for Agriculture and Rural Development, Mumbai.

———. (2006). *Progress of SHG Bank Linkage in India 2005–06*, National Bank for Agriculture and Rural Development, Mumbai.

———. (2007). *Status of Microfinance in India 2006–07*, National Bank for Agriculture and Rural Development, Mumbai.

———. (2008). *Status of Microfinance in India 2007–08*, National Bank for Agriculture and Rural Development, Mumbai.

———. (2009). *Status of Microfinance in India 2008–09*, National Bank for Agriculture and Rural Development, Mumbai.

———. (2010). *Status of Microfinance in India 2009–10*, National Bank for Agriculture and Rural Development, Mumbai.

———. (2011). *Status of Microfinance in India 2010–11*, National Bank for Agriculture and Rural Development, Mumbai.

Nair, Tara S. and Rutwik Gandhe. (2011). 'Liberal Cooperatives and Microfinance in India: Diagnostic Study of a Cooperative Federation', *Journal of Rural Cooperation*, 39(1): 19–34.

Nanda, Y.C. (2000). 'Marketing Microfinance in India—the NABARD Way', paper presented at the Workshop on Best Practices in Group Dynamics and Micro Credit, Manesar, Gurgaon, 15–17 February.

NCAER. (2008). *Impact and Sustainability of SHG Bank Linkage Programme*, National Council of Applied Economic Research, New Delhi.

Nirantar. (2007). *Examining Literacy and Power Within Self Help Groups: A Quantitative Study*, Nirantar. Available at http://www.nirantar.net/docs/ SHG%20Quantitative%20Report.pdf

Odell, Kathleen. (2010). *Measuring the Impact of Microfinance: Taking Another Look*, Grameen Foundation, Washington D.C.

Patel, Amrit. (2011). 'A Decade of Financing SGSY, a Self-employment Program for BPL Families', *Microfinance Focus*, 27 September.

Premchander, Smita, M. Chidambaranathan and Nikita Kaul. (2010). *Empowering Microfinance: A Critical Element of Women's Access to Productive Resources*, *Microfinance Focus*, 17 May.

Puhazhendi, V. (1995). *Transaction Costs of Lending to Rural Poor: Non-Governmental Organisations and Self-Help Groups of the Poor as Intermediaries for Banks in India*, The Foundation for Development Cooperation, Brisbane.

Puhazhendi, V. and K.C. Badatya. (2002). *Self Help Group-Bank Linkage Programme for Rural Poor in India: An Impact Assessment*, NABARD, Mumbai.

Puhazhendi, V. and K.J.S. Satyasai. (2000). *Microfinance for Rural People: An Impact Evaluation*, NABARD, Mumbai.

Rajagopalan, Shashi. (2003). 'Designing Secondary Institutions of Self-Help Groups (SHGs) (Engaged in Savings and Credit Services)', paper for discussion APMAS Workshop, Hyderabad, 21–23 June.

———. (2006). 'Sahakara Shakti—The Way Forward, A Report of the Study on Rural Women's Financial Services Cooperatives Registered with Orissa Self-Help Cooperatives Act, 2001', commissioned by CARE India, CASHE Project (unpublished).

Ramakrishna, R.V. and Jan Meissner. (2007). *Viability of SHG Lending through Banks and MFI—A Comparative Analysis: A Joint Study by GTZ-NABARD Rural Finance Program*, GTZ, New Delhi.

Reddy, Y. Venugopal. (2011). 'Microfinance Industry in India: Some Thoughts', *Economic and Political Weekly*, 46 (41, 8–14 October): 46–49.

Salomo, Wolfgang, G. Bhaskara Rao and N. Naveen Kumar. (2010). 'A Study of SHG Federations Structures in India: Core Elements for Achieving Sustainability' (draft), APMAS, Hyderabad, December.

Satish, P. (2005). 'Mainstreaming of Indian Microfinance', *Economic and Political Weekly*, 40(17, 23–29 April): 173–39.

Seibel, Hans Dieter. (2005). *SHG Banking in India: The Evolution of a Rural Financial Innovation and the Contribution of GTZ*, NABARD, Mumbai and GTZ, New Delhi.

———. (2006). *From Informal Microfinance to Linkage Banking: Putting Theory into Practice, and Practice into Theory*, European Dialogue No. 36, pp. 49–60, September.

———. (2011). *Development of Self-regulation and Self-supervision of the Self-help Group Federation System in Andhra Pradesh, India*, Evaluation of a Pilot Project of Andhra Pradesh Mahila Abhivruddhi Society (APMAS) implemented in partnership with Society for Elimination of Rural Poverty (SERP), Andhra Pradesh.

Seibel, Hans Dieter and Harishkumar R. Dave. (2002). *Commercial Aspects of Self-Help Group-Bank Linkage Programme*, NABARD, Mumbai.

Singh, Jaipal and Pranay Bhargava. (2010). 'Rajasthan Microfinance Report—2010', Centre for Microfinance, Rajasthan (unpublished).

Sinha, Frances with Ajay Tankha, K. Raja Reddy and Malcolm Harper. (2009). *Microfinance Self-help Groups in India: Living up to Their Promise?* Practical Action Publishing Ltd, the United Kingdom.

SERP. (2011). *Indira Kranthi Patham Progress Report for the Month of March 2011*, Society for Elimination of Rural Poverty.

Sridhar, G. Naga. (2011). 'First-ever Microfinance "Bank" to Begin Operations', *Business Line*, 14 September.

Srinivasan, Girija. (2000). 'Financial to Social Capital: Role of Banks'. In *Microfinance: Emerging Challenges*, K. Basu and K. Jindal (eds), Chapter 17, pp. 253–70. New Delhi: Tata McGraw-Hill Publishing Company Limited.

Srinivasan, Girija and Ajay Tankha. (2010). *SHG Federations: Development Costs and Sustainability*, ACCESS Development Services, New Delhi.

Srinivasan, Girija and N. Srinivasan. (2009). *Community Owned Microfinance Institutions: Enabling Double Bottom-line Impact*, ACCESS Development Services, New Delhi.

Srinivasan, Girija and P. Satish. (2000). *Transaction Costs of SHG Lending—Impact on Branch Viability*, Bankers Institute of Rural Development, Lucknow.

Srinivasan, N. (2008). *Microfinance India State of the Sector Report 2008*, ACCESS and SAGE Publications, New Delhi.

———. (2009). *Microfinance India State of the Sector Report 2009*, ACCESS and SAGE Publications, New Delhi.

———. (2010). *Microfinance India, State of the Sector Report 2010*, ACCESS and SAGE Publications, New Delhi.

———. (2011). *Microfinance India, State of the Sector Report 2011*, ACCESS and Sage Publications, New Delhi.

Sriram, M.S. (2004). *Building Bridges between the Poor and the Banking System: A Study of Sanghamithra Rural Financial Services*, research carried out under the SRTT fund for Research Collaborations in Microfinance and Indian Institute of Management, Ahmedabad.

———. (2010). *Impact of Kalanjiam Groups: A Study in Tamil Nadu and Karnataka*, report prepared for Sir Ratan Tata Trust, Indian Institute of Management, Ahmedabad.

Suran, B.S. (2011). 'Revisiting SHGs', presentation made at Third National Seminar on Microfinance—Issues and Challenges, Bankers Institute of Rural Development, Lucknow, 2–3 December. Available at http://www.birdindia.org.in/birdlatestpresentation/Seminar%20presentations/Other%20presentations/Microsoft%20PowerPoint%20-%20Revisiting%20SHGs-%20BIRD.pdf (accessed on 28 February 2012).

Swain, Ranjula Bali and Adel Varghese. (2008). 'Does Self Help Group Participation Lead to Asset Creation', Working Paper 2008:5, Department of Economics, Uppsala University, Uppsala, Sweden, May.

Swain, Ranjula Bali and Fan Yang Wallentin. (2007). 'Does Microfinance Empower Women? Evidence from Self Help Groups in India', Working Paper 2007: 24, Department of Economics, Uppsala University, Uppsala, Sweden, August.

———. (2011). 'Reassessing the Impact of SHG Participation with Non-Experimental Approaches', *Economic and Political Weekly*, Mumbai, 46 (11, 12 March): 50–57.

Tamil Nadu Corporation for Development of Women. (n.d.). *Completion Evaluation of the Tamil Nadu Women's Development Project by IFAD*.

Available   at   http://www.ifad.org/evaluation/public_html/eksyst/doc/
agreement/phi/tamil.htm
Tankha, Ajay. (2002). *Self-Help Groups as Financial Intermediaries in India:
Cost of Promotion, Sustainability and Impact*, a study prepared for
Cordaid and ICCO, the Netherlands, August. Available at http://www.
microfinancegateway.org/gm/document1.9.28136/3736SHGREPORT.pdf
(accessed on 28 November 2011).
————. (2006a). 'Who Needs to Borrow from Self-Help Groups?', *Small
Change*, Gurgaon, May.
————. (2006b). *Challenges and Potential for Indian Banks to Implement
Business Facilitator and Business Correspondence Models: A Status Report*,
GTZ, New Delhi, October.
————. (2009). 'Mission Drift: Much Ado about Nothing?', *The Pluralist*, 1
(1), Gurgaon, April.
Tankha, Ajay, Girija Srinivasan and Ramesh S. Arunachalam. (2008). 'Public
Systems: Major Central Government and Donor-supported Programmes
for Livelihood Promotion'. In *The State of the India's Livelihoods: The
4P Report*, Shankar Datta and Vipin Sharma (eds), ACCESS Development
Services and Basix, New Delhi.
Tankha, Ajay and Jan Meissner. (2007). *Viability Analysis of SHG Lending in a
Commercial Bank*, GTZ–NABARD, New Delhi–Mumbai, February.
The Hindu. (2004). 'RBI Rejects Plea to Convert Stree Shakti Groups into
Bank', *The Hindu*, October 29.
Vasimalai, M.P. and K. Narender. (2007). 'Microfinance for Poverty
Reduction: the Kalanjiam Way', *Economic and Political Weekly*, 42(13,
31 March–6 April): 1190–95.

INDEX

ABOUT THE AUTHOR

Ajay Tankha is an economist with over 35 years' experience of teaching, training and research in development studies, rural finance and microfinance. He has been associated with CARE-India's CASHE project, GTZ (now GIZ) Rural Finance Programme, American India Foundation, Sa-Dhan, Access Development Services, EDA Rural Systems and Small Industries Development Bank of India. In addition, he has prepared studies sponsored by the World Bank, International Finance Corporation, Ford Foundation, Rabobank, ICCO and Cordaid, the Netherlands.

Mr Tankha was International Head of Microfinance of ActionAid UK, where he directed a global review of its savings and credit programmes, including impact assessment studies in India, Bangladesh, Kenya, Ethiopia and Ghana. Earlier, he worked as Economist with the National Bank for Agriculture and Rural Development in India. He has also taught economics and development studies at leading universities in India, the Netherlands and Vietnam.

Mr Tankha has authored several research papers and publications on microfinance and rural livelihoods including two books on self-help groups. He is currently an independent consultant based in New Delhi.